ISOLATING THE ENEMY

STUDIES OF THE WEATHERHEAD EAST ASIAN INSTITUTE, COLUMBIA UNIVERSITY

STUDIES OF THE WEATHERHEAD EAST ASIAN INSTITUTE,
COLUMBIA UNIVERSITY

The Studies of the Weatherhead East Asian Institute of Columbia University were inaugurated in 1962 to bring to a wider public the results of significant new research on modern and contemporary East Asia.

Isolating the Enemy

DIPLOMATIC STRATEGY IN CHINA AND THE
UNITED STATES, 1953–1956

Tao Wang

Columbia University Press
New York

Columbia University Press
Publishers Since 1893
New York   Chichester, West Sussex
cup.columbia.edu
Copyright © 2021 Columbia University Press

Library of Congress Cataloging-in-Publication Data
Names: Wang, Tao (Diplomatic historian) author.
Title: Isolating the Enemy : Diplomatic Strategy in China and the United States, 1953–1956 /
Tao Wang.
Other titles: Diplomatic Strategy in China and the United States, 1953–1956
Description: New York : Columbia University Press, 2021. | Series: Studies of the Weatherhead
East Asian Institute, Columbia University | Includes bibliographical references and index.
Identifiers: LCCN 2020052484 (print) | LCCN 2020052485 (ebook) | ISBN 9780231198165
(hardback) | ISBN 9780231198172 (trade paperback) | ISBN 9780231552516 (ebook)
Subjects: LCSH: United States—Foreign relations—China. | China—Foreign relations—United
States. | United States—Foreign relations—1953–1961. | China—Foreign relations—1949–1976.
Classification: LCC E183.8.C5 W364 2021 (print) | LCC E183.8.C5 (ebook) |
DDC 327.7305109/045—dc23
LC record available at https://lccn.loc.gov/2020052484
LC ebook record available at https://lccn.loc.gov/2020052485

Cover design: Milenda Nan Ok Lee
Cover image: Looking for the road to death—let's break this open together.
The characters above the lever read: United States-Chiang Treaty.
Source: Yang Keyang (杨可扬), March 1955. Published by Renmin meishu
chubanshe (人民美术出版社).
Courtesy of IISH / Stefan R. Landsberger / Private Collection. www.chineseposters.net

In memory of my teachers:
Nancy Bernkopf Tucker
(July 12, 1948–December 1, 2012)
and
薛谋洪
(May 18, 1928–January 30, 2016)

CONTENTS

ACKNOWLEDGMENTS

I was fortunate to be Nancy Bernkopf Tucker's last graduate student. Throughout my years at Georgetown University, Nancy guided me with both patience and compassion, particularly in her last years when I was writing the dissertation on which this book is based. Despite her fight against cancer, she read dozens of drafts and wrote numerous recommendations. I can never forget the scene when she presided over my dissertation defense with her arm in a cast, and how she later attended my commencement in a wheelchair. I wish she had been able to see the publication of this book.

I was also lucky to have several other ideal advisors for this project. Warren Cohen provided mentorship and friendship after Nancy passed away. John Gaddis pushed me to distill the arguments; his postdoctoral fellowship broadened my horizons and enabled me to meet some most talented scholars. My dissertation committee members—Carol Benedict, Chen Jian, and David Painter—offered encouragement and suggestions. Adam Rothman's research seminar helped me launch this project.

A large number of scholars helped me improve the manuscript over the years. I appreciate the feedback from the four anonymous manuscript reviewers. Ang Cheng Guan, Gregg Brazinsky, Warren Cohen, and Kevin Shanley read the entire manuscript and offered ideas for revision. The following scholars gave suggestions and comments at various stages—in alphabetic order: Pierre Asselin, Su-Ya Chang, Shuhua Fan, Christopher

Goscha, Charles Hayford, James Hershberg, Mark Kramer, Steven Levine, James Matray, John McNeil, James Millward, Micah Muscolino, Timothy Naftali, Niu Jun, Christian Ostermann, Patrick Fuliang Shan, Yi Sun, Xiansheng Tian, Wang Jisi, Yafeng Xia, Xiong Zhiyong, and Qiang Zhai. Shen Zhihua and Li Danhui generously shared their collection of Soviet documents and directed me to other sources.

Several institutions provided funding for the project. My trips to archives and conferences were supported by Georgetown University Graduate School and the History Department, Yale University International Security Studies program, Iowa State University College of Arts and Sciences and the History Department, the Chiang Ching-kuo Foundation for International Scholarly Exchange, the Bou Family Foundation, and the Eisenhower Foundation. A generous Iowa State University Publication Subvention Grant has covered part of the publication costs.

Staff in the following institutions helped my research: the National Archives in Maryland, the British National Archives at Kew in England, the Eisenhower Presidential Library, the Foreign Ministry Archives in Beijing, the Universities Service Center of the Chinese University of Hong Kong, the Cold War International History program of Woodrow Wilson International Center for Scholars, the Hoover Institution of Stanford University, the Seely G. Mudd Manuscript Library of Princeton University, and several institutions in Taipei: the Institute of Modern History of Academia Sinica, Guomindang History Archive, and Academia Historica.

Fredrik Logevall generously allows me to use two excellent maps from his award-winning: *Embers of War: The Fall of an Empire and the Making of America's Vietnam*. I am thankful that the MIT Press allows me to republish chapter 1, which initially appeared in the Spring 2017 issue of *The Journal of Cold War Studies*. The annual conferences of the American Historical Association (AHA), Society for Historians of American Foreign Relations (SHAFR), and Association for Asian Studies (AAS) gave me opportunities to present my chapters and recruit feedback. I also thank Chinese Historians in the United States (CHUS) for sponsoring some of the panels.

I am grateful to Stephen Wesley from Columbia University Press and Ariana King from the Weatherhead East Asian Institute for their efficiency and diligence in moving my book project forward. I appreciate the editing help by Elizabeth Nygaard and Rosemi Mederos. Kate Blackmer drew the maps, and her professionalism made the process both interesting and instructive.

Over many years, my friends and colleagues have helped me with various issues. In particular, I am grateful to Meredith Oyen and Chichu Tschang for their support all these years. My Georgetown classmates Julia Famularo, Ben Francis-Fallon, Toshihiro Higuchi, Ma Haiyun, Shen Yubin, Anand Toprani, and friends Joseph Chan, Cindy Ewing, Jeremy Friedman, Jonathan Hassid, Hou Xiaojia, David Howell, Jason Kelly, Sulmaan Khan, Lin Mao, Lü Jie, Martin Rivlin, Gagan Sood, and Yi Guolin, have provided both comraderies and concrete assistance. Huang Zonghao, Jiang Zhaoxin, Ma Jianfu, Qiu Wenping, Zhu Hongbo, and Zhang Yaze facilitated my research in Taipei, Hong Kong, Shanghai, and Beijing. My thanks to my colleagues at the Iowa State History Department, who never hesitate to give me their hands when I need support. Particularly, I appreciate the advice and friendship Tim Wolters has offered.

Finally, this book is a family project. I am deeply indebted to my wife Qiao Lei, our son Allen, and our daughter Annabeth, who have spent countless months without a husband and father while I worked on this project. My parents and in-laws took my family responsibilities when I was absent. Without their love and support, this book would have been impossible.

ABBREVIATIONS

ANZUS:	Australia, New Zealand, United States Security Treaty
CCP:	Chinese Communist Party
CMC:	Central Military Commission (of CCP)
DRV:	Democratic Republic of Vietnam
EDC:	European Defense Community
FO:	Foreign Office
GMD:	Guomindang (Chinese Nationalist Party) government
JCS:	Joint Chiefs of Staff
MAAG:	Military Assistance Advisory Group
MDT:	mutual defense treaty
NEATO:	Northeast Asia Treaty Organization
NIE:	National Intelligence Estimate
PLA:	People's Liberation Army
SEATO:	Southeast Asia Treaty Organization
SNIE:	Special National Intelligence Estimate
SV:	State of Vietnam
VWP:	Vietnamese Workers' Party

ISOLATING THE ENEMY

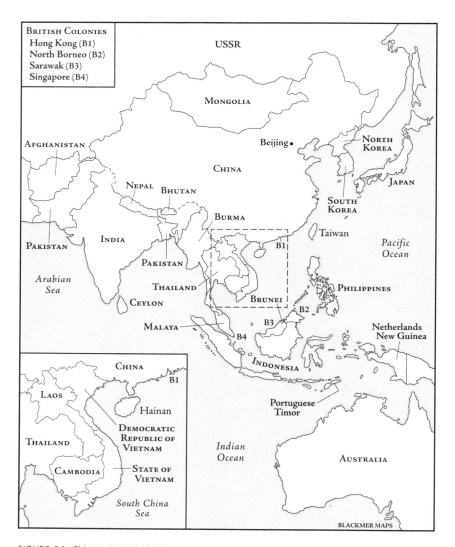

FIGURE 0.1. China and its neighbors
Source: Kate Blackmer

From 1953 to 1956, the People's Republic of China[1] made a series of peace overtures claiming to relax the tensions with the United States. Hence, Sino-American relations from 1953 to 1956 were marked by two seemingly contradictory tendencies: confrontation and conciliation. On the one hand, the PRC and the United States adopted very confrontational policies toward each other. PRC leaders viewed the United States as their archenemy who refused to recognize and militarily encircled the People's Republic. To meet the U.S. threat, Chinese leaders initiated the Taiwan Strait Crisis in July 1954. With the Chinese declaration of liberating Taiwan from the U.S.-supported GMD and capture of several small islands in the Taiwan Strait, the crisis brought the United States and China to the "edge of war."[2] Meanwhile, U.S. leaders saw China as "the primary problem" in Asia and tried to contain the Chinese Communist expansion.[3] During the crisis, the United States sent aircraft carriers to the Taiwan Strait, publicly threatened to use nuclear weapons against the PRC, and concluded a mutual defense treaty (MDT) with the GMD in December 1954, which provided security protection to a regime that the PRC considered illegitimate.

On the other hand, both the PRC and the United States took conciliatory actions, even as they were confronting each other. Beijing advocated peaceful coexistence with the United States, and its flexibility at the April–July 1954 Geneva Conference on Indochina led to the end of the eight-year war between its Communist comrade, the Democratic Republic of Vietnam (DRV), and U.S.-allied France. At the Bandung Conference in April 1955, during the Taiwan Strait Crisis, Chinese premier Zhou Enlai proposed to negotiate with the United States to reduce the tensions between the two countries. In response, Washington agreed to hold direct diplomatic talks with the PRC, a regime it had refused to recognize. The conciliation on both sides led to the ambassadorial talks between the two states, a means through which they communicated with each other at a time when there were no diplomatic relations between them.

How can these apparent contradictions in the two countries' policies be reconciled? Did they each adopt coherent policies? What were the motives of leaders of the two countries during this period? How did they perceive one another, and how did their perceptions or misperceptions of the other side shape their policies? What impact did each country's actions have on the other? What was the dynamic behind the crisis and conciliation in the bilateral relations? These are the questions this book answers.

The existing literature on Beijing's foreign policy in the 1950s gives three basic interpretations. Most scholars, such as He Di, Gong Li, Jia Qingguo, Thomas Stolper, Allen Whiting Zhang Baijia, and Qiang Zhai believe the PRC's diplomacy was driven by national security concerns and prompted by U.S. aggression. According to this interpretation, the Taiwan Strait Crisis broke out because of Beijing's anxiety about the threat to China's security and territorial integrity; China's intervention in Korea and Vietnam was based on its security concerns rather than shared ideology with the Korean and Vietnamese Communists.[4] In contrast, the prevailing New Cold War historiography stresses the predominance of ideology. According to Chen Jian, China's diplomacy was dictated by revolutionary nationalism. Obsessed with a tremendous sense of "post-revolutionary anxiety," China's top leader, Mao Zedong, created diplomatic tensions to promote the revolutionary enthusiasm of the Chinese people—who had a strong victim mentality and tended to support such policies—to promote his revolutionary programs at home, ultimately to restore China's central position in the world.[5] Lorenz Lüthi argues that ideological differences played a "vital role" in China's split with the Soviet Union.[6] Contrary to the above interpretations that see China as a rational actor, however, Michael Sheng sees Mao as an "erratic dictator" who "micromanaged China's military and political operations in the Taiwan Strait against the U.S.-Taiwan alliance with neither a long-term strategy nor a short-term plan." Out of fear and impulse, Mao abruptly reversed China's policy and initiated the Taiwan Strait Crisis in 1954, and later, the Second Taiwan Strait Crisis in 1958. Because of his continuous miscalculations, "China's national interest . . . suffered a great deal of damage."[7]

Interpretation of the Eisenhower administration's China policymaking has undergone three different phases: traditional, revisionist, and post-revisionist. The conventional interpretation is that the Eisenhower administration's policy toward China was dominated by John Foster Dulles, Eisenhower's secretary of state, and featured rigid anti-Communism. Believing that there was a monolithic Communism and China was the source of Communist expansion in Asia, Dulles pushed an inept President Eisenhower to a militant hostility toward the PRC; Washington refused to recognize the Communist regime, supported the GMD to contain the Communist threat, and was unnecessarily provocative during the Taiwan Strait Crisis, which almost led to a war with China. Over the Indochina crisis, Dulles refused diplomacy and sought allied intervention to stop the Communist expansion in Southeast Asia.[8]

The Eisenhower revisionists, however, see a pragmatic and flexible Eisenhower, who used Dulles's knowledge and experience to conduct a successful, if seemingly moderate, diplomacy; meanwhile, despite his bellicose rhetoric, Dulles turned out to be a rational leader.[9] Early revisionists focus on Eisenhower's leadership style and his successful crisis management.[10] Scholars praise Eisenhower's skillful ending of the Korean War,[11] "decision against war" during the Dien Bien Phu crisis,[12] and successful deterrence of the Chinese Communist aggression in the Taiwan Strait.[13]

Later revisionists stress a strategic China policy—in contrast to the blind anti-Communism traditionalists argue—based on a cooperative relationship between Eisenhower, Dulles, and their assistants. Nancy Tucker and Simei Qing argue that Eisenhower believed the United States should trade with China, despite the public rhetoric of hostility. Tucker also believes Dulles pursued a "Two Chinas" policy, accepting Communist control of the mainland and intending to prevent Chiang Kai-shek from provoking the PRC, which would drag the United States into a war. Eisenhower even considered allowing the PRC to enter the United Nations.[14] In the eyes of John Gaddis, Gordon Chang, and David Mayers, Washington was sensitive to the differences within the Communist camp and pursued a "wedge strategy" to split the Sino-Soviet alliance. By putting pressure on the PRC,

Washington aimed to force Beijing to demand more assistance than the Soviet Union could satisfy, which would ultimately strain and destroy the Communist alliance.[15] Shu Guang Zhang analyzes the U.S. embargo on China and argued that the "wedge strategy" worked just as Washington expected: in the long run, the consistent embargo hurt China's economy and forced China to seek Soviet assistance, which contributed to the final collapse of the Sino-Soviet alliance.[16]

Post-revisionists, however, are critical. Robert Accinelli, Su-Ya Chang, and Waldo Heinrichs find the U.S. policy was "indecisive" rather than "flexible." Instead of a consistent policy, the Eisenhower administration's policy toward China was crisis driven, and its commitment to Taiwan "emerged piecemeal in the context of crises," according to Accinelli.[17] Gordon Chang criticizes Eisenhower for his unnecessary and unwise provocation in the Taiwan Strait Crisis, which could have led to miscalculations and a war with the PRC.[18] Simei Qing argues that Eisenhower conducted an incoherent strategy for most of his presidency: while trying to ease the embargo to entice China away from the Soviet Union, he strengthened the GMD to confront China. And Eisenhower's trade policy was not supported by most of his assistants, especially Dulles.[19]

Unlike most of the aforementioned works that focus on either the U.S. or the Chinese perspective, the recent scholarship has stressed the interactions between the two countries. Qiang Zhai studies the trilateral interplay between China, the United States, and Britain, stressing China's security concerns.[20] Shu Guang Zhang and Simei Qing adopt a cultural approach. Zhang argues that mutual misperceptions, due to different strategic cultures, caused confrontations between the United States and China: each saw the other's deterrence as aggressive and responded accordingly, although neither really intended to threaten the other.[21] Qing argues that misjudgment based on different visions of modernity and identity transformed Sino-American relationship from allies to enemies.[22] Other scholars focus on different aspects of Sino-American interactions. Yafeng Xia studies the diplomatic negotiations and argues that the limited contact since 1949 paved the way for the historic rapprochement in the 1970s.[23] Meredith Oyen examines how the United States, the PRC, and the GMD conducted migration diplomacy in the Cold War: while the United States strived to contain the Communist expansion, the PRC intended to break the U.S. containment, and both the PRC and the GMD tried to legitimize their status and win the support of the overseas Chinese.[24] Gregg Brazinsky analyzes Sino-American competition in the Third World: China's efforts to promote its status through influence and leadership rather than material gains met strong but often unsuccessful response from the United States, which consistently exaggerated China's threat.[25] Hsiao-Ting Lin studies the interactions between the GMD and the United States and argues that the status quo in the Taiwan Strait today resulted from both the GMD's adaptions and its improvisations and accidents.[26]

Despite the recent stress on a balanced interpretation, due to limited access to the Chinese sources, the existing scholarship is still imbalanced and does not adequately reveal the complexity of Sino-American interactions in the mid-1950s. For one thing, the existing interpretation of Chinese diplomacy has not responded effectively to the Eisenhower revisionists and the post-revisionists. If there was a wedge strategy on the U.S. side, for example, how did Beijing perceive and respond to it? Were the Chinese leaders ever aware of Washington's indecision? Did they ever attempt to exploit it? To what extent did Beijing realize that Washington conducted a "Two Chinas" policy? And in this light, how did the United States view China's responses? What actions did they take against Beijing's reactions?

The current literature has also approached events in the 1950s in isolation. Most works focus exclusively on the confrontations without relating them to the conciliation between the two states. For the limited works that touch on China's peace initiatives, they often take China's statement of relaxing the tensions at face value. Therefore, the existing works do not effectively reveal the consistency in both the Chinese and U.S. policies. As a result, China's peace overtures in Geneva turned abruptly to the confrontation in the Taiwan Strait, which was then followed by a dramatic and seemingly out of the blue peace proposal in Bandung.[27] On the U.S. side, scholars also need to reconcile Washington's rhetoric about a tough policy toward China, especially the public threat of using nuclear weapons, and the decision to negotiate with Beijing, despite all the considerations about pressuring a split in the Sino-Soviet alliance.

Recently available government documents from China, the Soviet Union, and the DRV enable this book to reveal the intricacies in Sino-American interactions in the 1950s from a more balanced and multilateral perspective. This book makes extensive use of four crucial sources on the Communist side: the Chinese Foreign Ministry Archive, *Neibu Cankao*

(Internal Reference), Soviet diplomatic documents, and DRV Foreign Ministry sources. The documents from the Chinese Foreign Ministry Archives in Beijing are particularly insightful. During its brief opening from 2004 to 2012, this author was fortunate to obtain a valuable trove of internal diplomatic cables, policy reviews, and background reports. *Neibu Cankao* was a daily briefing prepared by Xinhua News Agency for China's leaders. It provides the most important domestic and international background for policymaking deliberations. These two sources give substantial information about Beijing's knowledge of the United States and the world and make possible a critical assessment of its diplomatic moves. My interpretation of the Soviet perspective benefited enormously from Shen Zhihua and Li Danhui, who generously shared their collection of sources on Sino-Soviet relations, including some crucial documents they obtained in Moscow shortly after the collapse of the Soviet Union. The DRV Foreign Ministry drafted a detailed sixty-nine-page policy review in 1976 about the Geneva negotiation. This invaluable document, complemented by declassified Chinese diplomatic reports about the Vietnamese Workers' Party (VWP) politburo meetings, sheds new light on the Vietnamese positions and the relations between the Communist states during the Geneva negotiation.[28]

My interpretation of the U.S. diplomacy is based on sources from the United States, United Kingdom, and Taiwan. The American sources are from the National Archives, the Eisenhower Presidential Library, and the John Foster Dulles Papers in Princeton's Seeley Mudd Manuscript Library, in addition to various published works. The British National Archives have some extremely prescient analyses of Chinese and American policies and numerous documents about British coordination with the British Commonwealth members. For the GMD's diplomacy, I researched the Foreign Ministry Archives (kept at the Institute of Modern History of Academia Sinica), the Chiang Kai-shek presidential documents (at Historica Sinica), and the GMD History Archive. Outside Taiwan, I studied the Chiang Kai-shek Diaries stored in the Hoover Institution of Stanford University.

Based on these sources, this book delineates the interactions between the PRC and the United States in the context of their relations with friends and allies in the mid-1950s. It concentrates on their perceptions and misperceptions of and actions and reactions to one another. While focusing on three major events—the Geneva Conference on Indochina, the Taiwan

Strait Crisis, and the Bandung Conference—this book highlights Beijing's underexplored peace initiatives at the Geneva and Bandung conferences. It delves into causes, China's motives, the influence of the Soviet Union and the DRV, the policy shifts between the conferences and Taiwan Strait Crisis, and, just as important, Washington's perceptions and reactions.

My research reveals that from 1953 to 1956 both China and the United States sought to eliminate the other's threat through uniting allies and mobilizing supporters to push the other to make concessions. And either side knew the other's strategy of isolating the enemy. While Beijing consistently took initiatives and conducted flexible diplomacy to alienate the United States, Washington always overestimated China's ambition and adopted rigid policies that failed to win support from its allies to contain the Chinese. Under the combined pressure from both its allies and the enemy, Washington had to retreat from its initial positions.

Apart from the prologue and epilogue, this book consists of an introduction, a conclusion, and six substantial chapters. The introduction analyzes U.S. and Chinese leaders' perceptions of each other and their policies after the Korean War. While Washington saw China as the source of Communist expansion in Asia and planned to weaken it and contain that expansion, Beijing wanted to break the U.S. encirclement of China. Both Beijing and Washington planned to pursue a strategy of isolating the other, and both knew their enemy's intention to alienate them.

Chapter 1 describes how Beijing perceived the U.S. threat in Indochina and the Geneva Conference and used the tactics of isolating Washington to neutralize Indochina. Worried about direct U.S. intervention in Indochina, Beijing exploited differences between the United States and its allies Britain and France to pressure Washington into accepting a peace settlement of the Indochina War in an attempt to forestall U.S. intervention. Aware of U.S. sensitivity to differences within the Communist camp, Beijing built a united front with the Soviet Union and the DRV and guided the latter to make concessions to reach the Geneva Agreements.

Chapter 2 interprets how Washington met the Chinese challenge and attempted to exploit Sino-Soviet differences in Geneva. Initially misperceiving the negotiation as a coverup for the Communist expansion in Indochina, Washington attempted to sabotage the negotiation and contain the Communists through united actions with Britain and France. However, the allies' resistance, Vietminh's military success, and China's diplomatic maneuvers combined to force Washington to accept a peace settlement. Though aware of the Communist tactics of isolating it from its allies, Washington's rigid positions strained relations with both France and Britain. The United States also found few opportunities to similarly exploit the differences within the Communist camp.

Chapter 3 interprets how Beijing continued its strategy of isolating the United States to prevent the conclusion of an MDT between the United States and the GMD. Chinese leaders initiated the crisis to warn Washington of the risk of concluding an MDT and mobilized Britain and Asian neutral states to pressure the United States to give up that idea. Meanwhile, Beijing demonstrated unity with the Soviet Union to press Washington. However, the Chinese misperceived the U.S. need for the MDT and overestimated the differences between Washington and London. As a result, the crisis ended up hastening the MDT and worrying the neutral states. Beijing then shifted to peace initiatives to both ease the worries of the Asian states and mobilize them to pressure Washington into negotiation.

Chapter 4 assesses U.S. responses to China during the crisis. Although Washington knew Beijing's intention to use Taiwan to separate it from allies, it was distracted and unprepared for the coming crisis. As a result, U.S. officials overestimated China's aggression after the crisis started, creating a dilemma: either help the GMD and risk a war or refuse to help and lose credibility. Obsessed with the misperceived Chinese aggression, Washington continued to overreact. That in turn strained relations with Britain and the GMD. Under pressure from both allies and the enemy, Washington had to make concessions to both the GMD and the PRC.

Chapter 5 shows how China used the Bandung Conference to exclude the United States from Southeast Asia. Beijing aimed to unite Asian states to develop a neutral zone of peace. Aware of U.S. attempts to manipulate the conference and contain China by sending proxies to the meeting, Beijing attracted major Asian states with increased trade, end of support of Communist insurgents, cooperation on the issue of overseas Chinese, and commitment to peaceful coexistence. Playing on the anxiety among its Asian neighbors about the Sino-American confrontation in the Taiwan Strait, China proposed direct negotiations with the United States; though it failed to develop the zone of peace, it was able to break the United States' imposed isolation and force Washington to the negotiation table.

Chapter 6 analyzes U.S. efforts to isolate China and its response to China's policy of alienating the United States in Bandung. Worried that China would exploit anticolonialism to alienate and isolate it, the United States initially attempted to sabotage the Bandung Conference, but finally decided to manipulate the conference through the use of friendly attendees. However, due to his misperception of the Chinese intentions, Secretary Dulles pushed allies to contain China's alleged aggression in the Taiwan Strait. Thus he created a warlike atmosphere that ultimately worked against the United States. When China made peace overtures, U.S. allies pressed Washington for a positive response.

The conclusion studies the ambassadorial talks after Bandung. Washington was reluctant to begin negotiations after a de facto ceasefire was achieved in the Taiwan Strait. Making use of U.S. allies' fear about war and the American concerns about U.S. nationals detained in China, Beijing successfully mobilized Britain and India to push Washington to start negotiations. But neither was willing to accommodate the other: Washington refused to upgrade to a foreign minister meeting, and China refused to renounce the use of force in the Taiwan Strait. Negotiations became deadlocked soon after they began.

China took more actions to alienate the United States in 1956. Pragmatic diplomacy was replaced by a confrontational policy as a result of changing domestic and international circumstances. The year 1958 marked the end of the so-called "Bandung moment," and Mao decided to start a tit-for-tat confrontation against the United States as he simultaneously sought "equality" with the Soviet Union. By launching the Second Taiwan Strait Crisis in the summer, Mao confronted the United States directly and indirectly challenged the Soviet leadership in the socialist camp and its quest for peaceful coexistence with the United States. China's assertive policy culminated in the revolutionary diplomacy of the 1960s. In retrospect, the mid-1950s was a brief aberration in China's diplomacy in the early Cold War.

SINO-AMERICAN RELATIONS AFTER THE KOREAN WAR

The United States and Communist China are now in effect engaged in a limited war (the battlefronts are in Korea, the Straits of Formosa, and Indochina and, in addition, we are at war in a general sense with respect to economic measures, mutual nonrecognition, etc.).[1]

—CHARLTON OGBURN, MARCH 26, 1954

[The Communists were] trying to divide the three of us [Britain, the United States, and France], just as we were trying to divide them.[2]

—ANTHONY EDEN, DECEMBER 1953

. . . the concept of leadership implied associates. Without allies and associates the leader is just an adventurer like Genghis Khan.[3]

—DWIGHT D. EISENHOWER, APRIL 29, 1954

U.S. PERCEPTION OF THE CHINESE THREAT

Participation of the People's Republic of China in the Korean War decisively changed U.S. leaders' perception of the Communist regime and its relations with the Soviet Union, eliminating any chance of an accommodation between the United States and China in the near future.[4] By the end of the war, China had emerged in the minds of Americans as a powerful and hostile Communist state closely aligned to the Soviet Union. Its threat to U.S. interests in Asia, according to Walter Robertson, assistant secretary of state for Far Eastern affairs, was even more active than the Soviet menace in Europe.[5] After conclusion of the Korean Armistice Agreement in July 1953, Secretary of State John Foster Dulles warned U.S. diplomats around the world not to be beguiled by China's willingness to stop fighting on the Korean peninsula, as "Armistice in Korea would not indicate Communist China had abandoned its basic objectives or its willingness [to] seek these objectives by armed force. Danger of aggression would continue, particularly in Southeast Asia, while

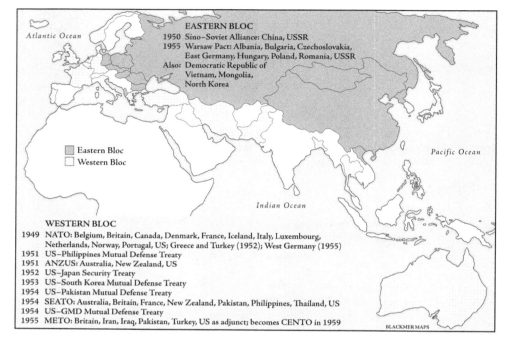

EASTERN BLOC
1950 Sino–Soviet Alliance: China, USSR
1955 Warsaw Pact: Albania, Bulgaria, Czechoslovakia,
East Germany, Hungary, Poland, Romania, USSR
Also: Democratic Republic of
Vietnam, Mongolia,
North Korea

Atlantic Ocean

Pacific Ocean

Eastern Bloc
Western Bloc

Indian Ocean

WESTERN BLOC
1949 NATO: Belgium, Britain, Canada, Denmark, France, Iceland, Italy, Luxembourg,
Netherlands, Norway, Portugal, US; Greece and Turkey (1952); West Germany (1955)
1951 US–Philippines Mutual Defense Treaty
1951 ANZUS: Australia, New Zealand, US
1952 US–Japan Security Treaty
1953 US–South Korea Mutual Defense Treaty
1954 US–Pakistan Mutual Defense Treaty
1954 SEATO: Australia, Britain, France, New Zealand, Pakistan, Philippines, Thailand, US
1954 US–GMD Mutual Defense Treaty
1955 METO: Britain, Iran, Iraq, Pakistan, Turkey, US as adjunct; becomes CENTO in 1959

BLACKMER MAPS

FIGURE 0.2. Eastern Bloc versus Western Bloc in the Eastern Hemisphere
Source: Kate Blackmer

[the] Communists would attempt [to] exploit armistice as [a] tactical device to weaken and divide [the] free world."[6]

In November 1953, the National Security Council (NSC) prepared a new basic policy toward China. NSC 166/1 ("U.S. Policy toward Communist China") identified China as "the primary problem of U.S. foreign policy in the Far East." China intended to dominate the Far East and exclude the Western forces from the area. In the short run, China menaced U.S. interests in several areas.[7] The Chinese increased their assistance to the DRV and planned to expand Communism throughout Indochina. Consequently, by late 1953, the DRV had the upper hand over France, and the NSC predicted that the situation would further deteriorate.[8] In other areas of Southeast Asia, China expanded its influence over the huge community of overseas Chinese and assisted indigenous Communist movements. At the same time, China wanted to capture Taiwan from Chiang Kai-shek's GMD, thus

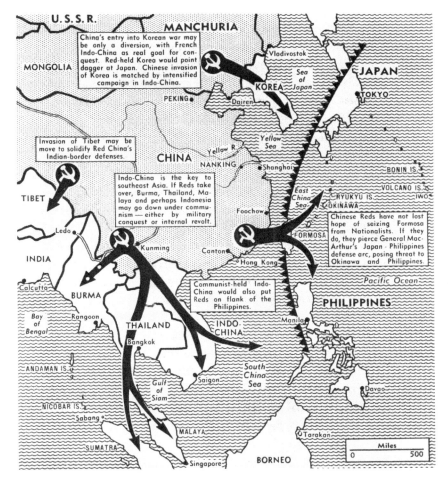

FIGURE 0.3. Map of Communist advances in East Asia, 1950
Source: Getty Images

breaking the U.S. island chain of defense in the Western Pacific.[9] By the summer of 1953, China had seized several offshore islands and was preparing to attack the strategically more important Dachen Islands.[10]

Elsewhere in Asia, China tried to neutralize these states to prevent them from being used by the United States against China. Politically, China advocated peace in order to form "the broadest possible alliance with all potentially anti-Western elements." Economically, China promoted trade with important U.S. allies such as Japan, Britain, and France as a way to win them over to the Communist side. Strategically, the Chinese would try to prevent "the establishment of strong Western military forces" in its bordering areas, especially North Korea, northern Burma, and Vietnam. And diplomatically, China aimed to enter the UN and set up diplomatic relations with more Asian states.[11] Among all of the mentioned areas, Indochina and Taiwan were critically important to U.S. national interests. According to the U.S. "Basic National Security Policy" (NSC 162/2), which was prepared right before adoption of NSC 166/1, these two places were "of such strategic importance to the United States that an attack on them probably would compel the United States to react with military force either locally at the point of attack or generally against the military power of the aggressor."[12]

In response to the challenge from China, according to NSC 166/1, the United States sought to eventually "secure a reorientation of the Chinese Communist regime or its ultimate replacement by a regime which would not be hostile to the United States." In the short run, the United States intended to weaken China's strength and influence in Asia, primarily by developing the political, economic, and military strength of non-Communist Asian countries, while also weakening or at least retarding the growth of Chinese Communist power in China and weakening Sino-Soviet relations.[13]

In the meantime, U.S. leaders realized that the Sino-Soviet alliance, a major source of China's strength, was established on the basis of both common ideology and mutual interest, so there was not much the United States could do to drive a wedge between them in the short run:

> The Chinese Communists and the Russians may eventually come into conflict, or at least cease to act as a unit, and the U.S. and the West may be able to capitalize on specific tensions and conflicts within the partnership. But in the last analysis a fracture of the alliance, if it comes, will stem primarily from the internal relationships of the partners and only secondarily from either the pressures or inducements of the West.[14]

Nevertheless, the United States pursued active policies to weaken the Chinese Communists through both containment and pressure. In terms of containment, the United States strived to contain the Communist expansion through the offshore island chain; be ready to fight back further territorial expansion; help non-Communist states in Asia against Communist subversion; assist China's neighbors, especially Korea, Taiwan, and Indo-china; help the development of Japan and other non-Communist states; and develop collective defense organizations.[15] Meanwhile, NSC 166/1 decided to "continue to exert political and economic pressures against the PRC, including unconventional and covert pressures." Politically, the United States sought to deny China "full status in the international community," including a UN membership, diplomatic recognition, and normal relations with the U.S. government. Economically, the United States intended to "impose difficulty and some delay" on China's industrialization, mainly by maintaining the embargo on trade, which the United States had imposed after the outbreak of the Korean War. Strategically, the United States would "employ all feasible means, covert and overt, to impair Sino-Soviet relations." In addition, it had increased assistance for France to defeat the Communists in Indochina and, in particular, funded the Navarre Plan, a major offensive named after the French commander in Indochina Henri Navarre to regain the initiative against the DRV.[16] Regarding Taiwan, the United States aimed to include the islands of Taiwan and Penghu (Pescadores) in its defense system, help the GMD defend the islands off the mainland, and assist the GMD forces to raid the Chinese mainland and disrupt its foreign trade.[17]

The success of this policy depended on cooperation with allies. As the NSC 166/1 indicated, both the political and economic pressures on China relied on the West "act[ing] in concert." Militarily, as NSC 162/2 showed, the French forces in Indochina and the British troops in Malaya and Hong Kong, as well as the military powers of the Republic of Korea (South Korea), the State of Vietnam (SV), and the GMD government provided indispensable ground forces. This was extremely important for the United States when its economy was in a recession and the Eisenhower administration pursued a national security policy named the "New Look," the gist of which was to contain the Communists at a lower price: through alliances and nuclear deterrence.

Meanwhile, however, the United States also realized that relations with its allies were strained by its hostility toward China. The Americans knew that their major allies worried about being dragged into either a general war with China or "indefinitely prolong[ed] cold-war tensions" in the Far East.[18] They also knew that the British were enticed by the Chinese market and preferred a conciliatory policy; the French wanted China to help them solve the Indochina problem; and the Japanese wanted more trade with China. In addition, the United States recognized that most states in

Southeast Asia supported the Indian policy of wooing China away from the Soviet Union through contacts with it instead of confronting China. In this circumstance, the United States expected that "any U.S. policy toward Communist China will encounter strenuous and vocal objections from at least some of the countries of the Free World."[19]

Even worse, U.S. leaders also knew the Communists were launching a "peace offensive" in order to "divide the West by raising false hopes [of peace] and seeking to make the United States appear unyielding," but the Communists had no intention of either giving up their expansion or settling the Cold War with the West.[20] These tactics did not cost the Communists anything, and they catered to U.S. allies very well. As a result, the NSC 166/1 concluded that the United States should be careful in its relations with allies and must avoid "excessive pressure" on them in order to "avoid the most dangerously divisive potentials of the Chinese Communist issue."[21]

CHINA'S POLICY TOWARD THE UNITED STATES

From the perspective of Chinese leaders, the United States had been the major security threat since establishment of the People's Republic in October 1949, and particularly after its entrance into the Korean War. In November 1950, after U.S. forces crossed the thirty-eighth parallel, China declared that the United States intended to invade China from one of three directions: Korea, Taiwan, or Vietnam.[22] After the Korean Armistice Agreement, Chinese leaders felt U.S. threats from these three directions still existed, although to a lesser degree.

To the northeast of China, U.S. troops stationed in South Korea directly threatened China's major industrial base in Manchuria. U.S. harassment of China, especially of the Shandong peninsula across the Yellow Sea from Korea, had increased unprecedentedly since the end of the war.[23] In October 1953, by concluding a mutual defense treaty with South Korea, the United States legitimized its long-term military deployment in the Korean peninsula and prevented an ultimate solution to the Korean problem.[24] And this was followed by a mutual defense assistance agreement with Japan in March 1954. From the Chinese perspective, this meant that the United States was rearming Japan in order to confront China.[25]

To the southeast of China, the U.S. Seventh Fleet had been protecting the GMD since the outbreak of the Korean War. After the war, the United

States attached greater importance to the position of Taiwan because the Eisenhower administration wanted to use the GMD troops to expand aggression. Consequently, it increased economic and military assistance to the GMD, strengthened control of its military, and expanded U.S. naval and air forces that had been stationed in Taiwan since June 1950.[26] Chinese leaders also suspected that the United States was planning to enter into a formal alliance with the GMD. Moreover, the United States encouraged the GMD to raid coastal areas, barricade mainland ports, and seize merchant ships in the Taiwan Strait.[27] After the Korean War, the GMD navy intensified its efforts to disrupt Chinese foreign trade by intercepting ships at the request of the United States, according to Chinese officials.[28] In the meantime, the United States reinforced its military bases in the Western Pacific. In 1951, the Australia, New Zealand, United States Security Treaty (ANZUS) came into effect, and the United States controlled the Filipino military through a mutual defense treaty. According to Chinese diplomatic reports, the United States was also considering a Southeast Asian military alliance based on the U.S.-Filipino treaty to carry out aggression against China.[29]

To the south of China, Chinese leaders saw U.S. involvement in Indochina increasing. Soon after Eisenhower came to power, China noted that the Americans sent more military assistance and pressured France to turn over the military command to the United States. Meanwhile, the United States pushed France to approve the agreement on the European Army, so that West Germany could join and send its forces to Indochina.[30] In September, Eisenhower declared support of France; the U.S. Congress approved $400 million in military assistance for France; and Dulles collaborated with the French to carry out the Navarre Plan.[31] In early 1954, China accused the United States of participating in the Indochina War by sending its air force and hundreds of military personnel to help the French, in addition to supplying money, equipment, and technicians.[32] Outside Indochina, based on a military assistance agreement with Thailand in 1950, the United States increased its military and economic assistance and pushed the Thais to expand their forces, which could then be used for aggression against China.[33] In early 1954, the United States and Pakistan were negotiating a military pact, and Eisenhower declared that the United States would provide military assistance to Pakistan.[34] Meanwhile, the United States was planning to organize an anti-Communist alliance with Thailand, Laos,

Cambodia, and Burma.[35] For Chinese leaders, all these actions were targeted at China.

In early 1954, the Chinese leaders were alerted to the New Look policy. From China's perspective, this new strategy meant a combination of U.S. air forces, equipped with atomic and other new weapons, and ground forces supplied by its allies would contain the Communists. To carry out this strategy, the United States planned to establish an Asian NATO and build military bases in Japan, the Philippines, and Thailand to develop a "global air force 'ring' " to encircle China and the Soviet Union.[36] Meanwhile, the United States was providing massive military assistance for the allies to develop their own armies, to be used as cheap manpower for the American strategy. In March, *Renmin Ribao* listed the network of bases the United States had built in the Asia-Pacific on the basis of the over two hundred bases from World War II, including those in the Pacific, South Korea, Japan, the Philippines, Australia, New Zealand, Thailand, and the Portuguese Goa and the Netherland New Guinea. The Chinese government mouthpiece attacked the U.S. deployments as threats to both China's security and world peace.[37]

The U.S. encirclement of China put Chinese leaders under great pressure—in Mao Zedong's words, the U.S. presence in China's neighborhood "made it hard for us to have a sound sleep,"[38] although China's experience in the Korean War convinced its leaders that a direct U.S. invasion of China was unlikely in the short run. In 1952, Mao predicted that the United States was not ready for a world war, and its strategic focus was in Europe rather than in Asia, so China would have ten years or so to concentrate on its domestic development. In June 1953, Zhou Enlai told Chinese officials that China's experience in Korea proved that the United States "did not dare to invade the mainland" of Asia.[39] Meanwhile, Mao Zedong told Chinese officials that China's participation in the Korean War had "put off the imperialist invasion of China and the outbreak of the Third World War." After the United States concluded the mutual defense treaty with South Korea and rejected China's proposal for a political conference on Korea in late 1953, Chinese leaders believed that the United States "dared not restore a war"; rather, they kept an "unstable ceasefire in Korea deliberately to *pressure* us."[40]

The U.S. threat prevented China from concentrating on domestic development, which the Korean War had proved to be vitally urgent. To meet the U.S. threat, Chinese leaders followed the peace initiatives the Soviet Union adopted after the death of Joseph Stalin in March 1953 and strived to ease tensions through diplomacy.[41] At the Soviet suggestion, the Chinese made new proposals, and the Korean Armistice Agreement was concluded largely due to China's concessions on the repatriation of POWs, which had been the principal obstacle for a truce.[42] As soon as the war ended, the Communists suggested building on the momentum to solve other international disputes by peaceful means.[43] Along with the Soviet suggestion in September to hold a five-power conference—including the United States, the Soviet Union, Britain, France, and China—to discuss tensions in Asia, Zhou Enlai proposed holding a political conference to discuss the withdrawal of foreign troops and settle the Korean problem.[44] Meanwhile, Soviet and Chinese leaders called for a peaceful solution of the Indochina problem.[45]

In addition to their alliance with the Soviet Union, Chinese leaders' confidence in diplomacy came from their perception of the relations between the United States and its allies. Chinese leaders, especially Zhou Enlai, found increasing contradictions among the Western imperialists. In early 1952, based on his observations of the relations within the Western camp during the Korean War and the process of concluding the Treaty of Peace with Japan, Zhou Enlai judged that the world order was much more complex than a simple confrontation between the Eastern and Western camps. The capitalist world was not a monolith. Rather, it was made up of progressive, neutral, and conservative states. This gave China enough room for diplomatic maneuver among them. Zhou pushed Chinese diplomats to conduct flexible diplomacy and distinguish these states from each other.[46]

When the Korean War came to its end, China concluded that U.S. foreign policy faced increasing opposition from both allies and Western colonial states and that contradictions between the Western imperialists had become exceedingly tense. Politically, Chinese leaders believed the United States struggled with the British and French for world leadership. As Zhou Enlai saw it, Britain and France wanted to maintain their colonies and the status quo in the world power configuration, but the United States wanted to expand its influence into their spheres of influence. According to Chinese diplomats, U.S. infiltration in India had led to the surfacing of U.S.-British conflicts, as well as the Indians' resistance to the United States.[47] In Indochina, the French feared that the United States would take over their interests, although France wanted U.S. economic and military assistance. Economically, despite the U.S. trade embargo on China, the British wanted to have more trade with China, and France had already concluded an agreement that allowed France to sell many kinds of strategic materials to China in order to beat the British in the profitable Chinese market. Japan, the most important U.S. ally in Asia, was also eager for business with China and sent trade delegations there, despite Japan still being under U.S. control.[48] Zhou Enlai told Chinese officials that China's peace policy since early 1953 had increased conflicts among the imperialists, and China should use this momentum to isolate the United States.[49]

While Chinese leaders planned to exploit the differences within the West, ever since 1949, they had known that the United States had conducted a "wedge strategy" to separate them from the Soviet Union.[50] In March 1953, China's leaders learned that a powerful group in the departments of state and defense had reached a new consensus to force China to seek extra assistance from the Soviet Union. The Soviets were busy with domestic issues and incapable of satisfying China's requests, and the Americans believed this was an effective way to disrupt the Communist alliance. These officials suggested taking strong actions in Korea, Indochina, and Taiwan to put more pressure on China, in addition to launching covert psychological warfare.[51]

But U.S. allies were not enthusiastic. The Chinese leaders learned from *Neibu Cankao* that the British believed pressure would only strengthen Communist unity, and U.S. provocative actions would lead to Chinese retaliation that could involve the British in a Sino-American war. Instead, the British advocated using carrots, such as trade, to draw China away from the Soviet Union.[52] Chinese leaders also knew that the French government, because of its interests in Indochina, wanted to grant China some kind of recognition, such as inviting China to the five-power conference the Soviets suggested, so that it could contact and convince China to stop assisting the DRV. Both Britain and France wanted to discuss the Soviet proposal at the four-power meeting between the Westerners and the Soviet Union.[53] Therefore, China concluded, the major U.S. allies were interested in negotiating with China, and their conciliation toward China added to tensions with the United States.

Deep hostility between the United States and China arose after the Korean War: China perceived the United States as a threat to its security and development, and the United States viewed China as the source of Communist expansion in Asia. Both states planned to separate the other from its allies to lessen the menace. U.S. leaders wanted to contain and pressure China to break the Sino-Soviet alliance, whereas the Chinese planned to use U.S. allies' interests in conciliation to isolate the United States through diplomatic maneuvers. Both states knew of the other's strategy and also realized the importance of unity with their allies, but their policies led to different consequences, as indicated in their interactions during the Geneva Conference, the Taiwan Strait Crisis, and the Bandung Conference.

PART I
Geneva Conference

Chapter One

NEUTRALIZING INDOCHINA

The Geneva Conference must not fail, but the United States obviously wanted to prevent the Geneva Conference from reaching any agreement, especially by threatening France to stop it from coming to an agreement on Indochina.... The Western states such as Britain and France should be told that they are facing two different roads: they could either have good relations with Asian people and maintain part of their interests or refuse this road and choose to walk the same road with the U.S., thus losing everything.[1]

—ZHOU ENLAI, APRIL 19, 1954

The two countries [Cambodia and Laos] must not have any foreign military bases, must not establish military alliances with other countries, and they should have guarantees from both sides or even from various sides.[2]

—ZHOU ENLAI, JULY 17, 1954

The Geneva Conference from April to July of 1954 ended the Indochina War between France and the Democratic Republic of Vietnam (DRV). As active participants of the Indochina War, both China and the United States played significant roles in the conference, leading to the Geneva Agreements on Indochina. Yet few works have approached the event from the perspective of Sino-American relations.[3] This chapter puts China's policy toward the United States in the broader context of its understanding of the relations within the Western Bloc. It explains China's objectives during the Geneva Conference and details its diplomacy with respect to its relationships with its allies, the Soviet Union, and the DRV.

This chapter shows how Chinese leaders perceived U.S. policy toward the conference and how that perception influenced China's policymaking. Beijing's objective in Geneva was to neutralize Indochina to prevent U.S. direct intervention, which would threaten China's southern flank. For that purpose, they mobilized the United Kingdom and France to pressure Washington to agree to end the Indochina War. Aware of the British and French resistance to U.S. intervention in Indochina, Chinese leaders adopted tactics of "showing a carrot to France while using a stick to deal

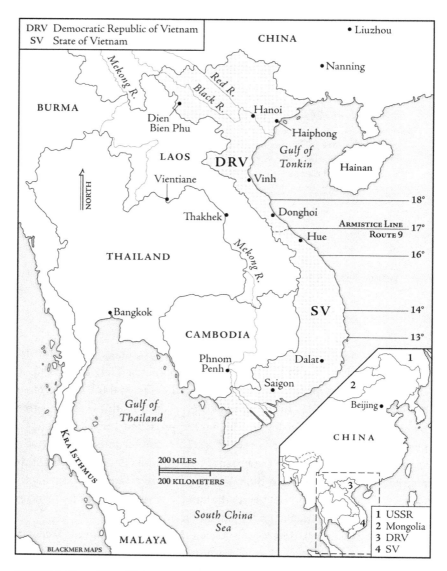

FIGURE 1.1. The partition of Vietnam
Source: Kate Blackmer

with the United States."[4] On the one hand, they helped the DRV take military offensives, which culminated in the French surrender in Dien Bien Phu; meanwhile, they coordinated closely with the Soviet Union and the DRV to press the Westerners at the negotiation table. On the other hand, understanding U.S. efforts to sabotage the negotiation, Chinese officials pushed the DRV to make concessions to mobilize British and French support for a peace settlement. In this process, they secured Laos's and Cambodia's promise that they would not ally with the United States. Ultimately, China succeeded in neutralizing these two states and securing a buffer area next to Vietnam.

CHINA'S POLICY IN GENEVA

The decision to hold the Geneva Conference was made in Berlin in early 1954, when foreign ministers of the United States, the Soviet Union, the United Kingdom, and France met to discuss the future of Germany. At that time, Soviet Foreign Minister Vyacheslav Molotov proposed a five-power conference, with the addition of China, to discuss relaxing the tensions in Asia. Although the United States opposed talking to China, Molotov won the support of the British and French leaders, and it was decided that the Geneva Conference would discuss the Korean and Indochinese issues. The participants included China and all other related states, but the U.S. government particularly declared that the conference was not a "five-power" one: China was not a sponsor, and U.S. agreement to sit together with it did not mean diplomatic recognition of the Communist regime.[5] U.S. Secretary of State John Foster Dulles deliberately clarified that "the Chinese Communist regime will not come to Geneva to be honored by us, but rather to account before the bar of world opinion."[6]

To a great extent, the Geneva Conference resulted from a well-coordinated "peace offensive," which the Communists launched after Joseph Stalin's death in March 1953. At Stalin's funeral, the new Soviet premier Georgy Malenkov declared that "there are no contested issues in U.S.-Soviet relations that cannot be resolved by peaceful means."[7] As the first behind-the-scenes step, the Soviets urged China to conclude the Korean Armistice Agreement. In September, the Soviets first suggested holding a five-power conference to discuss the tensions in Southeast Asia and the Pacific.[8] Chinese leaders readily endorsed the Soviet proposal and declared that "all international disputes can be solved through peaceful negotiation." Chinese premier Zhou Enlai immediately proposed a political conference to solve the Korean problem permanently. Soon China invited North Korean leaders to Beijing, and the two countries made a comprehensive proposal for the political conference.[9]

At the same time, the Communists started to call for a peaceful settlement in Indochina. Again, after the Soviets took the initiative, Beijing immediately declared its support.[10] In private, Chinese leaders tried to convince their Vietnamese comrades to consider a diplomatic solution. On November 23, 1953, Mao Zedong sent a telegram to Ho Chi Minh, urging him to take diplomatic actions:

> Currently the pressure from French people's quest to end the Vietnam War is increasing. Some members in the French ruling class also believe the invasion of Vietnam does not deserve the costs and advocate peace talk. [The French prime minister Joseph] Laniel also twice formally expressed willingness for negotiation. But the American imperialists have tried to expand the invaders' war in Vietnam since the end of the Korean War, and forced the French imperialists to fight to the end. In this circumstance, it is necessary and timely for the government of the Vietnamese Democratic Republic to formally express its willingness to end the Vietnam War through peaceful negotiations. Only in doing so can we take the banner of peace into our hands, encourage the struggle of the French people and all peace-loving people all over the world, and expose the lie of the French reactionaries who blame Vietnam for not wanting peace, and thus shift the responsibility for the war onto Vietnam. And only in so doing can we exploit and increase the contradictions between France and the United States.[11]

Mao seemed to convince DRV leaders, who realized the limit of their strength and, like the Chinese, worried about U.S. intervention. Although their confidence in negotiation might not have been as high as the Chinese, DRV leaders wanted to both demonstrate their goodwill and separate the United States from its allies.[12] Three days after Mao's message, making use of the Swedish newspaper the *Stockholm Expressen*, Ho declared that "if the French government has drawn a lesson in this war, wanting to reach a truce in Vietnam via negotiations and solve the Vietnam problem through peaceful means, then the Vietnamese people and the Democratic Republic of Vietnam government are ready to respond to that wish."[13] A month later, Ho repeated his willingness to negotiate with the French on the seventh anniversary of the beginning of the Indochina War.[14] Chinese and Soviet leaders, who urged Vietnam toward peace talks and demanded "further détente" in Asia, readily supported the Vietnamese position.[15]

Molotov's proposal in Berlin was a continuation of the Communist efforts. When the Soviets proposed the five-power conference, they did not hold much expectation, because they knew the United States would resolutely oppose it. The Soviets wanted to exploit the French and British interests in a diplomatic settlement of the Indochina War and win a political victory over the United States by advocating peace through diplomacy, in contrast to U.S. opposition to diplomacy. Contrary to the Soviet expectation, however, the United States ultimately agreed—after being cajoled by the British and French—to attend the conference.[16] Soviet leaders kept the Chinese informed about these developments throughout the meeting in Berlin. After reaching an agreement to hold a Geneva Conference, the Soviet Union immediately asked the Chinese to push DRV leaders to attend.[17]

Chinese leaders hailed the decision as "a move toward peace" and declared that China would attend the conference despite both the fact that China was not put on equal footing with the other four powers, which the Soviets had worried would displease the Chinese, and the apparent U.S. opposition to negotiate. According to Zhou, China attached great importance to the Geneva Conference and would actively participate to bring about some positive results.[18] Within two weeks after the Berlin meeting, the Chinese government prepared a plan for the conference. At the same time, Chinese leaders suggested to the Soviets that a partition line along the sixteenth parallel in Indochina would be "a very advantageous proposal for Ho Chi Minh." Zhou made the same proposal to Ho and encouraged him to seek a ceasefire through "diplomatic struggle."[19] Why were Chinese leaders so enthusiastic about the Geneva Conference? Why did they so eagerly want a ceasefire in Indochina? Why was Zhou confident that China's diplomacy would work in Geneva, given Washington's opposition to the conference and hostility toward China?

China's policy was basically a reaction to the threat that Chinese leaders perceived the United States posed. Since the outbreak of the Korean War, Chinese leaders felt pressure from the U.S. military presence in Korea and

Taiwan, but in early 1954, they believed the possibility of direct U.S. intervention in Indochina was increasing because the United States officially supported the French. In January, Dulles declared that China's military and technical assistance to the Vietnamese would lead to "grave consequences which might not be confined to Indochina" and that the United States would "retaliate, instantly, by means and at places of [their] choosing," which has since been known as "massive retaliation."[20] In late March, Dulles called for "united action" with allies to intervene in Indochina.[21] A week later, Dulles made what amounted to a public threat that China's aggression in Indochina might be responded to by retaliation against the mainland of China.[22] This was followed by U.S. President Dwight D. Eisenhower's warning of a "falling domino" in Asia if Indochina were allowed to be "lost" to the Communists.[23] Vice President Richard Nixon then told journalists that U.S. troops might be sent to Indochina.[24] Meanwhile, Dulles went to London and Paris to push for united action.[25] Chinese officials reported that although the Americans agreed to hold the Geneva Conference, they were pushing France to continue the war and wanted to sabotage the conference. Washington sent new military assistance to the French, and U.S. military leaders were striving to gain the power to command the indigenous Vietnamese troops now under French control, while officials from both the state and defense departments suggested that the negotiation was doomed. The Chinese newspaper *Renmin Ribao* reported that Washington would continue the war at any cost and had warned France not to seek peace.[26]

In these circumstances, the Geneva Conference provided Chinese leaders with an excellent opportunity to prevent U.S. intervention in Indochina through diplomacy, and they believed China could outmaneuver the United States by exploiting the differences between Washington and its allies. Beijing was aware that Washington's attempts to increase U.S. intervention in Indochina ran up against the French, who were unwilling to cede their interests in Indochina to the United States, despite their reliance on U.S. assistance.[27] Chinese officials believed that encouraging France to fight on and offering military and advisory assistance led the French to resent the United States' willingness to sacrifice French lives in pursuit of U.S. interests while being unwilling to send its own troops to Indochina.[28] Leaders in Beijing also sensed that France and the United States had opposing attitudes concerning the Geneva Conference. The United States downplayed the significance of the conference and opposed any possible solutions, including the division of Vietnam, a coalition government, or a free election in Vietnam. In contrast, French politicians attached a high value to negotiation. On the eve of the Geneva Conference, the question for many French officials was not whether they wanted war or peace but how to bring about peace. In the interest of peace, the French government was considering making concessions to China, including granting it diplomatic recognition or allowing it entry into the UN in return for agreeing to end its assistance to the DRV. French Prime Minister Joseph Laniel declared that he was considering moving ahead with the negotiations without consulting the United States. Because the United States was pressuring France to approve the European Defense Community (EDC), the French could use Indochina as leverage to maneuver on their own.[29]

In mid-February at a Chinese government conference held in preparation for the Geneva Conference, Zhou summarized China's perception of U.S.-French relations:

> On the Vietnam question, contradictions exist between France and the United States. France wants to have peace, and the United States does not want peace; France does not want to let the United States intervene in Vietnam, but the United States is attempting to gain control of France's command over military affairs and training in Vietnam, a step that has been rejected by France. Therefore, our general policy line should be *"showing carrot to France while using stick to deal with the United States."* In our propaganda, we should concentrate our criticism on America, and should leave France with some hope.[30]

To the satisfaction of Chinese leaders, U.S. policy was not supported by the United Kingdom, another major U.S. ally. The Chinese knew that the United Kingdom had supported the French invasion of Indochina and provided moderate military assistance for the sake of its colonial interests in Southeast Asia, especially Malaya. But when the Indochina War worsened in early 1954, the British became increasingly worried that the United States would intervene in Indochina, which would provoke China into participation, ultimately leading to a world war.[31] Moreover, British leaders were eager for trade with China and wanted to make use of Geneva to end the trade embargo on China, which the United States imposed in 1951. *Renmin Ribao* reported that the United States indeed had used the embargo to expel its allies from the world market and to enhance its control of these states. Chinese diplomats told Beijing that other European states, such as Italy and West Germany, supported British trade policy. They highlighted an article in a West German newspaper arguing that trade was the most powerful weapon China could use in Geneva.[32]

As disagreements between the United States and its major allies became more obvious, Chinese leaders believed they could frustrate any U.S. intention to move into Indochina by playing the Western powers against each other. In addition, Chinese officials believed that they could push U.S. allies to make major concessions to China, such as termination of the embargo, allowing trade, and even refraining from vetoing China's entrance into the UN. Their confidence was revealed by the issues they prepared to bring to the negotiation: In addition to a peaceful solution of the Indochina problem, the Chinese also wanted to expand the discussion to the Taiwan issue and U.S.-China relations.[33]

BUILDING A UNITED FRONT

While planning to separate the United States from its allies, Chinese leaders closely coordinated policies with their comrades. Documents and memoirs from China, the Soviet Union, and the DRV reveal the original positions of the three states for the first time. In early 1954, all three governments recognized the growing threat of direct U.S. intervention in Indochina and wanted to use the Geneva Conference to negotiate a ceasefire. The Soviet Union and the DRV also agreed to China's tactics of exploiting the conflicting interests between the Western states in order to realize peace in Indochina.[34]

However, the Communists differed somewhat on some major issues, especially the three most important problems they would later face at Geneva: the demarcation line, the status of Laos and Cambodia, and supervision of the ceasefire. China proposed the sixteenth parallel as a temporary partition line in Vietnam. Although the Soviet Union accepted a partition as the middle position they would seek in Geneva, the DRV had different ideas, despite Zhou's repeated suggestions. DRV leaders could not agree among themselves whether to pursue an on-the-spot ceasefire or a clear line of demarcation. The former option would give them about three-quarters of the territory and help them win an election if the French agreed to hold one right after the ceasefire. However, DRV leaders admitted that achieving this result would be difficult. Also, a demarcation line would require the DRV to withdraw its forces from southern Indochina and give up many bases it had built. Moreover, the DRV leaders who agreed to accept a demarcation line did not necessarily agree about where the line should be drawn. Because a line would suggest partition of Vietnam, at least temporarily, many DRV leaders regarded this as the least acceptable position.[35]

On the issue of Laos and Cambodia, the DRV stressed a shared destiny among the states in Indochina and demanded a general solution to the Indochina issue. At the same time, they acknowledged that the situations in these states differed from the situation in Vietnam. The Chinese accepted the Vietnamese position that the three states would ultimately form a Federation of Indochina, but they focused on the current phrase and aimed at "three unified and independent states" before they could move toward a Federation "on the basis of common will."[36] However, the Vietnamese did not put forward any concrete solution with regard to the differences between the three states.[37]

The Communist position on how to supervise the ceasefire is the best indication of the three states' differing concerns. Chinese leaders were most hopeful that a ceasefire in Indochina would preclude future U.S. intervention. Hence China was the only party to propose that the five powers guarantee any ceasefire reached in Geneva and that a supervisory commission be established to ensure that the Indochinese states did not allow foreign troops and weapons on their territory. The Soviet Union did not specify a position on this issue, emphasizing instead that key Soviet interests lay in Europe. For the DRV, adoption of the Chinese proposal would mean that the DRV could no longer get military assistance from China, which by this time was Hanoi's only source of aid.[38]

In addition, the Vietnamese still did not have high expectations of diplomacy, despite the Soviet and Chinese emphasis on the importance of negotiation.[39] For these two countries, the minimum objective in Geneva was to maintain direct negotiations between the French and the DRV, even if no agreement could be reached. Some DRV military leaders wanted to use military pressure to force the French to give up Indochina. Although China staunchly supported the DRV and helped it launch a series of successful operations, Chinese leaders responded to the start of the Dien Bien Phu campaign in March by stressing that military actions must serve diplomatic purposes. Zhou told Chinese military advisors in Vietnam to win several battles before Geneva "in order to gain diplomatic initiative," and Mao urged them to keep the military pressure on the French but not to expand the fighting.[40] Chinese leaders also ruled out the possibility of sending Chinese troops to join the war directly, despite repeated Vietnamese requests for China's direct intervention after their forces suffered heavy losses in the initial phase of the campaign.[41] Determined to neutralize Indochina through diplomacy, Chinese leaders got ready to stop assistance to the DRV once an armistice was concluded and ordered the Vietnamese Communist troops being trained in China back to the DRV as soon as possible.[42]

China's goal was not completely consistent with the DRV's goal. While the Chinese wanted a neutralized Indochina and were willing to accept a temporarily divided Vietnam, the DRV wanted a ceasefire and, ultimately, a Federation of Indochina, but they did not have a clear idea how they could achieve this, even as a short-term goal. Chinese leaders invited Ho to Beijing in late March to coordinate their positions, but they reached only general agreements: a solution to the Indochina problem included a military ceasefire and political elections; the two sides should regroup their troops after the armistice; the French should finally withdraw their forces from Indochina on schedule; and elections should be held to create a unified Vietnamese government. The DRV also agreed to stay within the French Union and maintain its economic and cultural ties with France as a way to induce France to negotiate. However, the two sides did not reach a consensus on whether they wanted a clear-cut demarcation line or an on-the-spot ceasefire, or how to handle Laos and Cambodia.

The Communist differences on these key issues persisted until they entered negotiation in Geneva. In early April, Zhou and Vietnamese leaders went to Moscow at the Soviet Union's request.[43] The three parties reached some general agreements: they would secure the DRV's independent participation in the conference and the participation of the resistance governments of Laos and Cambodia in the Vietnamese delegation if they failed to get them in as independent delegations[44]; their goal at Geneva was a ceasefire, guaranteed by the five powers, withdrawal of all foreign forces from Indochina within six months of the ceasefire; and the DRV's military action would continue until an acceptable political solution was reached, which meant that they would follow the policy of fighting while talking. But the three states failed to reach an agreement on the most important question of whether they wanted a demarcation line or an on-the-spot ceasefire, although both the Soviet and Chinese leaders once again suggested the sixteenth parallel, and they agreed that the French and Vietnamese troops would adjust their occupied territories after ceasefire.[45] The Soviets decided to let the Chinese and Vietnamese take the initiative on the Indochina issue in Geneva, and Soviet leaders told leaders in Beijing and Hanoi that the Soviet Union would respect whatever decision they reached.[46]

Nevertheless, preoccupied with the threat of U.S. intervention, the Communists made up their mind that "any agreement on Indochina . . . shall contain a clause on the end of U.S. interference in Indochinese affairs." To eliminate any excuse the United States might use to move into Indochina, the Communists decided to leave no impression that China was assisting the DRV.[47] In a series of instructions to the grassroots organizations of the VWP, DRV leaders warned that "the ruling circles in the U.S. have openly and directly been intervening in the war of aggression in Vietnam, Cambodia, and Laos" and were pushing France to "conscript troops and exploit our people with all methods in order to implement the policy of 'using Vietnamese to fight Vietnamese, feeding war with war.' " Due to these concerns, they called on the party to support the Geneva Conference to defeat the U.S. plan of intervention.[48]

On the eve of the Geneva Conference, Chinese leaders' determination to reach an agreement in Geneva was strengthened by reports about the differences between the United States and its allies. According to Chinese diplomats, France was eager for a solution. Although the current French administration was not sure what actions it could take in Geneva, it was not interested in pursuing united action with the United States.[49] Beijing was aware that Dulles's trip to Paris and London in mid-April failed to win either French or British support for united action. France simply rejected Dulles's request to make a joint statement about it. The British agreed to state that they would study the possibility of establishing a defense group in Southeast Asia, but they refused to make a joint communiqué about that in order to give diplomacy an opportunity in Geneva. The Indian government, whose policy on Indochina the Chinese leaders believed reflected the British position, called for a ceasefire in Indochina in opposition to the American desire for united action.[50]

To convey China's willingness to reach an agreement in Geneva to the United Kingdom, Zhou deliberately told the Indian ambassador to Beijing

FIGURE 1.2. Molotov prepares to shake Zhou's Hand
Source: Getty Images

before he left for Geneva that "the Geneva Conference must not fail." The Chinese delegation would do its best to bring about an agreement, especially on restoring peace in Indochina, despite U.S. efforts to sabotage the conference.

> The Western states such as Britain and France should be told that they are facing two different roads: they could either have good relations with Asian people and maintain part of their interests or refuse this road and choose to walk the same road with the United States, thus losing everything.[51]

Zhou was reminding the British leaders of the vulnerability of Hong Kong, a British crown colony.[52]

PREVENTING THE UNITED STATES FROM SABOTAGING THE CONFERENCE

The opening session on Korea confirmed Chinese leaders' perception of the tensions within the Western alliance. Chinese officials regarded Korea as a less serious issue, insofar as the war there had stopped, and the Communists had already concluded that the United States was not interested in a permanent solution.[53] Yet the Chinese delegation deliberately avoided mentioning Indochina in order to whet the French appetite for negotiation. At the same time, the DRV maintained military pressure on the battleground. After British and French leaders expressed eagerness to solve the Indochina problem, the Soviet Union pushed the French to invite the DRV delegation to the conference. Meanwhile, Chinese officials noticed that the two U.S. allies were indifferent to the Communist accusations against the United States on the Korean issue.[54] Despite Dulles's statement at his press conference that he would not meet the Chinese premier unless their cars collided, shortly after the conference started, the British foreign secretary Anthony Eden met Zhou. At the meeting, Eden expressed strong interest in developing relations, especially trade relations, with China. Moreover, Eden tried to distinguish the United Kingdom from the United States. He told Zhou that "[the United Kingdom has] nothing in common with the United States except the same language" and that the United Kingdom would be willing to let China co-sponsor the conference, making it a five-power conference, which was what the Communists had wanted.[55] Before the meeting, Chinese officials

FIGURE 1.3. 1954 Geneva Conference in session
Source: Frank Scherschel/The LIFE Picture Collection via Getty Images

learned that the United States would put off the Indochina negotiation until the Korean sessions succeeded, which meant it wanted to avoid the negotiation. Based on his observations in Geneva, Zhou now judged that the British sincerely wanted peace in Indochina, stating, "it is impossible for the U.S. to prevent the negotiations on the Indochina issue now."[56]

As soon as the Indochina session started, Zhou pushed the DRV delegation to agree to let the French withdraw their wounded soldiers in order to demonstrate sincerity. But it did not take long for the two sides to find the gaps between their positions. First, they did not agree on the general goal of the conference. France was interested in a ceasefire but refused to discuss the future of Vietnam, so it proposed to start negotiations about the ceasefire first. The DRV, however, wanted to discuss both a political solution that would unify Vietnam and a ceasefire simultaneously, and it would not stop military actions until a satisfactory result was achieved through negotiation, following the position it had agreed on with its Communist allies.

The second difference was about the supervision of the ceasefire. Although the two sides agreed about the necessity of supervision, they disagreed on the composition of the supervision commission. The French suggested an ambiguous international control of the ceasefire, but the Communists suspected the French proposal would lead to the U.S.-proposed military group, and they counter proposed a commission made up of neutral states, including India, Pakistan, Poland, Czechoslovakia, and Indonesia or Burma. The Westerners opposed this proposal because "Communist states were not neutral" and their membership would make the commission useless, as they had learned from the Korean Armistice Agreement.

The third difference concerned Laos and Cambodia. The Western side and the Laotian and Cambodian governments wanted to separate these two states from Vietnam on the grounds that the DRV indeed invaded these two states. No fighting was actually taking place between these two states and France, and the two so-called resistance governments in Laos and Cambodia were nothing but the DRV's puppets. Therefore, the Western delegations demanded the unconditional withdrawal of DRV forces from Laos and Cambodia before any negotiation about a ceasefire in Vietnam could be conducted. The Communists, however, refused to admit the existence of DRV forces in Laos and Cambodia and proposed an overall ceasefire in all of Indochina, which indicated that the DRV represented the whole of Indochina, in compliance with its ultimate goal of building a Federation of Indochina.[57]

To make matters worse, the United States was trying to exacerbate the conflicts between the two sides, which Chinese leaders believed was the major reason for the deadlock. Despite British and French requests, Dulles was uninterested in negotiations and left Geneva even before the conference entered the Indochina phase. While the conference was discussing a ceasefire, the U.S. government publicized its plan to assist France and the Indochinese states to resist "Vietnamese invasion." Meanwhile, the United States repeatedly demonstrated an intention to develop a "collective defense group" in Southeast Asia. These reports from Chinese diplomats only confirmed Chinese leaders' suspicion that the United States did not want the war in Indochina to stop and was determined to sabotage the Geneva Conference.[58]

To facilitate private discussions, the negotiation turned to restricted sessions at Molotov's request, but this did not lead to any progress because both the DRV and France increased pressure on each other, both expecting the other side to retreat first. While the Vietminh forces prepared for new offensives after Dien Bien Phu, the French started talking with the United States about internationalizing the war, and they deliberately released the news as a way to press the Communists.[59] When that did not seem to work on the Communists, leading only to British protests, French officials directly warned the Chinese that they would seek U.S. assistance if the Communists refused to make concessions. However, the French promised that they would consider establishing diplomatic relations with China if it could push the DRV to reach a satisfactory solution.[60] By late May, French officials became impatient and made a more serious threat: if the Vietnamese "did not make good use of their time," the French would have to "turn over the war to the U.S." The French requested holding direct meetings between the military representatives from France and the DRV to talk about the ceasefire.[61]

To break the deadlock, the Chinese encouraged the DRV delegation to make some concessions, particularly after Eden also warned Zhou that the military situation in Indochina would "deteriorate" if no agreement could be reached in Geneva.[62] The Vietnamese were reluctant to follow China's advice, despite their concern about U.S. intervention. According to Chinese diplomats, the victory of the Battle of Dien Bien Phu emboldened some DRV leaders, but more important, the Vietnamese remained divided on the question of how they could obtain a ceasefire. In this circumstance, Wang Jiaxiang, Chinese vice foreign minister, suggested starting discussion on the ceasefire issue while keeping on the agenda the proposal for a political solution, which retreated from the Communists' original position of simultaneous negotiation on the two issues. Wang also suggested that the DRV reconsider its position on Laos and Cambodia, reminding Pham Van Dong, the DRV's chief delegate, that a DRV's newspaper had once acknowledged the existence of Vietnamese forces in the two countries. Dong admitted this but preferred to avoid the issue in the conference.[63] Chinese officials also suggested a temporary division of Vietnam "along either the 14th, 15th, or 16th parallel," but the Vietnamese refused the idea as "politically disadvantageous" and instead proposed regrouping forces "according to the situation after the fall of Dien Bien Phu," which would give the DRV more than 80 percent of Vietnam's territory. The Soviets supported the idea of division, but they avoided getting involved in the dispute and asked the two delegations to work out their differences themselves.[64]

Under these circumstances, the negotiations failed to break the deadlock. On May 25, after repeated requests from the Chinese, Dong agreed to regroup military forces into the zones decided by the two sides, which

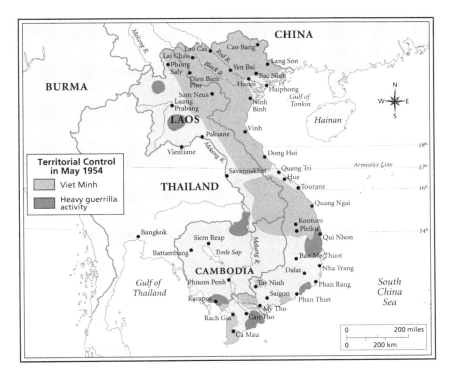

FIGURE 1.4. Territorial control in May 1954
Courtesy of Fredrik Logevall and Mapping Specialists, Ltd.

implied his acceptance of demarcation, and he also agreed to hold military-commander meetings with France in both Indochina and Geneva. The military talks started on June 1, but French officials soon complained to the Chinese that the DRV refused to talk about ceasefire details and were instead putting forth abstract principles.[65]

Chinese leaders were dismayed by the lack of development, in part because they simultaneously faced a surge of pressure elsewhere. In May of 1954, after the most serious conflicts since 1949 broke out between the Communists and the GMD in the Taiwan Strait, the United States sent aircraft carriers to the area.[66] Meanwhile, Beijing sensed that the United States was considering an alliance with Chiang Kai-shek and sent a series of military leaders to Taiwan to discuss it. According to Chinese diplomats, U.S. officials were also visiting Southeast Asia and pressuring the United Kingdom and France for their cooperation on establishing a Southeast Asian Treaty Organization (SEATO). Chinese officials were aware that the United States planned to sponsor the organization with Australia, New Zealand, the United Kingdom, and France, and wanted to include such Asian states as the Indochinese countries, Thailand, the Philippines, South Korea, and even the GMD. Eisenhower declared a willingness to move on without the United Kingdom if the latter hesitated to follow the United States.[67]

To safeguard Chinese interests against the United States, officials in Beijing wanted to use Geneva to pursue their original plan of ending the war by separating the United States from its allies. Their observations convinced them that this strategy was still feasible, insofar as serious differences still existed among the Western states. According to Chinese intelligence, the French still refused to let the United States command the Vietnamese troops, and, although the British agreed to the U.S. suggestion to hold a military staff meeting with other allies, they declared in advance that this conference would not include talks on the defense treaty in Southeast Asia.[68]

At the same time, the DRV's top leaders were anxious about U.S. intervention and pushed their delegation in Geneva for progress. In a telegram to the delegation on May 27, the VWP Central Committee warned that the French were magnifying and aggrandizing the military threat against them to justify the need for additional reinforcement and U.S. backing. Meanwhile, DRV leaders acknowledged that the Vietnamese people's demand for restoration of peace had intensified. Nevertheless, they admitted that they themselves were unsure of how to bring about peace, as they "[did] not have a clear understanding of the situation in France or of the international situation."[69]

The Chinese therefore took the initiative again. In a lengthy telegram to the central committees of the Chinese Communist Party (CCP) and the VWP, Zhou encouraged the Vietnamese to "enter discussions of substance" on the key issues of dividing zones, ceasefire supervision, and Laos and Cambodia. The DRV, he said, should "develop a more clearly defined solution" and "persistently take the initiative to pursue peace," instead of procrastinating in the negotiations, which would lead to failure. Zhou proposed dividing Vietnam at the sixteenth parallel and urged the VWP to be ready to make even more concessions. Zhou claimed that the Soviet Union approved this suggestion, and he called on the DRV to make concessions on Laos and Cambodia as well. The three countries in Indochina, Zhou argued, were clearly delimited by national borders, which existed before the French created the colonial state of Indochina. Also, the Communist forces in Laos and Cambodia were limited, and no independent Communist parties existed in either country, contrary to what the DRV had been claiming.[70]

At the same time, Zhou made overtures to France and the United Kingdom. In a meeting with the French foreign minister Georges Bidault, Zhou told him that China aimed to restore peace in Indochina and that he would do his best to realize that goal. He promised the French that both the regrouping and supervision issues could be solved, and that Vietnam would join the French Union after its independence. Zhou frankly told Bidault that China was worried about U.S. intervention in Indochina and that he believed China and France had a common interest in stopping the fighting in Indochina.[71] He encouraged the French to be more active and take more initiatives, while agreeing that the negotiations should work on the demarcation and supervision issues simultaneously. Chinese diplomats soon started to talk with their French counterparts about the two issues. After the French reiterated that the Vietnamese just talked about principles and refused to make concrete proposals, Wang Bingnan, general secretary of the Chinese delegation, assured the French that "problems could be solved," implying Communist concessions.[72]

When Zhou explored the British intentions, Eden told him that the United Kingdom sought better relations with China. He encouraged Beijing to send its diplomatic representative to London, even offering to visit China. This was a highly significant move, as no head of government, not even those of Communist states, had visited Beijing since the establishment of the PRC, and the British still supported the GMD government in the UN. On the issue of Indochina, Eden did not support Poland and Czechoslovakia as candidates for the supervision commission, but he wanted to include more Asian states, implying members of the British Commonwealth, through which the United Kingdom could exert influence. However, Eden also set up a deadline for the negotiation, saying he hoped the conference would be concluded "in 10 to 15 days."[73] In response, Chinese officials agreed to send a chargé d'affaires, which China had previously refused in protest to the United Kingdom's recognition of the GMD, and suggested exchanging trade delegations with the United Kingdom. At the same time, the Chinese wanted to make a public declaration on this to put more pressure on the United States.[74]

On June 4, the VWP Central Committee finally agreed to Zhou's suggestion of temporarily dividing Vietnam at the sixteenth parallel.[75] The DRV delegation's acceptance of partition was a significant step forward, but the Western states demanded more concessions on the issues of supervision and Laos and Cambodia.[76] The United Kingdom nominated the five Colombo powers—India, Indonesia, Burma, Ceylon, and Pakistan—as candidates for the supervision commission, and the West opposed granting the commission the right of veto, as the Communists proposed, because it would give Communist states so much power that it would make supervision impossible. On the issue of Laos and Cambodia, the French told the Vietnamese that an unconditional withdrawal of Vietnamese forces was "a prerequisite" for the negotiation to move forward.[77]

The Western side became increasingly impatient when the DRV leaders proved unwilling to retreat further from their positions and simultaneously pressed on with military actions on the battlefield. U.S. Undersecretary of State Walter Bedell Smith warned Molotov of U.S. intervention in Indochina if the Viet Minh had "too great appetites" and "over-reached themselves."[78] Eden told Zhou directly that the conference would fail if no progress was made.[79] At the same time, the British changed their attitude toward an exchange of chargé d'affaires with China and backed out of a Chinese trade delegation's visit to the United Kingdom.[80] A French diplomat also warned the Chinese that the United States wanted both the Korean and Indochinese negotiations to fail.[81] At the same time, the British government announced that Prime Minister Winston Churchill would visit Washington with Eden, and the military staff of the United States, the United Kingdom, France, Australia, and New Zealand would meet in Washington. Both of these things aimed to establish SEATO.[82] In the UN, using its position as chair of the Security Council, the United States successfully put a Thai proposal calling for an inspection of Indochina on the agenda. *Remin Ribao* saw this as a crucial step toward internationalization of the war that would pave the way for U.S. intervention.[83]

Anxious about these signals, Zhou expressed dissatisfaction with the lack of progress in the military talks and warned the VWP that the United States would disrupt the conference if the DRV failed to carry the negotiation forward.[84] He had urged the VWP to move the demarcation line to between the sixteenth and seventeenth parallels, and now he directly requested concessions on Laos and Cambodia in return for a French concession on the dividing zones in Vietnam.[85] After he probed the British attitude and was told that if an agreement was reached in Geneva the United Kingdom "cannot imagine that any participating countries would use such an agreement to establish [military] bases in Laos and Cambodia," Zhou directly proposed to the VWP to retreat on "the key issue" of Laos and Cambodia, so that the conference would continue.[86]

Under pressure from Zhou, the VWP finally agreed to withdraw its troops from Laos and Cambodia. Zhou immediately revealed this major concession to Eden, but he clarified that these two states should become "Southeast Asian type" countries, meaning neutral states, in which the United States would not build military bases.[87] When Zhou declared this concession in the plenary conference, he even agreed to allow Laos and Cambodia to import weapons for self-defense purposes, as long as they did not allow foreign military bases on their lands.[88] Dong also formally declared that the DRV would respect Laos's and Cambodia's independence and unity.

The Communist delegations' concessions kept the conference from failure. Bidault then told the Soviets that the UK-U.S. meeting in Washington did not matter and that the negotiation at Geneva should continue "at the highest possible level."[89] Eden also assured Molotov that the foreign ministers should continue to settle the problems of supervision and guarantees. Meanwhile, British diplomats declared that they were now ready to accept China's chargé d'affaires.[90] Under pressure from its allies, U.S. officials had to express that the Geneva Conference "should be kept going while there was hope of reaching reasonable settlement."[91]

In the meantime, political change in France also gave the Communists hope. On June 16, Laniel was replaced as prime minister by Pierre Mendès France. Chinese officials long believed he was much more pro-peace than Laniel, and the Soviets learned from his foreign policy advisor in early April that Mendès France wanted a ceasefire in Indochina and free elections in Vietnam.[92] Mendès France's promise to the French people that he would resign if he could not bring about peace in Indochina by July 20 further reinforced the Communists' impression that they could cooperate with the new French prime minister.

To build on the momentum, Zhou worked out a new position with the other two Communist delegations: To secure a solution in Vietnam, the Vietnamese should withdraw all their forces from Cambodia and strive

only for a political solution, and in Laos they would limit their regrouping areas to only two, one each in the north and the south. For Zhou, such
concessions were necessary because

> the current situation is: if we propose a reasonable plan in the military
> meeting, it would be possible to solve the problem with France and reach
> a ceasefire quickly. As a result, we could push the new French government
> to stand up to U.S. intervention, and at the same time, delay the European
> Defense Community issue. Therefore, *it would benefit both the East and
> the West.*[93]

To ensure that the Vietnamese leaders understood the significance of a
peaceful solution, he proposed holding a meeting with "a few more comrades in control in Vietnam Central Committee." The VWP leaders agreed,
seeing new indications of U.S. determination to get involved in Indochina.
On June 19, Ngo Dinh Diem became prime minister of State of Vietnam.
The DRV leaders saw this as a clear signal that Washington had its "lackey"
in place and that, if the Geneva Conference failed, the "Americans would
have free rein" in Vietnam.[94]

When the foreign ministers left the negotiation to their representatives
in late June, Chinese leaders believed their efforts to prevent the United
States from spoiling the negotiation on Indochina had worked well. Mao
optimistically predicted that an armistice could be reached in July.[95]
However, developments in Geneva were achieved at a price. The DRV's
agreement to separate Laos and Cambodia from Vietnam meant they
grudgingly accepted that these two states would differ from Vietnam in
their political complexions. Thus, the Communists had to put aside, at
least temporarily, the idea of the Indochina Federation.[96] The fact that it
was China that put forward the suggestion sowed seeds of disagreements
in Sino-Vietnamese relations, although at the time the two countries were
satisfied with the progress in Geneva and wanted to continue the negotiation.[97] Chinese leaders understood this, and they also knew that some
Vietnamese military leaders remained reluctant to resort to diplomacy. In
a telegram to Chinese military advisors in the DRV, Mao instructed them
to restrain the DRV from expanding the military actions before the end of
the Geneva Conference, when it was concluding a major military victory
against the French.[98]

ZHOU'S DIPLOMACY OUTSIDE THE CONFERENCE

Before Zhou left Geneva in late June, he started another round of intense diplomacy to make sure that the parties understood China's position on a neutralized Indochina. He consulted with the Laotians and Cambodians about their future as independent states. Zhou assured the two delegations that the DRV would withdraw its forces and guaranteed that their independence and security would be safeguarded. Also, Zhou warned them that China would not allow the United States to build military bases on their territory: "Once such bases were built, we [the Chinese] would have to get involved, because they would be a threat to our security." Therefore, remaining neutral was the only choice Laos and Cambodia could make. Zhou's meeting with the two delegations was significant, not only because it was his first meeting with officials from Laos and Cambodia but also because it paved the way for Dong's meetings with representatives of the two governments, which the DRV had branded as French puppets and refused to recognize.[99]

Zhou then proposed a meeting with the new French prime minister, and at Zhou's insistence, China and France made a joint statement about the meeting in advance. Mendès France was frank about his eagerness for peace in his meeting with Zhou, telling the Chinese leader that the difficulty in making progress came from the United States. Zhou, for his part, said that China's greatest concern was preventing the United States from internationalizing the war and building military bases in Indochina. Aside from that, China had no other requests. Mendès France responded that the "French government had not the slightest intention of allowing them [military bases] to be established."[100] Zhou then suggested leaving the demarcation line to be drawn by the French and DRV's military representatives; once a demarcation line was settled, the political problem was "not a big issue" and would be settled easily when the conference resumed in July. This suggestion indicated China's formal retreat from the Communists' agreement that a political solution must come before an armistice, which was in opposition to French attempts to only have a military ceasefire.[101] Zhou also told Eden that if the DRV's demands in Vietnam were satisfied they would make concessions on Laos and Cambodia.[102]

Zhou's concessions were based on his calculation of the international situation in late June. According to the Chinese Foreign Ministry, the British feared being dragged into a war in Indochina, and they also did not want to bend to U.S. leadership in a Southeast Asian group. Thus, Chinese leaders sensed that the British were trying to form their own version of a Southeast Asian bloc with countries like India, Indonesia, Burma, and Ceylon as a way to resist U.S. expansion into the United Kingdom's traditional sphere in Southeast Asia. Before leaving for Washington, Eden declared in the British Parliament that the United Kingdom wanted to build a Locarno-type pact in Asia, and that, more important, he would include Communist states in the pact. His purpose in traveling to the United States was to convince U.S. officials to give France a chance to reach a peace agreement. Eden also expressed satisfaction about the improvement in the United Kingdom's relations with China.[103] Encouraged by these statements, Chinese leaders concluded that the British leaders were not going to join the proposed united action during their visit to Washington. Meanwhile, the Chinese believed the French were also resisting U.S. pressure to continue fighting in Indochina because they worried that their sacrifice would only facilitate U.S. entry into the region, even if they ultimately won the war. Chinese leaders were confident that the United States would not be able to prevent China from neutralizing Indochina if they could keep the United Kingdom and France away from the United States and carry the conference forward.[104]

To gain Indian Prime Minister Jawaharlal Nehru's support, Zhou visited India in late June, following up on an earlier invitation he had declined. The visit to India reinforced Zhou's judgment that China could and should work with the British.[105] In New Delhi, Nehru tried to convince Zhou that London was still the center of diplomacy in the world, and that, "to some extent, London was even more important than Washington." According to Nehru, the United Kingdom was not interested in the defense group the United States had proposed, and its China policy was far different from the U.S. policy.[106] Chinese leaders may not have completely accepted what Nehru said, but his description of the UK-U.S. differences aligned with Zhou's observation in Geneva. Based on Zhou's experiences in Geneva and India, Chinese leaders concluded that the British government sincerely wanted better relations with China, despite U.S. opposition, and that China should exploit the opportunity to establish formal diplomatic relations with the United Kingdom.[107]

The visit by Churchill and Eden to the United States in late June confirmed for Chinese leaders that the United Kingdom could be used against the United States. In Washington, according to Chinese officials, British leaders refused to talk about any concrete steps toward a defense treaty in Asia and only agreed to a statement about some broad general principles, despite the great pressure the United States put on the British leaders. In the eyes of Chinese leaders, the British visit to Washington was nothing but a U.S. diplomatic failure. Mao gladly told the Soviet chargé d'affaires to Beijing that despite U.S. pressure on the United Kingdom to end the Geneva Conference fruitlessly, the British continued the negotiation, and, more significant, Churchill declared in Washington that he sought peaceful coexistence with the Communists. In response, the Soviets encouraged the Chinese to make good use of the chance to resolve the Indochinese problem.[108] Chinese officials offered several reasons to explain the British defiance of the position taken by the United States: the British feared being dragged into a nuclear war, the United Kingdom was under pressure from the world peace movement and members in the British Commonwealth, and, most important, the British economy was improving and no longer had to rely so heavily on the United States.[109]

In light of these developments, Chinese leaders became confident that their goal could be realized as long as they could convince the DRV. From July 3 to 5, Zhou held a series of intense meetings with the VWP leaders in Liuzhou, close to the Sino-Vietnamese border. In a presentation that lasted two days, Zhou stressed the necessity of an immediate ceasefire and the inevitability of U.S. intervention if the negotiation failed. He concluded, "The only task we are facing now is to accomplish peace." For that, Zhou made some specific suggestions regarding the demarcation line. The bottom line was the sixteenth parallel in Vietnam. If this was not possible, it could be moved to Route 9 to the north, at approximately the seventeenth parallel. In Laos, the Communists would demand one area each in upper, middle, and lower Laos but could only expect the two areas in upper and middle Laos. In Cambodia, the Communists could try requesting a regrouping area but should not have high expectations of achieving it.[110]

Ho was also worried about U.S. intervention and agreed that they should strive to reach a compromise on the demarcation issue and end the Indochina war as quickly as possible. He also agreed to Zhou's idea of neutralizing Laos and Cambodia. To make sure the DRV delegation understood the urgency of the situation, he sent a directive entitled "July 5 Document" to the VWP delegation in Geneva, which set the bottom line in Vietnam: a temporary demarcation line on the sixteenth parallel, a general election to take place six months to one year after the end of war, and two regrouping areas in Laos.[111]

Nevertheless, the meetings in Liuzhou also revealed that differences remained between the two states and that DRV leaders were divided among themselves. The fact that Zhou had to make repeated requests highlighted the unwillingness of the DRV to make concessions. Despite Zhou's insistence on the importance of peace, Ho maintained that the Vietnamese ought to be ready to fight an ongoing war. Although Ho agreed that "the main direction should be the pursuit of peace," he pointed out that "there were many difficulties" in "persuad[ing] our cadres" to accept the wisdom of seeking peace with the French.[112]

As soon as the meetings were over, Zhou met with the British chargé d'affaires in Beijing. The Chinese leader disclosed that he had reached an agreement with the Vietnamese leaders, adding that "it should not take very long now to settle matters at Geneva." Zhou also revealed he did not think "there was any danger of fighting on a significant scale in Indochina during this delicate time."[113] Soon the Chinese and DRV governments published editorials in their respective mouthpieces highlighting the meetings and their quest for peace.[114] This was the DRV's first public declaration that the chief goal in Geneva was peace.

After Zhou's meeting with the Vietnamese, Chinese leaders reviewed their policy in Geneva and concluded that an agreement in Indochina was most likely if the Communists could further exploit the conflicts between the United States and its allies.[115] They even believed the Eisenhower administration was riven by internal conflicts. The Chinese saw Smith, who led the U.S. delegation in Geneva, as a more reasonable figure than Dulles or Eisenhower, and they sensed differences even between Dulles and Eisenhower that might provide opportunities for maneuver.[116] Based on this analysis, Mao instructed the Chinese delegation to resume the consulate talks in Geneva in order to play on the differences between U.S. leaders and isolate the more aggressive figures.[117] En route back to Geneva, Zhou stopped over in Moscow and reached a final consensus with Soviet leaders. The Communists should put forward a simple, clear-cut proposal, acceptable to the French, which would help France resist U.S. pressure and bring about peace. Having reached this agreement, Zhou optimistically reported to Beijing that he was certain that China's goal could be achieved in Geneva.[118]

CHINA'S LAST EFFORTS

Zhou's first task back in Geneva, however, was to press the DRV delegation to accelerate the negotiations after failing to take any initiative during Zhou's absence. When the French proposed a demarcation line at the
eighteenth parallel, the DRV would only be willing to accept the fourteenth
parallel, despite Ho's July 5 Document and the requests from the Soviets
and Chinese. According to Zhou, the lack of progress resulted from the
DRV delegates' overestimation of their military strength and reluctance to
give up the idea of the Indochina Federation.[119]

Because French and British leaders were going to meet Dulles in Paris
the next afternoon, Zhou wasted no time.[120] After a meeting with Molotov,
Zhou held an overnight conversation with Dong to convince him that the
major task now was to strive to reach an agreement on Indochina. The Communist side, according to Zhou, must immediately let British and French
leaders know about its desire for a settlement and put forward new proposals that would be acceptable to France, in order to give Mendès France, in
particular, "enough capital to counterbalance" U.S. pressure in Paris. For
that purpose, Zhou suggested that Dong propose the sixteenth parallel as
a demarcation line, but that he be prepared to move the line a little further
north to get an agreement. As for the election, they could strive for a fixed
deadline, but it would be acceptable to reach an agreement in principle and
set the deadline later. On the issue of Laos, Zhou expected to send some
members from the resistance government to the national government to
form a coalition government. In Cambodia, most of the Vietnamese personnel should withdraw, with the remainder staying to work underground.
The key point, Zhou stressed, was to keep the negotiations going and give
up the unrealistic thought of unifying Vietnam through war. Dong finally
agreed to Zhou's proposals.[121]

Early the next morning, the three Communist delegations reached an
agreement on the basis of Zhou's position, and they met with the Western
leaders immediately to make the concessions known.[122] Zhou first assured
Mendès France that "we share common ideas and common goals, namely,
to restore peace in Indochina," so "we should be able to resolve the problem." He encouraged Mendès France to meet with Dong, who was ready
to make further concessions.[123] After that, Zhou turned to Eden when
Dong was talking with Mendès France.[124] Lest the British underestimated

the significance of his meeting with DRV leaders in Liuzhou, Zhou briefed Eden in person about the DRV's willingness for peace and assured him that neither the regrouping area in Vietnam nor neutralization of Laos and Cambodia was a problem, as long as Indochina would not allow foreign military bases or join a military alliance. He pushed Eden to "give a fair judgment" between China and the United States; while the former wanted peaceful coexistence with "any state," the latter planned to build a Southeast Asian military alliance to threaten China.[125]

Zhou shifted to Cambodia and Laos when the Western leaders were meeting in Paris. He reassured the two states that the DRV would observe the principle of peaceful coexistence and was willing to establish friendly relations with them, provided that the two countries remained neutral and did not allow any foreign bases on their territory. To demonstrate good-will, Zhou retreated further and allowed the Cambodians to import foreign weapons and even introduce French troops after the period of armistice, as long as the United States was kept out of Cambodia.[126] In private, the United States was not only pushing Laos and Cambodia to insist on the right to join SEATO but also enticing them with promises of military assistance, which made Zhou's overtures to the two states necessary and timely. Laos and Cambodia, for their part, had asked the United States for membership in the defense pact as protection against invasion by the DRV.[127]

After his meetings with British and French leaders, Zhou reported to Beijing that the French were willing to reach an agreement ahead of their self-imposed deadline and that they had already sent him a copy of a draft agreement. Zhou believed the French would finally agree to a demarcation line somewhere between the sixteenth and eighteenth parallels.[128] To get ready for the ceasefire, Zhou instructed Chinese military advisors in Vietnam to tell the Vietnamese to "quickly work out a plan for the [Vietnamese] People's Army to withdraw from the South, and promptly report the plan to the Vietnamese delegation [in Geneva]."[129]

The Communist concessions, however, were not reciprocated by French concessions. After the Western governments met in Paris, Molotov pushed Mendès France to show flexibility on the demarcation line and set June 1955 as the deadline for the election in Vietnam. He told the French that the Vietnamese concessions were made under "strong force of persuasion" and that the French should not expect more from Vietnam.[130] Based on the agreement they reached with allies in Paris, however, the French refused to retreat from the eighteenth parallel demarcation line and opposed the Soviet proposal for elections.

The Communist delegations had to make more concessions. Molotov suggested moving the demarcation line somewhere to the north of the sixteenth parallel and seeking a flexible election date—for example, no later than June 1955—as the date of the real election. Zhou readily agreed with Molotov and assured Dong that a flexible date had been approved by Ho in Liuzhou. He also suggested allowing French forces to stay in southern Vietnam until three months before the election, but as a negotiating tactic he suggested Dong start with the sixteenth parallel and insist on a fixed election date.[131] After Ho sent another telegram to Dong urging him to speed up negotiation as the July 5 Document instructed, Dong was finally ready to move ahead.[132]

When Zhou made these proposals, Chinese leaders were increasingly concerned about U.S. attempts to build SEATO. According to Chinese intelligence, the United States had already started to prepare for a ceasefire scenario in Indochina. U.S. leaders sent General James Van Fleet to the Far East twice in early July to conclude an alliance with Chiang Kai-shek and to push for bilateral military alliances between Taiwan, Japan, and South Korea.[133] Chinese leaders suspected that the United States would use these alliances as the basis for an overall North Pacific military pact modeled on NATO.[134] Zhou was suspicious that the United States, the United Kingdom, and France might have reached some agreement on SEATO during their meeting in Paris. If such a military group were built, Zhou told Molotov and Dong, and "the Americans manage to draw Bao Dai's Vietnam, Laos, and Cambodia into a military bloc, then the agreement we are drafting about a prohibition on creating foreign military bases on the territory of countries mentioned will lose the significance we are attaching to it."[135]

Nevertheless, Zhou believed that they could still exploit U.S. allies' worries about U.S. encroachments on their traditional spheres of influence in Southeast Asia. The United Kingdom seemed not to want to give up its Asian Locarno alliance.[136] Mendès France, according to Chinese leaders, was also strengthening cooperation with the United Kingdom, anxious for peace.[137]

To ensure that further concessions would not facilitate U.S. intervention in Indochina, Zhou wanted to receive guarantees from Eden and Mendès France. The Chinese leader told Eden directly that the Communists wanted peace, but that peace followed by a U.S. military treaty, especially one that included the three Indochinese states, was meaningless. Eden assured Zhou that the United States did not intend to build military bases in Laos and Cambodia, and the United Kingdom wanted the two states to be a buffer area between the two blocs. With regard to SEATO, Eden admitted that the United Kingdom and the United States were studying the possibility, but he did not think China should worry because the pact, if it materialized, would be "purely defensive," and "the better result we could achieve here in Geneva, the less we need to worry about the defense arrangement."[138] After double-checking with the United States, the British promised Zhou that the three Indochinese states would not join SEATO and that the final agreement, if reached, would include stipulations about this and the entrance of foreign personnel and arms. With that guarantee, Chinese officials promised the British that China would not ally with the DRV.[139] Zhou then assured Mendès France that the demarcation line and date of elections would not be problems if China was not threatened by the defense alliance in Southeast Asia. But if the United States built an alliance and included Indochina, Zhou warned, "all of our efforts to push for these compromises will become fruitless." He suggested including these stipulations in the final agreement.[140]

Zhou then reiterated his positions to the Cambodian and Laotian delegations. The Cambodians, however, remained suspicious of the DRV and warned that they would have to seek U.S. help, and were even considering joining SEATO if the DRV threatened their security.[141] Zhou assured them that this would not happen. To the Laotians, in addition to the promise that the Vietnamese forces would finally leave, Zhou said that Laos would be permitted to import weapons for defensive purposes and that the French would be allowed to retain two bases in Laos before the DRV troops withdrew. What China opposed, Zhou told the Laotians and Cambodians, was U.S. bases and an alliance with the United States. The Laotians promised Zhou they did not intend to join SEATO.[142]

With all these guarantees, the Communists were ready for further concessions. Dong finally agreed to a demarcation line drawn slightly to the north of Route 9. In return, he demanded French concessions on the timing of the election. Zhou agreed, but Molotov suggested another concession: setting a time period during which the election should be held. The Communists were also prepared to agree to the French proposal concerning the composition of the international supervision commission, which

FIGURE 1.5. Zhou Enlai and Pierre Mendès France
Source: Getty Images

would include Canada and Poland, with India as chair.[143] Zhou, however, pointed out that a new French draft he received did not include the provision about forbidding foreign bases in Indochina, and that this position was also not in the draft documents about Laos and Cambodia. Communist leaders decided to ask Laos and Cambodia to make a formal statement about this commitment.

Molotov immediately informed Mendès France of the new concessions, but the French prime minister wanted to stick with France's original positions. The impasse caused Molotov to wonder whether the French wanted a solution at all. During a restricted session on July 18, Molotov insisted that the Communists had made enough concessions and that failure of the conference at this point would not be their fault. Seeing no further concessions from the Communists, the British also became pessimistic, and Eden reported to London that the conference had "no more than [a] fifty-fifty chance of reaching agreement."[144]

The Communists, however, were determined to settle the issue, particularly after the U.S. delegation declared that it would not disrupt an acceptable agreement and the British promised that the final agreements would forbid foreign bases and alliances in Indochina. Zhou finally told Eden he agreed to the composition of the international supervision commission.[145] In addition to allowing French troops to stay in Laos for some time, he also pared the regrouping area for resistance forces.[146] The British emphasized that they guaranteed, on behalf of not just the United Kingdom but the British Commonwealth, that the Indochinese states would not be invited to join any military alliance. In return, Chinese officials made a package concession: the demarcation line could be ten kilometers north of Route 9; the election should be held two years after the signing of the agreement of armistice, but no later than June 1955, and representatives of North and South Vietnam must negotiate for a decision; and the regrouping of the armed forces within Vietnam would be completed within 245 days after the agreement. China requested that the final agreements be guaranteed by all conference participants, including the United States. The British side, however, revealed that the United States would only make a unilateral declaration.[147] On July 20, the Cambodians agreed not to allow foreign combat forces on Cambodian soil, but they wanted to keep some foreign technicians and experts and import weapons for their security. They also opposed the six-month withdrawal period suggested by the DRV. After

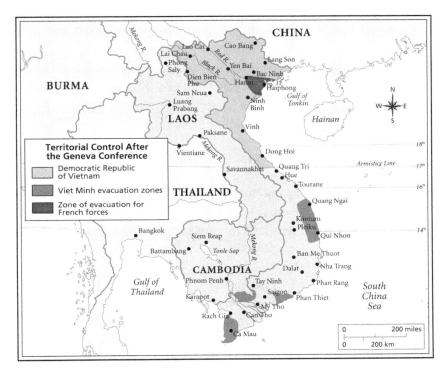

FIGURE 1.6. Territorial control after the Geneva Conference
Courtesy of Fredrik Logevall and Mapping Specialists, Ltd.

China realized its goal of neutralizing Cambodia, Zhou promised to convince the DRV to accelerate the withdrawal and agreed to allow Cambodia to import weapons. The key point, Zhou told the Cambodians, was that Cambodia must not lean toward the United States.[148]

The Communists largely achieved their goals. The Geneva negotiation ended on July 21, with a temporarily divided Vietnam and a neutralized Cambodia and Laos.[149] The two states could, however, appeal for foreign military aid if they were under threat from Vietnam. To convince the Laotians that they did not need foreign military assistance—especially from the United States—after the agreements were concluded, Zhou reassured the Laotian delegation of the good intentions of China and the DRV and encouraged Laos to develop friendly relations with the DRV. To demonstrate China's sincerity, Zhou expressed his understanding of the Laotian request to keep French troops in Laos until the Vietnamese Communist "volunteers" finally withdrew.[150] Before the foreign ministers left Geneva, Zhou again sought Eden's guarantee that the United States would not establish military bases in Cambodia. He was satisfied upon being told that the United Kingdom placed a great deal of emphasis on China and wanted to further develop relations with the Communist government.[151]

China played an instrumental role in bringing about the Geneva Agreements.[152] Zhou's timely concession to withdraw the DRV's forces in Laos and Cambodia prevented the Geneva Conference from coming to an early and fruitless end. China's agreement with the VWP leaders to seek peace as quickly as possible and its efforts to convince the DRV delegation to carry out this idea led to progress in the negotiation. Zhou's flexibility on the demarcation line in Vietnam and his concessions to Laos's and Cambodia's security concerns directly contributed to the final agreements.

China's actions in Geneva resulted principally from its security concerns. Seeing a U.S. military presence in its neighborhood as a serious menace, Chinese leaders strived to build a buffer area around China by removing the U.S. presence through diplomacy, following the Soviet peace initiatives. They started with the Korea issue. By the time Geneva convened, however, the war in Korea had stopped and North Korea insulated China from the U.S. military in Korea, so Chinese leaders concentrated their efforts in Geneva on Indochina. The Geneva Agreements built another buffer to the south of China, and thus decreased U.S. pressure on China.

China's strategy of isolating the United States by winning over the majority of the participants of the Geneva Conference contributed to the final agreements. Although Chinese leaders had limited access to information about the relations between the Western powers, their perceptions of differences among them were largely correct. Zhou's efforts to play the British and French against the United States may not have exacerbated tensions within the Western camp as much as Beijing expected, but the demonstration of good intentions kept the United Kingdom and France in the negotiations, and this gave the Chinese an opportunity for diplomatic maneuvering. China's assurances and concessions to Laos and Cambodia helped draw them away from the West and led to their approval of the Geneva Agreements.

China's experience in Geneva had a strong influence on its policy toward the United States. By the time the Geneva Conference ended, officials in Beijing were satisfied that the United States had been isolated and was vulnerable to diplomatic pressure. They aimed to continue the strategy of separating the United States from other states, and they were especially impressed with the United Kingdom's interest in better relations with China, sensing that British policy was fundamentally different from U.S. policy.[153] The initiation of the Taiwan Strait Crisis was China's effort to mobilize U.S. allies and Asian neutral states to push the United States not to conclude a mutual defense treaty with the GMD government on Taiwan.

Throughout the Geneva Conference, China, the Soviet Union, and Vietnam closely coordinated their positions and maintained a division of labor because of their common anxiety about U.S. intervention in Indochina. The Soviet Union was instrumental in bringing China and the DRV into the conference and organizing the Communist states' action. For appearances' sake, however, Soviet leaders let China and the DRV initiate most of the proposals.[154] Soviet officials tried, with considerable success, to convince Western governments that differences existed between China and the Soviet Union. All of this was just for show. Molotov's remarks to Western leaders, such as his statement that "China is very much her own master in these matters," were nothing but a negotiation tactic.[155]

The DRV's role was much more complicated. The DRV leaders' worries about U.S. invention in Indochina were real, and their need for peace urgent.[156] However, some DRV leaders were reluctant to give up their military advantage, especially after the Battle of Dien Bien Phu. Yet they had neither concrete plans nor material means to realize their goal. Due to their reliance on China for ideological guidance and material assistance, it was natural for China to provide advice. Vietnamese leaders also admitted their need for the Chinese leaders' guidance. Consequently, the Chinese initiated most of the important proposals and pushed Vietnam to make concessions.

Although the Geneva Agreements served China's interests, they did not necessarily damage the DRV's interests. The DRV welcomed the Geneva Agreements when they were reached and believed their interests to be well served.[157] When the situation in Indochina later did not develop as they expected, however, both the Chinese and the Vietnamese put forward different interpretations of the Geneva Conference. Chinese leaders regretted that they pressured the DRV into the Geneva Agreements and Zhou even admitted his "mistake" in pushing the DRV to retreat from its original positions, whereas the Vietnamese portrayed themselves as innocent victims of Chinese pressure. As Chen Jian points out, "Beijing's handling of the Indochina issue at Geneva in 1954 . . . sowed a seed of potential discord between the Chinese and their Vietnamese comrades."[158] Furthermore, Chinese leaders' admission of "mistakes" added to the Vietnamese resentment toward China, which contributed to the conflict between the two Communist states that flared in 1979. Ironically, the war between the former Communist allies contributed to China's normalization with its former enemy, the United States, and led to the tacit alliance between the two countries in the 1980s.[159]

Chapter Two

BETWEEN THE UNATTAINABLE AND
THE UNACCEPTABLE

Every effort will be made by the enemy to divide France and the United States, to contrast a peace-loving, reasonable France anxious to stop the death of her sons with a warmongering United States eager to continue a slaughter in which American soldiers are not engaged.[1]

—PHILIP W. BONSAL, MARCH 15, 1954

The British people would not be easily influenced by what happened in the distant jungles of S.E. Asia; but they did know that there was a powerful American base in East Anglia and that war with China, who would invoke the Sino-Russian Pact, might mean an assault by Hydrogen bombs on these islands.[2]

—WINSTON CHURCHILL, APRIL 26, 1954

What is certain, it's that internationalization of the war is the end of French influence in Indochina—in one definitive stroke it draws down one hundred years of effort and eight years of sacrifice.[3]

—HENRI NAVARRE, APRIL 21, 1954

This chapter assesses U.S. policy toward the Geneva Conference from the perspective of its relations with China.[4] It establishes how U.S. leaders saw Chinese intentions in Indochina and their objectives at the Geneva Conference, and how that perception influenced U.S. actions in Geneva. This chapter also discusses the consequences, if any, of China's policy of separating the United States from its allies.

In this chapter, I argue that Washington initially knew of China's efforts to separate the United States from its allies through a "peace offensive," but they misperceived China's objective in Geneva, believing the peace talk was a cover-up for the Communist military domination of Indochina. So, reluctantly agreeing to hold the conference at the request of allies, U.S. leaders hoped to disrupt the negotiation and contain the Communists expansion through a united action with allies. However, Washington failed to win the support of France and the United Kingdom. And it also failed to isolate a more aggressive China from a supposedly moderate Soviet Union. Finally, under pressure from both U.S. allies and the Communist military advances on the battlefield, Washington had to adjust its position and finally acquiesce to the neutralization of Indochina that the United Kingdom and France had reached with the Communists.

RELUCTANT PARTICIPATION

For the Eisenhower administration, Indochina was America's "first concern in the Far East," ahead of Taiwan and Korea.[5] The importance of Indochina principally resulted from the belief that the Chinese Communists were striving to dominate Indochina, the gateway to Southeast Asia, which, with its rich resources and vast market, was critical to the survival of Japan and the economy of the Western world.[6] With establishment of the PRC in 1949, the Americans realized that they faced the danger of losing Indochina to the Communists. Beijing's immediate recognition of and assistance to Ho Chi Minh's DRV led to the Truman administration's belief that China had targeted Southeast Asia for expansion. As a result, the United States started to provide assistance to the French in early 1950.[7] The NSC 68 in Spring 1950 defined the global containment of Communism as the primary goal of U.S. diplomacy.[8] The Communist initiation of the Korean War, and particularly China's participation, confirmed the belief that there was a Communist conspiracy for expansion; Southeast Asia, with its weak governments and indigenous Communist insurgents, made an ideal next target. Immediately after the outbreak of the war, Washington started to send arms and military advisors to Indochina. By 1952, the United States contributed to one-third of the French war cost.[9] The NSC 124/2 approved in June 1952 warned that the Chinese aggression in Southeast Asia was an immediate threat.[10]

The Eisenhower administration inherited this policy. According to Dulles, "Korea and Indo-China are two flanks. There is a large force [Communist China] in the center. If that force in the center can be without danger shifted to one flank or then the other flank it is very difficult to see how any satisfactory peace can be established either in Korea or in Indo-China."[11] With the Chinese assistance, the DRV invaded Laos and Cambodia in early 1953. Washington suspected that the Vietnamese wanted to dominate the whole Indochina under a federation. The capture of Laos was the first step toward the Communist capture of the whole of Southeast Asia. The end of the Korean War freed the Chinese to assist their Vietnamese comrades, even if they did not participate directly in the war in Indochina. Eisenhower warned that the development in Indochina was critically significant for U.S. interests in Southeast Asia. Washington provided additional support for the French to carry out the Navarre Plan.[12] However, by January 1954, the Vietminh forces frustrated the resolve of France and the Associated States to continue the war. A French military defeat or forced withdrawal would give Indochina to the Vietminh, and hence lead to Chinese domination in the region; consequently, the West would lose the whole of Southeast Asia to the Communists. That in turn could lead to the disaffection of India, Japan, and the Middle East, which would seriously endanger the stability and security of Europe, according to the NSC.[13]

To deter the Chinese, both Eisenhower and Dulles repeatedly warned that any overt aggression in Indochina would have grave consequences for China. When the Communists first proposed a five-power conference to discuss relaxing tensions in Asia, Dulles publicly cautioned the world not to be deceived by the proposal:

> Communist China has been and now is training, equipping, and supplying the Communist forces in Indochina. There is the risk that, as in Korea, Red China might send its own army into Indochina. The Chinese Communist regime should realize that such a second aggression could not occur without grave consequences which might not be confined to Indochina.[14]

In January 1954, Dulles made his well-known speech about massive retaliation against the Communists, which implied using nuclear weapons against Chinese expansion in Indochina.[15]

In this circumstance, the Communist proposal for a peaceful settlement in Indochina was seen as nothing but a peace offensive, a different yet more dangerous way to seek domination in Southeast Asia, in addition to boosting China's and DRV's international positions. When the Soviets first made the peace initiative in March 1953, Washington believed the Soviet move was "a skillful effort to promote dissension within the US Government, between the US Government and the American people and, above all, between the US and the rest of the non-Communist world."[16] When the Communists proposed to settle the Indochina war, U.S. officials concluded that they were using this to divide the Western powers and weaken the French will to fight, and they believed the Communists would not agree to any negotiations and settlement in Indochina.[17] After a field trip to Asia,

Nixon told the NSC in December 1953: "If there is negotiation now, the only thing that will result is Communist domination."[18] Dulles warned Bidault: "even to initiate discussion, puts us on slippery ground and might lead to further deterioration [of] morale in Indochina and France."[19]

But U.S. allies had different ideas. Under the pressure of war weariness from the French public, Bidault had attempted to include a diplomatic solution in Indochina in the Korean armistice talks in July 1953. When his suggestion was refused by the United States, he pointedly asked the Americans "why negotiation was fit and honorable for Korea and not for Indochina."[20] The French were unwilling to accept the duality of an armistice in Korea but continued war in Indochina.[21] Paris wanted a five-power conference that included France, the United States, the United Kingdom, the Soviet Union, and China, but it opposed talking to the DRV directly.[22] Meanwhile, the British, who were pushing for détente with the Soviet Union and a modus vivendi in the Far East, not only supported the Communist proposal for a Korean political conference but also attempted to include in it a "wide agenda" of solving the "China problem" permanently.[23] Both France and the United Kingdom pressed the United States for a positive response to the Communist proposal, and U.S. leaders bent to this pressure and agreed to hold a four-power meeting with the Soviet Union when leaders of the big three met in Bermuda in late 1953, although U.S. leaders warned allies that the Communists were merely launching a peace offensive to split the Westerners. As Eisenhower told Churchill, "Russia was a woman of the streets and whether her dress was new, or just the old one patched, it was certainly the same whore underneath. America intended to drive her off her present 'beat' into the back streets." Meanwhile, U.S. officials predicted that the Communist diplomatic offensive would turn to Indochina.[24]

When leaders of the four states meet in Berlin in early 1954, the Soviet Union successfully manipulated U.S. allies to include Indochina in the agenda. Subsequently, the United States had to agree to the allied request for the Geneva Conference because, in the words of Dulles, it was "apparent that if Bidault had not gone back to Paris with something to show on Indochina, the Laniel Government would have fallen at once and would have been replaced by a government which would not only have a mandate to end the war in Indochina on any terms, but also to oppose French ratification of EDC," which was a U.S. top priority in 1953–1954.[25] But Dulles made

FIGURE 2.1. (*left to right*) Georges Bidault, John Foster Dulles, and Anthony Eden, at Berlin Foreign Ministers' Conference.
Source: Frank Scherschel/The LIFE Picture Collection via Getty Images

it clear that this did not indicate a U.S. recognition of China and that the PRC was not a sponsor of the conference, as the Soviets suggested and the British and French connived. For Dulles, "It is . . . one thing to recognize evil as a fact. It is another thing to take evil to one's heart and call it good."[26] Therefore, he set up preconditions for the negotiation: the Geneva Conference would only take place after China stopped its aggression, and the Communists must first prove their sincerity in the negotiations on Korea, the issue with which the conference would start.[27]

Soon after the Berlin meeting ended, the Policy Planning Staff of the State Department concluded that none of the possibilities that might come out of the conference was acceptable. A ceasefire and an end to Chinese military aid to the DRV did not guarantee a French victory, given the growing strength of the Vietminh forces. An overall political settlement would result in the Vietminh's victory in elections and was the "most dangerous" result. Partition of Indochina along the sixteenth parallel, as the Soviets suggested, would give the Communists the Tonkin Delta, "the key to the whole of Southeast Asia." Moreover, if the United States was involved in this arrangement, it would be seen as selling out its ally, the State of Vietnam (SV), and thereby discredit the United States in Asia. Neutralization and demilitarization of Indochina seemed the "least dangerous formula" for the United States, but the Communists would not accept this. Indeed, the decision to hold the conference itself would prompt the Vietminh to increase military pressure on the French to gain a diplomatic initiative, as Dulles warned the French in Berlin. On the French side, negotiations could end up lessening, rather than increasing, the chance of the French ratifying the EDC because the prospect of peace would further decrease both the French fighting morale and the urgency in approving the EDC.[28]

An estimate of the Communist's intentions made U.S. leaders even more pessimistic. A National Intelligence Estimate (NIE) in mid-March 1954 concluded that "the Communists probably will not make any major concessions in the interest of relieving international tension in Asia, but will attempt to impress free world countries, particularly Asian neutrals, with their willingness to negotiate."[29] According to Philip Bonsal, aware of the United States' difficult position among its allies and encouraged by their diplomatic victory in Berlin, the Communists would spare no effort "to divide France and the United States, to contrast a peace-loving, reasonable France anxious to stop the death of her sons with a warmongering United

States eager to continue a slaughter in which American soldiers are not engaged."[30]

In contrast, the apparently close relations between the Communists did not seem to leave much room for U.S. exploitation. Although Dulles was suspicious about Soviet sincerity in promoting Beijing's status and other officials speculated that the rise of China's prestige after the Korean War and Stalin's death had made the Soviets uneasy about their alliance with the Chinese, they were never sure if the perceived differences within the Communist alliance really existed.[31] Meanwhile, with its attention concentrating on Europe, the Soviet Union seemed content to let China play a leading role in Asia, lacking interest in getting involved in a conflict in Southeast Asia.[32]

Given the fact that China's security interests were at stake, U.S. officials acknowledged that "the United States and Communist China are now in effect engaged in a limited war (the battlefronts are in Korea, the Straits of Formosa, and Indochina and, in addition, we are at war in a general sense with respect to economic measures, mutual nonrecognition, etc.)."[33] Therefore, the Americans concluded that China would be the principal actor on the Communist side and play a central role in Geneva. To better meet the Chinese challenge during the conference, Walter Robertson, U.S. assistant secretary of state for Far Eastern affairs, suggested establishing a working group focusing specifically on China.

In early March, both the military and civilian leaders concluded that negotiations would not produce any acceptable result. While planning to delay the discussion of the Indochina issue in Geneva, Washington tried to help France win a military victory without using U.S. troops. At this moment, the NSC was still optimistic about the military situation in Indochina.[34] To assist the French, Eisenhower publicly declared that the United States was helping France and the SV fight the war. Having provided cargo airplanes and training technicians, Washington now pushed France to continue fighting until a satisfactory settlement was achieved.[35] Meanwhile, Dulles suggested helping Taiwan launch some "harassing tactics" along China's coast to distract the Chinese Communists from Indochina. The Bureau of Far Eastern Affairs proposed starting negotiations with Chiang Kai-shek on a mutual defense treaty (MDT) to "strengthen our negotiating posture at the [Geneva] Conference by making clear at the outset our completely firm position on the Formosa issue."[36]

If the United States had to go to Geneva, according to Dulles, it should approach the conference as a "holding action" to make time for the French to win the war on the battleground and ratify the EDC. The U.S. delegation intended to stipulate their settlement terms with China with the intention of ending the conference inconclusively.[37] On April 7, Eisenhower publicly poured cold water over the Geneva negotiation and warned of a domino effect if Indochina was lost to the Communists.[38] To delay the conference, Dulles instructed U.S. diplomats not to make preparations with the British and French officials and to leave all the procedural and substantive problems until he arrived at Geneva. Meanwhile, Dulles resisted the Soviet efforts to make China appear to be a sponsor of the conference and warned the United Kingdom and France not to consult with China about anything related to the composition of the conference.[39]

The deteriorating military situation in Indochina, however, pushed U.S. leaders to consider direct intervention. As Dulles had warned, after the Berlin meeting, China increased assistance to the DRV. In mid-March, the DRV started the Dien Bien Phu campaign with Chinese help, and Dulles said this verged on overt aggression.[40] By late March, French forces were facing a collapse and repeatedly requested U.S. intervention. The American leaders worried about a French surrender, but they recognized that U.S. intervention could not be approved by Congress unless several conditions were met: joint action with allies, continued French fighting, independence granted to the three Indochinese states, and an invitation for U.S. intervention from France and the three Associated States of Indochina.[41] In these circumstances, building a collective defense organization to deter the Communists and prepare allies for further actions seemed to be the only feasible strategy. Dulles and Eisenhower publicly called for united action with allies, which they hoped would both daunt the Chinese and stiffen the French positions.[42]

However, U.S. efforts for united action found few supporters.[43] France requested U.S. intervention to save Dien Bien Phu but worried that internationalization of the war would help the United States take control of Indochina from them. "What is certain," French general Henri Navarre, the commander in Indochina, told the French government, is "that internationalization of the war is the end of French influence in Indochina—in one definitive stroke it draws down one hundred years of effort and eight years of sacrifice."[44] Therefore, Bidault refused to internationalize the war.

All Paris wanted was a one-time unilateral air strike by the United States to save Dien Bien Phu, not the united action of Western allies. Once the military situation was stabilized, the French calculated, they could start peace negotiations with the Communists from a position of strength.[45] They also expected that the talk about U.S. intervention itself would have the added effect of pressuring the Communists to relax their military offensive. Therefore, to press the United States for assistance, the French warned that if they lost the fortress they would have to seek peace with the Communists, and due to public pressure, disapprove the EDC. In the meantime, the French ambassador told Eden that his country sought a deal with the Chinese, trading the transit and port facilities in Haiphong for China's agreement to push the DRV to end the war.[46]

The United Kingdom was even less willing to follow the United States. Although the British generally agreed with the Americans about the strategic importance of Indochina, they did not think the loss of it would hurt their own interests in Southeast Asia, which focused on Malaya and Hong Kong. Moreover, they did not even think the loss of Dien Bien Phu would lead to the loss of the whole of Indochina. Even if the Communists captured Indochina, the United Kingdom could still withhold Malaya at the Kra Isthmus.[47] The British also thought China was unlikely to intervene openly in Indochina. According to the British chargé in Beijing, in the short term, the Chinese priority was domestic development. For that purpose, they needed a period of

easier relations with the West, while they built up their strength and seated themselves in the United Nations. There was no sign in Peking since the end of the war that they intended to undertake aggressive action which might produce American counter-action, such as a more obvious form of intervention in the war in Indo-China, or a move against Formosa.[48]

Furthermore, both France and the United Kingdom worried that U.S. intervention would provoke China's intervention and lead to a general war with the Communists. With the world entering a new era of thermal nuclear weapons, a world war would mean destruction of the whole world. The British, who were shocked by the fact that Washington kept them in the dark about their acquisition of the hydrogen bomb for over a year, were particularly scared by U.S. rhetoric about massive retaliation and its tests of deployable hydrogen bombs in the Pacific Ocean, given U.S. nuclear deployment in the United Kingdom and the fact that the Soviets already possessed hydrogen bombs. Despite Eisenhower's personal request for united action, Churchill was most worried about potential Communist retaliation. He told Arthur Radford, chairman of the Joint Chiefs of Staff, who was visiting London to seek allied intervention in late April,

> the British people would not be easily influenced by what happened in the distant jungles of S.E. Asia; but they did know that there was a powerful American base in East Anglia and that war with China, who would invoke the Sino-Russian Pact, might mean an assault by Hydrogen bombs on these islands.[49]

The French and British also believed that Beijing's real concern was its own security, not expansion into Indochina, and that its objective in the negotiation was a buffer area in northern Vietnam.[50] For the French, a cease-fire on the basis of a partition of Vietnam was one achievable solution, given their military disadvantage and domestic divisions, but for political reasons France did not want to be the country that initiated the proposal.[51] For the British, a divided Vietnam with an independent Laos and Cambodia was the "least undesirable" solution, as the British ambassador told the Americans in early April.[52] But according to Dulles, "Communists would infiltrate south of any agreed line," so a partition would just delay, not stop, their aggression and the loss of all of Indochina.[53] When the British interest in partition became public in late April, Eisenhower told a press conference that division or partition of Indochina was unacceptable to the United States.[54]

Both France and the United Kingdom believed the DRV was indeed China's satellite and that the Westerners could induce the Chinese to push their Vietnamese comrades toward concessions. The French themselves had little to offer, but they expected the United States to make concessions to Beijing, such as diplomatic recognition, UN membership, or a trade agreement, and in return the French would approve the EDC.[55] The British agreed that détente with Beijing would work. As Eden confided to Churchill in May, "I have always believed that these negotiations involve concessions to the communists probably entailing a buffer state on China's southern border."[56] But Dulles stated that

> any settlement negotiated in [the] immediate future could only result in ultimate complete control of all Indochina by Communists, there is no

possibility whatsoever of concessions by US to Communist China in return for any promises or agreements they might indicate their willingness to enter. Long experience has taught us that exchange of US performance for Communist promises is a swindle and we will have no part in it.[57]

To sum up, both the British and the French thought the Geneva Conference provided an opportunity to reach a negotiated peace. The French hoped to find a settlement through a deal with China, and the British publicized its solution, a partition of Vietnam,[58] a position supported by Australia and New Zealand, two other important allies of the United States.[59]

To win allied support for united action before the Geneva Conference, Dulles visited London and Paris in early April, but his trips were not successful.[60] The British did not think Dulles had a well-developed idea about united action, so Eden only agreed to start informal talks about a defense group, but declined to even make a declaration about it.[61] Moreover, when Dulles returned to Washington to call for the meeting, Eden changed his mind and asked the British ambassador not to attend it.[62] In Paris, Dulles found that the French were reluctant to displease the Chinese and could not even agree among themselves about what they wanted other than a military ceasefire. Dulles believed that the French would seek peace in Geneva "at almost any price," and the United States refused the French request for unilateral intervention on the grounds that the United States would not intervene without UK participation.[63]

The three foreign ministers met together in Paris right before the Geneva Conference, but Dulles failed to make any progress. The United States requested UK participation to save Dien Bien Phu, which would soon be lost to the Communists, and the French warned of a complete collapse of the French resistance in Indochina. But Eden was unwilling to discuss the possibility and refused to give even moral support to an intervention. Despite Dulles's protest that the British opposition to action might lead to French capitulation, Eden was only willing to start working on a defense group after the Geneva negotiation ended. The British leader believed that intervention would "be the first step towards a third world war" and stated that the United Kingdom would do its best to help France reach an agreement in Geneva instead of preparing for united action. He told Dulles that he would accept a demarcation line at the seventeenth or eighteenth parallel as a solution.[64] Meanwhile, Churchill announce at the Parliament that London would not do anything that might hurt the Geneva negotiation.[65]

Infuriated by the allies, U.S. leaders had kept open the option of a unilateral intervention, but without British support they were clear that Congress would not support the action.[66] And perhaps more important, they had to agree with the British that U.S. unilateral actions in Indochina would likely lead to Chinese intervention, which might lead to a world war involving the Soviet Union.[67] Finally, the NSC decided to hold up any military action on Indochina, but the United States should continue to push for the establishment of a defense group in Southeast Asia.[68]

On the eve of the Indochina negotiation, great gaps existed between the United States and its allies. State Department officials believed only two results were possible in Geneva: disguised capitulation either by the French or by the Communists. In this circumstance, the U.S. delegation would simply specify terms for the Communists to reach. A ceasefire was only possible after some rigid conditions were satisfied, including disarming the DRV forces to a controllable limit, control of the Sino-Vietnamese border under international supervision to stop Chinese assistance to the Vietminh, withdrawal of the DRV's forces from Laos and Cambodia, and ultimate incorporation of the DRV into the SV.[69] The French government, incapacitated by internal divisions, could only agree on a peaceful settlement, and would not do anything that might hurt that possibility in Geneva.[70] The British were increasingly worried that Washington was seriously considering replacing France in Indochina.

Although the Western leaders realized the vital importance of unity, especially when the Communists were exploiting the differences between them, U.S. relations with its allies were frayed.[71] French officials resented that the United States was putting them in a difficult position by refusing to help them either on the battleground or at the negotiation table. Many French believed that Washington was simply sacrificing the French lives for its own interests, meanwhile sabotaging negotiations.[72] On the other side, Washington was worried that France would seek peace at any cost, knowing the French were talking secretly with the Soviets to trade the EDC for an Indochina settlement. The Americans were so infuriated by the British intransigence about united action that they considered establishing a coalition without British participation.[73] According to Livingston Merchant, the assistant secretary of state for European and Eurasian affairs, "our alliances have been put under greater and more sudden strain in the last few weeks than at any time since the war ended."[74] And the U.S. ambassador in Paris, Douglas Dillon, pessimistically predicted that "we may find ourselves in uncomfortable isolation" in Geneva.[75]

In contrast, U.S. leaders did not find many differences between the Communist countries. Dulles toyed with the idea of pressuring China through the Soviet Union and tried to feel out the Soviets on this possibility when he reached Geneva. At his meeting with Molotov, Dulles suggested the United States and Soviet Union should both restrain their junior partners, meaning France and China, but to his disappointment, Molotov did not bite at "any of the flies I [Dulles] had cast."[76] Before Dulles went to Geneva, the NSC had concluded that there was no open friction between the Chinese and the Soviets, and driving a wedge between the two remained a long-range objective. After his meeting with Molotov, Dulles concluded that there was no indication of "anything but complete Communist bloc unity."[77]

HOLDING ACTION

Communist actions after the Indochina negotiation began simply confirmed Washington's estimate about their aggression in Southeast Asia. The Communist proposals at the conference were absolutely unacceptable to the United States. A ceasefire leaving the Vietminh forces intact would lead to Communist control of Vietnam; without effective supervision, the Vietminh would use the ceasefire to build up military and political strength. Moreover, the DRV's request for a "general solution" of the Indochina problem revealed its ambition was not limited to Vietnam, just as the Americans had suspected.[78] In addition, Communist actions on the battleground removed any doubt about their ambitions. After capturing Dien Bien Phu, the Vietminh forces were quickly moving toward the Tonkin Delta and would be able to start a new offensive in weeks, according to the director of the CIA.[79] Shortly after the negotiations began, a joint estimate made by the State Department and the CIA concluded that the immediate goal of the Communists was "victory in Vietnam" with the objective of capturing the whole Indochina.[80] Their peace proposal simply exploited the French and British interests in peace to prevent U.S. intervention. Therefore, talking with the Communists played right into their hands.

However, U.S. allies disagreed. The French were eager for a respite from the war and only reluctantly added the issue of supervision to their proposal under the threat that the United States would end its assistance and its participation in negotiations. But according to the U.S. ambassador to Paris, the French secretary of state for foreign affairs, Maurice Schumann, implied that with the loss of Dien Bien Phu France had lost its hand and "may eventually be forced to accept pretty much any settlement put forward by the Viet Minh and the Chinese Communists."[81] The British agreed with the United States on the importance of supervision, but in contrast to the U.S. position of a guarantee by united action of the United States and its allies, they suggested a general guarantee by both the Communist and the Western powers, which U.S. officials believed would give the Communists opportunities to make the supervision useless.[82] Eden told the UK cabinet that the British goal in Geneva was to "draw a line and create a *modus vivendi* in Asia of the kind already created in Europe." He instructed the British Foreign Office:

> It is important to coordinate our line with French. Two things are essential:
> (a) that French should make up their minds as to what they will take and say so soon. We will back them.
> (b) Americans should not press French to stand out for more than they can hope to get. We should speak out firmly against any such US tendency.[83]

Washington considered withdrawing from the meeting, but after some hesitation the Americans decided to stay; they feared that the French government would collapse and surrender everything to the Communists if the United States did not stand by them in Geneva. In addition to restraining its allies from surrendering to the Communist requests, U.S. participation would demonstrate its willingness to seek peace, and thus help it win over allied support for the defense group to be built in Southeast Asia. According to Charles Stelle, advisor to the U.S. delegation, "U.S. participation in negotiation of a settlement would keep the U.S. in a better position to play off the Associated States against the French, to stimulate the Communists to overreaching themselves, and in general to attempt to whittle down the degree of unacceptability of an Indochina settlement."[84] Dulles, who had left Geneva to downgrade the negotiation even before the Indochina phase began, told Smith to limit the U.S. role to a mere "interested nation," whose goal was to protect people in this area from being "amalgamated into the Communist bloc of imperialistic dictatorship." The United States would not give "express or implied approval" to any settlement that would not protect the current Indochinese governments and their territorial integrity. Dulles also told Smith to be ready to leave the conference, in case an unacceptable settlement was reached. At Dulles's request, Smith warned Bidault that the United States would not accept a partition that would ultimately lead to a Communist takeover. And U.S. diplomats also made sure the SV delegation would refuse any "unsatisfactory solution" and would withdraw from the conference should an unacceptable settlement be reached.[85]

Behind the scenes, Dulles talked with Eisenhower again about the possibility of U.S. intervention, but they concluded that it was too risky; unilateral intervention would be vetoed by the British and subsequently "encourage Chinese Communist aggression to a point where the whole position in the Pacific would be endangered and the risk of general war increase."[86] Indeed, even a united intervention with allies would likely lead to Chinese intervention. After his short stay in Geneva, Dulles became increasingly worried about a possible Chinese intervention under the scenario of U.S. overt entrance into Indochina. At the same time, U.S. leaders understood that U.S. intervention would also be opposed by the other Asian states.

U.S. efforts toward united action made little progress. Eden finally agreed to Dulles's suggestion of starting preliminary talks through the Five-Power Military Staff Agency—including the United States, the United Kingdom, France, Australia, and New Zealand—but opposed even publishing his agreement on the grounds that it would decrease the chance of agreement at the negotiations and alienate Asian states, especially those British Commonwealth members he hoped to bring along into the future organization.[87] Dulles then started negotiations with France about internationalizing the war behind Eden's back, hoping the French realized that internationalization was "preferable to the harsh terms which no doubt [the] Communists will seek to extract."[88] The French, however, refused to meet the conditions the United States set. Although they reluctantly agreed to let the United States train and advise SV's troops, the French were unwilling to meet the other conditions the United States had insisted on for intervention.[89] In private, Bidault told Eden that he was using the negotiation about U.S. intervention to "play on fears of [the] Chinese and Russians."[90] Dulles figured out that France sought U.S. intervention independent of united action and instructed U.S. officials not to accept the training program. Finally, French officials frankly told the Americans that they would only be willing to consider internationalization if an "honorable armistice" could not be obtained at Geneva.[91]

Washington concluded that "the French were practicing a form of blackmail, holding a sword of Damocles over our heads." According to Dulles, "Laniel is creating an alibi and he, or his successor, will in the end tell the French people that they had to capitulate because US terms were so rigorous that they were obviously unacceptable and that therefore [the] US is to blame."[92] When France released the Franco-U.S. secret talks to newspapers in an effort to pressure the Communists, Churchill publicly denied British participation in the secret talks and declared

> our immediate task is to do everything we can to reach an agreed settlement at Geneva for the restoration of peace in Indo-China. Her Majesty's government are resolved to do their utmost to achieve this aim and to exercise their influence to ensure that any acceptable settlement shall be backed by effective international guarantees.

Meanwhile, Eden proposed a dangerous ceasefire. According to Dulles, the acceptance of the proposal "would bring about a *de facto* partition of all three of the Associated States." It would pave the way for the Communist infiltration and ultimately "complete control of all three States."[93]

Infuriated by the British, Eisenhower told reporters that he might go ahead with united action without UK involvement,[94] and he told Dulles that he "would not necessarily exclude sending some Marines" to Indochina, had the United States decided to intervene. The condition was that Washington got support from some allies, including Australia, New Zealand, the Philippines, Thailand, and the Associated States. The two agreed that the intervention "did not make U.K. active participation a necessary condition." Eisenhower had asked six government agencies to prepare "with the highest urgency and secrecy" studies on the topics of U.S. military intervention and China's reactions. Dulles once again suggested that some GMD "diversionary activities along the China coast" with U.S. air and navy support might soon be needed to stop China from dominating Southeast Asia. Eisenhower agreed. Simultaneously, the tension between the Communists and the GMD escalated to the highest level in the Taiwan Strait in May 1954. At the same time, Dulles declared at a press conference that the United States had had military staff meetings with major allies in Washington to discuss united action to protect Southeast Asia against Communist expansion.[95]

Negotiations in Geneva were deadlocked. The Communists retreated a little from their original positions, such as agreeing to start the military talks first, reaching a ceasefire on the basis of demarcation, and setting up armistice negotiations with the French, but they refused to admit the existence of DRV forces in Laos and Cambodia or to accept U.S. requirements for ceasefire supervision. U.S. officials ignored the Communist concessions as a delaying tactic. The NSC concluded in late May that the Communists were exploiting the British and French interest in a diplomatic settlement to protract the negotiations and prevent allied intervention so they would win the war in Indochina.[96]

Communist actions in early June confirmed this judgment. The Vietminh refused to discuss substantial issues in their meetings with the French; Zhou refused to separate Laos and Cambodia from Vietnam; and Molotov, whom the Westerners initially regarded as relatively moderate, started to take a "tougher line," leading to the speculation that the Communist delegates were instructed by Moscow not to retreat.[97] Reports from various channels indicated an imminent Vietminh attack on the Tonkin Delta. While Soviet advisors were helping the Vietminh forces, the Chinese forces were in a good position to help the DRV's offensive on the Tonkin Delta. According to an NIE prepared by the CIA in late May, Beijing could send over half a million troops into Indochina and had sufficient capabilities to "overcome any conventional US assistance" requested by France. The Chinese could also help its intervention by attacking the Dachen Islands in the Taiwan Strait to draw away the U.S. navy from supporting the Marines in Indochina. Indeed, the U.S. ambassador in Taiwan reported that Chinese air and naval forces were gathering along the Chinese coast for an attack on Dachen.[98]

In Geneva, the Chinese were also launching an offensive. Making use of Washington's concerns about its nationals detained in China, the Chinese delegation suggested direct negotiations with the United States. Washington saw this as a ploy to both promote China's international standing and exploit differences between the United States and the United Kingdom, which had always been interested in mediating between China and the United States. However, under pressure from the American public, it had to seek the return of the Americans and finally agreed to start consular talks with the Chinese. But Dulles instructed U.S. diplomats to stop the talks as soon as they got back the detained American citizens.[99]

With negotiations deadlocked, the United States saw increasingly serious Chinese aggression in early June. Smith even believed China was

> willing to risk the chance of what we might do in Indochina. They probably would welcome the introduction of some US ground forces there because of the opportunity this would give them directly to intervene for the ostensible purposes of repelling US aggression and because of the initially adverse effect our participation would have on Asiatic public opinion for many reasons well-known to you.[100]

In late May, U.S. officials had warned Chinese leaders not to take actions, and now the NSC started to discuss the U.S. response to a Chinese Communist "overt unprovoked military aggression" in either the Western Pacific or Southeast Asia. Dulles met with Australia's and New Zealand's ambassadors, requesting their support to get ready for a Chinese threat to the three states in the Western Pacific, under the scenario that the Chinese Communists would "run amuck" after their successes in Indochina "[went] to their heads."[101] On June 8, Dulles publicly warned against the Communist tactic of "dragging out" negotiations "while the Communist military effort [had] been stepped up in Indo-China itself."[102]

U.S. leaders worried that their allies could not withstand the Communist pressure. Given the United Kingdom's and France's determination to get a settlement, Smith pessimistically predicted that a settlement could be reached in ten days, despite U.S. opposition, and that the French may be forced to "accept almost any face-saving cease-fire formula."[103] Dulles instructed the U.S. ambassador to France to "warn Laniel that no statement implying anything like final agreement should be made to his Cabinet or in Parliament or otherwise now or at any time without careful prior agreement between our Governments as to [the] precise form of words."[104] Dulles also asked the U.S. delegation in Geneva to "avoid formal identification with open partition or the creation of two states where one now exists." In case the French and British could still be lured into an agreement when the Soviets "put up a proposal which would salvage a little something for the French" at the last minute, Dulles told the U.S. delegation to warn Eden and Bidault that the United States would disassociate itself from such a settlement. Dulles also instructed Smith to push France and the United Kingdom for an agreement to let Thailand appeal to the UN Security Council against Vietnamese invasion of its neighbors.[105] Smith also warned the Soviets that if the Vietminh "appetites were too great and if they over-reached themselves a crisis could ensue, which . . . might well lead to US armed intervention."[106]

To the Americans' relief, a breakthrough did not materialize, and their allies lost patience with the Communist intransigence. The French sensed the Communists were stalling for time, and Eden finally concluded that a settlement was impossible and "it was a Communist rather than a Western advantage to continue the Conference," so he agreed to end the negotiation in a few days.[107] To make use of the British impatience with the Communists, Eisenhower and Dulles instructed Smith to end the conference as soon as possible in order to begin discussing united action. As another ally, Australia, also came to agree to carry out the plan of the defense group, Dulles told the U.S. delegation that "final adjournment of [the] Conference is in our best interest."[108]

Just at this moment, however, the Communists made major concessions: Molotov compromised on the composition and authority of the international supervision commission; Zhou agreed to withdraw all "foreign forces" from Laos and Cambodia; and Dong told the two states directly that DRV "volunteers" would leave their territories. The United Kingdom and France were immediately attracted. Eden concluded that Beijing seemed to want a settlement in Laos and Cambodia, and the French officials trusted the Communist sincerity in negotiation and told the Americans and British that they had decided to continue their military talks with the DRV on an official basis, instead of the previous unofficial conversations.[109]

COMING TO TERMS WITH REALITY

Washington attributed Communist concessions to the pressure they had exerted, including the British change of policy, British leaders' upcoming visit to Washington, and the threat of allied intervention.[110] Yet the Americans neither increased the pressure on the Communists nor withdrew from negotiations to let the conference fail, which was the best result Washington had expected. Instead, U.S. leaders privately accepted partition of Vietnam and, on this basis, reached an agreement with the British as the foundation for a diplomatic settlement to the Indochina war, which they had originally opposed.

This shift of position was due to several factors. First, after the Communists made the concessions, U.S. officials modified their previous estimate

of the Communist's objectives. Zhou's obsession with the United States setting up bases in Laos and Cambodia, indications about China's objective
of neutralizing Indochina, and a willingness to push the DRV to withdraw
from the two states were a "considerable advance" over his previous positions.[111] Based on the observation of China's significantly "less doctrinaire"
actions, the State Department realized that the Chinese really wanted a
ceasefire in Indochina and were attempting to reduce tensions, although
it did not give up the ultimate goal of dominating Asia. Restricted by its
limited forces, Beijing would be unwilling to take actions that could provoke a war with the United States.[112] For the first time, Washington articu-
lated a clear statement of China's actual objectives in Geneva. According
to both Smith and an NIE prepared in early June, the Communists wanted
the partition of Vietnam; control of about one-third to one-half of Laos;
withdrawal from Cambodia, on condition that Cambodia did not join the
U.S.-sponsored defense group; and an ineffective international supervisory
commission.[113]

If the Americans still had any doubt of the Communists' sincerity
about a diplomatic settlement, their allies were certainly convinced by the
Chinese. The British and French leaders pressured the United States for
responses to the Chinese concessions.[114] From their meetings with Zhou,
Eden and Pierre Mendès France, who was by now the French prime minister, "received a strong impression" that Zhou wanted peace urgently and
was willing to make concessions for a settlement.[115] According to French
diplomats, the Chinese pressed the DRV for a settlement based on partition at the sixteenth parallel, and the Vietminh seemed impatient to reach
an agreement as soon as possible. Therefore, French officials optimistically told their U.S. ally that they were going to reach tentative agreements
with the DRV soon. British diplomats believed that France had decided to
accept a partition of Vietnam that would leave the Tonkin Delta to the Vietminh.[116] The U.S. delegation in Geneva was anxious that the French were
"moving rapidly toward [a] Franco-Vietminh agreement on respective
zones of occupation under cease-fire, with almost complete lack of agreement on supervision."[117] Before leaving for Washington, Eden declared in
Parliament that a collective defense group in Asia must wait for the result
of the Geneva Conference, and the British wanted a Locarno-type pact to
guarantee the ceasefire in Indochina, which involved both Communist and
non-Communist states.[118]

In the meantime, the Communist military advance on the battleground forced Washington to accept a diplomatic solution. After Dien Bien Phu, the Vietminh forces quickly moved toward the Tonkin Delta, ready to launch a comprehensive offensive by September.[119] By mid-June, Washington and its allies recognized that without U.S. intervention the French were going to lose the delta, making it difficult to establish a defense line to contain Communism in Indochina. U.S. participation, however, risked a global war and use of nuclear weapons.[120] Moreover, U.S. negotiations with the French over U.S. intervention had already failed. Dulles acknowledged that the best time to intervene in Indochina had passed. The NSC had also decided against intervention, even on the basis of united action. Indeed, both Eisenhower and Dulles had publicly declared that the United States would not send troops to Indochina. Intervention at that time would make the United States "appear in the unenviable position of being against both peace and democracy." It would not only "split our basic coalition" but also "appear to [the] world and US opinion as a desperate US move to frustrate a cease-fire and free elections."[121] For these reasons, Washington could not afford to let the Geneva Conference fail at this point.

Washington now realized that a partition of Vietnam might not be as disastrous as they had originally imagined. The Five-Power Military Staff Meeting held in early June accepted the British view that division of Vietnam was inevitable. After carefully calculating the military situation in Indochina, the meeting made a pessimistic prediction about the prospect of the war. At the same time, however, the military leaders reached a conclusion that provided them some relief: if a ceasefire was obtained, they believed the Western alliance should be able to stop the Communist advance at the Thakhek-Donghoi line, a little north of the seventeenth parallel, even if the Tonkin Delta was lost. Under the scenario of Chinese intervention, the allies could still expect to hold the stop line at the Kra Isthmus of southern Thailand.[122] Against this backdrop, Dulles changed his attitude toward the partition. He told Smith to reconsider the U.S. position. Smith first indicated to the Australians his agreement with partition. Washington finally decided to accept a partitioned Vietnam because they now believed they could still "draw a line" to stop the Communist expansion.[123]

Moreover, a settlement of the war would pave the way for united action, as U.S. allies had refused to move on with the collective defense organization before conclusion of the conference. Indeed, accepting the negotiation was the only option available to the United States; Washington could not afford a unilateral withdrawal from Geneva. It would be seen as abandoning the Associated States, and Washington would lose whatever restraining power it had on the French. This became particularly important when the new French prime minister was determined to achieve peace, and even set up a deadline for the Geneva negotiations. Therefore, Washington agreed to let the U.S. delegation stay in Geneva to "assist in salvaging as much as possible from a most unhappy situation."[124]

The U.S. policy shift led to an Anglo-American consensus for the first time since the beginning of the Geneva Conference, which greatly relieved the British, who were anxious about the rift with Washington. According to Churchill, the British should make it clear which side they were on, although he did not completely give up the idea of détente with the Communists.[125] In these circumstances, U.S. and UK leaders reached the Seven Points during Churchill's and Eden's visit to Washington in late June, an agreement that included the integrity and independence of Laos and Cambodia, a divided Vietnam that "does not exclude the possibility of the ultimate unification by peaceful means," and effective international supervision of a ceasefire.[126] Eden also gave up his Locarno Pact after Eisenhower bluntly rejected the idea.[127] On this basis, the U.S. and UK leaders declared their intention to "press forward with plans for collective defense."[128] The French were not happy about their exclusion from the meeting, but they were satisfied that the joint declaration met their request for pressure on the Communists and were willing to follow the U.S. positions.[129]

Nevertheless, despite the agreement with the British, Dulles was worried "that the British look upon this merely as an optimum solution and that they would not encourage the French to hold out for a solution as good as this." Meanwhile, he had little idea about the French plan, other than their eagerness for a settlement, because the French did not keep the Americans informed of their negotiations with the Vietminh. Dulles was worried that France would reach a settlement that superficially resembled the Seven Points but would enable the Communists to control Laos, Cambodia, and Southern Vietnam soon after the settlement. He was also worried, as he told the GMD ambassador to Washington, that France would include recognizing China in the deal, as both Churchill and Eden had implied their willingness to admit China into the UN after a successful settlement of Indochina at the Geneva Conference. In a memorandum Dulles prepared for Eisenhower, he warned that "we have to expect that the French will not succeed in getting our terms from the Communists."[130]

Dulles instructed the U.S. delegation to call upon the French delegation to remain firm on the positions the United States and the United Kingdom had reached. Lest the French reach an agreement unacceptable to the United States, Dulles kept open such options as withdrawal of the U.S. delegation from Geneva or public disapproval of the French position. In the meantime, Dulles told the U.S. diplomats in Paris to remind the French that in addition to meeting the Seven Points positions, a settlement should also get the approval of the Associated States. Moreover, when newspapers speculated that the French might trade the EDC for a favorable Indochina settlement, Dulles decided neither he nor Smith would attend the last phase of the negotiations on Indochina.[131]

Dulles's decision met strong opposition. When he met Eden and Mendès France in Paris to prepare for the final session of the negotiations, the French and British leaders strongly pleaded with Dulles to return to Geneva as an indication of his support for the negotiations. London had pressed for the return of Smith to Geneva, and in Paris, Eden warned that if Mendès France failed at Geneva, there would be no French support of EDC.[132] Mendès France promised that "France will do its best to get a settlement within the framework of the seven points, . . . If there is no agreement by July 20, the war will continue, with intensification." While Dulles demurred, Eisenhower was afraid that the absence of the United States in the negotiations would certainly be exploited by the Communist propaganda and "also by propaganda of our allies, particularly the French, who will then blame us for everything that goes wrong."[133] The U.S. ambassador in Paris also warned Dulles that his absence would reveal divisions between the Western states and be interpreted as disapproval of the negotiation and its result.[134] Finally Dulles agreed to send Smith back to Geneva, after he clarified with the British and French leaders that "the US could never join in any guarantee to the Communists of the fruits of their aggression."[135]

SALVAGING AS MUCH AS POSSIBLE

The concluding phase of the Geneva Conference was generally regarded as having been anticlimactic, and Smith as having "exercised scant influence on the settlement."[136] The currently available documents, however, indicate a neglected aspect of U.S. diplomacy during the last week of the negotiation. Instead of being a passive and reluctant audience, the U.S. delegation indeed contributed to the Geneva Agreements, although in an indirect way. Rather than supporting the positions of the Associated States, which Dulles had encouraged, U.S. officials pushed them to meet the Communist request, and hence facilitated the conclusion of the agreements.

Once U.S. leaders were convinced that the Chinese wanted a ceasefire, they no longer interpreted Communist intransigence as delaying tactics and started to distinguish the DRV from China. When the French military talks with the Vietminh deadlocked because the Vietminh delegate "made [an] unacceptable proposal of demarcation line along [the] thirteenth parallel" and requested a political election in 1955, U.S. officials believed that the DRV leaders were emboldened by their military gains. They also speculated that the DRV suffered from internal differences.[137] The Chinese, however, seemed to want a ceasefire "as badly as the French and would be disposed to force the Viet Minh" to make concessions.[138] The perception was confirmed by Communist concessions before the Western leaders' meeting in Paris: the Vietminh agreed to move the demarcation line up to the sixteenth parallel and give up the request for a fixed date for elections. Zhou Enlai told Mendès France that "present difference of [the] demarcation line must be settled," and he implied that the Vietminh would make further concessions.[139]

Dulles believed the Communist retreat, despite their apparently favorable military standing, resulted from their anxiety about potential U.S. intervention in Indochina.[140] Throughout his meetings with officials of both U.S. allies and the Associated States, Zhou was obsessed with his concerns about the United States building bases in Indochina or including these states in military alliances. He repeatedly expressed willingness to make concessions to prevent these prospects.[141] When the Communists made strong requests on the issues of a regrouping area in Laos and exclusion of Cambodia from the military group, U.S. officials believed they were dissatisfied with an unexpectedly firm Mendès France and worried about the Associated States' participation in the Southeast Asia defense pact. They were upset by the firm position of the French on both Indochina and the EDC, and wanted to force Mendès France out of the government, not ruin the opportunity for a settlement.[142]

Nevertheless, U.S. leaders wanted to make sure their allies kept their promise of sticking to the Seven Points. Dulles instructed Smith to limit his role to that of "the representative of a nation friendly to the non-Communist states primarily interested . . . in arriving at a just settlement."[143] When the British pushed the United States to endorse the final armistice agreement, as requested by the Communists, despite the U.S. position that it would only be willing to make a unilateral statement, Dulles told Smith that the U.S. Constitution did not give the president the power to guarantee the settlement. He was worried that Eden would "try to push Mendès-France into [an] agreement far short of 7 Points which will confront us with [the] dilemma of either agreeing to 'respect' it or repudiation which might involve our responsibility for breakup."[144] Dulles instructed Smith to tell the French that Eisenhower was preparing for the failure of the negotiation and would make a public statement indicating "a very grave view of the failure of the Conference as creating a likelihood of the war being intensified and enlarged, both in terms of the area of combat and of the belligerents," in an effort to both "buck up" the French and pressure the Communists.[145]

In private, however, the U.S. delegation pushed Cambodia and Laos to compromise their original positions, which the United States had requested. U.S. officials had collaborated with the two delegations to influence the result of the negotiation through them, and Washington was well informed of their meetings with the Communists. In June, Dulles welcomed the two states to join SEATO and warned them not to make any commitment that would exclude the possibility of their memberships in the organization. He also offered military training and weapons to Cambodia to consolidate their position.[146] As the final negotiation was starting, Dulles told the Cambodian ambassador in Washington that he hoped Cambodia would join the collective defense group planned by Washington and London, knowing his resistance to neutralization of Cambodia, which the Cambodians believed would ultimately lead to a Communist takeover. And U.S. delegates in Geneva assured the Laotians that their security would be covered in the future SEATO.[147]

In the last days of the negotiation, however, Smith wanted the two states to give up their original positions. Although he was well aware of their resistance to neutralization and eagerness for direct U.S. assistance, Smith suggested to the Cambodian delegation that Cambodia could make a declaration, as requested by the Communists, that it did not intend to have foreign bases on its territory nor to join military alliances. Smith also implied that neither membership in the upcoming Southeast Asia defense group nor U.S. weapons were indeed necessary, because its status in the French Union would enable Cambodia to get "adequate desirable means of securing through France necessary arms some of which would be American as well as necessary instructors and technicians some of which might well be American trained."[148] U.S. officials knew that Zhou was using both sticks and carrots to press for the two states' neutralization, so what Smith said amounted to pressuring them to surrender to the Communist request.[149]

Washington also ignored the SV's opposition to a peace settlement, which reversed the initial U.S. position. At the beginning of the conference, Dulles worked together with the SV delegation and secured the Vietnamese agreement to withdraw from the negotiation if it went against their positions. When the Communists made aggressive requests in June, Dulles pressed U.S. allies to agree that a final settlement must get the approval of the Associated States in case France made unacceptable concessions to the Communists. He then repeatedly reminded the French of this position, and U.S. officials were also aware that the French never bothered to consult the SV government about their negotiations with the Communists and wanted the United States to press the Vietnamese to accept whatever results they could get. When the French and Communists reached agreement about partition in Vietnam, the SV was strongly opposed. However, instead of supporting the Vietnamese, Washington sided with the French and Communists, and ignored the SV's opposition.[150]

Therefore, Washington did contribute to the final agreements, although Dulles refused to guarantee them. Under pressure from both the United States and the Communists, Laos and Cambodia had to make unilateral declarations stating their neutralization, and the SV had to accept a divided Vietnam. By withdrawing their support to the Associated States, Washington accepted the agreements as an accomplished fact, so that they could start united action with allies—building SEATO, as Eisenhower and Dulles declared when the Geneva Agreements were reached.[151]

U.S. leaders originally misperceived Beijing's intentions in Geneva, and as a result, they exaggerated the Communist aggression. Instead of a peaceful settlement in Indochina, U.S. leaders believed the Geneva Conference served the Communist expansion scheme. Therefore, they ignored Communist demonstrations of conciliation and set up unrealistic objectives in the beginning phase of the negotiations. Under allied pressure for peace, and also in the face of a worsening military situation in Indochina, U.S. leaders compromised their original positions and developed a more accurate judgment of Communist objectives. However, the initial U.S. intransigence reinforced the Communists' worries about U.S. intervention and led to their concessions, which were critical to the peaceful settlement of the Indochina War.

Although leaders in Washington understood the Communist tactics of exploiting the differences within the Western alliance, they failed to meet the challenge effectively. The uncompromising U.S. response to the misperceived Communist aggression strained its relations with the United Kingdom and France, both of which had a better understanding of Communist intentions and were interested in a peaceful solution in Indochina. These differences further undermined the effectiveness of the U.S. policy of relying on alliances to contain the Communist expansion. In Geneva, under pressure from both Western allies and the Communists, Washington had to accept an initially unacceptable settlement: a divided Vietnam with the Tonkin Delta in the hands of the Communists, and neutralized Cambodia and Laos.

Washington's tacit acceptance of the Geneva Agreements betrayed its ally, the Indochina Associated States, and its apparent intransigence alienated most other states in Southeast Asia. Shortly after the Geneva Conference, the British commissioner general for Southeast Asia reported to London:

> The conduct of American foreign policy towards Asia during recent months has left the United States with few friends, many enemies and almost universal critics amongst Asian Governments and peoples. It has done America's reputation shattering harm, appears sometimes to Asians to support the Communist contention that the United States are the real "war-mongers" in the world, and has left the United States virtually isolated here except for the support of some of the least influential Asian nations, like Siam and Chinese Nationalist Formosa. . . . It is appalling that American statements and actions have caused such gigantic misunderstanding, and that the vast influence which America could exert for good has been turned to grave disadvantage to us all.[152]

Although Washington attempted to exploit the differences within the Communist Bloc, it did not get much chance. Lacking information about relations between the Communists, their observations of emerging tensions remained speculative and uncertain. U.S. diplomats often overread differences between China and the Soviet Union, as can be seen in currently available government documents from these two states. Compared to Sino-Soviet relations, the Americans were relatively ignorant of differences between China and the DRV, and they often mistook the Vietminh's military actions on the battleground for China's intentions to dominate Indochina. Although they were aware that China would play a principal role in Geneva, there was no way they could exert influence on the Chinese due to their hostility toward and isolation from the People's Republic.

U.S. actions during the Geneva Conference added to the tensions between China and the United States. Its intransigence about negotiation and hostility against the Chinese Communist government—especially its attempts to use the GMD to contain China—enhanced Beijing's hostility toward the United States and drew its attention to the yet to be restored territory of Taiwan. The willingness of Washington to make compromises under pressure from its allies and Communist military actions encouraged the Chinese to further mobilize U.S. allies to push the United States to compromise its policy.

PART II

Taiwan Strait Crisis

Chapter Three

PREVENTING THE MUTUAL DEFENSE TREATY

Right now, an important issue in our relations with the United States is the Taiwan issue. This will be a long-lasting problem. We must prevent the possible US-Taiwan [military] pact.[1]

—MAO ZEDONG, JULY 7, 1954

Making use of the contradictions between the United States and Britain, [China] should expose U.S. aggression policy in Asia, to substantially separate the United States from Britain. [China should] propagandize Sino-British friendship and trade, in order to win over Britain and isolate the United States.[2]

—ZHOU ENLAI, AUGUST 12, 1954

On July 23, only two days after the Geneva Agreements concluded, China abruptly began a massive propaganda campaign claiming it was determined to liberate Taiwan from the GMD. On September 3, 1954, the People's Liberation Army (PLA) severely bombarded the GMD-held Jinmen Islands off the coast of Fujian province, despite the fact that the United States' Seventh Fleet had been deployed in the Taiwan Strait to protect the GMD since the outbreak of the Korean War. The United States sent warships to the Jinmen area, and tensions quickly escalated in the Taiwan Strait. The United States and China participated in a nine-month military confrontation, which is commonly known as the Taiwan Strait Crisis. The crisis reached its peak in March 1955, when the United States threatened to use nuclear weapons against China, and ended abruptly when Zhou declared at the Bandung Conference in April 1955 that China was willing to negotiate with the United States to resolve tensions between them.

This chapter investigates why Chinese leaders initiated the confrontation with the United States when they sought peace in Indochina and how the radical move in the Taiwan Strait served the Chinese leaders' strategy of isolating the United States. This chapter weighs in on whether Beijing had a coherent policy; the Communists' objectives in bombarding the Jinmen Islands; how they perceived the U.S. response; and the factors leading to China's subsequent conciliation.[3]

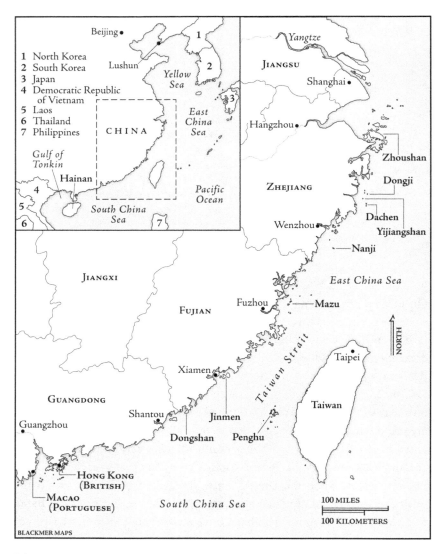

FIGURE 3.1. Eastern China and the Taiwan Strait
Source: Kate Blackmer

Highlighting China's neglected diplomatic moves during the crisis, I argue that Beijing's actions in the Taiwan Strait were a continuation of its efforts to reduce tensions in its neighborhood—in this case, the U.S. attempts to build an MDT with the GMD. To achieve that objective, Chinese leaders continued to separate the United States from its ally, the United Kingdom, and from the neutral Asian states. The military actions in the Taiwan Strait were a warning to Washington of the risk of allying with the GMD and aimed to mobilize the United Kingdom and Asian states against the United States. While bombing the Jinmen Islands, China invited the British, Indian, and Burmese leaders to Beijing and pushed them to convince the United States not to ally with GMD. China also exerted pressure by receiving the first secretary of the Soviet Communist Party, Nikita Khrushchev, and demonstrating the Sino-Soviet unity. However, Mao misperceived the Americans' need for an MDT and overestimated the differences between the United States and the United Kingdom. Therefore, his initiation of the crisis inadvertently hastened the conclusion of the MDT. When the crisis caused anxieties among the Asian countries, China turned to peace initiatives. In addition to soothing tensions among the Asian states, the conciliation was aimed to mobilize them to push Washington to negotiate with China, thus granting it de facto recognition.

INITIATING THE CRISIS

The Taiwan Strait Crisis began immediately after the Geneva Conference, when China started its propaganda campaign.[4] On July 23, the day after *Renmin Ribao* hailed the peaceful settlement of the Indochina War as a big diplomatic victory, the Chinese government stated in the same newspaper that the Chinese people "are determined to liberate" Taiwan, and "they will not stop until their aim is achieved."[5] To add to the tensions, the PLA air force shot down a British Cathay Pacific airliner on the same day, killing ten passengers including three American citizens, as the plane was flying from India to Hong Kong over the Hainan Island. Tensions escalated when the U.S. Air Force shot down two Chinese fighters in retaliation three days later. While protesting the U.S. action, Chinese press published numerous articles warning against U.S. attempts to sign the MDT with the GMD government and its efforts to whip together a Southeast Asian military group.[6] On August 1, Zhu De, the PLA commander in chief, declared that China's determination to liberate Taiwan would not waver even if the U.S. intervened. On August 11, Zhou published a report on foreign affairs, warning:

> If any foreign aggressors dare to try to hinder the Chinese people from liberating Taiwan, if they dare to infringe upon our sovereignty or violate our territorial integrity, if they dare to interfere in our internal affairs, they must take all the grave consequences of such acts of aggression upon themselves.

Soon a joint declaration by "all democratic parties and people's organizations" in China was published, claiming Taiwan as Chinese territory and warning the United States not to conclude the MDT with Taiwan.[7] The PLA shelling of Jinmen on September 3 was a culmination of China's actions.

The Chinese leaders initiated the crisis because they felt an MDT between the United States and Taiwan was imminent.[8] According to the Chinese Foreign Ministry, after the Geneva Agreements ended the war in Indochina, U.S. leaders were worried that they would be under greater diplomatic pressure on the Taiwan issue. To forestall that and continue to use Taiwan to contain China, the United States wanted to consolidate relations with the GMD using the MDT. At the same time, the United States was enlarging its military advisory group in Taiwan, strengthening its control of the GMD military, and expanding the activity of the Seventh Fleet to cover offshore islands including Jinmen and Dachen. Chinese officials worried that the MDT would become part of a broader Pacific military alliance, which would include both SEATO and the Northeast Asia Treaty Organization (NEATO). When U.S. efforts to set up SEATO did not meet with enthusiasm from the United Kingdom and the Asian states, according to the Chinese estimate, Washington wanted to begin with the MDT and build NEATO on the basis of bilateral treaties between Taiwan, Korea, and Japan. Chinese officials were particularly alerted by Van Fleet's repeated visits to Taiwan in April and July and believed his objective was an MDT.[9] *Renmin Ribao* reported that GMD officials said that the MDT would be signed in September, and Dulles said at a press conference in early August that the United States was already negotiating with the GMD over this. Meanwhile, Washington was supplying jet fighters and two destroyers to Taiwan.[10]

The Chinese anxiety is demonstrated in a telegram Mao sent to Zhou on July 27, when Zhou was on his way back from Geneva via Moscow:

FIGURE 3.2. Looking for the road to death—let's break this open together. The characters above the lever read: United States-Chiang Treaty.
Source: Yang Keyang (杨可扬), March 1955. Published by Renmin meishu chubanshe (人民美术出版社). Courtesy of IISH / Stefan R. Landsberger / Private Collection. www.chineseposters.net

The Central Committee recently discussed the situation related to the Geneva Conference, and it believes that after the armistice in Korea and Indochina, the US is unwilling to accept its failure at the Geneva Conference, and will inevitably continue to carry out the policies of creating international tension for the purpose to further taking over more sphere of influence from Britain and France, expanding military bases for preparing for war, and remaining hostile to our country. In Southeast Asia, in addition to active efforts to set up an organization of defense and rearming Japan, the US surely will continue to use Taiwan to carry out pirate-style robberies of the ships from various countries to come to our country, and is likely to expand the sphere of blockade of our country to the areas off the Guangdong coast and to the Gulf of Tonkin area. Recently the US and Chiang Kai-shek have been discussing signing a US-Chiang treaty of defense, and the US has repeatedly increased military aid to the Chiang bandits in Taiwan. All of this is worthy of our main attention. According to public information, *it seems as if the US still has some worries about signing a US-Chiang treaty of defense, and it seems as if they had not made the final decision.* But if the US and Chiang sign such a treaty, the relationship between us and the US will be in tension for a long period, and it becomes more difficult for the relationship to turn around. *Therefore, the central task of our struggle against the US at present is to break up the US-Chiang treaty of defense and the Southeast Asian treaty of defense.*[11]

The same document further laid out the tactics Chinese leaders would adopt to achieve their objective. Politically, they launched a propaganda campaign to increase diplomatic pressure on the United States by highlighting to the world the domestic nature of the Taiwan issue and China's determination to liberate Taiwan. Militarily, the PLA prepared to take actions against the GMD forces in the Taiwan Strait to demonstrate to the United States the risk of intervening in the Chinese civil war. However, Chinese leaders strictly limited the military targets to the GMD forces and forbid PLA generals from raiding U.S. planes and warships to avoid a direct conflict with the United States.[12] As they did in Indochina, Chinese leaders used military actions to serve their diplomatic purposes. And diplomatically, China would take advantage of the tensions to mobilize U.S. allies, especially the United Kingdom, and China's Asian neighbors to pressure the United States not to ally with the GMD. Such a program would have a bonus effect—it could "raise the political consciousness and political alertness of the people of the whole country" and "stir up" their "revolutionary enthusiasm," promoting the socialist construction.[13] This was particularly important in the summer of 1954, when an unprecedented flood in the Yangtze River was causing serious losses and damage to the morale of the Chinese people.

This policy was based on Chinese officials' perception of U.S. isolation on its China policy. Beijing had noticed that U.S. hostility toward China was criticized by neutral Asian states. It was happy to see that India, Burma, and Indonesia sought peaceful coexistence with China and supported the PRC's entry into the United Nations at the Colombo meeting in April. Zhou's visits to India and Burma in June, according to the Chinese Foreign Ministry, further increased China's affinity for these countries. Consequently, when Eisenhower reiterated opposition to China's entry

FIGURE 3.3. Liberate Taiwan, annihilate the remnants of the bandit Chiang Kai-shek
Source: Wu Yun (吴耘), Zhao Yannian (赵延年), Yang Keyang (杨可扬), 1954. Courtesy of IISH / Stefan R. Landsberger / Private Collection, www.chineseposters.net

into the United Nations and the U.S. Congress passed a resolution supporting this position in July, most Southeast Asian states criticized the U.S. position. Most important to the Chinese leaders, these states were also opposed to U.S. efforts to build SEATO and instead advocated building a neutral zone of peace in Asia.[14]

Moreover, the Chinese leaders believed they could exploit the differences between the United States and its closest ally, the United Kingdom. Instead of uniting to fight Communism, Chinese diplomats believed the British were struggling with the United States for its sphere of influence in Asia. This was best demonstrated by their attitude toward SEATO: the British proposed a Locarno-type pact in Asia and advocated peaceful coexistence between the two camps, but the United States wanted to build a Western military group, which, according to the Chinese Foreign Ministry, would serve the dual goals of both containing Communism and expanding U.S. influence into the traditional British sphere in Asia.[15] Chinese officials also pointed out that the American China policy hurt several British interests. The British suffered heavy losses in the American-supported GMD harassment of merchant ships in the Taiwan Strait and were opposed to an MDT, which would encourage GMD raids on the mainland and consequently drag the United States, and possibly the United Kingdom, into a war with China. Chinese leaders believed that after losing over forty ships and becoming the biggest victim of the GMD harassments in the Taiwan Strait, the British were sympathetic to the PLA's actions to eliminate the GMD forces from the strait.[16] In addition, as British leaders showed in Geneva, the British government wanted to coexist with China and planned to improve the relationship with the PRC, in opposition to U.S. hostility toward China. In particular, the British wanted to improve trade with China. They invited a Chinese trade delegation to visit the United Kingdom despite the U.S. embargo on China. According to an analysis by Chinese diplomats, the British independent policy was bolstered by its economic condition. Although the United States was experiencing an economic crisis, the United Kingdom was not influenced by the crisis. Instead, its economy had developed well. Therefore, Chinese diplomats wondered whether the British government was even attempting to get rid of U.S. "economic control" of the United Kingdom.[17]

Chinese leaders concluded that the United States was becoming increasingly isolated on its China policy. As Zhou observed, in the Korean War, the United States rallied a dozen or so supporters. In Indochina, it had become difficult for the United States to find followers. On the Taiwan issue, the United States was virtually alone.[18] Mao concluded that the successful Geneva negotiation indicated that in diplomatic isolation the Americans would make concessions under pressure from allies.[19]

The Chinese idea got support from their Soviet comrades.[20] During Zhou's stay in Moscow on his way back to Geneva on July 11, he talked to the Soviet leaders about China's concerns regarding the Taiwan issue. The Soviet leaders believed that U.S. policy was still uncertain, and Washington might not be willing to bind itself with the GMD while facing a mid-term election in November. Therefore, the Soviets encouraged the Chinese to give "stern warnings" to U.S. leaders to enhance their indecision, in addition to criticizing the U.S. "conspiracy" in the press, instead of showing weakness before the United States.[21] When Zhou was in Moscow in late July, he consulted the Soviets again about China's plan to prevent the MDT. Malenkov agreed that "the gap between policies adopted by the US and Britain and France was widening." Indeed, at this moment, Moscow even believed the conflicts between the Westerners indicated that the U.S. leadership was over.[22] Therefore, the Soviet leader endorsed both Beijing's goal of preventing the MDT and its tactics of exploiting differences between the United States and its allies. Moreover, Malenkov supported China's plan to strengthen its navy and air force for the defense of the coastal area. He agreed to let Soviet military leaders look into China's request for the most up-to-date long-range heavy jet bombers.[23]

As the Chinese leaders prepared to mobilize the United Kingdom to pressure the United States, the PLA's accidental attack on the British plane worked against efforts to separate the United Kingdom from the United States. Mistaking the British passenger plane for a GMD plane, two PLA fighters escorting a Soviet merchant ship, without seeking approval from their commanders, opened fire and destroyed it. To make up for the accident, Beijing promptly acknowledged the mistake and granted a full apology—to the extent that the British chargé d'affaires Humphrey Trevelyan expressed "utter astonishment." The Chinese government paid the compensation the British demanded in full, and Trevelyan even speculated that "the offending pilots had probably been shot" for their mistake.[24] In private, Mao immediately ordered the PLA not to attack any foreign ships or planes when they were patrolling the high seas or convoying merchant ships. He also instructed the PLA to carry out an education campaign to prevent future accidents.[25]

In the meantime, Chinese leaders made good use of a visit by a British Labour Party delegation led by former prime minister Clement Attlee. In early May, when learning that the Labour Party, which recognized the PRC in 1950 but was now in opposition, was interested in a trip to China, Chinese leaders immediately embraced the suggestion and even offered to fund the visit.[26] When the Labour Party's trip was decided, Zhou criticized *Renmin Ribao* for not highlighting the event sufficiently and instructed the editors to consult the Foreign Ministry and the Central Publicity Department to better utilize this event. In Zhou's judgment, the Labour Party could not visit China without the British government's approval, and the fact that the UK government supported this trip, despite U.S. hostility toward the

PRC, indicated that the United Kingdom was willing to challenge the U.S. publicly. Therefore, Chinese officials must not miss the golden opportunity to exacerbate the conflicts between them.[27] Before the delegation's arrival in mid-August, Zhou held a central government conference to emphasize the importance of exploiting the visit to highlight U.S.-UK contradictions. He told Chinese officials that, although the British visitors also wanted to feel out Sino-Soviet differences, their principal purpose was to expand the Sino-British exchange and normalize relations with China. Therefore, China could form a united front with the United Kingdom against the United States.[28] The day before the delegation's arrival, all Chinese newspapers published Zhou's report on foreign affairs declaring China's determination to liberate Taiwan and protest U.S. aggression toward China, which Trevelyan correctly interpreted as a deliberate move to play off the United Kingdom and the United States against each other.[29]

In their meetings with the Labour Party delegation, both Zhou and Mao tried their best to convince the British to push the United States to change its policy toward China. When meeting with some Labour Party leaders in Geneva in May, Zhou had encouraged the British to publicize their position on China to pressure the United States when he learned about the differences between the United Kingdom and the United States on China's entry into the UN.[30] In Beijing, Zhou stressed that it was "universally recognized" that Taiwan was part of Chinese territory; the Taiwan problem resulted from U.S. support of the GMD; and it was "unreasonable" for the United States to "occupy" Taiwan.[31] Mao Zedong assured the British visitors that China wanted a peaceful environment and was willing to exist peacefully with different countries. He "wished the United States would adopt a policy of peaceful coexistence. If such a Big Power as the US does not want peace, China would not have tranquility, nor did the others." He pushed the British to convince the United States:

1. To remove its Seventh Fleet [from the Taiwan Strait], and no longer meddle with the Taiwan issue, because Taiwan belongs to China; 2. Not to set up SEATO, as it is against the history, and to establish a collective peace pact instead; 3. Not to arm Japan, which aims at China and the Soviet Union, and would ultimately hurt [the US] itself and the states in the Southwestern Pacific. It is likely to "shoot itself [the United States] in the foot"; 4. Not to arm Germany, for that would not end well and may also "shoot itself in the foot."[32]

Indeed, Mao went so far as to push the United Kingdom to *"make up its mind between friendship with the United States or friendship with China."*[33]

The British got the message. According to Trevelyan, what Mao said represented "the policy which they would like Her Majesty's Government to follow. They look to us to exercise a moderating influence on American policy and in particular to get the United States government to withdraw from Formosa the protection of the 7th Fleet."[34] However, Trevelyan continued, "the Chinese failed to understand our position correctly." "For all their subtlety and intelligence, the Chinese did not understand the British political scene at this time," as the Labour Party delegation did not represent the official British policy. Indeed, the British government was not consulted about the visit and tried to avoid leaving the impression that the Labour Party delegation stood for official British policy.[35] For Trevelyan, the Chinese underestimated "the strength of the Anglo-American alliance, which was of much greater importance to us than our relatively small interests in China." The British, according to Trevelyan, "were not going to abandon the American alliance in favor of a neutralist position" and did not have "as much influence on American policy as the Chinese seemed to think."[36] Indeed, the British government officials thought the visit was poorly timed and were anxious about U.S. displeasure.

Beijing, however, believed its maneuvers worked.[37] Even after the trip, Chinese diplomats still reported that the Labour Party spoke for the British government.[38] The trip infuriated the United States and worsened U.S.-British relations.[39] The Communist Party of Great Britain confirmed that the visit changed the Labour Party's attitude toward China, strengthened the position of its left wing, and deepened the contradictions between the United Kingdom and the United States.[40] Satisfied with the result, the Chinese Foreign Ministry instructed its diplomats to pay closer attention to the possible British change of attitude toward the MDT and SEATO, and their differences with the United States. The Chinese leaders also questioned whether the United States treated Taiwan differently from the offshore islands; was ready to intervene under the scenario of China attacking Taiwan; would invade the mainland should they decide to fight; and had internal divisions on the Taiwan issue.[41] In response, Chinese officials saw that the British took conciliatory actions around the time of the Labour visit. In mid-July, Churchill supported putting Taiwan under a UN trusteeship, which meant he denied the GMD regime statehood, and actually disagreed with the U.S. plan to conclude the MDT with the GMD. After Zhou declared China's position on the Taiwan issue, the British Foreign Office declared that SEATO did not cover Taiwan, and the United Kingdom did not assume responsibility for protecting Taiwan. According to Chinese officials, following the Joint Declaration, the British Foreign Office further declared that Taiwan had already been returned to China and denied that the United Kingdom would propose to neutralize Taiwan in the UN.

U.S. policy also had some subtle changes, according to the Chinese Foreign Ministry Intelligence Department. In late August, the U.S. government avoided mentioning the MDT, and the U.S. press generally disagreed with the idea following publication of Zhou's diplomatic report. The United States worried about being dragged into a war with China and hesitated to get into a longtime deadlock in relations between the two countries. Moreover, Eisenhower indicated that the United States might change its policy regarding China's entry into the UN. On the defense of Taiwan, although the United States declared its willingness to protect the island, it did not promise unconditional intervention. On the offshore islands of Jinmen and Dachen, U.S. leaders—including Dulles, who was the most overtly hostile—took China's warnings seriously and distinguished these islands from Taiwan. The U.S. Navy declared that these islands were beyond the protection of the Seventh Fleet, and U.S. warships would not take actions if the PLA attacked them. Chinese officials concluded that the U.S. did not have a set policy and was indeed looking for an exit. Furthermore, they believed the U.S. quest for SEATO had relaxed when Eisenhower publicly stated that he did not like calling it a defense group, and rather wanted it to be a loose ANZUS-style organization, instead of a militarized organization like NATO.[42]

Based on these observations, Beijing concluded that the United States could find no supporters on the Taiwan issue and feared China's follow-up actions. To further demonstrate the risk of concluding the MDT with the GMD, the PLA bombarded the GMD troops on the Jinmen Islands on September 3. The heavy shelling lasted five hours and killed two U.S. military advisors. Unlike the previous tensions in May, this attack was coercive diplomacy aiming to deter the United States from concluding the MDT. The Chinese leaders had originally planned to attack the Dachen and Jinmen Islands simultaneously in mid-August, around the time the British Labour Party was visiting China, to reinforce the pressure on the United

States, but they had to put off the bombing because the flood in the Yangtze River blocked transportation. When the bombing took place, Dachen was dropped from the target because there were U.S. forces in the area, and Mao did not want a conflict with the United States.[43]

For Chinese leaders, the bombardment exacerbated the differences between the United States and the GMD over the MDT. According to the Chinese Foreign Ministry, the U.S. leaders did not agree to cover the off-shore islands, and the bombardment added to the hesitation about con-cluding the MDT with the GMD. The U.S. ambassador to the GMD. Karl Rankin, disclosed that the offshore islands were the biggest problem in U.S. considerations about the MDT—if they were included in the treaty, the United States would face the risk of fighting China, but if they were not covered, the treaty would invite China's attack on the islands. There-fore, Rankin suggested not concluding the treaty at this point. Dulles was meeting with allies to establish SEATO in the Philippines when the bom-bardment took place. He declared his intention to visit Taiwan after the meeting, which the Chinese interpreted as a meeting to discuss the MDT with Chiang, but the bombing forced him to change the plan. The U.S. Embassy in Taipei refused to release the purpose of the trip and only said his stay in Taipei would be short.[44] The British government also reiterated its position that the United Kingdom was not committed to protecting Tai-wan, and Taiwan was not covered in the newly established SEATO.[45]

The bombardment also successfully revealed the U.S. position on the offshore islands. According to Chinese diplomatic reports, after the shell-ing, both the White House and the Defense Department refused to commit to the protection of Jinmen, although the Americans declared they would protect Taiwan. The U.S. State Department stated that it would not protest against the killing of the U.S. officers. The NSC was divided on the issue of whether the United States should prevent China from attacking Jinmen. Some U.S. officials wanted to help the GMD, but many others were worried that would lead to a Sino-American conflict, which would split the alliance between the United States and the United Kingdom and alienate Washing-ton from many other European and Asian states. And the U.S. press stressed the difficulties in stopping China from liberating the offshore islands.[46]

To increase pressure on the United States and also in retaliation for GMD air raids of the coastal mainland area in response to the bombardment of Jin-men, the PLA shelled the Jinmen Islands again on September 22.[47] After that the military actions were adjourned until November. Chinese leaders may have felt that the military actions had backfired. According to a Chinese Foreign Ministry analysis after the second bombardment, the GMD had withdrawn its proposal to include the offshore islands in the MDT, and the final treaty would not specify its accurate coverage. As a result, although some U.S. officials were still doubtful about the necessity of the treaty, the U.S. government increased its pace of negotiating with the GMD in order to conclude the MDT as a way to deter China from invading Taiwan.[48] The PLA was also incapable of carrying on lasting attacks. According to new sources, PLA artillery forces had just enough resources to take limited actions. Indeed, short of air force coverage, after the bombardment, the artillery troops relocated immediately to avoid destruction by GMD air attacks.[49]

Still, the military action achieved some success. Through the two bombardments, Chinese leaders figured out the U.S. position on the offshore islands, highlighted the Taiwan issue to the world, and pushed the United States to stop the GMD from raiding the coastal areas. After the second bombing, the GMD air raids on the mainland stopped.[50] Subsequently, the Chinese leaders shifted to diplomacy to mobilize more pressure. They received a series of important visitors in Beijing and sent a Chinese diplomat to London.[51]

INCREASING PRESSURE

While attempting to alienate the United States, the Chinese leaders carefully maintained a united front with their own ally. Making use of a Soviet visit to China for the fifth anniversary of the establishment of the PRC, the two countries demonstrated the strength of their alliance, which was particularly important when Chinese leaders noticed that U.S. leaders were interested in the Sino-Soviet differences.[52] During his stay in Beijing in late September and early October, Khrushchev declared that the Soviet people supported the Chinese exercise of their sovereignty rights by liberating Taiwan. The two states made a joint communiqué accusing the United States of a "direct invasion" of China through its "occupation" of the Chinese territory Taiwan and its economic and military assistance to Chiang, who was "the common enemy of the Chinese people." In the UN, the Soviet Union twice accused the United States of both invading China and infringing on free shipping in the Taiwan Strait. On October 8, during the Soviets' stay in

Beijing, Zhou telegrammed the UN General Assembly, accusing the United States of infringing upon China's sovereignty and threatening peace in the Far East.[53] As the Soviet delegation was leaving Beijing, *Renmin Ribao* declared that "China and the Soviet Union were completely in agreement on the cooperation between the two states and issues of the international situation." The two states wanted to build relations with other countries on the basis of peaceful coexistence, and they protested the U.S. denial of China's UN membership and support of Taiwan as against the requirements of relaxing tensions.[54]

The Soviet leaders, especially Khrushchev, who had just become the first secretary of the Soviet Communist Party and was the number two leader after Malenkov, also needed Beijing's support as a struggle for leadership was going on after Stalin's death. So Khrushchev offered to join the delegation to visit Beijing, although the original plan did not include him.[55] During his stay in Beijing, Khrushchev agreed to help China launch its nuclear program. Although he hesitated to support Mao's plan to develop nuclear weapons, which he thought was both "expensive" and "unnecessary" because China already had Soviet nuclear protection, the Soviet leader was willing to help China build an experimental nuclear reactor, which would lay the foundation for China's nuclear weapon development.[56] In addition to their support of China's foreign policy, the Soviets signed a series of agreements ranging from scientific and technological cooperation to government loans to assist in China's massive industrial modernization. Moreover, Khrushchev decided to return Lushun, formerly Port Arthur, which had been under Soviet control since 1945, to demonstrate their respect for Chinese sovereignty, despite opposition from the Soviet Foreign Ministry. The Soviets also sold Soviet shares in four Sino-Soviet joint ventures in Xinjiang and Manchuria to the Chinese, which were set up in 1950 and had been a subject of criticism by Chinese intellectuals. Khrushchev's visit started the honeymoon in the Sino-Soviet alliance.[57]

In Beijing's efforts to isolate the United States, it was important to unite the neutral states of India, Burma, and Indonesia. These states were preparing to hold the Bandung Conference of Asian and African countries to promote Third World unity, and Nehru advocated a neutral zone of peace in Asia, in opposition to the U.S. military alliance system. According to the Chinese Foreign Ministry, India not only refused to join SEATO but also dissuaded other Asian states from entering because Nehru believed

SEATO increased the risk of war.[58] After Beijing launched the propaganda campaign, these states expressed sympathy for China's position, although they feared war and wanted to see a peaceful resolution.[59] Based on these observations, as well as his experience in Geneva, Zhou divided the capitalist camp into three groups: (1) the belligerent group led by the United States; (2) the status quo group headed by the United Kingdom and France; and (3) the neutral group led by India. China's policy was to isolate the belligerent group, win over the status quo group, and unite with the neutral powers. In addition to trying to secure Indian support on Taiwan, the Chinese leaders were particularly interested in the Bandung Conference and believed they could work with India to carry out the idea of a zone of peace at the conference.[60]

To improve China's relations with India, Chinese leaders invited Nehru to Beijing shortly after the Soviets left. During Nehru's stay in China, Chinese leaders did their best to impress him with China's goodwill. Zhou explained that China's action in the Taiwan Strait resulted from GMD raids of the mainland and U.S. interference in China's domestic affairs. If the United States withdrew its forces from Taiwan, the problem would be solved peacefully among the Chinese. Zhou assured Nehru that China wanted peace and cooperation with other countries, including the United States, and did not want to provoke a war, but it must take actions to protest against the U.S. occupation of Taiwan. China's primary goal was to isolate the U.S. war policy, and it was careful not to provoke a war despite its declaration to liberate Taiwan.[61] Mao also reassured Nehru that China wanted peace, but the U.S. frontlines in Korea, Taiwan, and Indochina kept the Chinese vigilant; therefore, China needed friends and supported the establishment of the zone of peace.[62]

Chinese leaders believed they won Nehru's support. In his conversation with the Chinese, Nehru did not hide his disdain about Dulles and the U.S. policy, saying Dulles was "a man with exceedingly limited outlook but with some kind of bigoted zeal about it, he is a danger in a position of high responsibility"; and "a man like Dulles is a great menace. He is a Methodist or a Baptist preacher who religiously goes to Church and he is narrow-minded and bigoted. He thinks everyone must agree with him, and a man like him might take any move."[63] According to Chinese diplomatic reports, back in India Nehru reiterated his recognition of One China and told the press that he trusted China's peace intention and was sympathetic to China's position on Taiwan. In contrast to China, Nehru believed the United States was creating obstacles to peace and wanted to dominate Asia.[64] Needless to say, Chinese leaders were satisfied that they had successfully alienated India from the United States. Soon the Soviet chargé d'affaires in Washington reported to Moscow that the U.S. Congress was worried about deteriorating relations with India.[65] However, what the Chinese leaders did not know was that the United States and the United Kingdom were considering taking the crisis to the UN Security Council. Nehru supported this plan because it was consistent with his idea of solving international tensions peacefully, and more important, it might give the Communist leaders a chance to go to the UN, thus helping solve the "China problem."[66] But in Beijing, Nehru did not say anything about the plan.

Although the United Kingdom joined the United States in setting up SEATO, Chinese leaders still distinguished the United Kingdom from the United States at this point. According to Zhou, British participation in SEATO and its support of the GMD in the United Nations "created barriers for the improvement of the Sino-British relations," but the United Kingdom remained a power to win over he told Chinese officials in private. Zhou encouraged the British to take actions to improve cooperation with China, as Beijing was eager to do with the United Kingdom.[67] Beijing's attitude toward the United Kingdom was primarily based on its analysis of SEATO. According to the Chinese Foreign Ministry, the establishment of SEATO indeed enabled the United Kingdom to get into the ANZUS sphere of influence, which London had wanted but the United States had refused, and the pact was consistent with the British concept of the Locarno Pact because it kept a balance between the United Kingdom and the United States. The British also successfully aborted the U.S. plan to include the Communist invasion as the target of the organization and to cover Taiwan in the SEATO Pact. Therefore, Beijing believed London was still pushing for the Locarno Pact in Asia and pressuring the United States to start peaceful negotiation with China.[68]

To enhance their relations with the United Kingdom, the Chinese leaders made more efforts. They sent Huan Xiang as the PRC's first chargé d'affaires to the United Kingdom in late October. Once in London, Huan wasted no time in telling British officials that the only solution to the Taiwan problem was U.S. withdrawal of its support to Chiang. He reminded the British of the "obligations borne by the British Government as a result of its signing the Cairo Declaration and the Potsdam Proclamation." At the same time, he also assured the British that China "would never wish to start a war with the United States."[69] Leaders in Beijing attracted the United Kingdom with trade, following their trade initiatives during the Geneva Conference.[70] At the request of the Chinese, the Sino-British Trade Committee was set up in London in July, and it sent a business delegation to China in November. In Beijing the British found a hospitable host, that "adopted a more realistic stance" and no longer demanded items on the U.S. embargo list. The *Financial Times* reported that "this Chinese position marked 'a notable change from the experience of earlier British business visitors to China who came back with masses of conditional contracts which were never fulfilled.' " Trevelyan believed the Chinese would "no doubt make incidental political capital" out of the trade relations with the United Kingdom.[71]

Despite all of these efforts, Chinese leaders failed to prevent the MDT, and in November they felt the U.S.-GMD military alliance was inevitable. As a clear indicator, on November 16, Dulles declared at his press conference that the United States would not give up protecting Taiwan. In his meeting with British diplomats in mid-November, Huan disclosed that Beijing expected the MDT would soon come into being,[72] and *Renmin Ribao* published a series of articles protesting the imminent MDT.[73] China's goal then turned to preventing the MDT from including the offshore islands. To deter the United States from doing that, on November 23 a Chinese court sentenced eleven U.S. pilots to imprisonment as spies, despite the U.S. protest that these Americans were POWs from the Korean War.[74] A week later, Chinese military leaders instructed the PLA troops to get ready to attack the Yijiangshan Island off the Zhejiang coast around December 20, an important defense point in the Dachen Islands. The purpose, according to the order, was to warn the United States and the GMD not to include the offshore islands in the MDT.[75]

Just as the PLA was preparing to attack Yijiangshan, the MDT was declared on December 3. In response, *Renmin Ribao* stated that China would not tolerate the U.S. invasion of Taiwan and would carry its liberation cause to the end. Zhou stated that the U.S.-GMD treaty was illegal and invalid.[76] The Soviet Union immediately declared its support for China.[77] However, in private, Chinese leaders took the MDT seriously. Mao once again put off the planned attack on Yijiangshan when the U.S. Seventh Fleet sent warships to patrol the Dachen area in response to the PLA's attacks on the GMD forces.[78]

In the eyes of the Communist leaders, although their diplomacy did not prevent the MDT, it successfully controlled the damage: because of British pressure, the United States excluded the offshore islands in the MDT. According to Chinese sources, British Foreign Office officials visited Washington three times to pressure the United States to neutralize Taiwan instead of concluding the MDT and to trade the offshore islands for China's promise not to attack Taiwan. But Eisenhower wanted to use the treaty to bolster Chiang, although he agreed with the British on the status of the offshore islands. Sentencing the U.S. pilots, however, according to the Chinese Foreign Ministry document, helped the Americans because it gave U.S. leaders an excuse to inhibit British pressure and conclude the MDT promptly.[79]

After the treaty was concluded, the British policy changed, according to the Foreign Ministry document. The British press defended the United States by stressing that the treaty was defensive and that its coverage did not include the offshore islands and stating that the GMD must get approval from the United States to attack the mainland. The British government turned to supporting the U.S. publicly: it attacked China for sentencing the U.S. pilots and warned China not to attack the islands. British representative to the United Nations Anthony Nutting even publicly warned that an attack on Taiwan was invading a UN member and would lead to UN collective action, in which the United Kingdom had to participate. According to Chinese Foreign Ministry analysis, the Conservative Party needed to demonstrate strength to win the upcoming general election. It might also have mistaken China's previous display of goodwill as its weakness.[80] In this situation, Beijing's attitude toward the United Kingdom changed. Zhou attacked the British as followers of U.S. aggression. Such a policy, Zhou warned, hurt Sino-British relations and went against British commitments in the international treaties regarding Taiwan.[81]

At this time, Chinese leaders also tried to win Burmese support on the Taiwan issue. They invited the Burmese prime minister U Nu to Beijing in early December. Playing on the Burmese concerns about the GMD forces in Burma, Zhou stressed that the United States indeed legitimized the GMD regime as the official representative of China by signing the MDT. The MDT also legalized U.S. occupation of Taiwan and encouraged the GMD to raid the mainland. The goal of the United States was to encircle China with a Pacific Pact built on the basis of SEATO and the MDT. To prove U.S. aggression, Zhou handed U Nu a detailed record, which showed that the U.S. Air Force had invaded Chinese territory thousands of times in the past four years.[82] In contrast to U.S. aggression, Zhou assured U Nu, China wanted peace and supported Burma's efforts, with India and Indonesia, to build a zone of peace in Asia. To demonstrate China's sincerity in good relations with neighbors, Mao asked U Nu to help China improve relations with Thailand.[83] Apparently Chinese leaders believed China's diplomacy toward Burma paid off. According to a Chinese diplomatic report, U Nu trusted China's goodwill, agreed with the Chinese position on Taiwan, and regarded U.S. forces in Taiwan as unbearable. U Nu even declared the Sino-American détente must build on the U.S. withdrawal of its forces from Taiwan. He also proposed to solve the Taiwan issue in the UN, on condition of China's participation in the organization.[84]

The conclusion of the MDT delayed China's attack on Yijiangshan, but it also made the action inevitable. Facing naked aggression from the United States, Chinese leaders could not afford to retreat given their original intention to mobilize the Chinese people by showing strength. *Neibu Cankao* showed that the conclusion of the MDT caused great anxiety among some Chinese. Indeed, many people lost confidence in the government's capability of liberating Taiwan, and some even questioned the validity of the CCP's policy.[85] In this situation, Beijing protested the MDT with strong actions to bolster Chinese confidence. Militarily, the PLA was ready for the attack and pressed Chinese leaders to capture the island. Strategically, the attack would test the U.S. position on the offshore islands and might also mobilize the United Kingdom to pressure the United States, given the different British position on these islands.[86]

Nevertheless, Chinese leaders carefully avoided potential U.S. intervention. They warned the local PLA generals several times not to start the action unless they had "absolute confidence." With prior knowledge that there were no U.S. forces in the Yijiangshan area, the PLA started the attack on January 18 and took the small island within two hours. After the action, Mao again restrained PLA commanders from carrying out their initial plan to attack Dachen. When the United States forced the GMD to withdraw from the Dachen Islands under its military protection after losing the shelter of Yijiangshan, Mao once again instructed the PLA not to chase or attack the GMD forces lest the United States intervened.[87]

The PLA attack led to a strong American response. Although the United States had to push the GMD to evacuate the Dachen Islands, Dulles sent a signal to the Soviets warning China not to use the evacuation to attack the GMD forces.[88] The U.S. Congress responded with the Formosa Resolution on January 28, which authorized Eisenhower to use force to defend Taiwan and Penghu and "related positions and territories."[89] At the request of the United States, New Zealand asked the UN to discuss the hostile situation in the Security Council, which in turn led to strong opposition in the Chinese press and a Soviet counterproposal to discuss the U.S. invasion of China instead.[90] The Security Council invited the PRC to the UN for the discussion, but China rejected the invitation on the grounds that the UN was intervening in China's domestic affairs.

SHIFTING TO CONCILIATION

Just as the tension seemed to be escalating out of control, Beijing turned to conciliation. On February 2, Zhou told J. Lomakin, Soviet chargé d'affaires ad interim in Beijing, to propose a ten-power conference.[91] Two days later, the Soviet Union publicly proposed to discuss the Taiwan Strait Crisis via a meeting with delegates from the United States, China, the Soviet Union, the United Kingdom, France, and the five Colombo Powers: India, Burma, Indonesia, Pakistan, and Ceylon.[92] Zhou then told Sweden's ambassador to Beijing that China was willing to negotiate directly with the United States to resolve tensions.[93] He then made the same suggestion to the Indian ambassador.[94] Chinese leaders maintained this conciliatory position until the Bandung Conference in April, where Zhou reiterated China's willingness to hold bilateral talks with the United States.

China's gesture of conciliation aimed to mobilize its Asian neighbors to pressure the United States, which became even more important after China accepted the invitation to attend the Bandung Conference in late January.[95] Mao stressed to the Soviet ambassador that China "attached great significance" to Bandung for the opportunity to unite other Asian states against the United States.[96] After Beijing sentenced the U.S. pilots, UN Secretary-General Dag Hammarskjöld asked to visit China because these pilots were viewed by the United States as POWs from the Korean War. Although Chinese leaders hated that Hammarskjöld was helping the United States "divert people's criticism and opposition" away from the "aggression treaty" the United States had just signed with Taiwan, they agreed to receive Hammarskjöld because, as Zhou told the Soviet Ambassador to Beijing,

> if we refuse, we would be put into a passive situation. They would still push this issue through the neutral states; and Ceylon would raise this issue among the Colombo Powers, thus putting us in a disadvantageous position. This would *even* influence negatively our participation in the coming Asia-African Conference.[97]

Before the crisis escalated in late January, India, Burma, and Indonesia were sympathetic to China.[98] Nehru and U Nu expressed understanding when Chinese leaders blamed the U.S. "invasion" of Taiwan as the cause of the tensions. By late December, Nehru was still convinced China was "anxious to avoid war, anxious even to avoid friction and possibilities of conflict."[99] But these states became anxious when hostilities between the United States and China intensified after the Yijiangshan takeover and subsequent passage of the Formosa Resolution. Although they still acknowledged China's right to liberate its territory, they worried that an attack on Taiwan would "directly endanger world peace." On January 30, Burma called for a peaceful solution, and U Nu offered to immediately visit the United States to help end the crisis. The Indonesian cabinet proposed that the Colombo Powers hold a conference to discuss this issue.[100] It cautioned China that an action on Taiwan would put China in a disadvantageous position in the upcoming Bandung Conference.[101]

It was Nehru who drew Beijing's closest attention. Nehru kept expressing to Chinese diplomats that "Taiwan's legal position is indisputable, and the Chinese position was completely correct." But he also worried about a war between the United States and China.[102] Nehru was then attending a meeting of the British Commonwealth prime ministers, the main purpose of which was to coordinate positions on the Taiwan issue. Chinese leaders feared Nehru would switch to the U.S. position because they knew the United Kingdom was pushing Nehru to put pressure on China.[103] Their worry seemed confirmed when one of Nehru's assistants suggested to Chinese diplomats in London that India would have to accept a "military deadlock" in the Taiwan Strait.[104] To make sure the Indians understood China's conciliatory attitude, Zhou immediately told the Indian ambassador that

China was willing to negotiate with the United States at an international conference, as long as Taiwan was excluded, and China rejected the invitation to the UN Security Council because that was a plot to create two Chinas.[105] Catering to Nehru's desire to play the role of the leader in Asia, Zhou encouraged India to propose the international conference, which would help all of Asia.[106] Zhou also instructed the Chinese chargé in London to send the same message to Nehru.[107]

However, the ten-power conference proposal was rejected by the United States on the grounds that it would not talk about the Taiwan Strait Crisis without the GMD's presence. In London, the Commonwealth prime ministers followed the United States, and the United Kingdom supported the GMD's participation in negotiations between Washington and Beijing. Moreover, Beijing was told that under Western pressure Nehru failed to stand for China's position and also suggested that the GMD could attend any proposed negotiation.[108] Worried that India was switching to the U.S. side, the Chinese Foreign Ministry immediately instructed its diplomats to confirm whether this was the case. To their relief, Nehru soon switched back to supporting China's position.[109] To consolidate Nehru's support, Zhou promptly reiterated to the Indian ambassador that the simplest way to solve the Taiwan problem was a direct U.S.-China negotiation.[110] Meanwhile, Chinese diplomats kept the Indonesians and Burmese informed of their conciliatory stance to maintain their support. That was particularly important because Chinese leaders now knew the United States was attempting to sabotage the Bandung Conference.[111] According to the Chinese Foreign Ministry, to split the unity of the Colombo Powers, which the Americans believed was critical to the result of the conference, the U.S. diplomats offered India economic assistance and even atomic materials to lure it away from China. They also increased economic assistance to Indonesia and promised to enlarge U.S. investments.[112]

In addition to uniting the neutral states, Beijing's conciliation was a diplomatic offensive designed to alienate the United States from its allies. The proposed conference was to discuss tensions in the Taiwan Strait—a deliberately ambiguous phrase—instead of a ceasefire or solution to the Taiwan problem, which were China's internal issues and not to be discussed internationally. As Beijing had made known, tensions in the Taiwan area resulted from U.S. intervention and "occupation" of Taiwan. So, if the United States agreed to hold the conference, China would propose discussing withdrawal of U.S. forces from Taiwan, according to what Zhou told the Soviets.[113] By displaying their willingness to accept a diplomatic solution, Chinese leaders put the ball back in the United States' court. The United States would then face a dilemma between sitting together with China in an international conference, thus giving it de facto recognition, and rejecting the proposal, which would be interpreted as U.S. unwillingness to solve the problem diplomatically, further alienating the Asian states. Moreover, the proposal for direct talks without Taiwan's attendance would strain U.S. relations with the GMD. The Communist leaders knew that the GMD never had complete confidence in the U.S. commitment to its security, despite the conclusion of the MDT. A meeting between China and the United States would also exacerbate differences between the United States and the United Kingdom, Chinese diplomats told their Soviet comrades.[114] The Chinese leaders were already aware that the British had pushed the United States to force the GMD to withdraw its forces from Jinmen and Mazu in return for the Communists' promise not to attack Taiwan. If an international conference were ever held, Chinese leaders hoped that the U.S.-UK difference would come to the front, providing China with opportunities to mobilize the United Kingdom against the United States.[115]

In coordination with the diplomatic moves, Beijing maintained military pressure on the United States, as long as that did not provoke a conflict, playing on the fears about a conflict to separate the United States from the Asian states.[116] When two U.S. fighters entered the airspace of Zhejiang province on February 9, PLA antiaircraft artillery opened fire and shot one down.[117] On February 21, Mao instructed the PLA not to retreat before the U.S. threat: "if we show any fear, the enemy will consider us weak and easy to bully. In other words, if we give them an inch, they will take a mile and intensify their military expansion. Only by adopting an unyielding, resolute, and calm stance can we force the enemy to retreat."[118] Subsequently, the PLA air force bombed the Nanji Island, which forced the GMD to give up the last island it held off the coast of Zhejiang province.

When the United States responded with threats of using nuclear weapons later in March, however, Chinese leaders were alarmed and refrained from further actions.[119] In early March, PLA leaders planned to carry on the momentum and attack the Mazu Islands, expecting the United States to push the GMD to withdraw from the Jinmen Islands, as they did on Dachen. But Mao vetoed the plan and ordered the PLA not to attack, even if the GMD forces withdrew from Mazu or any other island.[120] In late March, Chinese leaders twice held conferences discussing the possibility of a U.S. surprise attack. Mao warned Chinese officials to prepare for the worst in the current nuclear age: "If we are prepared beforehand, . . . the atomic and hydrogen bombs the imperialists use to scare us will not be that terrifying." In mid-April, PLA troops stationed across the Taiwan Strait prepared for U.S. air raids on Shanghai and the coastal areas along Fujian and Zhejiang.[121]

Making use his presence in Bandung, Zhou publicized China's suggestion for direct talks with the United States, and the Americans finally agreed to hold direct negotiations with the Chinese, having exhausted all other ways of defusing the crisis.

Beijing's initiation of the Taiwan Strait Crisis was based on an incorrect judgment that the United States was negotiating with the GMD about the MDT. Apparently, Chinese leaders were misled by the frequent visitors, especially Van Fleet's conspicuous visits, to Taiwan, and the rhetoric made by both the United States and the GMD officials about the MDT. As American sources show, the U.S. leaders were not seriously considering such a treaty and hesitated to make a commitment to the GMD in the summer of 1954, although the idea had existed, and the GMD urgently pushed for such a treaty. Van Fleet's visits were to inspect the U.S. assistance program, just as the United States declared. Although he personally supported the MDT, he was not authorized to discuss it and was blamed for suggesting the MDT in his report to the NSC.[122] As a result of this misperception, the crisis the Chinese started did indeed expedited the MDT; in their efforts to defuse the crisis, U.S. leaders concluded the MDT to get the GMD's support in the United Nations, as discussed in chapter 4.

Chinese leaders also misunderstood relations within the Western alliance. Although they were correct that the United States suffered from diplomatic isolation on its China policy—which was commonly recognized by the British, the Soviets, and even the Americans themselves—it was simplistic to believe that the British were still struggling against the Americans for world leadership. It was ridiculous for Mao to believe he could ask the

British to choose between China and the United States. Chinese leaders also enormously exaggerated both the British interest in China and their capabilities to push the United States. In addition to skillful British diplomacy, the Chinese lack of experience contributed to this miscalculation. After all, attendance at the Geneva Conference was the CCP's diplomatic debut in the world. The Chinese also misunderstood British politics, and China's diplomacy toward the British failed to exert much influence on the U.S. decision regarding the MDT.

Beijing's efforts to mobilize neutral Asian states to pressure the United States did not work out as expected either. Its diplomacy with India and Burma won their sympathy, but these states wanted to remain neutral and did not have much influence in Washington on the Taiwan issue. U Nu's role was limited to transmitting China's messages to the Americans. Nehru indeed followed the United Kingdom, which was helping the United States defuse the crisis.

China's diplomacy with its Soviet ally played a limited role, although the Chinese obtained Soviet support throughout the crisis. Beijing's decision to initiate the crisis was based on the agreement with the Soviets. Khrushchev provided diplomatic pressure to help prevent an MDT. China's shift to conciliation in early February was a joint decision made by the Chinese and the Soviets together. In addition, the two states agreed on the follow-up actions China would take to break the deadlock in the Taiwan Strait and avoid a military conflict with the United States.[123] At the peak of the crisis in January 1955, the Soviet leaders declared support for China's nuclear research.[124] Although the Sino-Soviet alliance failed to prevent the United States from concluding the MDT with the GMD, it successfully deterred Washington from taking aggressive actions in the Taiwan Strait, as the following chapter explains.

Despite the failure to prevent the MDT, China's efforts did achieve some success. Militarily, the PLA took over all the islands off the coast of Zhejiang province and forced the United States to stop the GMD from raiding the mainland in late 1954.[125] Diplomatically, Chinese leaders successfully focused international attention on Taiwan and created tensions between the United States and its allies. Caught in the dilemma of fighting the Communists and losing allies and giving up protection of the GMD and losing prestige, Dulles and Eisenhower constantly modified their position on the offshore islands and finally accepted the British suggestion to give them up, which strained U.S. relations with the GMD to the breaking point. Had the Chinese continued the pressure, they might have been able to obtain Jinmen and Mazu without a fight. Tactically, Beijing's shift to conciliation was a wise move. While easing Asian states' anxiety about a war, this policy enabled China to play on the tensions to mobilize their support. In Bandung, China would continue alienating the United States in Asia.

Chapter Four

"A HORRIBLE DILEMMA"

The Communists are clearly out to maintain tension with the U.S. and to cause difficulties between us [Britain and the U.S.] over the Formosa question.[1]

—BRITISH COMMONWEALTH RELATIONS OFFICE, AUGUST 31, 1954

The Communists might estimate that this [attacks on the offshore islands] would exacerbate relations between the US and such states as the UK and India over China policy, and possibly deter the US from extending a long-range commitment to Chiang Kai-shek.[2]

—SNIE, SEPTEMBER 4, 1954

They (the Chinese Communists) are certainly doing everything they can to try our patiences. It's awfully difficult to remain calm under these situations. Sometimes I think that it would be best all around to go after them right now without letting them pick their time and the place of their own choosing.[3]

—PRESIDENT EISENHOWER, FEBRUARY 3, 1955

With access to new Chinese sources, in this chapter I assess the U.S. response to China's challenge during the Taiwan Strait Crisis.[4] I focus on how U.S. officials perceived the Chinese threat and how effectively the Americans met the Chinese challenge. China's initiation of the Taiwan Strait Crisis put the United States in "a horrible dilemma," in the words of Dulles: helping the GMD defend the offshore islands would risk a war with China and would not be supported by U.S. allies; but refusing to help would cost U.S. credibility to allies, which were already hurt in Indochina.[5] Throughout the crisis, U.S. leaders were caught in this dilemma.

I argue that Washington was not initially ready to conclude an MDT with the GMD. Although U.S. officials knew of China's plan to use the Taiwan issue to separate the United States from its allies, they were distracted and failed to examine Beijing's tactics and objectives. Shocked by the bombardment of the Jinmen Islands, Washington exaggerated Beijing's aggression and forced itself into the dilemma of either fighting a war or losing accountability. Dulles sent the Seventh Fleet to deter Beijing and sought a UN resolution condemning China. The goal was to both contain the Chinese aggression and split the Sino-Soviet alliance by forcing the Soviets to choose between supporting China, which would alienate other UN members, and endorsing the resolution and thus offending China. To win GMD's support for the UN move, Washington precipitately concluded the MDT.

However, although U.S. allies accepted the MDT, they exerted pressure from different directions: the United Kingdom pressed the United States to push the GMD to evacuate from the offshore islands and to seek détente with China, whereas the GMD resisted U.S. requests to abandon the islands and instead sought a U.S. commitment to the islands. In deep frustration, Washington ignored China's peace overtures as a hoax and mistakenly believed Beijing was preparing to attack Taiwan. When U.S. leaders threatened to use atomic weapons to deter the alleged Chinese aggression, their rhetoric further strained relations with the United Kingdom and created a bellicose atmosphere, which would be exploited by the Chinese during the Bandung Conference.

AMBIVALENT POLICY

When the Geneva Conference ended, U.S. leaders concluded that the conference promoted the PRC's prestige and increased its capacity to expand Communism in Asia. Despite the Communist concessions in Geneva, Washington believed Beijing would continue its peace offensive to separate the United States from its allies and attract other Asian states to the Chinese side. Therefore, according to the Joint Chiefs of Staff (JCS), China "was the heart of the problem for U.S. policy in Asia."[6] CIA Director Allen Dulles suggested in early August that the Chinese Communists would not give up Indochina and would change their tactics to subversion and infiltration, although they were not likely to break the armistice openly. He also predicted that Chinese leaders "would make Formosa a major diplomatic issue" and that "diversionary attacks on the offshore islands near Formosa were possible."[7] Indeed, since early 1954, both civilian and military officials had warned of the possibility that the Communists would attack the offshore islands. In a major confrontation between the CCP and the GMD in

May, the PLA captured the Dongji Islands off the coast of Zhejiang Province.[8] In late May, the CIA reported to the NSC that the PLA was preparing to attack the Dachen Islands.[9]

Although the situation in the Taiwan Strait was a pressing challenge, the top U.S. priority after the Geneva Conference was "drawing a line" in Southeast Asia to deter Communist aggression.[10] As the British ambassador to the United States Roger Makins observed, after Geneva Washington was preoccupied with the creation of a defense system in Southeast Asia,[11] and Taiwan was of secondary importance. Also, Washington was eager to restore U.S. prestige and leadership in containing the Communists, which had been hurt by supporting France and failing to obtain united action in Indochina. Furthermore, while Taiwan was a divisive issue in U.S. relations with allies, American leaders reached consensus with major allies on building SEATO. Therefore, on the day the Geneva Agreements were reached, Eisenhower announced that the United States was pushing for the "rapid organization of a collective defense in Southeast Asia in order to prevent further direct or indirect Communist aggression in that general area."[12] Dulles soon laid out his plan for this organization at a press conference and had his staff study the legal basis of potential membership for Cambodia, Laos, and SV in SEATO.[13] U.S. leaders remained preoccupied with SEATO until it was set up in early September.[14]

Washington failed to study China's intentions in the Taiwan Strait and responded to the Chinese instinctively. Despite warnings about the possibility of the CCP attacking the offshore islands, this prospect was not seriously studied. When the PLA fighters shot down the British airliner around Hainan Island killing three American passengers, Washington considered it an isolated event caused by some "trigger-happy" PLA pilots.[15] To deter the PLA, while filing a protest to the PRC government through the British, Washington sent two aircraft carriers to the area, and the U.S. Air Force soon shot down two Chinese fighters. While Communist propaganda was claiming to liberate Taiwan, the NSC discussed tensions in the Taiwan Strait on August 5.[16] Dulles asked for more U.S. Navy visits to the area to deter China, and Eisenhower confirmed that American warships had made regular visits. Without thinking through the Communists' intentions, Eisenhower told Dulles that "if the Communists tried an invasion of Formosa by a fleet of junks, this might make a good target for an atomic bomb."[17]

When the possibility of a Communist attack of the islands was raised again at the NSC meeting on August 18, the JCS chairman Admiral Arthur Radford suggested protecting all the coastal islands. Eisenhower regarded these islands as "vital outposts for the defense of Formosa" and believed in going "as far as possible to defend them without inflaming world opinion" against the United States.[18] Consequently, the Seventh Fleet was sent to the most vulnerable Dachen area again, now ordered to return fire if attacked by the PLA.[19] The commander of the Pacific Fleet Admiral Felix Stump visited Dachen and then Taiwan. In private, Stump told Chiang that Radford intended to protect these offshore islands, but this was not yet approved by the NSC.[20] In public, Dulles told the press on August 24 that the security of these islands "might from a military standpoint be so intimately connected with the defense of Formosa that the military would be justified in concluding that the defense of Formosa comprehended a defense of those islands." And a week earlier Eisenhower had told reporters that "any invasion of Formosa would have to run over the 7th Fleet."[21]

These statements were consistent with a tendency toward an increasing commitment to these offshore islands.[22] When Truman sent the Seventh Fleet to the Taiwan Strait in 1950, he excluded the islands from the coverage. But after China participated in the Korean War, the State Department encouraged the GMD to defend these islands and were willing to provide assistance for that.[23] After Eisenhower "unleashed" Chiang in February 1953, the United States pushed the GMD to use the coastal islands as bases to raid the mainland. Consequently, the GMD forces launched more raids and even attempted to capture the Dongshan Island off the coast of Fujian province in the summer.[24] In August, when the GMD set up a new command on Dachen, General William Chase, head of the Military Assistance Advisory Group (MAAG) in Taipei, attended the opening conference.[25] While declining the GMD request to include these islands formally in the coverage of the Seventh Fleet, Eisenhower agreed to provide some navy vessels, and in late 1953 the NSC included these islands in the U.S. military assistance programs under the control of MAAG. At the request of Chase, Washington also agreed to involve MAAG in the command of GMD operations from these islands.[26] Entering 1954, the GMD intensified its raids of both the merchant and fishing ships in the Taiwan Strait. After the PLA moved its navy and air force to Zhejiang, conflicts quickly escalated. U.S. Ambassador Karl Rankin visited Dachen and Jinmen islands in early May, followed by Chiang's inspection of Dachen. In mid-May the PLA captured the Dongji Islands, threatening Dachen.[27] However, Eisenhower was ambivalent at that time: He refused to commit U.S. forces to the protection of the islands but at the same time believed some were "really an integral part of the Formosa defense" and must not be lost to the Communists. As a compromise, he sent the Seventh Fleet to the Dachen area to deter the Communists.[28] In July, the NSC decided to provide the GMD with more ships to help it protect these offshore islands.[29]

U.S. support was neither a formal policy nor an official commitment to the offshore islands, and despite GMD pressure for coverage of these offshore islands, neither the Department of State nor Defense believed they were essential to the defense of Taiwan. The basic U.S. policy, as indicated by NSC 146/2, was to use U.S. forces to protect only Taiwan and the Penghu Islands.[30] When Radford recommended covering the offshore islands in mid-August, Dulles suggested that the administration may need congressional authorization to enlarge the coverage of the Seventh Fleet. Although Eisenhower said the United States would cover the islands, he would only do so on the condition that covering the islands did not turn world opinion against the United States.[31] As a Policy Planning Staff memorandum prepared on August 20 indicated, there were "no U.S. commitments of any kind, public or private, to defend the islands."[32] When the British minister Robert Scott expressed anxiety about the offshore islands on August 31, Dulles assured him that deployment of U.S. Navy forces in the Taiwan Strait was a "flexible position," and "it should not commit the U.S. to a long-range, permanent defense of these islands" because their status was different from that of Taiwan. London interpreted the U.S. policy as deterrence rather than commitment to the defense of the islands.[33]

Similarly, Washington was ambivalent toward an MDT with Taiwan. Since Eisenhower came to power in January 1953, and especially after the United States signed an MDT with Korea in October 1953, Chiang had striven for a similar treaty.[34] While the GMD ambassador Wellington Koo pressured U.S. officials in Washington, Chiang won the support of a series of U.S. visitors in Taipei, including Nixon (November 1953), Secretary of Defense Charles Wilson, and General James Van Fleet, who was on an inspection tour of mutual defense programs (May and July 1954).[35] The Chinese Communist participation in the Geneva Conference prompted

Chiang to increase his efforts in July 1954. To lessen U.S. worries that he intended to drag the United States into a war with the Communists, Chiang reiterated that he would not take any military action against the mainland without prior U.S. agreement.[36] However, the GMD government started a campaign of "negotiation through journalism" and made the MDT a "hot topic," in the words of historian Su-Ya Chang, in the press in both Taiwan and the United States. The GMD Ministry of Foreign Affairs suggested that negotiation of the MDT was ongoing, and the GMD's mouthpieces clamored that the treaty would be signed before the end of the year.[37] The *New York Times* reported in late June that an agreement was reached during Van Fleet's visit, and the United States would protect both the offshore islands and Taiwan.[38]

Washington's response was ambiguous. Ever since 1951, U.S. officials had pondered a long-term goal of establishing a comprehensive Pacific security organization—to some extent, the GMD's quest for the MDT was encouraged by the Americans.[39] In March 1954, Dulles thought of including Taiwan in a Western Pacific organization as his "united action" to deal with the Indochina crisis. After American and British leaders reached agreement on SEATO in June, U.S. officials again attempted to include Taiwan in the organization. They had to give this up due to British opposition, but they sought British agreement that SEATO would be open to additional participants. Soon U.S. diplomats told GMD officials that they might be allowed to join the organization later.[40] The idea of a broader security pact in the Western Pacific lingered among U.S. policymakers. At his press conference in early August, Dulles suggested this possibility and Taiwan's potential participation.[41] The NSC 5429, which was later published in November 1954, also included the long-term goal of a broad defense group.[42]

However, preoccupied with SEATO in Asia and the EDC in Europe, U.S. leaders did not seriously consider the MDT.[43] In late March, Robertson suggested concluding an MDT both to prevent China from using Taiwan to separate the United States from allies and to pressure China in the Geneva negotiations. But Dulles put off a decision.[44] Eisenhower thought an MDT was "too big a commitment of U.S. prestige and forces."[45] Nevertheless, both Eisenhower and Dulles told the press that the possibility of the MDT was being studied.[46] In late August, Robertson again suggested concluding the MDT to "remove the basis for the pressures and undermine the effectiveness of the Communist propaganda campaign." Dulles once again delayed the decision, although he agreed that the United States might ultimately need an MDT with the GMD.[47] He had planned to visit Taiwan after SEATO's opening conference in Manila, mainly to assuage Chiang, who was aggrieved by the exclusion of the GMD from SEATO. Expecting Chiang to press him for the MDT, Dulles considered canceling the trip but finally decided to restrict it to a "purely social call" and limit the stay in Taipei to a mere two hours, which he hoped would deprive Chiang of any chance to discuss the MDT. Still, Chiang pushed for the MDT in their meeting, and Dulles demurred.[48]

The British were nervous about the American ambivalence.[49] They had a better understanding of Communist intentions and worried their American ally would take reckless actions without understanding the seriousness of the situation. The day after China started the propaganda campaign, Trevelyan told the British Foreign Office that the main reason for the campaign was the "fear" about an MDT between the United States and GMD.[50] According to Trevelyan, the Communist propaganda aimed:

(1) To try and deter the Americans from making a defense treaty with Chiang Kai-shek; (2) To provide a new pretext for attacks on American Far Eastern Policy in substitution for intervention in Indo-china, as suggested by Robertson; (3) To provide a substitute for "Oppose America, Aid Korea" as an incentive to further efforts on the home front; (4) To raise the temperature in the hope of mobilizing international pressure on the Americans to modify their attitude; (5) As a diplomatic counter order to recover the islands off the coast, not only for protection of shipping but also for obvious security reasons.[51]

The British Foreign Office agreed with the judgment.[52] After the Labour Party delegation left Beijing, Trevelyan concluded that China wanted to use the British to push the United States: "They look to us to exercise a moderating influence on American policy and in particular to get the United States government to withdraw from Formosa the protection of the 7th Fleet."[53] In late August, British officials predicted that the Communists would not attack Taiwan, but they might attack the offshore islands, such as Jinmen, Mazu, or Dachen. However, the United States seemed unaware of the Communist threats. London was extremely worried that the United States would either rush into the defense of these islands or leave the situation to the judgment of military leaders on the spot. Either way it would significantly increase the chance of a clash between China and the United States that would ultimately hurt British interests in Hong Kong and peace in the Far East in general. To prevent such a scenario, British officials requested that Washington keep the GMD under control and stop it from provoking the PLA.[54]

In the meantime, however, the British hesitated to pressure the Americans. Ironically, the Chinese efforts to split the Western alliance contributed to the British hesitancy. Fully aware that Chinese leaders would "take every opportunity for wedge-driving between the United States and the United Kingdom,"[55] the British remained careful in their relations with the United States with respect to China, although they had an accurate analysis of Chinese intentions.[56] British leaders were reluctant to talk to the Americans directly about their judgment, knowing China's exploitation of UK-U.S. differences had caused an "unfavorable impression" and led to U.S. suspicion of the United Kingdom.[57] In this circumstance, further suggesting restraining the GMD could be interpreted by U.S. leaders as appeasing China. Indeed, when British officials conveyed to Washington what Mao told the Labour delegation, they felt "slightly embarrassed by the whole thing."[58] As a result, they held their tongues and waited for a "suitable opportunity" to tell Dulles their concerns when the Taiwan issue came up at the Manila Conference.[59] Unfortunately, they did not have such an opportunity before the PLA bombed Jinmen Island on September 3.

Throughout this period, the attention of U.S. leaders continued to be occupied elsewhere. Despite pressures from both the GMD and China, policymakers in Washington had neither a clear understanding of the nature and extent of the Communist threat nor a clarified policy toward either the offshore islands or the MDT with Taiwan, although they roughly knew the Chinese wanted to use Taiwan to alienate the United States. In late August, Robertson believed that Beijing intended to "generate increasing international pressures for a negotiated change in the status of Formosa as a means of removing a serious cause of tension."[60] According to a Special

National Intelligence Estimate (SNIE) prepared before the bombing, "the Communists might estimate that this would exacerbate relations between the US and such states as the UK and India over China policy, and possibly deter the US from extending a long-range commitment to Chiang Kai-shek."[61]

However, Washington was confident that they could handle the Communists. When the U.S. ambassador to Japan expressed anxiety about the "uncoordinated US Government activity in [the] Far East" in mid-August, Dulles assured him, saying, "I do not believe that the Chinese Communists are in fact now prepared to challenge us in any major or sustained way and provoke further our sea and air power along their coast."[62] As late as August 25, Robertson still told Scott that he had not even thought about Communists attacking the coastal islands.[63] Washington had good reasons to believe that the deterrence would work: when the Seventh Fleet visited Dachen in early June, the PLA stopped military actions.[64] For contingency, the NSC asked the JCS to submit recommendations under the scenario of Communists attacking the coastal islands on September 9, which would be six days after the PLA's bombing of Jinmen.[65]

Washington was also unable to produce a clarified policy toward China on the basis of the post-Geneva situation. After several discussions over different options, the NSC decided to temporarily maintain the current policy of preventing Chinese aggression by deterrence. A softer policy similar to the British request for peaceful coexistence was against the basic U.S. policy. A "tough" policy, however, would require resources unavailable to the United States, given its priority in Europe and the financial difficulty in 1954. And it would certainly strain relations with allies, whose attitude toward China had recently changed significantly. Dulles said that he would put on hold a clarified China policy until he had the time to "give the problem of Communist China a great deal more thought." Nevertheless, U.S. leaders did reach some basic consensuses, including that the Sino-Soviet alliance was going to last, and it was difficult to split it from outside in a foreseeable period of time, which according to Dulles was about twenty-five years; U.S. policy toward China was facing increasing pressure from allies, such as the United Kingdom and France, as well as neutralist states like India; and the United States could not afford to get involved in a war with the Chinese.[66] These guidelines would dictate U.S. responses to the Taiwan Strait Crisis as it later developed.

MEETING THE CHINESE THREAT

The Chinese bombardment of the Jinmen Islands was "a rude shock" for the Americans, in the words of Gordon Chang and He Di.[67] The timing had an extraordinary psychological impact. It took place despite the presence of the Seventh Fleet in the Dachen area and Washington's public warnings about military intervention, and in the midst of the establishment of SEATO to contain the CCP. Washington noticed that the Communist propaganda even acknowledged that the United States would guarantee the defense of the off-shore islands. Yet the PLA still bombed Jinmen, and the JCS worried that it would attack Jinmen. According to Rankin, the PLA buildup continued and would have the capability to invade Jinmen soon.[68] Had U.S. officials studied more carefully, they might have realized that the bombardment took place not in Dachen, which the Seventh Fleet was poised to protect, but in Jinmen, where there were no U.S. forces. What they did not know was that Mao cautiously stopped a planned bombing of Dachen to avoid a conflict with the United States.

Frustrated that previous measures had failed to deter the Chinese, Washington exaggerated both the intentions and the capacities of the Chinese. The two SNIEs prepared around the bombing estimated that the PLA had superior air power in the coastal area and the potential to capture any of the offshore islands if the United States did not help the GMD.[69] This judgment largely exaggerated the PLA's strength, but it guided U.S. policy in the crisis. Acting Secretary of Defense Robert Anderson predicted that the Communist action may lead to an all-out attack on the islands.[70] An SNIE dated September 10 concluded that "the Chinese Communist objective is to take over the Nationalist occupied islands at some time, and they look upon such action as an essential part of the consolidation of their control of all China."[71] The British Labour Party delegation, which China used to pressure the United States, might also have contributed to the U.S. overestimate of the Chinese aggressiveness. When the Labourites visited Japan after their stay in China, a delegation member reported to the U.S. embassy that the PLA would soon attack Taiwan "in order to provoke U.S. countermeasures and thereby split the Western powers." Meanwhile, Labour leader Attlee stressed the CCP's determination in his public talk in Hong Kong.[72]

U.S. leaders worried that the PLA would attack the offshore islands and fretted over whether the United States should protect these islands. Indeed, the bombardment only lasted five hours, and even the GMD did not see it as the beginning of a large-scale invasion and seek U.S. assistance.[73] The British Joint Intelligence Committee was not sure if it was "a propaganda gesture designed to embarrass the Manila negotiations for SEATO or actually portended a Chinese Communist attempt to seize these islands."[74]

Given the failure in Indochina, however, Washington could not risk further loss of prestige and credibility of containment in Asia. So, when the NSC discussed the crisis, nobody doubted China's intention to attack the offshore islands. The only question was how to meet the threat. The spontaneous response was sending warships to the Jinmen area to deter the Communists, but the question of whether the United States should protect the islands became a "horrible dilemma" that divided the policymakers. Dulles initially intended to help the GMD protect Jinmen.[75] The majority of the JCS recommended using force to defend the islands, which may involve attacking targets on the mainland and using atomic weapons.[76] However, Wilson suggested that "the choice was between the loss of morale resulting from the loss of the islands, and the danger of precipitating war with Communist China." Eisenhower followed that "this was not just a danger but would constitute precipitating such a war."[77] According to Dulles, "almost certainly a committal under present circumstances to defend Quemoy etc. would alienate world opinion and gravely strain our alliances, both in Europe and with ANZUS. This is the more true because it would probably lead to our initiating the use of atomic weapons."[78] Facing the prospect of a general war, Eisenhower retreated from his previous position and argued that Jinmen was not worth U.S. protection because it "was not really important except psychologically" to the GMD.[79]

Finally, the NSC decided to deter the Chinese by deliberate ambiguity: withholding its position on the offshore islands to "keep the enemy guessing." Meanwhile, Dulles proposed that the United States take the issue to the UN Security Council and accuse China of menacing international peace. Such a policy would kill two birds with one stone, according to the secretary of state:

> This move could put a serious strain on Soviet-ChiCom [Chinese Communist] relations. If the SU [Soviet Union] vetoed the move, that would gravely impair its "peace offensive" and then the US would win a measure of support from allies and world opinion now lacking. If the Soviets did not veto, the

ChiComs could react adversely, and might, indeed, defy the UN. In that case the ChiComs would again become an international outcast.[80]

The success of this policy, however, relied on support from allies—first and foremost, the United Kingdom. However, the British initially disagreed over the status of the offshore islands and U.S. reaction to the Chinese challenge. Eden believed these islands were part of the mainland, both historically and geographically, although he supported the U.S. commitment to Taiwan. The British JCS said Jinmen was "indefensible and inessential" to the defense of Taiwan. So it would be a bad play if the United States became embroiled in a large-scale war over Jinmen. Therefore, Eden pushed the United States to get the GMD to withdraw its forces from the offshore islands and stop raiding the mainland. The best way to solve the problem, London suggested, was direct negotiation between the United States and China.[81]

Finally, Eden reluctantly agreed to cooperate with the United States on the UN move to control the damage under the misperception that the United States would settle the general China problem. He was shocked by the frightening prospect Dulles described: the PLA might attack Jinmen or Dachen at any time, and the majority of U.S. military leaders wanted to assist the GMD, with atomic weapons if needed.[82] The Communist renewal of bombardment of Jinmen in late September probably reinforced Eden's worries. What really interested Eden, however, was Dulles's suggestion that "his object was to start a process of negotiation that might overcome some of the present difficulties in the Far Eastern situation and that above all would resolve the differences that still divided our two countries on Far Eastern policy."[83] To Eden's understanding, this meant the United States would ultimately be willing to find a general solution to the China problem after the Chinese attended the UN discussion of the proposed resolution and accepted a ceasefire.

Since early 1954, British officials had expected the United States to adopt a more flexible China policy. Dulles suggested in June that the United States might consider recognition of the PRC after the congressional election in November.[84] In July, the secretary also indicated to Eden and Nehru that India might take China's place in the UN Security Council and the two Chinese regimes (PRC and GMD) could join the General Assembly simultaneously.[85] The United States also seemed to have accepted the British position that GMD raids of the mainland were the source of tensions in the Taiwan Strait.[86] After the PLA resumed bombing Jinmen in late September, Eisenhower decided to "suspend 'encouraging and assisting the Chinese Nationalist Government [GMD] to raid Chinese Communist territory and commerce,' " as a means to help Dulles reach an agreement with the British.[87] Therefore, Eden judged that the Americans may finally agree to reconsider their China policy.

Eden knew the importance of maintaining unity with the United States, especially when the press was reporting how the Taiwan issue was splitting the Western alliance.[88] So he finally suggested letting New Zealand, a British Commonwealth member, introduce the UN Security Council resolution—code-named Oracle—on condition that Beijing was invited to the UN when Oracle was discussed. To improve the chance of Communist cooperation, the British would inform both the Chinese and the Soviet Union in advance.[89] After the discussion started, however, the British found out that Dulles limited the scope to the ceasefire over the offshore islands. Eden found this "unduly restrictive" and pushed for a "wider settlement" on the grounds that a mere neutralization of the offshore islands would not prevent the GMD from provoking the mainland elsewhere. He got the New Zealanders' support, but Dulles argued that a broad discussion would only expose differences between the United States and the United Kingdom over China and warned Eden that the situation would be "fraught with perilous possibilities" if they failed to act immediately. Eden had to agree to introduce the resolution after the United States informed the GMD.[90]

To move on with the plan, however, the Americans had to get the GMD's support, as it had veto power as a permeant member on UN Security Council. Rankin and Robertson suggested inducing Chiang with an MDT. Eisenhower readily agreed, on condition that the GMD "was prepared to assume a defensive posture on Formosa and Pescadores" and would not drag the United States into a war with China. Spectacularly, the decision was made without careful discussions at the NSC.[91] While Chiang was glad to get the MDT, he worried a ceasefire would be the first step leading ultimately to the Communist taking over GMD in the UN Security Council, so he pushed the United States to give up Oracle. American officials tried to convince Chiang that the UN move would indeed help him protect these islands because the United States would not make a public commitment to the offshore islands in the MDT anyway. Chiang finally agreed to the

MDT, but on condition that the United States declare its intention to conclude the MDT before New Zealand introduced Oracle in the UN—and more important, the United States should privately promise to defend the offshore islands in an exchange of notes with the GMD, with which the Americans had to agree.[92] Once the meeting was over, however, Chiang instructed GMD diplomats in the United States to try their best to derail Oracle and to secure the MDT as early as possible.[93]

When the United States informed the UK government of the development, the British supported the decision, in contrast to blocking the MDT, as Beijing had expected. Eden just suggested moving ahead with the MDT first, so that the United Kingdom had better knowledge about it when they informed and invited the PRC to the UN. Knowing that the United States had thought about such a treaty for some time and would probably conclude it anyway, the British felt their opposition would only add to the tensions with the United States.[94] The British also understood that the Americans would never give up Taiwan and Penghu, with which the United Kingdom agreed, so the MDT virtually reiterated the current U.S. policy, as long as it did not extend the coverage to the offshore islands, which the U.S. officials promised.[95]

Most important, the British accepted Dulles's suggestion that a combination of the MDT and Oracle would ultimately settle the China problem: Oracle would neutralize the offshore islands, the MDT would limit the GMD to Taiwan and virtually accept Communist rule on the mainland. In effect, this would lead to de facto Two Chinas, which the United Kingdom had pursued.[96] The British assumed the Chinese Communists would also find the MDT acceptable; neutralization of the offshore islands would give them some hope that they could obtain these islands through peaceful means. Once the ceasefire was realized, the British calculated, the Americans might also shift to a pragmatic policy, such as relaxing the trade embargo and becoming more flexible on China's status in the UN. They expected the Communists could still be tempted to attend the UN, which might lead to an ultimate settlement of the China problem.[97] Therefore, the British requested the United States not provoke China by recognizing the GMD as the official representative of China or including the offshore islands in the coverage of the treaty.[98]

In the process, Washington watched Sino-Soviet relations closely.[99] The Communist alliance, however, failed to deter Washington from moving on with either Oracle or the MDT. Although Charles Bohlen, U.S. ambassador to the Soviet Union, believed Khrushchev's speech in China placed the Soviet Union "solidly behind [the] Chinese position," and the "increasingly threatening tone of Chinese Communist utterances now supported by [the] Soviet Union are not to be lightly dismissed,"[100] the CIA director thought Khrushchev was a "rather brash fellow" whose remarks did not carry much weight due to his secondary position within the Soviet regime.[101] Bohlen's follow-up report seemed to confirm the CIA's judgment, and the Soviet government "appeared to be trying to avoid further public commitment to the Chinese Communist position regarding Formosa."[102] Instead of being deterred by the Communist unity, Robertson believed Khrushchev's support of China accentuated the need for an MDT to clarify the U.S. position on Taiwan, lest the Communists miscalculate and attack the island.[103] When Eisenhower decided to start negotiation for the MDT, the Soviet response was not a factor in the U.S. leaders' consideration. The Soviet move in the UN came after Washington had decided to pursue the MDT. It caused doubt among some American officials about whether China would attack the islands but only led to a suggestion that Oracle should be carried out more quickly to prevent further Communist aggression.[104] Washington also found the Sino-Soviet communiqué "only mildly endorse[d] the present Chinese Communist campaign regarding Taiwan."[105]

Nevertheless, Washington still had to think twice when it was considering using force in the Taiwan Strait. According to Robertson, the Sino-Soviet joint communiqué declared in Beijing promoted China's status in the Communist camp and put the Chinese on equal footing with the Soviet Union. It indicated that China remained "firmly integrated in the Communist bloc under the leadership of the Soviet Union."[106] This judgment reinforced Eisenhower's assessment of the strength of the Communist alliance. When Dulles suggested at the NSC that protecting the offshore islands may lead to a general war with China, Eisenhower warned that "when we talk of general war with Communist China, what we mean is general war with the USSR also." In his judgment, the Soviets were certain to join the war, even if just for the credibility of the alliance, because "in any event, if the Soviets did not abide by their treaty with Communist China and go to war in support of their Chinese ally, the Soviet empire would quickly fall to pieces."[107]

Dulles was also worried about India's response to U.S. plans. Initially, officials in charge of both South Asia and the CIA worried that the MDT would alienate India and drive it closer to China. The Indians would see the MDT as an "unnecessary provocation to Communist China" and "further evidence of US imperialistic interference in Asian affairs."[108] Nehru, however, was now collaborating with the British behind the scenes.[109] Instead of pushing the United States not to conclude the MDT, as both the Chinese and Americans had expected, Nehru supported the MDT, with a condition that the GMD stop attacking the mainland to lessen Communist worries. Although the Communist leaders would protest, Nehru told U.S. officials, they would finally accept the accomplished fact. Nehru also supported Oracle and suggested he would be able to convince the Chinese to send a representative to New York; the British chargé in Beijing Trevelyan believed Nehru's "persuasion might have a powerful effect" on Beijing.[110]

Just as Washington decided to move on with both Oracle and the MDT, the PLA shelled the Dachen Islands and also renewed bombardment of Jinmen on November 1, in an effort to prevent the MDT. But the actions prompted U.S. leaders to carry out the MDT and Oracle. As in September, the shelling convinced Eisenhower and Dulles that U.S. protection of the islands would lead to a war with China, which would alienate both allies and the American people alike and, most important, could trigger a war with the Soviet Union. Therefore, the NSC concluded that pushing for Oracle and the MDT was the only practicable option.[111] This judgment was supported by a CIA estimate, which said the MDT would not lead to Communist military action against Taiwan, and if Oracle was introduced to the UN Security Council, it could deter the Communists from attacking the offshore islands.[112]

U.S. and GMD officials started the negotiation over the MDT on November 2 and finished on November 23.[113] According to the treaty, the United States agreed to protect "Taiwan, the Pescadores and such other territories as may be determined by mutual agreement," which was consistent with U.S. strategic ambiguity. The two sides agreed on this ambiguous statement because the GMD wanted to avoid the impression that its territory was restricted only to Taiwan and Penghu islands, and the United States tried not to commit their protection to the offshore islands. In a subsequent exchange of notes, the GMD also agreed to subject their military dispositions and use of forces to U.S. agreement. These stipulations reflected Dulles's concerns that the GMD would transfer their force to the offshore islands and leave the defense of Taiwan completely to the United States or that Chiang would try to restore his rule in the mainland and drag the United States into a war between the Chinese. GMD officials protested loudly but had to include this in the notes—instead of a formal protocol, as Washington originally wanted—but did not want them to be published by the United States.[114]

By this time, however, the British were unwilling to move on with Oracle. Before the MDT was concluded, Eden requested the United States first declare that Taiwan would not be "established as a protected base for attacks against the mainland." Dulles refused but said Eden could tell China and the Soviet Union "in private communication" that Taiwan would not be a "privileged sanctuary." Eden was not satisfied because the British chargé in Beijing warned that Chinese leaders saw the offshore islands and Taiwan as an integral part of China and would regard the MDT as a "notice that Formosa was to be permanently separated from the mainland" and acceptance of Oracle as "tantamount to acquiescence in such a separation." Moreover, British support of U.S. actions would "make the Chinese associate the United Kingdom with U.S. Formosa policy and give up all hope that the British might secure any modification in U.S. Far Eastern policy."[115] Chinese diplomats also warned British officials that the MDT would only lead to further tension and deterioration of the situation in the Far East, and they pushed the United Kingdom to request that the United States withdraw its forces from Taiwan.[116]

After the MDT was concluded, Eden insisted that the United States publicize both exclusion of the offshore islands in the treaty and the secret exchange of notes with the GMD, which forbid Chiang from using force without U.S. approval. Eden believed these would assure Beijing of the defensive nature of the treaty and give the Communists the "minimum willingness" to "play along" with Oracle. Otherwise, the UN move would only stimulate China to take "further acts of aggression." Apparently, the British still did not give up the idea of an ultimate settlement of the China problem and wanted to strive for China's attendance at the UN discussion. When Dulles refused to meet Eden's requirements, the two countries had to put off raising Oracle in the UN.[117]

The U.S. actions failed to deter the CCP. Unaware of the development on the MDT, the Chinese made its last effort to influence the MDT by sentencing captured U.S. pilots to imprisonment as spies on November 23.[118]

Instead of deterring U.S. officials from proceeding with the MDT, however, this action caused strong repercussions in Washington. The Americans generally saw this as a provocation and requested retaliation. The Defense and State Departments and the CIA recommended seeking congressional authorization for a blockade of Chinese ports, but Senate majority leader William Knowland, known as the "Senator from Formosa" for his support of the GMD, publicly called for a blockade of the Chinese coast to force Beijing to release the detainees. Eisenhower rejected the proposal because he deemed that blockade to be an act of war that would alienate the United States from both allies and Asian neutral states. He was furious about Knowland's "most irresponsible statements of late which are hurting us very much with our allies." He asked his press secretary: "Can't he [Knowland] see that this move by the Chinese is part of the general Communist plot to divide us from our western allies and try to defeat ratification of the Paris agreements?" Dulles believed the Chinese were collaborating with the Soviets: while the latter called for peaceful coexistence to attract U.S. allies, the former took provocative actions to create divisions between the United States and allies.[119] Therefore, responding strongly would play into the hands of the Chinese Communists. Finally, U.S. leaders decided to let Hammarskjöld go to Beijing to seek the release of the pilots, on the grounds that these pilots were under UN command.[120]

"A HORRIBLE DILEMMA"

After the conclusion of the MDT was finally declared on December 2, Washington again misperceived China's response. Chinese leaders rejected Hammarskjöld's request and merely offered visas for the families of the pilots to visit them in China, which historian Su-Ya Chang sees as a tactic designed to mobilize public pressure on U.S. policymakers.[121] Meanwhile, the PLA air force bombed the Dachen Islands on January 10 and a week later captured the Yijiangshan Island in the north of Dachen in protest against the MDT. The director of the CIA speculated that China might either make a "suicide" attack on Taiwan or invade the offshore islands, whereas Dulles was worried that an attack on Dachen was imminent and China also planned to capture the rest of offshore islands in the Taiwan Strait.[122] When the NSC met to discuss the Communist threat in late January, Eisenhower worried that "the Soviets were undoubtedly doing all they could to involve the United States in Asia and in a general war with Communist China." And Dulles concurred.[123]

Ironically, there was no evidence indicating PLA preparations for an attack on either the offshore islands or Taiwan, as Dulles admitted to the British.[124] However, based on this misunderstanding of Chinese aggression, Dulles concluded that the previous policy of keeping China guessing had failed. He suggested asking the GMD to withdraw from the indefensible Dachen while publicizing U.S. willingness to help the GMD hold both Jinmen and the Mazu, in order to restore the credibility of the U.S. commitment to its ally. Radford promptly supported the suggestion, and Eisenhower agreed that Jinmen and Mazu "were the outposts for the defense of Formosa." The NSC then decided to seek congressional authorization to use force to protect these islands. To prevent Beijing from miscalculating, Dulles suggested that the United States make its positions on the offshore islands "crystal clear" because strategic ambiguity had failed to deter China. Meanwhile, he resumed the quest for Oracle.[125]

Facing the new crisis, the United States needed British support—as recognized by Eisenhower at this moment, the British were "good sturdy old allies" in a crisis.[126] The United Kingdom, however, opposed the move. The British cabinet worried that the U.S. guarantee of Jinmen would extend the MDT's coverage and lead to the GMD's permanent occupation of the offshore islands, which went against the United Kingdom's basic objective of neutralizing the Taiwan Strait. Moreover, U.S. protection of Jinmen would eliminate any possibility that the Chinese Communists would go to the UN, and Eden wanted to secure China's attendance.[127] He reminded Dulles via Makins that Dulles himself said the United States would have to use atomic bombs if they wanted to defend Jinmen. Therefore, Eden threatened to withdraw the support of Oracle unless the United States withheld its guarantee on offshore islands.[128]

To gain British support, Dulles had to agree not to declare the commitment to Jinmen and Mazu.[129] The Congressional Formosa Resolution only granted Eisenhower the power to use force to protect Taiwan, Penghu, and "related positions and territories of that area now in friendly hands." Therefore, instead of a "crystal clear" position, the U.S. defense of the offshore islands remained ambiguous. Believing that the United States had relinquished the commitment to the islands, the British gave the green light to Oracle.[130] Finally, New Zealand submitted the proposal to the UN on

January 28, and the Security Council invited China to the UN to discuss a ceasefire in the Taiwan Strait.

Beijing attacked the congressional resolution as "a war message" and rejected the UN invitation. In private, however, Chinese leaders made peace initiatives. Through the Soviet Union, they proposed a ten-power conference to discuss tensions in the Taiwan area.[131] Zhou suggested through the Swedish ambassador, who was forwarding Hammarskjöld's invitation for China's attendance to the UN discussion, holding direct negotiations with the United States.

U.S. leaders saw the overtures as another peace offensive to alienate the United States from allies and neutral states. According to Bohlen in Moscow, the Communist proposal for a ten-power conference was mainly propaganda supporting China. It was meant to please neutral Asian states and exploit the differences between the United States and the United Kingdom, as it "made quite a point of Great Britain's position."[132] In the face of China's threat to the offshore islands, according to Robert Bowie, director of the Policy Planning Staff,

> such a conference would be the worst possible context for a solution. The very fact that the ChiComs [Chinese Communists] took part would brand any outcome as appeasement. Moreover, it would be hard to prevent such a conference from taking up other questions such as ChiCom membership in the UN, especially if the ChiCom made this the price of settlement.[133]

This analysis was consistent with the position the Office of Far Eastern Affairs and the CIA reached in November 1954, which opposed a potential negotiation with China in the context of the crisis and saw such a proposal as China's trick to split the Western alliance and please neutral states.[134] Washington rejected the Communist suggestion on the grounds that they would not discuss this issue without the GMD's participation.[135]

While rejecting Chinese initiatives for negotiation, U.S. leaders were especially disturbed by the Chinese refusal to discuss Oracle in the UN. Initially, Bohlen told Washington that the Soviets implied that China would accept the invitation.[136] Eden and Nehru also suggested Beijing might attend the UN discussion. The CIA director believed the Soviets were restraining China in the Taiwan Strait.[137] The unexpected rejection, in addition to British and GMD pressure for clarification on U.S. positions on the coastal islands—both pushing in opposite directions—brought U.S. leaders to the limit of their patience. In deep frustration, Eisenhower groaned to his correspondence secretary in private:

> they (the Chinese Communists) are certainly doing everything they can to try our patiences. It's awfully difficult to remain calm under these situations. Sometimes I think that it would be best all around to go after them right now without letting them pick their time and the place of their own choosing.[138]

U.S. officials severely overestimated Chinese aggression and believed that China's rejection of the UN invitation indicated its willingness to attack Dachen. The CIA was worried that China intended "to press on regardless of the consequences," but Eisenhower suspected that there was a Soviet plan to "get the United States bogged down in a debilitating war with Communist China."[139] To avoid that prospect, Washington requested the GMD evacuate immediately, but Chiang insisted that the United States must declare its protection of Jinmen and Mazu in advance. Washington rejected the request and warned the GMD not to unilaterally declare U.S. commitment to these islands, otherwise the United States would have to deny this commitment.[140] Eisenhower threatened to withdraw assistance in the evacuation if Chiang further delayed the action. Finally, Chiang had to give up Dachen. Furious that the United States had broken its promise, a helpless Chiang cursed the British for their manipulation of the Americans as the cause of this policy shift.[141]

In the meantime, Dulles pressed the United Kingdom for more actions in the UN, but Eden refused again on the grounds that further moves in the Security Council would only provoke a Communist attack. Instead, he held that the GMD withdraw from all the coastal islands was the only solution to the crisis. In Parliament, Eden publicly declared that these islands were in a "different category from Formosa and Pescadores since they undoubtedly form part of territory of People's Republic of China." To increase the pressure, Eden told the Americans that his suggestion got the support of all the British Commonwealth leaders. Simultaneously, Australian and Canadian leaders joined the United Kingdom in pressuring the United States for the evacuation.[142] Meanwhile, Churchill wrote to Eisenhower, stressing that evacuation was the only way to frustrate the Communist desire to drive a wedge between the United States and its allies.[143] Moreover, Eden protested that a statement in which Dulles implied willingness to protect the offshore islands "amount[ed] to a public commitment," from which the

United Kingdom had to "dissociate" itself. As a result, Dulles had to revise his statement when it was formally published.[144]

Instead of the UN move, Eden suggested negotiating with China at an international conference, as the Soviets suggested, or through Hammarskjöld, or directly with Chinese officials. The British ambassador pushed Washington to accept the Soviet proposal, which he thought was a "serious one and not designed for propaganda purposes." But Dulles accepted none of these options: Washington was unwilling to negotiate with the Communists without GMD's participation; Hammarskjöld's "meddling" in the issue without authorization may cause misunderstanding and was "extremely dangerous." Moreover, the United States could not retreat further before the Chinese aggression.[145] When Eden and Dulles met at the SEATO conference in Bangkok in late February, Eden told Dulles that he did not see the need to hold the islands and questioned the desire of the United States to secure them. If the United States gave up the offshore islands, its position on Taiwan would get more support from the British Commonwealth and Western European states. Finally, Dulles had to agree to let Eden seek a meeting with Zhou to feel out whether the PRC would promise not to attack Taiwan in return for the GMD's abandonment of the offshore islands.[146] Apparently, he was moving closer to the British policy.[147]

By now, however, Chinese leaders had concluded that it was meaningless to deal with the British because they were collaborating with the United States.[148] Zhou virtually rejected the British proposal by suggesting that Eden come to Beijing to discuss the "cessation of United States aggression against China and the withdrawal of United States forces from Formosa and the straits."[149] In private, the Chinese were shifting their attention to the Bandung Conference, and they decreased tensions in the Taiwan Strait to reduce the worries among Southeast Asian states. In early March, *Renmin Ribao* publicly called for support of the Soviet proposal for a ten-power conference.[150]

At this point, Dulles misperceived China again. Although U.S. intelligence indicated that PRC's propaganda had declined "to the lowest point since last summer," both navy and air force leaders confirmed that the PLA did not have sufficient air force to attack Taiwan, and State Department officials speculated that the Communists were probably "adopting a tacit ceasefire." Dulles's judgment was that Beijing was building up its forces and was "determined to capture Formosa." He thought the United States was now indeed "in a battle for Taiwan," although he admitted that he did not have adequate intelligence to support this judgment.[151] In addition to the

war scare created by U.S. media,[152] Dulles's trip to attend the SEATO conference in Bangkok in late February contributed enormously to his misperception. While meeting Stump in Hawai'i on the way to Bangkok, Dulles
learned that the PRC was conducting a massive military build up and preparing for actions in the Taiwan Strait. In Burma after the conference, U Nu
confirmed that China was determined to "take Taiwan by force" because its
leaders feared Taiwan would be used as a base to invade the mainland.[153]
Ironically, when Dulles met Chiang to formally sign the MDT in Taipei
on March 3, Chiang did not indicate anxiety about such a threat from the
PRC.[154] When Zhou rejected Eden's proposal for a meeting, Dulles's pes-
simism was reinforced. He told the New Zealand ally that "there was a
likelihood that severe fighting might break out and there was a danger that
the U.S. might be drawn in."[155] And Dulles told Eisenhower:

> The situation out there in the Formosa Strait is far more serious than I
> thought before my trip. The Chinese Communists are determined to capture
> Formosa. Surrendering Quemoy and Matsu won't end that determination. If
> we defend Quemoy and Matsu, we'll have to use atomic weapons.[156]

Eisenhower agreed to consider using "atomic missiles" to defend Jinmen and Mazu, and he recommended that Dulles include a paragraph in
his radio and television address to be delivered two days later showing that
the United States "would use atomic weapons as interchangeable with the
conventional weapons."[157] When the issue was brought to the NSC, Radford offered his ready support: "the Joint Chiefs of Staff have consistently
asserted that we should have to use atomic weapons. Indeed our whole military structure had been built around this assumption." The U.S. military prepared an extensive plan for nuclear attacks on China,[158] and the commander
of the Seventh Fleet discussed with GMD joint actions against China, to the
effect that Chiang wondered if a war was imminent.[159] Dulles, Eisenhower,
and Nixon, publicly and on three consecutive days, threatened China with
nuclear weapons.[160] According to the historian Gordon Chang, at this time
Washington "actually brought the country to the 'nuclear brink.'"[161]

In the face of a nuclear war, Eisenhower once again realized "we could
not afford to be isolated from our allies in the world," particularly when
the United States urgently needed their help in Europe and there was a
risk of Soviet retaliation.[162] According to a British diplomat in Beijing, Mao
warned the Finnish ambassador that "if the Americans atomic-bombed

Shanghai or Peking, 'they' [the Soviets] would retaliate by wiping out American cities," and the Soviet ambassador confirmed to the Finnish that "if the Americans bombed the Chinese mainland, the Soviet Government would give the Chinese *all possible support* under the Sino-Soviet agreement."[163] Finally, Eisenhower returned to the basic guideline of avoiding direct U.S. intervention. He reversed his thinking and asked U.S. officials to strive to delay Beijing's attack on Jinmen and Mazu in a way that would not accidentally provoke it. Meanwhile, he took measures to reduce public fear about a war with China.[164] What he did not know, however, was that Mao tried to avoid a confrontation as well and restrained PLA generals from taking further actions at the same time.

Consequently, Dulles resumed his push on the British to pursue Oracle in the UN, but the British were now "fairly unhappy over this proposal," believing that move had everything to lose but nothing to gain. It would provoke China to attack the islands, expose differences between the United States and the United Kingdom, and alienate the Asian neutral states. Instead of the UN move, London again requested that the United States "find some means of getting Chiang Kai-shek out of the coastal islands before an attack." Meanwhile, Eden strongly pushed Dulles to use the Asian states to restrain China in Bandung instead. He also suggested letting the United Kingdom, India, and the Soviet Union explore diplomatic means, but Dulles refused on the grounds that all of the three states recognized the Chinese Communist regime, and thus were biased.[165]

The United Kingdom's perception of the Chinese threat was once again accurate. According to the British chargé in Beijing, China kept a rigid position to mobilize diplomatic pressure on the United States. London believed that instead of looking for a "showdown," as Dulles feared, China's "objective seems more likely to be to isolate the U.S.A. and to consolidate opinion on their side." Beijing intended to "win over Asian opinion and lull Asian suspicions by appearing moderate and peace-loving while at the same time pursuing their objectives under cover." Therefore, Washington faced a "long drawn out struggle for the support of Asia" instead of a Communist attack, which they knew would invite U.S. retaliation. If there were conflicts, they resulted from Communist miscalculations rather than deliberate design. The Asian states were crucial, and London urged the United States to "exercise moderation in our statements and attitudes lest we frighten the Asians into China's arms." They believed that Washington must force the GMD to evacuate the offshore islands.[166]

The British Commonwealth members joined London in exerting pressure. When Dulles sought the support of the Canadian and Australian prime ministers, both of them pushed the United States to remove GMD forces from Jinmen and Mazu in return for their support in defending the island of Taiwan.[167] The Indians offered to set up "informal contact" so the Americans could talk with Beijing directly. When Dulles said that at present China, emboldened by its successes in Korea, Indochina, and the Taiwan Strait, was a bigger threat to the world than the Soviet Union, the Indian envoy Krishna Menon retorted that "he and his Government felt absolutely confident that the Peking regime had no expansionist ambitions." He pushed the Americans to negotiate with the Chinese, and he "felt confident that tensions in the Far East would be relaxed" once the talks started.[168]

Finally, Washington accepted the British policy. Dulles told the British ambassador that he agreed to use the Bandung Conference to restrain Beijing on the offshore islands. He planned to urge U.S. friends to propose a ceasefire in Bandung and sought British help with their influence in Asia.[169] More important, Washington also accepted the British position on the offshore islands. State Department officials had indeed thought of pushing the GMD to give up these islands, and Eisenhower himself had wondered if these islands were a liability.[170] The president now feared that a military response to Beijing's attack on the islands would lead to a world war and split the Western alliance. Hence, he redefined the status of the islands and concluded that they were "outposts, not citadels," which implied they were expendable. Dulles then announced at a news conference, "We have no commitment of any kind, sort, or description, expressed or implied, which binds the United States to anything except the defense of Formosa and the Pescadores."[171] At a White House meeting with the national security team, Eisenhower summed up the U.S. position:

> an all-out fight with the Chincoms, involving the United States, in an effort to retain Quemoy and Matsu, would be undesirable from the following viewpoint:
>
> (a) The military position of the islands is not favorable and the ultimate objectives of such an operation are obscure.
> (b) Little or no support from our allies is forthcoming to support our position.

(c) Public opinion within the U.S. would be divided.

(d) Impact on the domestic economy could be serious.

. . . A desirable solution would be to convince Chiang that he should:

(a) Voluntarily evacuate Quemoy and Matsu.

(b) Entrench himself on Formosa, await internal developments on the mainland, and provide a constant military and psychological threat to the Chicom régime.[172]

At the same time, Eisenhower was concerned that further retreat before the Communists would damage both the morale of the GMD and U.S. prestige, leading to "the disintegration of all Asian opposition to the spread of Communism in that continent." On further reflection, however, he felt that if Chiang could be convinced to give up the islands willingly neither the United States nor the GMD needed to commit to the defense of the islands, and thus the credibility of containment would not collapse after Communist capture of the islands.[173] Bowie suggested making a public statement announcing the U.S. intention not to commit to the defense of the offshore islands, both to prevent prestige loss and to pressure Chiang to evacuate from the islands, and an NIE confirmed that losing Jinmen and Mazu might not necessarily damage U.S. prestige, as long as Washington gave "convincing evidence of a US determination to resist further Communist aggression."[174]

Communist pressure demanded an immediate action, and the urgency of the situation in the Taiwan Strait intensified in mid-April. General Chase, director of MAAG, reported that the PLA air force buildup across the Taiwan Strait was "genuine and becoming more and more threatening." He believed the PLA would soon challenge U.S. control of the Taiwan Strait. He recommended approving the GMD request to attack the airfields in the coastal mainland. And Chase and Rankin suggested "a blockade of the China coast of all shipping" from Shantou in the south to the boundary between Zhejiang and Fujian in the north. Meanwhile, Stump strongly recommended allowing the GMD to launch air strikes against the PLA inland airfields that could be used to attack the offshore islands or even Taiwan. If the Communist buildup continued without obstruction, he warned that the United States might have to use atomic weapons to retaliate against this attack.[175]

Finally, Eisenhower made up his mind: he negated the GMD request to strike China's airfields and pushed the GMD to evacuate the offshore islands, although he wanted to avoid leaving the impression that the United States forced the GMD. Eisenhower also recognized that in the long run "it might be necessary to accept the 'Two China' concept."[176] To offset the withdrawal, Washington would provide the following inducements to Chiang: the United States would cover the evacuation, blockade the Chinese coast from Shantou to Wenzhou until Beijing renounced the use of force to capture Taiwan and Penghu, station atomic bombs on Taiwan, and commit not to recognize the PRC.[177] When he made this decision, Eisenhower seemed to have forgotten his earlier position that a blockade was an act of war that would definitely create repercussions among allies and from China. Also, the decision was made without deliberations at the NSC.

Even though U.S. officials promised that the United States would maintain forces in Taiwan and assist Chiang's recovery of the mainland when the time was ripe, Chiang bluntly rejected evacuating the islands. Chiang understood that the United States had to change its position, but evacuation would be disastrous to his leadership in Taiwan. "Soldiers must choose proper places to die. Chinese soldiers consider Quemoy–Matsu are proper places for them," the generalissimo told Robertson and Radford, whom Eisenhower believed were trusted by Chiang and had been sent to convince him.[178] Chiang's rejection pushed U.S. leaders back into the dilemma again.

As the Americans were once again struggling for a way to defuse the crisis, Zhou declared in Bandung that China was willing to negotiate with the United States to ease tensions. For Washington, China's timely conciliation, according to historian Robert Accinelli, "offered an escape from the dilemma,"[179] and the crisis ended, to the surprise of U.S. leaders, just as how it had started.

The U.S. response to China during the Taiwan Strait Crisis featured a series of misperceptions and overreactions. China's ambivalent attitude toward the GMD prompted Beijing to start the crisis, and Washington paid insufficient attention to China's actions after the Geneva Conference. The United States failed to recognize Beijing's motives in the Taiwan Strait and were not ready to meet its challenge. When the bombardment of Jinmen took place, Washington was frustrated by the failure of its deterrence and became preoccupied with the alleged Chinese military threat, neglecting the diplomatic implication of Beijing's military action. Ironically, U.S. efforts to defuse the crisis led to the hasty conclusion of the MDT, which the Chinese leaders wanted to prevent and which policy makers in Washington initially had delayed considering.

Throughout the crisis, U.S. leaders overestimated both China's capabilities and ambition. In the U.S. estimate, the Chinese had the strength and the determination to invade the offshore islands, or even Taiwan, but according to Chinese sources, neither was correct: The PLA was not even able to maintain a lasting bombardment of Jinmen, and the Chinese military ambition was limited to the capture of Dachen.[180] Yet the Americans believed they must protect the Jinmen and Mazu islands to prevent PLA capture and worried about a general war with China, which would trigger a global war involving the Soviet Union. When China reduced tensions in March 1955, Washington worried that it was planning to attack Taiwan, which was completely groundless. The exaggeration of Chinese aggression further added to American anxiety.

In this self-inflicted crisis, the United States overreacted to the misperceived Chinese threat. The hurried decision to protect the offshore islands forced the United States into a corner. The MDT was decided without careful deliberations. The rhetoric about using nuclear weapons scared allies and neutral states and stood in contrast to China's peace initiatives. Eisenhower's decision to blockade the Chinese coast reversed his previous considerations and would lead to greater pressure from allies. Moreover, like the MDT decision, this one was made without discussion among the top national security officials.

Although U.S. leaders were aware of the Communist tactics of alienating the United States from allies and neutral states, the Taiwan Strait Crisis "threaten a split between the United States and nearly all its allies," as Eisenhower later admitted.[181] U.S. reliance on allied cooperation in handling the crisis gave allies, especially the United Kingdom, leverage to influence U.S. policymaking. Under this pressure, the Americans constantly modified their policies and retreated from their original positions, can best be seen in their shifting positions on the offshore islands.[182] Finally, the Americans had to accept the British position of giving up these islands to neutralize the Taiwan Strait. Had the Communists not made the peace initiatives in Bandung, U.S. leaders would have been in a deeper dilemma between

British pressure to force the GMD to withdraw from the offshore islands and the GMD's rejection of that request.

Eisenhower and Dulles claimed that their management of the crisis prevented a war with the Chinese.[183] Eisenhower revisionists also praise them for their diplomatic skills. However, as Chinese sources indicate, throughout the crisis, Chinese leaders worked to avoid a direct military confrontation with the United States. Before the crisis, U.S. leaders had also decided not to fight China, therefore there would have been no war to avoid at all. Instead of preventing a war, however, Eisenhower's handling of the crisis might have led to a conflict. His decision to impose an aggressive blockade of the Chinese ports might well have provoked China into military a response, as Gordon Chang has argued.[184]

PART III

Bandung Conference

Chapter Five

FORMULATING A ZONE OF PEACE

The strategic goal [of China] is to maintain a neutral group in Southeast Asia, and to unite Britain and France through these Asian states, so as to block the US infiltration and defeat its conspiracy to establish an aggression group in Southeast Asia.[1]

—ZHOU ENLAI, JUNE 17, 1954

We do not want to see our neighbors allow foreign interveners to build military bases [on their territories]. The Burmese, along with India and Indonesia, did not approve of US efforts to build the aggression group in Southeast Asia, and opposed establishment of [foreign] military bases. This demonstrated that there was the foundation for our friendship and cooperation.[2]

—ZHOU ENLAI, JUNE 29, 1954

From April 18 to 24, 1955, twenty-nine Asian and African states gathered in the small Indonesian city of Bandung to make their united voice heard in a world whose destiny had long been controlled by the Westerners.[3] An important milestone in the history of the Non-Aligned Movement, the Bandung Conference was also a critical moment in Sino-American relations because it came in the midst of the Taiwan Strait Crisis and the subsequent U.S. threats of using nuclear weapons against the PRC. China made a strong response to the United States, but surprisingly Zhou declared in Bandung that China was willing to negotiate with the United States to solve the problems between the two countries. This proposal virtually ended the Taiwan Strait Crisis and led to ambassadorial talks between the two countries, the only channel for Chinese and American diplomats to talk to each other when there were no diplomatic relations between them.

How can Zhou's conciliation in Bandung be reconciled with China's confrontation in the Taiwan Strait? What were China's motives in Bandung? What tactics did the Chinese adopt to achieve their objectives? This chapter situates China's policy toward the United States in the context of China's perception of the world and its relations with its Asian neighbors.

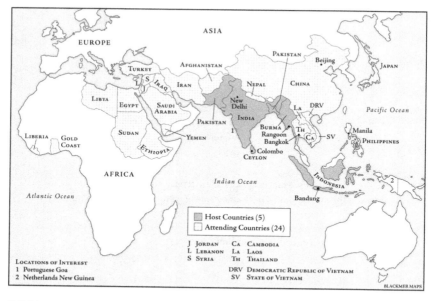

FIGURE 5.1. The twenty-nine countries that participated in the Bandung Conference, April 18–24, 1955
Source: Kate Blackmer

I argue that the Chinese leaders continued their strategy of isolating the enemy to remove the U.S. threat. In Bandung, China's objective was to unite Asian states to develop a neutral zone of peace to exclude the United States from Southeast Asia. Aware of U.S. attempts to manipulate the conference against China by sending proxies to the meeting, China relied on Asian neutral states to push for the zone of peace. To encourage the neutral states, Beijing made concessions on the issue of overseas Chinese living in Southeast Asia, suspended its support of Communist parties in neighboring countries, and demonstrated goodwill over territorial disputes with neighbors. In Bandung, the Chinese delegation attracted participants with trade and a commitment to peaceful coexistence, which Chinese leaders hoped would secure their opposition to U.S. alliances. Playing on the anxiety among Asian states about the Taiwan Strait Crisis, Zhou proposed negotiations with the United States, which successfully mobilized the conference attendees to press Washington to agree to negotiate with China, although he failed to develop the zone of peace.

ENTHUSIASM FOR THE CONFERENCE

The Bandung Conference was initiated by the Indonesian prime minister Ali Sastroamidjojo when the prime ministers of Burma, Ceylon, India, Indonesia, and Pakistan met in Ceylon's capital Colombo in April 1954 to exchange their ideas on such issues as the situation in Indochina, colonialism, nuclear weapons, and international Communism. The proposal did not immediately generate enthusiasm from the other prime ministers, but the Indonesians, largely because of their need for diplomatic accomplishments to bolster their regime, struggled to keep the idea alive.[4] In late September, Sastroamidjojo received support from Nehru and U Nu, who were worried about tensions in Asia created by SEATO and the Taiwan Strait Crisis, and advocated unity of Asian and African states. When the Colombo Powers met again in Bogor, Indonesia, in late December, they finally made up their minds to hold the conference and invite the PRC, instead of Chiang's GMD, to represent China.[5]

From the beginning, Chinese leaders demonstrated greater interest in this conference than did the sponsors. Shortly after Indonesia proposed the meeting, Zhou visited India to encourage a reluctant Nehru to move on with the idea. During Nehru's visit to China in October, Chinese leaders explicitly underscored their eagerness to take part in the proposed conference. When U Nu visited Beijing in December 1954, Chinese leaders once again expressed their enthusiasm. These visits happened before the Colombo leaders had made up their minds about the meeting and when they still disagreed over whether the PRC should be invited at all. The Chinese leaders were well aware of this, but they continued to push for it.[6] Why were they so enthusiastic about the conference?[7]

Beijing was interested in these Asian states because the Chinese leaders were anxious about the U.S. threat and wanted to improve relations with them to forestall U.S. infiltration in China's neighborhood. China's goal was to commit Asian states to a neutral zone of peace, so they would not join the U.S. alliance or accept U.S. bases on their territory. The Bandung Conference provided the Chinese with an opportunity to push for this zone of peace.[8] China's diplomacy in Geneva aimed to neutralize Indochina by separating the United States from its allies. However, just as the Geneva negotiation was going on, Chinese leaders were alerted to the fact that the United States was setting up a new military alliance in Southeast Asia. On

May 19, Eisenhower publicly declared that the United States would formulate a military pact in Southeast Asia without British participation, despite British insistence that such an organization should not be considered before the end of the Geneva Conference. Meanwhile, the Chinese leaders anxiously watched a series of U.S. officials visit Taiwan in the summer of 1954, which they believed were focusing on an MDT with the GMD.

The moves of these Asian nations coming as they did at this time immediately attracted the attention of Chinese leaders. Nehru made a statement on April 24, calling for a peaceful solution and the independence of Indochina. In opposition to the united action against the Communists that the United States sought, both India and Burma refused to allow U.S. airplanes carrying French troops to Indochina to fly over their airspace. Instead he called for developing a neutral zone of peace in Asia.[9] And India signed an agreement with China over Tibet, in which the two countries declared they would build their relations on the basis of Five Principles of Peaceful Coexistence.[10] Then, in Colombo, the Asian prime ministers discussed admitting China into the United Nations and the Indonesian prime minister proposed the Bandung Conference. The prime ministers also discussed the possibility of signing an agreement of non intervention with China.[11] Shortly after the meeting, Indonesia declared interest in a non aggression treaty with Burma, India, and China. Subsequently Indian and Indonesian diplomats probed China's intention toward such a treaty.[12] Meanwhile, Nehru repeatedly promoted the idea of a zone of peace to be built on the basis of the Five Principles, and he publicly criticized U.S. policies of "mass retaliation" and "united action."[13]

Eager to find a way to break the U.S. encirclement of China, Chinese leaders wanted to explore the possibility of uniting these Asian states, although they knew that Burma, Ceylon, and Pakistan were more or less anti-Communist. They suspected that both the Colombo meeting and the proposal for a non aggression treaty were manipulated by the United Kingdom to resist U.S. efforts to exclude British influence in Southeast Asia, in addition to moderating U.S. behavior in Geneva.[14] *Renmin Ribao* first showed China's willingness to join the Asian leaders in an editorial on May 12: "If the Asian countries, with more than half of the world's population, can undertake joint responsibility to safeguard peace and security in Asia, all imperialist schemes to start war in Asia will be defeated."[15] Then on June 13, Chinese leaders in Beijing sent a telegram to Zhou, who was attending the Geneva Conference, urging him to:

take active actions to win over these Southeast Asian states, in order to consolidate peace in the Far East and the world and isolate the US and defeat
American imperialist aggression policy and frustrate its conspiracy to put
together an aggression group in Southeast Asia. In the current circumstance,
it was advantageous for China to conclude either bilateral or multilateral
treaties with India, Indonesia, and Burma, or a collective security pact with
them. That will be conducive to both the peace in Asia and to the policy of
isolating the US. The situation is favorable since it was India and Indonesia
who initiated to negotiate such a treaty.[16]

Zhou Enlai immediately consulted Molotov, and with the Soviet support,
Zhou further proposed some concrete actions to take:

Concerning a non-aggression treaty, or a collective security treaty, with
Southeast Asian states, after studying this issue, we all agree that it is advantageous for China to conclude such a treaty to safeguard peace in current
circumstance, as that will enable us to defeat US conspiracy, safeguard our
national security, and relax international tension. We have exchanged opinion about this issue with comrade Molotov. He expressed approval of our
diplomacy. As for the steps to be taken, it is preferable to begin with bilateral
treaties, and then follow up with a multilateral pact. But if possible, we are
not against concluding a multilateral treaty directly. The strategic goal is to
maintain a neutral group in Southeast Asia, and to unite Britain and France
through these Asian states, so as to block the US infiltration and defeat its
conspiracy to establish an aggression group in Southeast Asia.[17]

To actively pursue the Asian prime ministers' proposals, Chinese leaders
decided that Zhou should immediately visit India and Burma, and probably
also Indonesia, when the Geneva Conference was suspended in late June.[18]
Previously the Indians had invited Zhou to visit New Delhi, but China
declined for fear that the Indians would pressure China on the boundary
disputes between the two states and China's support to Asian Communist
parties. Earlier that year Chinese officials had also refused the Indian suggestion to reassure Burma that China sought to peacefully coexist with the
Burmese because they were reluctant to stop assisting the Communists
in Burma.[19] But to separate these states from the United States, Chinese
leaders were now willing to sign whatever type of treaty they wanted. To

prepare Zhou for that, Beijing sent him the "Draft Treaty for Safeguarding Peace in Asia." The gist of this treaty included withdrawing foreign troops from and dismantling foreign bases in Asia, abolishing aggression treaties, and non participation in military alliances.[20]

In New Delhi, Zhou played on Nehru's worries about tensions in Asia and emphasized China's policy of peaceful coexistence, in contrast with U.S. military alliances. On his part, Nehru confided in Zhou that India's relations with the United States were not good, and he opposed U.S. attempts to build a military organization in Southeast Asia, which would only create new tensions. Instead, he proposed a zone of peace composed of neutral states that "have no foreign bases in them." Zhou offered his ready support. The two agreed to apply the Five Principles to Asian states to formulate such a zone to prevent U.S. military blocs. As the first step, Nehru suggested that China make a bilateral declaration with Burma based on the Five Principles; then India, Indonesia, Burma, and China would make similar bilateral statements with each other. Satisfied with Nehru's response, an ambitious Zhou suggested they should aim to include "as many states as possible" in this zone of peace. Preliminarily, Zhou suggested including India, Indonesia, Burma, Laos, Cambodia, and even Ceylon, after efforts were made to draw it away from the United States.[21] To demonstrate China's commitment to the cause, Zhou issued a joint communiqué with Nehru, declaring the importance of the Five Principles for international relations. Chinese enthusiasm indeed rekindled Nehru's interest in the Bandung Conference.[22]

Zhou then moved on to Burma and issued a similar communiqué there. He was frank with U Nu on his purpose and stated that China

> does not want to see our neighbors allow foreign interveners to build military bases [on their territories]. The Burmese, along with India and Indonesia, did not approve of U.S. efforts to build the aggression group in Southeast Asia, and opposed establishment of [foreign] military bases. This demonstrated that there was the foundation for our friendship and cooperation.[23]

To better develop a united front with Burma, Zhou had to work out the Burmese worries about China's support of the Communist insurgents in Burma.[24] In addition to the commitment to the Five Principles, Zhou clearly promised U Nu that China would not export revolution. He admitted the presence of some Burmese Communist leaders in China, but he assured U Nu that these people were only granted political asylum and not allowed to engage in political activities. This was a position Nehru had pushed China to take that the Chinese government had refused before.[25]

Zhou's visits to India and Burma convinced Chinese leaders that they could work with these states to develop a zone of peace in Southeast Asia. And Zhou's experience in Geneva confirmed the effectiveness of their tactics of isolating the United States. In early July, after hearing Zhou's report, Mao picked up the "intermediate zone" theory he had first put forward in 1946. He concluded that China should continue its policy of uniting countries in the intermediate zone between the United States and the Soviet Union to exclude the United States from Asia.[26] After neutralizing Indochina in Geneva, China should build on the momentum and strive for a zone of peace in Southeast Asia. Consequently, the CCP politburo decided to launch a diplomatic offensive to develop an international united front with states in Asia.[27]

DIPLOMATIC OFFENSIVE

Chinese leaders knew they had to overcome some obstacles in China's relations with Southeast Asia. Although major states in the area were opposed to U.S. military alliances, they were also suspicious of China. Three issues contributed to this suspicion: anxiety about Communism, overseas Chinese, and territorial disputes with China.

The first concern of these states was Communism. Since establishment of the PRC in October 1949, most Chinese neighbors worried that China would export Communism into their territories. This anxiety was not groundless. Indeed, Chinese leaders were interested in supporting Communist parties in Southeast Asia, especially after Stalin encouraged the CCP to play a leading role in an "Asian revolution." Even before the CCP came to power, it had started to teach its experience to Communist parties from Burma, India, Indonesia, Malaya, the Philippines, Vietnam, and Thailand. In 1951, the CCP established the International Liaison Department, which was put in charge of interactions with other Asian Communist parties. In 1952, the International Liaison Department started various training programs to help these Asian Communists apply the Chinese experience in their own countries.[28] After the Korean War, the Western press and the GMD in Taiwan published numerous reports about a Communist conspiracy to conquer Southeast Asia. These claims culminated in Eisenhower's domino theory.[29] China was reported to be training and supplying the Burmese and Thai Communist insurgents and planning to expand Communism into Southeast Asia. The Chinese leaders were aware of these reports.[30] Yet they had hesitated to pledge not to support these Communists when it was requested by Nehru.[31]

Southeast Asian states' second concern was the existence of a vast overseas Chinese population in this area. The Chinese had been migrating into Southeast Asia for centuries. By the mid-1950s, about twelve million of them lived in the area, including about two and a half million in Indonesia, over two million in Malaya, between two and three million in Thailand, and about a quarter of a million in Burma.[32] Southeast Asian states generally observed *jus soli* (birthright citizenship), but China had followed *jus sanguinis* (citizenship by the right of blood), so a large portion of these ethnic Chinese had dual citizenships. Southeast Asian states in general worried that China would use these ethnic Chinese to expand Communism, and this became a particularly urgent problem for Indonesia. The votes from over one and a half million overseas Chinese holding dual citizenships would be critical for the result of its first general election in late 1955. Since the beginning of the PRC, the Chinese government had promised to protect the interests of overseas Chinese and refused to negotiate with Southeast Asian states over this issue.[33] When the Indonesian government requested negotiation to solve the issue of dual citizenship in early 1954, Chinese officials ignored the request. Indeed, the first Chinese People's Congress, which was held in September 1954, had delegates representing the overseas Chinese.[34]

Territorial disputes was the third issue that strained China's relations with its neighbors. China had never drawn clear boundary lines and thus had territorial disputes with most of its neighbors, including India and Burma, which China relied on to isolate the United States. The status of Tibet had been the biggest problem in China's relations with India, which had regarded Tibet as a buffer area between the two states. When Chinese troops moved into Tibet in 1950, India condemned this action as an invasion. Eventually Indian leaders decided to accept the fait accompli. In late 1953, China and India started negotiations over Tibet, and in April 1954, the two countries reached an agreement that recognized Tibet as Chinese territory. India and China had other territorial disputes, but they both chose to shelve them at this moment.[35] Burma also had border issues with China.

Zhou assured U Nu that China would maintain the status quo and solve the problem through negotiations in the future. The two countries started negotiation in 1956 and soon reached a basic agreement based on China's concessions. A formal border treaty was signed in 1960.[36]

To unite these Southeast Asian states against the United States, Chinese leaders began addressing these issues, but they had limited resources. In Southeast Asia, China had diplomatic relations with five states: India, Indonesia, Burma, Pakistan, and the DRV. India was the most important state for China's policy of isolating the United States because of Nehru's influence, his initiation of the idea of the zone of peace, and India's status in Asia.[37] Nehru believed the future of Asia depended on good relations between China and India, two of the leading members in the emerging Third World, and India was the first non-Communist state to establish diplomatic relations with China in April 1950. He also understood that China needed peace so that it could concentrate on domestic development. By pushing for the Five Principles with China, Nehru hoped to allay Chinese fears about a U.S.-Indian collusion against China, and more important, to compel China to keep its peace commitments. Hence it was also a policy of "containment through friendship," in the words of scholar G. H. Jansen. Beyond Asia, India adopted a policy of neutralism because Nehru believed India should play a role of leadership instead of being a mere "camp follower." In a practical sense, non alignment served India's interests because it forced the United States and the Soviet Union to compete for India's favor, while sustaining a fragile domestic political consensus.[38] Chinese leaders knew Nehru's intentions, so they used the Five Principles to ease Nehru's worries. Furthermore, realizing that India suffered a shortage of food, China signed the first trade agreement with India in 1954. Despite China's own food problems, Beijing started to sell foods to India.[39] Beijing was also aware that the Indians were alienated by the U.S. alliance with Pakistan and wanted to exploit this. Chinese officials noticed that Dulles had pushed for a defense organization in the Middle East, which led to a military pact between Turkey and Pakistan in February 1954.[40] Three months later, the United States itself concluded a mutual defense assistance agreement with Pakistan. Nehru warned that Pakistan's alliance with the United States upset the balance of power in the area and would lead to a future world war. In response, he repeatedly called for a zone of peace.[41]

Burma was the only state that suffered all three of these problems with China, so it was extremely suspicious about China. Meanwhile, it suffered from Chiang's military remnants that fled to Burma after losing China's civil war. The Burmese held the Americans responsible for the problem, as they believed the United States was using these forces to harass China.[42] As a result, Burma was the first non-Communist state to recognize the PRC. With India, Burma refused to join the United States in condemning China as an aggressor in Korea in 1950. It also supported the PRC to represent China in the UN and turned down U.S. offers of a mutual security treaty and economic assistance in 1952.[43] The Burmese also blamed the United States for their financial difficulty and worried about the sale of rice, which made up about 70 percent of its export earnings. The United States was making the situation worse by outpricing Burma on the market, which had suffered from a worldwide surplus since 1953.[44] China was sensitive to this and offered a trade agreement to buy Burma's rice in April 1954. Later that year, it twice increased the amount of rice it purchased from Burma and also started to sell machinery products to Burma, even though China itself was agricultural and urgently in need of such products.[45]

Indonesia had pursued a neutralist policy since its independence in 1949. The Truman administration provided limited economic, technical, and military assistance in 1950, but Indonesia refused to accept military assistance in order to maintain its neutrality. In 1952, it also rejected the U.S. invitation for a defense pact, as did Burma.[46] The Indonesian government formed in 1953 was allied with the Indonesian Communists. It was offended by U.S. support of the two rightist opposition parties and its neutrality over Western New Guinea (also known as Western Irian or Netherlands New Guinea), the part of Indonesia still under Dutch colonial control. Moreover, according to Chinese diplomats, the Indonesian leaders also suspected that the United States was involved in a GMD attempt to overthrow the Indonesian government in order to revoke recognition of the PRC.[47] Sensitive to the Indonesian concerns, the Chinese leaders publicly supported their decolonization struggle. Knowing its needs for economic assistance, China sent a delegation to Indonesia and concluded a trade agreement in June 1954, which resulted in Indonesia starting to sell rubber to China.[48] This was a significant move because trade relations might decide which side Indonesia would tilt toward.[49]

Ceylon recognized the PRC in 1950, but the two countries did not exchange ambassadors. The Ceylonese prime minister was very anti-Communist, but he had to find a market for rubber, Ceylon's principal product, and to purchase rice to feed the Ceylonese.[50] The Chinese moved in and signed a trade agreement with Ceylon in 1952, solving Ceylon's two big problems simultaneously: China would sell rice to Ceylon at the market price and purchase Ceylonese rubber at a price 5–8 percent higher than the market price.[51] The Ceylonese were excited by this profitable deal, but Chinese leaders were willing to pay extra money to woo Ceylon away from the United States.[52] In late 1954, China increased its imports of rubber, which gave the Ceylonese even more benefits. Needless to say, the Ceylonese were satisfied with these arrangements.[53]

Pakistan was a member of multiple military pacts the United States sponsored in 1954. In February, it signed a military pact with Turkey in Dulles's efforts to build an alliance of so-called northern tier states, including Iran, and Iraq.[54] In May it signed a mutual defense assistance agreement with the United States. Pakistan also offered to join SEATO when it came into being in September 1954.[55] But Beijing believed Pakistan joined the U.S. alliances simply out of an expectation of U.S. economic assistance and support for its conflicts with India over Kashmir rather than hatred against Communism or China, so there was a possibility of drawing Pakistan to the Chinese side.[56] Aware of Pakistan's need to sell cotton, the Chinese pleasantly became its largest buyer in 1952, and China signed its first trade agreement with Pakistan in 1953, which allowed Pakistan to exchange its cotton for China's coal.[57]

While the Chinese were attracting states in Southeast Asia with both trade and assurance of peaceful coexistence, they saw more hope of a united front when the establishment of SEATO alienated these same states from the United States in September 1954. Despite U.S. efforts to recruit Asian members, Beijing noted, most of the Southeast Asian states rejected the organization, and only three Asian states—Pakistan, the Philippines, and Thailand—joined SEATO. Nehru was the first to opposed it. He announced that the military group created new tension in Asia, and its establishment was unfortunate. Nehru rejected the Ceylonese prime minister's proposal for a meeting to discuss the possibility of the Colombo Powers joining SEATO. Burma and Indonesia supported the Indian position, seeing SEATO as "Western colonialism in a new and more subtle disguise." Under their pressure, Ceylon also declined the U.S. invitation.[58] Moreover, SEATO provoked Indonesia to reinitiate the Bandung Conference, which aimed at concluding treaties of non aggression to maintain peace in Asia.[59]

Chinese leaders were satisfied that SEATO was not popular in Asia, but they were upset that SEATO was finally established. Cambodia, Laos, and South Vietnam were put under SEATO's protection, and from China's perspective this violated the principle of the Geneva Agreements. What worried the Chinese even more was the fact that the United States continued its efforts to recruit the Colombo Powers into SEATO.[60] They noticed that the United States was offering both carrots and sticks to Indonesia, and Australian and Filipino foreign ministers went to Burma and Ceylon to push them to join SEATO. Chinese officials believed Afghanistan and Japan were also U.S. targets for recruitment.[61] They also knew that major neutral states were interested in U.S. assistance, although they did not like the strings the Americans attached to their assistance. Beijing feared that these Southeast Asian states would bend to the U.S. lure of economic assistance.[62]

To consolidate relations with states in Southeast Asia, the Chinese Foreign Ministry directed its diplomats to take effective actions to convince these countries that they could coexist peacefully with China.[63] And Beijing adopted three major moves to further this policy. First, it reversed its original policy toward the overseas Chinese. In late September, Zhou declared that China did not acknowledge dual citizenship and sought to solve the issue through negotiations with Asian neighbors. He publicly encouraged the overseas Chinese to give up their Chinese citizenship if they chose to stay overseas.[64] This was a radical departure from the previous policy, and Chinese leaders knew it was unpopular among the overseas Chinese. Most of those holding dual citizenships wanted to maintain both citizenships. But compared to the priority of uniting Southeast Asian states to exclude the United States in Asia, the interests of overseas Chinese became secondary. In November, China started negotiations with Indonesia, and the two countries quickly reached an agreement. Chinese officials were willing to subject the "partial interests of the overseas Chinese" to friendship with Indonesia and "avoid raising issues that the Indonesians would disapprove of" to speed up the negotiation.[65]

The second initiative Chinese leaders took was to invite Nehru as the first head of government to visit China in October. As the leader of the neutral states, Nehru's support was crucial for the success of China's policy. Zhou specifically held a government meeting to prepare Chinese officials for receiving Nehru. He told the officials that the central issue he wanted to discuss with Nehru was how to make use of the Bandung Conference to formulate the zone of peace in Asia. According to Zhou's plan, this area would ultimately cover Southeast Asia (except Pakistan), pass over Afghanistan, and ultimately reach through North Africa.[66]

The Chinese did all they could to impress Nehru with China's goodwill. About two hundred thousand people welcomed Nehru along Beijing's streets; the common experience as victims of colonialism was stressed in conversations with Nehru; and the shared need for economic development was pointed out. Chinese leaders once again assured Nehru that China wanted peace and pursued international cooperation. The United States, however, threatened China's security by putting its frontlines in Korea, Taiwan, and Indochina, according to Mao. Zhou raised the topic of the Bandung Conference and told Nehru China supported it and was willing to participate, because "it will work towards the zone of peace," despite the fact that Nehru had not yet invited China.[67] Instead, Nehru was more interested in actions China would take to lessen the fear among some Asian states about China. In reply, Mao Zedong assured him that China would prove its faith by adhering to the Five Principles. He also disclosed to Nehru that China would find a reasonable solution to the overseas Chinese problem.

The Chinese leaders were pleased to be told that their efforts toward Nehru received very positive responses in Southeast Asia. Satisfied with the visit, Nehru proceeded with the Bandung Conference proposal.[68] The other Colombo Powers saw the respect the Chinese people showed to Nehru as indicative of China's goodwill toward neighbors.[69] More important, Nehru's visit worsened India's relations with the United States.[70] Chinese leaders learned that after the visit Nehru declared his belief that China should be admitted into the United Nations, the Five Principles should be used to establish a zone of peace, and SEATO was an obstacle to peace. He trusted China's goodwill and agreed to hold the Bandung Conference.[71]

As their next move, the Chinese leaders welcomed U Nu in early December. In Beijing, the Chinese officials made a package deal to address both Burma's political and economic needs. After stressing China's new policy toward the overseas Chinese, they made other assurances to the Burmese: China would solve boundary problems through negotiation; it would neither interfere with Burma's internal affairs nor support the Burmese Communists; and more important, it would not cross the border to attack the GMD remnants in Burma, which had been Burma's biggest fear. To further demonstrate China's trust in Burma and its need for friendship with neighbors, Chinese leaders asked U Nu to help China improve its relations with Thailand.[72] In addition, Beijing offered a two-year trade agreement that allowed Burma to export rice and import manufactured goods and industrial equipment from China. Finally, the Chinese leaders stressed their enthusiasm for the Bandung Conference, despite U Nu's suggestion that Pakistan wanted to invite the GMD instead of China. "If we were able to attend the Conference, we would feel glorious," Mao told U Nu.[73] Mao and Zhou did not forget to stress their support of the idea of a zone of peace: "once such a Peace Area is expanded . . . future war will be delayed or prevented." To demonstrate China's goodwill, Zhou once again stressed China's commitment to the Five Principles in the joint communiqué with Burma.[74] U Nu in turn assured Chinese leaders that Burma would not allow China's enemies to establish bases in Burma.

China's efforts secured its participation in the Bandung Conference. U Nu's interest in the Bandung Conference grew after his visit to China.[75] When the five Colombo Powers met to finalize planning for the Bandung Conference, India and Burma strongly suggested inviting China despite the Ceylonese and Pakistani opposition and pressure from the United States and the United Kingdom against the PRC's participation.[76] When Pakistan proposed inviting the GMD to represent China, U Nu threatened to withdraw from the conference, and he got Nehru's immediate support. Finally the prime ministers agreed to invite China.[77] The Chinese leaders determined that the communiqué of the meeting "was consistent with the spirit" of the Five Principles.[78] Moreover, they were pleased to hear that U.S. leaders worried China would make use of the Bandung Conference to frustrate the American plan to expand SEATO and develop closer relations with U.S. ally Japan, which was eager for trade with China.[79] Encouraged by these messages, the Chinese Foreign Ministry prepared its plan for China's participation in the Bandung Conference. China's most important goal in Bandung was to expand the zone of peace by promoting relations with Asian and African states on the basis of the Five Principles.[80] In late January, Zhou pleasantly accepted Indonesia's invitation to the Bandung Conference.[81]

STRIVING FOR PEACEFUL COEXISTENCE

As Chinese leaders prepared for the Bandung Conference, they were fully aware of the U.S. threat. The SEATO meeting in Bangkok in February 1955 initially aimed to establish a permanent military force in Asia, according to Chinese diplomats. The United States promised to provide air and sea forces and asked the other members to contribute ground troops. However, this request met with broad opposition, especially from the three Asian members who were only interested in U.S. economic assistance, according to Chinese officials. The Americans failed to fulfil their promise to satisfy the demands of assistance from the Asian allies, and the SEATO meeting failed to reach any concrete agreement, Chinese leaders observed with satisfaction.[82] Moreover, the Americans further alienated the Asian neutral states, despite their gesture of sympathy toward Bandung.[83] Perceiving it as a new move to create tensions, Burma not only rejected a U.S. invitation to attend the Bangkok meeting but also pushed other Asian countries not to attend.[84] The Indian public generally criticized the SEATO conference as dangerous interference in Asian affairs and felt that the U.S. claim to protect this area was an "insult" to Asian states. The Indian government declared that the U.S. military bloc infringed upon the Geneva Agreements and would harm the upcoming Bandung Conference.[85]

In the meantime, however, Chinese leaders were alerted by U.S. efforts to sabotage the Bandung Conference. According to Chinese diplomats, U.S. leaders were worried that Bandung would give China an opportunity to promote Asian neutralism and formulate an area of collective peace in Asia.[86] According to the Chinese Foreign Ministry, the U.S. leaders tried to attract the sponsors of the meeting with economic assistance to prevent China from dominating the conference. Harold Stassen, director of the Mutual Security Agency, visited Asia and pledged to increase assistance. Chinese officials predicted that the U.S. government would also publish an assistance program worth one billion dollars before the Bandung meeting.[87] In Indonesia, in addition to economic assistance, the United States increased its investment and tried to influence the country through religious and cultural exchanges. Via Taiwan, the Americans also attempted to manipulate Indonesian politics through Indonesian opposition parties.[88] To win the support of India, former U.S. ambassador to India Chester Bowles visited New Delhi. U.S officials attracted India with economic assistance and aid to its industrialization. The Americans again promised to provide more nuclear materials to help India with its nuclear program, in addition to selling ten tons of heavy water and committing to help construct atomic power plants a month earlier.[89] More important, the Chinese leaders learned, the United States sent proxies such as Japan, Pakistan, the Philippines, Thailand, and Turkey to discredit the Five Principles in Bandung. To separate China from Asian neutral states, these U.S. allies would attack Communism as "new colonialism."[90] And the United Kingdom was using its influence in Southeast Asia to help the United States contain China in Bandung.[91]

Chinese leaders adopted a conciliatory stance in Bandung, focusing on convincing the attendees of China's peace intentions instead of mobilizing them against the United States. China's objective in Bandung was limited to establishing a permanent organization for the attendees to meet every two years and committing the conference to the Five Principles, which would lay the foundation for the zone of peace in Asia.[92] Such a position was consistent with the suggestions of the three major sponsors China relied on to realize its goals. As Nehru and U Nu indicated, China still needed to work out the suspicions about the PRC among Asian states. India informed PRC leaders that a regional pact was premature.[93] And Indonesia hoped China would not be too ambitious in Bandung. None of the neutral states expected the conference to solve any major problem.[94]

Chinese officials analyzed the attendees of the conference and deemed their plan was practicable. According to Chinese officials, the participants of the conference consisted of four groups: (1) pro-peace neutral states, including India, Burma, Indonesia, and Afghanistan; (2) states holding positions close to the neutralists: Egypt, Sudan, Nepal, Syria, Lebanon, Yemen, Saudi Arabia, the Gold Coast, Cambodia, Laos, Ceylon, and Pakistan; (3) states holding positions close to anti-neutralism: Japan, South Vietnam, Jordan, Libya, Liberia, Iran, Iraq, and Ethiopia; and (4) anti-neutralist states: Thailand, the Philippines, and Turkey. Accordingly, China would unite the neutralist states, win over countries in group two, influence group three, and isolate group four. The Chinese delegation gave particular attention to Egypt and Japan, but even for such anti-neutralists as Thailand and the Philippines, it would not give them up and tried to influence them through frequent contacts.[95]

The Chinese Foreign Ministry decided to pursue several tactics. First, the Chinese delegation would focus on Western colonialism, from which most of the attendees had suffered, to mobilize the conference against the United States and its Western allies. In response to U.S. attempts to attack Communism to separate China from the attendees, the Chinese delegation would make every effort to prevent the conference from discussing the topic of Communism, although Chinese officials would in private reassure Asian states that China would not interfere in their domestic affairs.

Second, Chinese leaders decided to demonstrate a willingness to help the other attendees instead of asking them to support China. Therefore, the Chinese delegation would not raise the Taiwan issue, but outside the conference it would disclose the nature of the issue: the United States intervened in China's domestic affairs, and China acted to oppose U.S. attempts to occupy Taiwan and create "two Chinas." Therefore, the liberating Taiwan campaign was part of the anticolonial efforts the conference promoted. Chinese officials would assure the conference that although China insisted on its right to liberate Taiwan and the U.S. withdrawal of its forces from Taiwan, it was willing to solve the Taiwan Strait Crisis through negotiation with the Americans; if the United States withdrew, China would strive to liberate Taiwan peacefully.[96]

Third, catering to the concern about the citizenship of overseas Chinese, Chinese leaders reiterated their willingness to solve the problem through negotiations. Meanwhile, China should publicize its conclusion of negotiation with the Indonesians. In Bandung, the Chinese delegation should hold a grand signing ceremony before the meeting to address Southeast Asian states' concerns about this issue and improve their trust in China.

Fourth, Chinese leaders planned to use commerce to win over friends because they knew that most neutral states had expectations of China on trade. Although the United States was influencing Asian states with assistance, Chinese officials believed China was the only country that could provide profitable trade to those who suffered from both Western monopoly of world trade and lack of funds and export materials. Therefore, the Chinese Foreign Trade Department made a long-term plan to improve trade relations with Asian states. The Chinese delegation in Bandung would focus particularly on Indonesia and Egypt, and also take some concrete actions toward India, Burma, Ceylon, Pakistan, Syria, Afghanistan, Japan, and Thailand. Chinese officials calculated that over time trade with China would push such U.S. allies as Ceylon, Pakistan, Japan, and Thailand out of the orbit of the United States.[97]

Last, Chinese officials realized that the success of their diplomacy in Bandung relied on the cooperation of the three neutral states: Burma, Indonesia, and especially India. To consolidate relations and reassure them that China had a conciliatory approach toward the United States, they informed these three states of China's plan to release four U.S. pilots before the Bandung Conference.[98] To coordinate positions with leaders of the neutral states, Zhou went to Burma to meet with U Nu and Nehru before he flew to Bandung. He clarified China's position on Taiwan and got their agreement that Communism would not be discussed at the conference. However, China's suggestion for a permanent organization did not arouse U Nu and Nehru's interests because the conference, according to U Nu, would just discuss "general principles," not concrete issues.[99] Chinese leaders were careful not to displease Nehru. The Chinese delegation was

FIGURE 5.2. Bandung Conference, Indonesia, 1955.
Source: Howard Sochurek. The LIFE Picture Collection via Getty Images

FIGURE 5.3. Nehru, Nu, and Sukarno
Source: Lisa Larsen/The LIFE Picture Collection via Getty Images

told not to leave the impression that China was stealing the thunder from Nehru, which "would give imperialism and its running dogs opportunities to alienate India from China."[100]

In Bandung, the Chinese delegation met three major challenges from U.S. allies, which Chinese leaders had expected, but Zhou, the head of the Chinese delegation, maintained a conciliatory approach throughout the conference.[101] During the opening speeches, Iran and Iraq suddenly started to condemn Communism as a "subversive religion" despite the topic being excluded from the agenda.[102] Immediately Pakistan, the Philippines, and Turkey joined them. Then Cambodia questioned the sincerity of the DRV in applying the Five Principles toward Cambodia, and Thailand accused China of supporting Thai Communists for subversion. Zhou had to defend China and push the conference toward China's goal.[103] He gave a firm denial to Thailand's accusation and emphasized the importance of the Five Principles for collective peace. The Chinese delegation came "to seek unity and not to quarrel; to seek common ground and not to create divergence." Zhou tried to get the participants to concentrate on their common enemy, pointing out that China had not raised such issues as the tensions over Taiwan caused by the United States or China's membership in the United Nations because that would only lead to unnecessary controversy.

Then the Ceylonese prime minister, who had been in close consultation with the Americans, initiated a second challenge. At a meeting about colonialism and national independence, he surprisingly declared Communism "a new form of colonialism" and drew an analogy between Soviet satellites in East Europe and imperialist colonies in Asia and Africa. Then other U.S. allies—Turkey, Iran, Iraq, Lebanon, Pakistan, the Philippines, Sudan, and Liberia—introduced a resolution condemning "all types of colonialism," although the Pakistani prime minister distinguished China from the Soviet Union.[104] The conference attendees debated this issue for a long time. Although he got strong support from India, Burma, and Indonesia, Zhou finally had to accept a compromise formulation: "colonialism in all its manifestations is an evil which should be brought to an end." According to Zhou, this meant colonialism had manifestations in political, economic, social, and cultural fields; but other people could interpret it as "different types of colonialism," including the "new colonialism" of the Soviet Union.[105]

U.S. allies did not give up. Iraq, Turkey, Pakistan, the Philippines, and Thailand launched a third challenge to the foundation for the final resolution, the Five Principles, which was the most important goal of the Chinese delegation. Nehru, China's ally, tried to convince the participants that military blocs threatened peace and a neutral area was the only way to safeguard peace, but U.S. allies defended military alliances and their membership in the U.S. alliances. Pakistan claimed that military alliance belonged to collective self-defense, which the UN Charter permitted. It also proposed including the obligation to settle peacefully all international controversies as a principle in the final resolution, with the dual purpose of both pressuring India over Kashmir and preventing China from taking actions in the Taiwan Strait. Other U.S. allies cooperated with the Pakistanis. Iraq and Turkey regarded the Five Principles as vague slogans, but the Philippines justified its military alliance with the United States as a necessary means for small states to defend themselves against Communist aggression.

Zhou stepped in to push for the Five Principles. He finally made a seven-point peace declaration, which was based on the Five Principles but in different wording. To ensure the conference acceptance of these principles, Zhou again reassured China's neighbors when he explained his statement.

China respected Burma's sovereignty and territorial integrity and would negotiate with its neighbors to define the border lines. Recognizing the Thai and Filipino concerns about a Chinese invasion, Zhou invited their leaders to visit China to inspect the situation with their own eyes. To win the support on Cambodia and Laos, he stressed China's adherence to the Geneva Agreements and its promise of non intervention in the internal affairs of these two states—the day before Zhou had already asked DRV to make the same pledge to the two states. Zhou also admitted that, as a big country, China tended to ignore smaller states, but he promised that China would be alert against such a tendency.

Most important, Zhou played up concerns about the tensions between China and the United States and initiated peace talks with the United States, which both drove home China's policy of conciliation and posed a peace offensive on the United States. When elaborating on the principle of mutual respect, Zhou stated that "we respect the way of life and political and economic systems chosen by the American people." Moreover, he added that "China was willing to settle its conflict with America by peaceful means" and welcomed those who would like to facilitate the settlement of disputes between the United States and China.[106]

The effect of the peace initiative was further promoted by the Indonesian prime minister. Concerned about the tensions in the Taiwan Strait and worried that China's position was expressed in closed sessions and thus would not be known by the public, he held a press conference for Zhou. Using the opportunity, Zhou made an influential statement:

> Chinese people are friendly to the American people. Chinese people do not want to have war with [the] USA. The Chinese government is willing to sit down and enter into negotiations with [the] US government to discuss [the] question of relaxing tension in [the] Far East and especially [the] question of relaxing tension in [the] Taiwan area.[107]

This was actually the position China had made in early February,[108] but as scholar A. Doak Barnett observed, it was "really a skillful trial-balloon" because Zhou "made no specific offer. He did not say where he would sit down, or with whom, or exactly what he would be willing to discuss. Exactly what he meant was undefined." Moreover, when Zhou repeated his offer of talks with the United States in his closing speech the next day, he modified the previous statement: "However, this should not in the slightest degree affect the just demand of the Chinese people to exercise their sovereignty rights in liberating Taiwan."[109]

For most of the delegations in Bandung, Zhou's public statement was dramatic and "a major peace move." U Nu, as the first attendee to comment officially on the initiative, declared that this "was a great step toward easing world tension."[110] The foreign minister of Indonesia, who had believed that China had not been willing to negotiate with the United States and that Zhou had just made a brand-new proposal, observed that "this was the first time that such a statement had been published from the mouth of Prime Minister Chou En Lai. The Western world in general and the American public in particular, did not hear many direct statements from the leaders of the People's Republic of China."[111] The statement quickly raised enthusiasm among countries both at the conference and outside for the possibility of mediation between the United States and China. Soon after the meeting, the United Kingdom, India, Indonesia, Burma, and even Pakistan offered to facilitate a U.S.-China dialogue.

Zhou's efforts worked. The Bandung Conference finally reached a compromise on its final communiqué and incorporated the right of self-defense, the principle of peaceful settlement of disputes, and the Five Principles, with some modifications.[112] Building on the momentum, Zhou visited Indonesia to further China's policy of establishing a zone of peace. He made a joint communiqué with the Indonesian government, repeating the importance of the Five Principles. A month later, the Indonesian prime minister visited China and offered to help start negotiations between China and the United States.

The Bandung Conference provided China with a rare chance to present itself to the world. Chinese leaders seized the opportunity to develop a united front with the Southeast Asian states. Following the Geneva Conference, China launched a series of diplomatic offensives toward India, Indonesia, and Burma to win their support, including exchanging visits, terminating support to the Communist insurgents in these countries, making political deals of foreign trade, and solving the dual citizenship problem of the overseas Chinese. China's efforts secured its participation in the conference and cooperation of major sponsors.

FIGURE 5.4. Zhou offering autographs
Source: Howard Sochurek/The LIFE Picture Collection via Getty Images

Chinese leaders failed, however, to achieve the two major objectives they had planned toward building a zone of peace. Zhou managed to include the Five Principles in the Bandung communiqué, but they did not have much binding power. Within a month after Bandung, Cambodia signed a military assistance agreement with the United States despite its pledge to observe the Five Principles. The communiqué also acknowledged the rights for "collective security," which justified U.S. military alliance in Asia. The Chinese also failed to create a permanent organization to further push for the zone of peace. Zhou's proposal failed to attract India and Burma even before the conference. Although he raised the issue again at the conference, few participants were interested. The final communiqué only mentioned the necessity of having a liaison office, but even that did not materialize. Furthermore, China's proposal to convene another such conference did not get much support. An enthusiastic Indonesia suggested that it should take place "within the next year," but a second Asian-African conference never took place.[113]

Chinese leaders had succeeded in breaking the U.S. isolation of China, even if the plan of isolating the United States was too ambitious. First of all, making use of the publicity given to the meeting, Zhou made the peace overture, which played on the fear about a U.S.-Chinese conflict and successfully mobilized pressure on the United States for the ambassadorial talks. The negotiation with the United States not only enhanced the PRC's international prestige but also indicated the failure of the U.S. nonrecognition of the Communist regime.

Second, although on the defensive during the most of the conference, Zhou exploited his stay in Bandung and achieved a big "social success," in the words of the noted China expert A. Doak Barnett, who witnessed the event.[114] The Chinese delegation invited over twenty delegations to its numerous banquets, at which Zhou made assurances, demonstrated friendliness, and issued invitations to visit China. As a result, China won the sympathy of many participants, including some U.S. allies. The Pakistani prime minister told Zhou that Pakistan did not oppose China and was not afraid of the PRC's aggression. He even promised Zhou that Pakistan would not join the United States if a war broke out between the United States and China, despite Pakistan's alliance with the United States.[115] The Lebanese delegate, which the United States sent to contain China, confided in Zhou that his country was willing to establish an "intimate relationship" with China.[116] Even Prince Wan of Thailand and General Romulo of the Philippines were convinced of China's peace intentions.[117] In Bandung, Chinese officials held their first official meeting with Japanese officials, following two years of unofficial trade contact.[118] China started relations with the Arab states, most of which still had diplomatic relations with the GMD. Following Zhou's meetings with the Egyptian prime minister in Bandung, the two countries continued negotiations, leading to formal diplomatic relations in 1956. Other Arab states, such as Syria and Saudi Arabia, also became friendlier to China after the conference.[119]

Finally, Bandung paved the way for China's diplomacy with the Third World. When reviewing the conference, Zhou concluded that China's original categorization of the attendees was right, and the policy of establishing a united front with Asian and African countries was "completely correct."[120] According to this judgment, the Chinese Foreign Ministry formulated a comprehensive plan to promote China's relations with Asian and African countries.[121] The next states China should win over—following India, Burma, and Indonesia—were Egypt, Pakistan, and Ceylon.[122] Only three days after the Bandung Conference, Mao assured the Pakistani ambassador to China that Pakistan's fear about China was groundless and the two countries should work out misunderstandings and improve relations.[123] Later in 1955, Chinese leaders invited the prime ministers of Pakistan and Ceylon to China. As a result of China's active diplomacy, the number of states having diplomatic relations with China doubled in the following decade. Except for France, all these states belong to the Third World.[124]

Chapter Six

A BLESSING IN DISGUISE?

If France, Great Britain and the U.S. are excluded from Asian affairs then the entire region will fall under the domination of China and the Soviet Union.[1]

—JOHN FOSTER DULLES, FEBRUARY 8, 1955

The question of peace or war in the Far East may be determined at the [Bandung] conference.[2]

—JOHN FOSTER DULLES, APRIL 9, 1955

U.S. leaders were anxious from the very beginning. The Bandung Conference provided China with an international forum, which the United States had tried to prevent, so China's participation was "clearly inimical" to the interests of the United States and the Western camp.[3] In the absence of Western countries, the Chinese Communists would make use of anticolonialism and drive a wedge between the conference attendees and the West. To meet the Chinese threat, U.S. leaders first attempted to sabotage the conference, but finally decided to manipulate the conference through friendly attendees. The State Department pushed pro-Western states to attend the meeting as U.S. proxies. As a result, although the United States was not an official attendee of the conference, it was an active participant behind the scenes.[4]

However, on the eve of the meeting, Dulles's obsession with the Taiwan Strait Crisis caused him to overestimate the Chinese aggression. Misbelieving that China would seek the conference attendees' support of its invasion of Taiwan, Dulles pushed U.S. allies to contain China by condemning the alleged Chinese aggression. Thus Washington created a war scare that worked against it when Zhou made the peace initiative. After realizing China was conciliatory instead of belligerent, as Dulles had suggested, both U.S. allies attending the conference and the American public pressured Washington to agree to negotiate with the PRC, although the Americans knew Zhou's overture was merely another peace offensive.

ATTEMPTS TO SABOTAGE THE CONFERENCE

The U.S. leaders were alerted to the threat China would pose in Bandung even before the Colombo Powers made up their minds about the conference. From the spring of 1954, U.S. officials anxiously observed China's exchanges of visits with India and Burma.[5] Shortly after China decided to pursue active diplomacy in Asia, CIA director Allen Dulles stated in August 1954 that the Communists "would emphasize Asia for the Asiatics and seek to increase neutralism to prevent the establishment of additional U.S. bases."[6] When the Bogor meeting finally decided to hold the Bandung Conference and invite China to attend in late December 1954, the assistant secretary of state for Far Eastern Affairs Walter Robertson immediately concluded that "the Bandung meeting would provide Chou En-lai [Zhou Enlai] with an excellent forum to broadcast Communist ideology to a naive audience in the guise of anti-colonialism."[7] Secretary Dulles warned U.S. diplomats that the conference

> might become a step forward for [the] Communists in their design of driving [a] wedge between Asian states and US. [The] Communists hope that they can develop such splits between non-Communist Asians and US that US will find it difficult politically cooperate with Asian states against Communists. In such circumstance Asian states would be exposed to eventual Communist engulfment.[8]

The State Department soon prepared a fairly accurate analysis of China's policy with regard to Bandung. As a part of the Communist peace offensive, Chinese leaders sought to formulate an Asian area of collective peace to exclude the Western influence, and the Bandung Conference would provide China with a great opportunity to advance that objective by both settling differences with Asian states and expanding China's influence in Asia.[9] Moreover, the Chinese threat would go beyond Asia. According to Dulles, "if the nations invited to Bandung, acquired the habit of meeting from time to time without Western participation, India and China because of their vast populations will very certainly dominate the scene and that one by-product will be a very solid block of anti-Western votes in the United Nations." He also linked Chinese intentions in Asia with Soviet efforts to exclude the United States in Europe and warned about a "Communist engulfment" of states in Europe, Asia, and Africa through "continental groupings" excluding the United States.[10] In addition to the obvious anti-colonialism theme, the Chinese would seek the conference's support of the Five Principles of Peaceful Coexistence and China's entry into the UN. The Americans generally agreed that although the Communist invitees—China and the DRV—were in the absolute minority, China would still dominate the conference because none of the other attendees would have "the stature to rebut Communist propaganda effectively on behalf of the free world." Robertson was impressed by Zhou's "skillful diplomatic machinations at Geneva" and predicted that Bandung would be a "rigged conference."[11]

When U.S. officials started to seriously deliberate the issue, they found themselves in a dilemma: The United States definitely did not want China to get its way, but it could not oppose the conference because that would lead to attendees' resentment about the United States infringing upon their sovereignty and prompt an "anti-western orientation of the conference." State Department officials concluded that Western opposition to the conference could only help the Communist propaganda, which was already playing on colonialism and imperialism to unite the conference invitees against the West.[12]

Their best policy option was to get the conference delayed or canceled in a way that did not alienate Asian and African states. The U.S. embassy in Ceylon believed that if "a considerable number of nations declined to attend the Afro-Asian Conference, the sponsoring countries would very probably postpone it."[13] Meanwhile, U.S. officials learned that France opposed the conference and instructed its embassies in Africa to dissuade the Gold Coast, Liberia, Ethiopia, and the Central African Federation from attending the Bandung Conference.[14] A study of responses to the conference invitation in early January also suggested that the invitees generally lacked interest.[15] Based on this information, Robertson and Director Dulles concluded that the United States "might be able to delay and forestall the meeting by suggesting to friendly countries that they ask sponsors to furnish a detailed agenda and information regarding procedures to be followed at the meeting place."[16] This process would be both time consuming and embarrassing for the sponsors because they themselves remained ambivalent about the purposes of the conference and had disagreed over whether they should invite China and DRV, instead of the GMD and SV, according to a State Department estimate.[17]

Secretary Dulles concluded that "if, without using strong-arm methods we can prevent the Conference from taking place we would welcome the outcome; but we are not prepared openly to oppose it or to threaten lest such a posture elicit an unwanted counter reaction."[18] The State Department sent a circular telegram to U.S. ambassadors in the area requesting them to privately ask local governments to "withhold decision on [the] invitation and also refrain from taking [a] public position on [the] question of attendance" in an effort to either delay the conference or get it canceled with more invitees dragging their feet.[19] Dulles believed that the Arab states were "the key to the success of the Conference," so U.S. diplomats started to pressure representatives of these states in Cairo not to attend the Bandung Conference.[20] Washington paid particular attention to Egypt, the leader of Arab states. In the UN, U.S. Ambassador Henry Cabot Lodge Jr. warned Egypt's representative not to attend the conference, and he hoped Egypt decision would lead to the absence of other Arab states, although Dulles knew that "the price for wrecking the Afro-Asian Conference by using our influence in Egypt's might be extremely high."[21] Meanwhile, Dulles wanted to feel out the British. He told British ambassador Roger Makins that "it would be vastly preferable that the conference should not meet at all. This result could only be achieved if the Arabs stayed away. Egypt might be the key here. If the Arabs went, they, plus the convening powers, would be a quorum, and the conference could not be prevented."[22]

However, the United Kingdom opposed the policy.[23] Makins told Dulles bluntly that "London believes that it would be a mistake to oppose holding of the conference or to attempt to keep invitees from attending," and it believed there was no chance to get the conference postponed. Instead, according to the British, the best policy was to "encourage good people to attend from friendly countries but otherwise develop an attitude of aloofness" in public to avoid alienating the attendees.[24] The British had come to this conclusion after learning a hard lesson. Due to its colonial interests in Asia and Africa, the British government responded to the Bandung problem much earlier than Washington. In October, after learning most Colombo Powers were not very interested in the Bandung proposal, the British diplomats had attempted to dissuade the Commonwealth members, particularly Pakistan and Ceylon, from supporting the conference proposal.[25] Before the Bogor meeting, Eden told Krishna Menon, who was visiting London on behalf of Nehru, that "any conference which included the Chinese Communists at this time together with all the Colombo Powers would make a bad impression here and in the U.S."[26] Nehru's response was quick and furious. He told the Indian officials: "For us to be told, therefore, that the US and the UK will not like the inclusion of China in the Afro-Asian Conference is not very helpful. In fact, it is somewhat irritating. There are many things that the US and the UK have done which we do not like at all."[27] Therefore, after the Bogor meeting, the British immediately reversed the policy and started to privately encourage friendly states to attend the conference on behalf of the United Kingdom.[28]

Other major U.S. allies agreed with the British. The French supported Asian states attending the conference to fight Communism, although they prevented African states from going to Bandung.[29] An Australian diplomat told his American colleagues that his country believed that "the Conference would take place and that free countries would participate. With that in mind, it would be important that the non-Communist delegations coordinate together and present a solid front to thwart the Communist manipulation of the Conference."[30] The GMD government, whom the Americans did not consult, believed that neither the United States nor the GMD had the means to disrupt the Bandung Conference. Indeed, the GMD leaders made an accurate prediction of the Communist policy: Beijing wanted to expand the zone of peace to weaken U.S. power; through promoting peaceful coexistence, it wanted to pressure the United States to remove its forces from Taiwan and to admit the PRC into the UN.[31]

Reports from U.S. diplomats in the region confirmed the British judgment. Indeed, U.S. embassies in Burma, Ceylon, Indonesia, Pakistan, and Turkey had reported that it was unlikely to prevent the conference.[32] A State Department intelligence report drafted in late January concluded that the Bandung Conference would be "well-attended," even if the Westerners persuaded some invitees from going to Bandung. Out out of the thirty invitees, the United States and the United Kingdom could influence the decision of a maximum of fourteen states, including eight states the United States could swing—Japan, Turkey, Iran, Thailand, Laos, the Philippines, Ethiopia, and South Vietnam, all of which would otherwise choose to attend the conference had the United States not resisted—and six states the United Kingdom could convince: the Gold Coast, Sudan, the Central African Federation, Iraq, and Jordan.[33] If pro-Western nations failed to attend, the conference attendees would blame Western intervention for their absences. That resentment would alienate the neutralist countries and allow China to exert more influence in Bandung. Indeed, alleged Western interference had already created more publicity for the meeting. U.S. diplomatic reports confirmed that both the Soviet Union and China used their propaganda to exploit Western intervention to separate Asian and African states from the United States. According to the State Department analysis, if these pro-Western states attended, they could probably prevent the conference from supporting the Communist agenda. If they could convince more attendees, they should even be able to stop the Chinese Communists from either dominating the conference or getting the endorsement to its Five Principles or denunciation of the West.[34] According to the U.S. embassy in Turkey, if the United States could "encourage [the] maximum attendance [of] anti-Communist countries" to send their "strongest possible" representatives to attend the conference, the Bandung Conference could "actually provide [a] real opportunity [to] confound Chinese Communist and counteract neutralist tendencies."[35]

RECRUITING ALLIES

The State Department reversed its policy in late January. When Dulles received confirmation that China was attending the conference and would "miss no opportunities to turn [the] conference emotions against the US and to present subtly its own case as 'leader and liberator of colonial peoples,' "[36] he started to encourage U.S. friends to "send ablest possible representation" to meet the Chinese threat. On January 25, the State Department sent a circular telegram requesting U.S. embassies to warn local governments:

(a) Communists will attempt "rig" Conference (b) Main Communist purpose at Conference will be divide free Asian countries from their Western friends (c) Conference will be used by Communists as vehicle for propaganda purposes throughout area (d) Unless non-Communist countries exercise utmost caution and alertness they will find themselves joining in adoption of resolutions suggesting common purposes with Communist bloc and which could only be misunderstood by non-Communist nations not participating in Conference.[37]

Tactically, the Chinese would play on colonialism and imperialism to challenge U.S. relations with these newly independent states and to convince the conference to endorse the Five Principles, which would commit Asian and African states against cooperation with the United States and incorporate them into the so-called zone of peace. Unfortunately, China seemed to have successfully recruited four of the five Colombo Powers, excluding Pakistan, according to a State Department intelligence report. All of them had recognized and developed good relations with the Communist regime. Still worse, they more or less shared China's opposition to U.S. military alliances in Asia. U.S. diplomats predicted that China would continue to use "sweet reasonableness" to separate more Asian states from the United States in Bandung.[38]

In response to the Chinese threat, the U.S. tactic was to turn anticolonialism against the Communists by attacking the Soviets as new colonialists and convincing the attendees that the "major division in Conference is between Communist countries and all others, not (as Communists will try have it) between 'U.S. stooges' and all others." Therefore, while collaborating with European allies behind the scenes, Washington publicly kept a distance from these colonial powers. The focus of U.S. diplomacy was to encourage its allies in Bandung to make use of anti-Communism to attack Soviet colonialism and discredit the Five Principles China was promoting.[39] The major objectives were: "(1) successful rebuttal of Communist charges, and (2) encouragement of an affirmative attitude by the Conference toward Free World and U.S. achievements and goals."[40] U.S. diplomats were cautioned to refrain from showing "undue interest" that might be perceived as the United States using the conference for its own gain, lest the Chinese exploit U.S. actions to provoke anti-Western sentiments.[41]

U.S. policy required close cooperation with the United Kingdom, which was pleased that the United States shifted its policy and eager to collaborate with the United States.[42] The British government was most worried that the Bandung Conference would enable Asian nationalism to influence the African attendees and form an anticolonial bloc, devastating its colonial interests. To prevent that, the British relied on concerted efforts with allies to influence the participants. After a careful analysis of the attendees, the Foreign Office instructed its diplomats to cooperate with the Americans to hold "full and frank discussions" with friendly and allied countries, especially the Philippines, Thailand, Pakistan, Turkey, Iran, and Japan.

Meanwhile, British officials were busy mobilizing Ceylon, SV, Lebanon, Burma, and Nepal for support.[43]

For Washington, the Bangkok Conference of the SEATO members in late February provided an important opportunity to coordinate positions with allies. During the meeting, Dulles worked hard to convince the attendees that there was a well-coordinated Communist strategy to dominate Southeast Asia, and hence unity among the SEATO members was crucial to meet the Communist threat. He warned the French ally,

> If France, Great Britain, and the U.S. are excluded from Asian affairs then the entire region will fall under the domination of China and the Soviet Union. Accordingly, it was of first importance that the Bangkok Conference should present a success to the world and thereby demonstrate that free Asian countries and western countries could deal together with profit and harmony.[44]

Throughout the meeting, Dulles stressed the danger of Communist expansion as a common threat to SEATO members. Meanwhile, he demonstrated goodwill to please the Bandung Conference attendees. At his request, the conference communiqué included a "guarded welcome" to the Bandung Conference that Dulles hoped was a "good touch, which, if properly played, can have an excellent propaganda value, and to some extent put the conference on the spot."[45]

In the meantime, the Americans started intense diplomacy focusing on the "uncommitted elements in neutralist countries" and Western allies.[46] While U.S. diplomats sought help from these governments, the State Department was busy preparing "ammunitions," such as background briefings, draft statements, resolutions, and communiqués, for them to use on behalf of the United States in Bandung. To their relief, the Americans found several ardent supporters from both allies and sponsors of the Bandung meeting.[47]

The government of the Philippines, a U.S. ally and former colony, followed the U.S. diplomacy and adopted an anti-Communist, anti-neutralist policy.[48] It did not recognize the PRC and continued diplomatic relationship with the GMD. It was initially reluctant to participate in the Bandung Conference because most Filipinos believed China's participation would "subvert the conference to communist aims."[49] At the U.S. suggestion, the government agreed to attend and promised to report the development of the Bandung Conference. The Filipino ambassador to the United States, General Carlos Romulo, was eager to serve as the U.S. agent in Bandung.[50] But he needed U.S. help to send him to Bandung in the first place, a request the Americans were more than happy to satisfy, because the conference invited premiers or foreign ministers, and thus Romulo was not an eligible candidate.[51] Soon Romulo reported that he learned from the Indonesian ambassadors that the conference would seek two resolutions: anticolonialism and admittance of China into the UN. He asked the Americans to provide counter resolutions to be used in Bandung.[52] Romulo also requested background briefings and suggestions about the subjects China would be likely to raise. He strongly suggested cooperating with other pro-Western states, such as Thailand, Pakistan, and Turkey, as well as some Arab delegations.[53] U.S. officials satisfactorily observed that Romulo would "likely be one of the most effective spokesmen [of the] free world at Bandung."[54]

Washington also successfully mobilized the support of Turkey, which had been a member of NATO since 1952. At the request of the United States, Turkey initiated to coordinate positions with Greece and Yugoslavia on common interests, including military matters. It also joined the Middle East Treaty Organization, or Balkan Pact, with the United Kingdom, Iran, Iraq, and Pakistan as a proxy of U.S. interests in February 1955. Before the Bandung Conference, the Turks urgently needed U.S. economic and military assistance, but they worried that U.S. attention had been diverted from Turkey, so they were eager to work for the United States. The Americans were well aware of this. Washington in turn pushed the Turks to stand up to the Communists on behalf of the United States, and Dulles pushed Egypt to collaborate with the Turkish delegation in Bandung.[55] To encourage the Turks, the United States signed a loan agreement worth twenty million dollars on April 22, 1955, right in the middle of the Bandung Conference. Although the Turks were unprepared for the conference and reluctant to stand publicly on the side of the West among fellow Asian and African countries, they decided to serve as a U.S. "Trojan horse" in Bandung.[56]

Pakistan was an extremely important ally for the United States and was also one of the sponsors of the Bandung Conference. As a U.S. ally, the Pakistanis opposed participation of the PRC, although it had diplomatic relations with the Communist regime.[57] When approached by the Americans, the Pakistani diplomats informed Washington of their plan for conducting the conference. They predicted that the Five Principles would be proposed, but they assured the Americans that they would oppose any resolution adopting this—nevertheless, Pakistan would agree to admit China into the UN—and would fight for the principle of collective security to defend U.S. military alliances if they were raised in the conference.[58] The Pakistani prime minister was optimistic and believed pro-Western states would be able to "deflate Communists and neutralists." He asserted:

> why should we be afraid [of] Chou En-lai[?] I am not afraid of him, I am not afraid to fight. This will be the first time he has crossed the equator and if all anti-Communist nations attend we can clobber him and any neutral efforts of Nehru. I promise you we will not give one inch. Let's show the world that this man they are so afraid of can come out into the world and not pollute the anti-Communist bloc. We can and will deflate him.[59]

Although the Americans were satisfied with his "spirit and intentions," and trusted the "wholehearted cooperation [of the] GOP [government of Pakistan] in combatting Communist efforts," they worried that "his abilities may not equal his spirit." The Americans were also aware that the Pakistanis may hesitate to play an active role to avoid alienating the conference, if it was dominated by the neutralists. But if more anti-Communist states went to Bandung, especially under the leadership of someone with "real courage and resourcefulness," the prime minister could be expected to play a more effective part. Therefore, the U.S. State Department encouraged the Pakistanis to join other allies, such as Turkey, Thailand, Philippines, and Japan, to work out the avenues to better counter the Communists in Bandung.[60]

Ceylon, another sponsor of the meeting, also agreed to help, which probably resulted from the British effort.[61] The Ceylonese had posed an anti-Communist stance at the Colombo conference opposing Communist interference in Asia. After the Bogor meeting, both its prime minister and foreign minister confided in the Americans that Burma was mainly responsible for inviting China, against the resistance of Ceylon and Pakistan, and India had attempted to force the Five Principles into the Bogor summation report. The U.S. ambassador in Colombo concluded the premier could be counted on as an ally against the Chinese in Bandung, due to his anti-Communist stance.[62] Indeed, the Ceylonese were not disappointing; they assured the Americans that they were determined to oppose the Chinese Communists, although the latter would dominate the Bandung Conference with the support of India and Burma on anticolonialism. To better meet the Chinese threat, they requested background briefings on the Five Principles and on issues of peaceful co-existence. The Ceylonese also sought American suggestions on counter proposals and tactics to fight the Communists in Bandung. Ceylonese prime minister John Kotelawala promised he would "ask Zhou Enlai 'blunt questions'." He offered to send the U.S. ambassador the speeches he would make at the conference.[63]

After extensive exchanges with the Ceylonese officials, the U.S. embassy in Ceylon concluded that "it can be expected that the Ceylonese delegation will be strongly anti-communist, anti-neutralist and generally favorable to the principles and ideals of the western world." However, the officials were concerned that "the Prime Minister and other members of his delegation will neither be strong enough, well enough briefed or sufficiently versed in international affairs to cope with such giants as Nehru and Chou En lai."[64] Indeed, according to a State Department intelligence estimate, the prime minister appeared "to indulge in considerable wishful thinking regarding the influence he expects to exert." They also knew that "Ceylon would be reluctant to seriously offend China so long as its trade agreement with that country continues in force."[65] Therefore, Ceylon's contribution was limited to following other anti-Communist states. The Americans pushed the Ceylonese to consult with the other anti-Communist non-neutral states, including Japan, Turkey, Thailand, Pakistan and the Philippines.[66]

While encouraging allies to meet the Chinese threat in Bandung, Washington was relieved by reports from diplomats in the region: the two leading neutralist states, India and Burma, would take a moderate position in Bandung. According to the U.S. embassy to Burma, China would not be able to dominate the conference, and the final communiqué would be general. The Burmese delegation would not take sides if the Taiwan issue was discussed, although Burma believed Taiwan legally belonged to China. Indeed, Burma was still vigilant regarding China's interference in its internal affairs, and U.S. diplomats in Rangoon thought it was not likely to ally the Chinese in Bandung.[67] The U.S. embassy in New Delhi reported that India had a "rather half-hearted interest" in the conference and had "a strong desire to avoid becoming involved in highly contentious exchanges." Therefore, it would be unwilling to discuss specific issues like Taiwan and would rather propose a "broad outline" on economic development and cooperation, cultural exchange, and cessation of nuclear experiments.[68]

Based on these reports, the State Department concluded that China would focus on promoting the unity of Asian and African states instead of pursuing specific objectives. Earlier, U.S. officials had concluded that the Chinese knew the limit of their influence and would avoid pushing the conference to endorse their agenda. Therefore, State Department officials predicted that the conference resolutions would not have any operative clauses and would just include an agreement on general principles, such as a peaceful solution to world problems, independence of former colonial countries, equality of races, the danger of hydrogen bomb tests, cultural and economic exchanges between countries, and settlement in Vietnam and the integrity of Laos and Cambodia.[69]

DULLES'S OBSESSION WITH THE TAIWAN STRAIT

Dulles's obsession with the Taiwan Strait Crisis had caused him to reestimate Chinese aggression. After his trip to Asia to attend the SEATO conference in Bangkok, Dulles overestimated Chinese aggression and in early March believed a Chinese invasion of the offshore islands or even Taiwan was imminent, although ironically, at this time tensions in the Taiwan Strait were cooling down. Eisenhower agreed with his judgment, and based on this misperception, Washington publicly threatened China with atomic bombs. But the threats did not seem to deter Communist aggression. In late March, Washington was worried about "a real probability of war with Communist China." Dulles feared that the Chinese would enlist the Bandung Conference's endorsement of its invasion plan and start the attack after the meeting.[70] U.S. officials in Taiwan added to his anxiety; they warned of the Communist buildup and requested approval for the GMD to launch a preemptive attack on the Communist airfields.[71] Dulles accepted the British suggestion to use the Bandung Conference to restrain the Chinese, and he told the British ambassador to the United States that he worried the conference may pass a resolution supporting the Chinese:

If any resolution or statement came out of Bandung which seemed to give a green light to the Chinese Communists to take Formosa, the possibility of hostilities which could not be confined to the offshore islands and Formosa was greatly enhanced. If, on the other hand, some resolution or statement could come out of Bandung calling for a cease-fire and calling on both parties not to resort to force, the chances of maintaining peace in that area would be very considerably enhanced. In other words, *the question of war or peace in the Far East could be significantly affected by what happens at Bandung.*[72]

Dulles said he had decided to urge friendly countries to propose a ceasefire if the subjects of peace or Taiwan came up at the conference. He urged the British to use their influence in Asia "so that both the Formosa situation and the over-all problem of pan-Asianism might not become more aggravated" in Bandung.[73] In addition, the State Department sent telegrams to the U.S. ambassadors to Turkey, Japan, Pakistan, Thailand, Iran, Iraq, and Egypt pushing their delegations to restrain China in Bandung.[74]

Although the British had originally concluded that the Chinese had limited ambition in the Taiwan Strait, they also became anxious after the crisis had lasted for more than eight months. On the one hand, they were worried that the Americans would lose their patience and rush into a nuclear attack on China. Makins warned:

> there is a large element of face involved on the American side, which combines with hatred of Communists, particularly Chinese Communists, dislike of further retreat in the face of Communist pressure and other emotional attitudes to induce in some people a kind of resignation and disposition to bow to the inevitable. Dulles himself is not immune from the infection of fatalism.[75]

On the other hand, they believed the Chinese had the capabilities to attack the offshore islands. An estimate by the British Joint Intelligence Committee in late March said, "the Chinese Communists are serious in their declared intention to capture these two islands [Jinmen and Mazu]. It is believed that they have the immediate capability to carry out the invasions successfully against Nationalist [GMD] opposition." The British predicted that "it is probable that the Chinese Communists will try air and artillery action in the next 3 months, although they may not feel it safe to risk an invasion. Nevertheless an attempt at a landing is a possibility which should not be excluded and if it is made Matsu is the more likely objective."[76] Agreeing with Dulles on using the Bandung Conference to restrain Chinese aggression, the Foreign Office telegrammed the British embassies in the area:

Our first objective in trying to deal with the problem of Formosa and the coastal islands has been to get both sides [to] renounce the use of force. The Chinese Communists have so far steadily refused to do so. We do not of course know whether the Bandung Conference will pass a series of resolutions or simply issue a final communiqué; nor whether the Chinese will press for specific support in some form of their claims to Formosa and the islands. If they do we hope the Conference will resist the suggestion.[77]

The Commonwealth Relations Office sent a draft resolution calling for the Chinese to renounce the use of force for the Commonwealth members to use in Bandung.[78]

In the meantime, Dulles pushed other allies for help. When he met Romulo to discuss the opening statement the latter planned to make in Bandung, the secretary of state again stressed the seriousness of the situation in the Taiwan Strait. It was "possible that the Chinese Communist decision as to whether they should attack Quemoy [Jinmen], Matsu [Mazu] and Taiwan might depend on the attitude which they found among the powers meeting at the Bandung conference," the secretary said, "the Chinese Communists have publicly and at great length announced their intention of attacking Taiwan." In that scenario, he wanted Romulo to introduce a resolution to push the Chinese toward both a ceasefire and the renunciation of the use of force in the Taiwan Strait. He suggested that if the Communists agreed to those, the United States would reconsider its policy of helping Chiang protect Jinmen and Mazu. Dulles gave Romulo a draft resolution to be used in Bandung to push the Chinese to renounce the use of force in the Taiwan Strait area.[79]

U.S. officials continued to look for new allies to contain the Chinese aggression. They pushed Charles Malik, the pro-American Lebanese ambassador to the United States, to attend the Bandung Conference on behalf of the Western states because they believed Malik, a famous diplomat and philosopher, could influence the Arab states.[80] Immediately after the State Department officials approached Malik, Dulles personally met Malik and told him that "the question of peace or war in the Far East may be determined at the conference" because "the Communist Chinese would probably use the conference as a means of ascertaining whether their use of force to capture Formosa would have the moral support of the countries of Asia as a whole." Moreover, "there was a very real danger that it [the conference] might establish firmly in Asia a tendency to follow an anti-Western and 'anti-white' course, the consequences of which for the future could be incalculably dangerous." Dulles encouraged the Lebanese to stand up to the Chinese threat in Bandung.[81]

Three days before the Bandung Conference, State Department officials concluded that "there is no doubt that Chou En-lai will raise the Taiwan issue under the general category of colonialism, which is now defined by the Communists to mean direct Western military intervention in the affairs of Asian countries." To form a united front with India and Indonesia, China would include under the theme of colonialism such issues as Korea, Indochina, and Goa in India and Western New Guinea in Indonesia. According to the State Department memorandum,

> The major unknown factor in Communist behavior at Bandung concerns the degree to which Chou En-lai will play upon fears of war by threatening action against Taiwan. Chou will certainly attempt to convince the conferees that responsibility for any war over Taiwan rests with the US. At the same time, he will probably press for a ten-power conference on Taiwan, as endorsed by the recent New Delhi conference, and will maintain that "peaceful liberation" is possible only if the US withdraws its forces from the area. *No real Chinese Communist concessions on Taiwan and no new and startling proposals concerning negotiations appear imminent.*[82]

The State Department took several actions to meet the Chinese threat. It instructed U.S. diplomats to request U.S. friends to "stress an offensive rather than defensive approach," and it took concerted actions "not only to prevent the Communists from exploiting the Conference to the detriment of the U.S., but also to turn the Conference to the positive benefits of the free world."[83] Dulles called the CIA deputy director of plans to make sure people in the agency "[have] done enough imaginative thinking on it [Bandung]," which was understood to mean an expectation of spreading information to influence the conference to the benefit of the United States. He was glad to be told that CIA officials "have put their most able and imaginative people on the job. They have irons in the fire in the field and are using contacts . . . and seeking to influence them."[84] When discussing how to win the support of the conference attendees at NSC, Eisenhower "remarked facetiously that perhaps the best way for the U.S. to handle this matter was to give a few thousand dollars to each of the delegates." Subsequently, the week before the Bandung meeting, Eisenhower declared the mutual defense program. He promised to send more economic assistance to states in South and Southeast Asia, in addition to stressing intensified cooperation.[85] The congressional debate over the bill of the Asian Development Fund took place simultaneously with the Bandung Conference.[86] The day before the meeting, Dulles made one final effort; at a press conference, he said that he and the president had "discussed the grave implications of an extensive build-up, now in progress, by the Chinese Communists of offensive airpower on the China mainland opposite Formosa" and that the president hoped the Bandung Conference would "voice the peaceful aspirations of the peoples of the world and thus exert a practical influence for peace where peace is now in grave jeopardy."[87]

BACKLASH

In Bandung, the U.S. allies launched a series of offensives just as Washington planned, attacking Soviet colonialism and challenging the credibility of the Five Principles. Their fear of a war in the Taiwan Strait, however, one which had been exaggerated by Dulles, played into the hands of Zhou. Making use of the publicity in Bandung, Zhou initiated another peace offensive by proposing to negotiate directly with the United States.

The initial U.S. reaction to Zhou's overture was an immediate rejection. On the same day Zhou made his proposal, after consulting James Hagerty, Eisenhower's press secretary, the State Department issued a statement that requested the Chinese to provide evidence to demonstrate their sincerity, taking such actions as declaring a ceasefire in the Taiwan Strait, releasing the Americans detained in China, and agreeing to go to the UN to discuss the Taiwan Strait Crisis. In addition, the Americans wanted Taiwan to join any potential talk as an equal party, a request that was bound to be rejected by Chinese leaders. This response was based on the understanding that the Chinese initiative aimed to "establish a basis for throwing the onus for Far Eastern tensions on the United States, thus enabling the Communist propagandists to utilize the fear of war as a means of isolating the United States." Simply put, it was just another hoax, because Zhou did not indicate that China gave up its plan of invading Taiwan.[88]

The U.S. response provoked a big backlash in Bandung. Conference attendees generally welcomed China's peace initiative, and U.S. Asian allies pushed Washington to negotiate with the Chinese. Convinced of Zhou's "sincere desire for Sino-American negotiations leading to a peaceful settlement," the Ceylonese, Pakistani, and Thai prime ministers immediately informed their U.S. ally of this "significant departure" from China's previous belligerence. They pushed the Americans to consider the Chinese proposal seriously.[89] Indeed, the U.S. rejection made these allies feel betrayed; they thought the peace initiative was exactly what Dulles wanted and they had worked hard to achieve. The Pakistani prime minister believed Zhou's initiative was "a great move," and the Ceylonese prime minister blamed the Americans for dismissing "without thinking" such a "reasonable and sincere" proposal.[90] The frustration of U.S. allies was later best summarized by Romulo, who told the Americans that, for U.S. allies, the State Department response was "a slamming of the door which put them in a very bad position vis-à-vis Chou En-lai after their strong attack on Communism."[91] Under the allied pressures, Washington had to make concessions, as Dulles later admitted.[92]

These Asian allies disliked the State Department statement, but the Western allies were equally disappointed. For the British diplomats in Washington, the statement was "hasty and unimaginative" and regarded as "a serious mistake in tactics."[93] Although the British were clear that Zhou's initiative was "no more than a skillful and plausible version of the previous position of the Chinese government," and it did not "indicate any softening of the Chinese position," they felt the proposal could lead to a peaceful solution to the problem and get the United States off the hook in the Taiwan Strait.[94] Therefore, the British Foreign Office told its diplomats that "we can hardly urge a renunciation of force and the peaceful settlement of disputes on the one hand, but at the same time refuse to negotiate on the other."[95] When Dulles asked the British to help the United States figure out if the Chinese were really "sincere," the British Foreign Office responded that it would not talk to the Chinese unless the United States first agreed to negotiate with China. The reason was that if the United States was "prepared to discuss the Formosa question subject to certain conditions, this would put the ball back in the Chinese court and might enable us to discover whether the Chinese were sincere in their professions more readily than would the posing of any direction question."[96] The Australian diplomats believed the U.S. response to Zhou's initiative was "disturbing to some normally pro-western delegates whose hopes for an Asian settlement had been raised high by Chou's offer."[97] Meanwhile, the French prime minister told a press conference that Zhou's proposal "should be considered as serious and interesting." Furthermore, he criticized the U.S. containment of China in general: "one cannot continue to ignore a government which controls more than half a milliard human beings."[98]

Back at home, both the American public and Congress criticized the State Department and favored a direct talk with the Chinese. According to a Gallup poll, the Americans were so nervous about a conflict with China over Taiwan that by mid-April over 80 percent of the Americans polled felt the United States should talk to the Communists "to see if a peaceful solution can be worked out in the Formosan dispute."[99] In his radio talk, Adlai Stevenson, the influential Democratic Party's presidential candidate in both 1952 and 1956, strongly attacked the U.S. policy of getting involved in the offshore islands.[100] In keeping with public opinion, Congressional leaders attacked the State Department's rigidity. On the same day Zhou made the overture, Walter George, the powerful chairman of the Senate Foreign Relations Committee, told the American Society of Newspaper Editors that the United States "should be big enough and great enough, through its highest officials, to talk to him [Zhou]," regardless of his sincerity.[101] Three days later, he directly said he "would be willing to waive the condition that the Nationalists should be presented" to talk to the Chinese.[102] George's suggestion got the support of other heavyweight Democratic leaders. Soon senators J. William Fulbright and John F. Kennedy, and Chester Bowles, former U.S. ambassador to India, pushed the administration to start a serious dialogue with Beijing. When the Democrats controlled both the Senate and the House, their pressure exerted a critical influence on Dulles and Eisenhower, as Dulles admitted.[103]

Under these pressures, U.S. leaders promptly reversed their policy.[104] Only three days after the State Department's statement, Dulles, who had just returned from a vacation and was not involved in the first statement, told a press conference that the United States would be willing to enter into talks with China, without Taiwan's participation, to see if China's proposal was sincere.[105] The next day, Eisenhower also announced that the United States was willing to discuss issues such as a ceasefire in the Taiwan Strait and American citizens detained in China with the Chinese.[106]

To this new position, London offered its ready support. The Foreign Office wasted no time in instructing British diplomats to "concentrate on exploiting the new situation created by Mr. Dulles' reaction to Chou

En-lai's statement" to bring about a direct U.S.-China talk, which the British expected would not only push the Chinese to refrain from using force in the Taiwan Strait but also lead to a final solution to U.S.-China confrontation.[107] The Foreign Office was most "anxious not to miss an opportunity where we could play a useful part" and told Trevelyan to "seek an interview with Mr. Chou En-lai as soon as possible after his return to Peking [Beijing]" to help set up the U.S.-China talks.[108] Meanwhile, the Commonwealth Relations Office told British diplomats to immediately encourage the Commonwealth members to exploit the new situation.[109] The Australians realized that there was an "opportunity to explore settlement much wider than that of the offshore problem," and the prime minister promptly suggested Dulles invite China to the proposed four-power conference to make it a five-power conference.[110]

When the Bandung Conference was over, U.S. officials, especially Dulles, found the meeting was actually a "gift" to the United States.[111] Admitting that Zhou made some personal success, Washington was glad that the Chinese failed to achieve anything substantial: a unity of neutralism and Communism did not come true; an anti-Western bloc failed to materialize; instead of getting the conference support of China's invasion of Taiwan, Zhou was forced to seek peace and initiated negotiation with the United States; and the Five Principles were watered down and juxtaposed with justification of U.S. military alliances containing China. As a result, the Bandung Conference communiqué turned out to be "a document which we ourselves could subscribe to. Even its references to colonialism were in accord with what we feel in our hearts (though we are unable to say them publicly)." Dulles suggested that the conference also restrained the PRC as Washington expected and the Taiwan Strait was closer to a ceasefire. "This is a good development but we don't boast about it." He attributed the success to the "great amount of pressure which was put on Chou to refrain from acts of violence" by U.S. allies. During the conference, Dulles sent numerous telegrams to thank those allies who "put on an amazing performance at Bandung with a teamwork and coordination of strategy which was highly gratifying—even though none of them enjoyed the personal prestige of Chou."[112] After the meeting, he expressed appreciation in person to Romulo of the Philippines and Malik of Lebanon, as well as some Turkish officials.[113]

On second thought, however, the Americans were less sanguine. First of all, the United States was not able to alienate China from the conference, hence it was a failure of the policy of containment. U.S. officials realized that while attacking Soviet Communists none of the delegates targeted China directly. Indeed, the Pakistani prime minister publicly singled out China by saying "China is by no means an imperialist nation and she has no satellites."[114] Zhou's conciliation convinced most conference attendees of China's peace intentions, including U.S. allies such as Thailand, the Philippines, Ceylon, and Pakistan. The Pakistani prime minister emerged as "the great disappointment" for the United States. After two meetings with Zhou in Bandung, the Pakistani leader found China gave him "virtually everything we asked for. We found nothing to fight." According to British diplomats, the Ceylonese prime minister was "obviously impressed by Chou's behavior at Bandung." As a result, both prime ministers planned to visit China soon.[115] The Pakistani prime minister finally paid his official visit to China in 1956, following the Egyptian leaders, and Ceylon established formal diplomacy with China in 1957. Romulo told the Americans that the Thai prime minister was "completely 'beguiled'" by Zhou and "took an increasingly soft attitude toward Chinese Communism and apparently believed all their promises to him."[116] One month after the conference, both the British and American officials realized that anti-Communism was indeed diminished in Asia, and they predicted that a tendency toward neutralism would grow. As Malik told Dulles after his return from Bandung:

> The most important result [of the conference] was the strengthening of Communist China; it won friends and good will. In fact, the conference appeared staged for this purpose. Three things are now clear: (1) it will be difficult for the US now not to negotiate with Communist China; (2) it will be difficult for the US to counter the good will generated towards Communist China; (3) it will be difficult for the US to keep Communist China out of the UN.[117]

Furthermore, Dulles's exaggeration of the Chinese aggression in the Taiwan Strait backfired. Chinese leaders did not seek the conference support of its invasion of either Taiwan or the offshore islands, as Dulles had predicted.[118] So the secretary's obsession with Taiwan indeed misled U.S. allies and contributed to the war scare in Bandung. This in turn gave Zhou the opportunity to play on the momentum to mobilize U.S. allies to push the Americans to negotiate with China. The Americans had to admit that Zhou's "inexpensive tactical maneuver" was very successful. According to an OCB evaluation of the conference, "Chou's maneuver on Taiwan favorably impressed the delegates, placing the U.S. on the defensive. Chou utilized effectively the old Soviet trick of catering to the universal desire for peace, by appearing to make concessions, even though such a concession was simply a slight deviation from a previous attitude of complete refusal to discuss any phase of question."[119] Under pressure from allies and the U.S. public, and also out of a sense of relief that China finally sought peace after all the other moves failed to end the Taiwan Strait Crisis, Washington agreed to negotiate with Beijing, easily relinquishing their original position about nonrecognition of the Communist regime and Taiwan's participation. Moreover, the U.S. leaders reversed their policy without careful deliberations.[120] Worse still, in a desperate effort to get off the hook, Washington inadvertently gave the Communist regime more legitimacy: it declared it would negotiate with "the People's Republic of China," which was Washington's first public use of the official name of the regime it had refused to recognize.[121]

THE AMBASSADORIAL TALKS

They [the Chinese leaders] use prisoners as hostages to bargain for political advantages.[1]

—JOHN FOSTER DULLES, JUNE 14, 1955

It [negotiating with China] is minimum needed to preserve de facto cease-fire in Formosa Straits.[2]

—JOHN FOSTER DULLES, JULY 16, 1955

Although Eisenhower and Dulles agreed to negotiate with the Chinese, they were unwilling to start the talk. China's peace initiative resulted in a de facto ceasefire, so the United States had achieved its objective in the Taiwan Strait. Therefore, the Americans had "no reason for haste in establishing the contact," according to deputy undersecretary of state Robert Murphy, especially since the Chinese did not take any favorable actions on the issue of the American nationals detained in China.[3] Eisenhower told a press conference on April 29 that the United States adopted "a wait-and-see attitude" toward negotiation with the Chinese. If the Chinese upset the de facto ceasefire, they would be held responsible for changing the status quo.[4]

Accordingly, Washington adopted a delaying tactic. As Dulles told the British ambassador Roger Makins, "a détente [with China] at this time might change the situation and it is in our interest to play for time."[5] In response to the Australian prime minister's suggestion that China be included in the upcoming four-power summit that was to be held in Geneva in July 1955 alongside the United States, the United Kingdom, France, and the Soviet Union, Dulles replied that the PRC must first take actions to prove its sincerity in peace. He did not want to improve China's prestige, and U.S. public opinion opposed adding the PRC to the meeting.[6] Meanwhile, Dulles and Robertson reassured nervous GMD ambassador Wellington Koo that the United States would not take steps to contact the CCP unless the latter renounced the use of force in the Taiwan Strait.[7] When the Belgian foreign minister pushed Dulles to give up Chiang, whose "role in Asia was over," and negotiate with China to resolve the Taiwan question, "just as it had been necessary to deal with him [Zhou] to make peace in Korea and Indochina," Dulles demurred on the negotiation, while defending the alliance with Chiang.[8] In private, Dulles and Eisenhower decided to prevent any solution to the Taiwan issue at this time.[9]

Although Washington was "being flooded with" mediators, in Dulles's words, the secretary of state "had no intention whatsoever of going further (than getting Communist agreement to a ceasefire) without [the] Nationalist participation." He told the New Zealand ambassador that "he had no real confidence in a successful outcome of bilateral talks. They were a concession to friendly countries in Asia."[10] Washington declined numerous offers to mediate between the United States and China to facilitate the negotiation. Dulles told the Indonesian and Lebanese ambassadors that the United States was not short of intermediaries and their help was not needed.[11] Similarly, he refused the Pakistani premier, when the latter offered to let the Colombo Powers, the Philippines, and Thailand bring together the United States and China. Indeed, he was angry that the Pakistani premier was scheduled to visit China and told the U.S. ambassador to Pakistan to be aware of the consequences of the first visit to the Communist regime by a U.S. ally.[12]

Nevertheless, U.S. leaders had to contact the Chinese because the American public was concerned about those U.S. citizens detained in China. According to a national poll conducted in early May, about 70 percent of Americans and the majority of the U.S. media supported direct talks with the Chinese, and twelve leading Republican senators publicized their support of negotiation.[13] Under this pressure, Washington tried several means to get back the American detainees in China. U.S. representative to the UN Henry Lodge Jr. told UN Secretary-General Hammarskjöld to continue his efforts to get the U.S. pilots out of China as soon as possible, as "we were drawing near to the end of our hope here in the US and the situation could become ugly."[14] The State Department told the U.S. Embassy in New Delhi to encourage the Indians to push the Chinese for the same objective.[15]

In Geneva, U.S. diplomats sought more consular meetings with China that first started during the Geneva Conference.[16]

The Chinese leaders were clear about both Washington's needs and the differences between the Western states. The Chinese embassy in Switzerland reported to Beijing that the Europeans were excited by Zhou's initiative in Bandung. Although the press reports generally saw China's overture as a collaboration with the Soviet Union to split the Western states and win over neutral states, Britain and France wanted to get involved in the Sino-American negotiation.[17] Moreover, the British continued to press the United States for the GMD's evacuation from Jinmen and Mazu. Under allied pressure, the United States would have to negotiate with China. According to Chinese diplomats, Washington would set four conditions: (1) a peaceful solution of the Taiwan issue; (2) neutralization of the Taiwan Strait; (3) cessation of military action in the strait and coastal area; and (4) release of the detained American personnel.[18]

Beijing consequently exploited the general interest in diplomacy to pressure the United States. In contrast to the United States' rejection to offers of help, China welcomed all the intermediaries. Mao told the Pakistani ambassador that China wanted to coexist peacefully with the United States and solve any problem through negotiation.[19] Zhou welcomed the Indonesian offer of mediation. During the Indonesian prime minister's visit to China in late May, Mao stressed China's need for a peaceful environment and even offered a peace treaty with the United States, which could be effective for up to fifty or even a hundred years. Zhou told the Indonesians that China accepted all venues of negotiation with the Americans, as long as the GMD was not a party. He proposed two initiatives: (1) China would release some U.S. nationals and seek to liberate Taiwan peacefully, once tensions in the Taiwan Strait were reduced; (2) in return, the United States should revoke its trade embargo on China.[20]

China's diplomacy focused on Britain and India. On May 9, Zhou clarified with British chargé Humphrey Trevelyan that the subject of negotiation with the United States was reducing tensions, not ceasefire, as Dulles suggested, because there was no fighting between the two states.[21] Two weeks later, Zhou told Trevelyan that China was flexible about the venues of negotiation.

Chinese diplomats could meet the Americans either in a multilateral setting, such as the ten-power meeting suggested by the Soviet Union, or through direct bilateral negotiation. Zhou disclosed that China would take some initiatives to facilitate the negotiation. The Chinese government also planned to negotiate with Chiang directly and seek a peaceful liberation of Taiwan.[22]

Making use of India's enthusiasm in negotiation, Chinese leaders carefully designed a tactic to mobilize its support during Krishna Menon's visit to China as Nehru's emissary in mid-May. Catering to the Indian interest in leadership in international affairs, Chinese officials told Menon that although many countries wanted to mediate between the United States and China, China chose to work with India and would not share their ideas with other states. Meanwhile, Chinese officials deliberately told Menon different stories. While some military leaders expressed the determination to fight the Americans to play on Menon's worry, Zhou assured him that China was willing to negotiate with the Americans to reduce tensions.[23] The Chinese premier agreed to release some Americans detained in China, but asked Menon to press the United States to return the treatment, taking such actions as ending the trade embargo and releasing Chinese students and scholars stranded in the United States.[24] If the United States gave up its intervention in China's internal affairs and withdrew its forces from Taiwan, the Taiwan problem could be solved satisfactorily. Encouraged by the Chinese conciliation, Menon proposed an ambitious plan to fundamentally solve the Taiwan problem in three steps: first, the two countries should take actions to reduce tensions; second, they should consolidate the situation; and third, they should find an ultimate solution through long-term efforts.[25]

Beijing took two actions to demonstrate its good intentions. On May 13, 1955, at the Standing Committee of the First National People's Congress, Zhou declared that there were two different ways to retrieve Taiwan, through either war or peaceful means, and the PRC would seek peaceful means when possible.[26] Meanwhile, the Chinese government deported four U.S. pilots after they were judged by a Chinese court in late May. In addition to broadcasting this news, the Chinese diplomats approached their American counterparts in Geneva to brief the latter about China's efforts to reduce tensions.[27]

The Chinese leaders were confident they successfully mobilized support. Mao confided in the Soviet ambassador to Beijing how the Chinese maneuvered Menon. He was so satisfied with the tactic that he believed the

Indians would not even share the information with the British.[28] Zhou told the Soviet diplomat that he believed the United States needed negotiation, and major Asian neutral states supported China: Burma wanted China to negotiate with Chiang; Indonesia supported China's position on Taiwan and expected direct Sino-American talks; and India encouraged China to take the initiative to start the negotiation.[29]

The Chinese diplomacy worked. The litany of, in the words of Burmese prime minister U Nu, "peace brokers" put the Americans under great pressure. Britain, Indonesia, and Burma conveyed the Chinese message to the Americans, and the Indians launched an aggressive diplomacy in Washington, despite the fact that they were not even welcomed.[30] Menon assured Eisenhower and Dulles that the issue of detained Americans could be solved easily if the United States started direct negotiation with China. Because China had released some U.S. pilots, he suggested that the United States release Chinese students and allow journalists and relatives of the detained Americans to visit China, as Zhou requested.[31] Menon also pushed the United States to get Chiang out of the offshore islands as the first step toward a final solution of the Taiwan problem. He blamed the Americans for misunderstanding the Chinese leaders, who "wanted good relations with the US because it was not happy to remain dependent on the friendship of only one great power." Dulles told Menon bluntly that the United States would not put pressure on Chiang and that he found negotiation to find a "quick solution to the entire problem very dangerous because they would be more likely to end in war than in peace." But Menon did not give up and pressed for more meetings with Dulles and Eisenhower.[32]

Eisenhower and Dulles were "getting fed up with all the intermediaries," especially the "troublesome" Menon,[33] but they started to worry whether the ceasefire in the Taiwan Strait would last, as the CCP might lose patience. According to acting assistant secretary for Far Eastern affairs William Sebald, the United States had to negotiate with China to prevent the situation in the Taiwan Strait from becoming worse:

It seems unlikely that the Communists will be content to extend a de facto cease-fire situation indefinitely. We should avoid being pushed into a position where we (a) either must negotiate under disadvantageous conditions or

(b) face increasing Communist military activity against the off-shore islands putting us in the dilemma of allowing them to be lost or engaging ourselves in hostilities which would not have the support of our allies.[34]

The U.S. military agreed that the worry was reasonable. On June 30, CIA Director Allen Dulles briefed the NSC on the Chinese military buildup across the Taiwan Strait: while the Soviets transferred bombers, fighters, submarines, and destroyers to China, the Chinese were quickly "improving the road and rail network from the interior to the coast opposite Formosa." Director Dulles believed the CCP was unlikely to attack the offshore islands or Taiwan in the near future, but Radford seemed unconvinced. Instead, Radford stressed that the infrastructure project "was proceeding rapidly and urgently" and could be ready "in another month or six weeks."[35] Meanwhile, British foreign secretary Harold Macmillan sent a letter to Dulles, suggested negotiating with the PRC to "prevent any foolish or headstrong action by the Chinese Communist Government."[36]

Negotiating with the Chinese would also forestall the diplomatic pressure the Soviets were exerting on the United States. During a meeting in San Francisco in late June, Molotov told Dulles that the Soviet Union would propose a six-power conference to discuss Far Eastern affairs, including the Big Four, China, and India.[37] In early July, Macmillan told Dulles that the Soviet Union would strive to either raise the Chinese issue at the Geneva summit of the four powers or "press for a separate conference about the Far East."[38]

Eisenhower and Dulles accepted Robertson's suggestion to start negotiation with the Chinese, although they were clear the Chinese "use prisoners as hostage[s] to bargain for political advantages." They deliberately avoided the expression "exchanging commissioners," because the word "commissioners" had "a representative and quasi diplomatic status of sorts," and hence could be interpreted as implying diplomatic recognition.[39] Dulles immediately informed Britain, India, and Burma.[40] Still, the Indians continued the pressure. Menon pushed Dulles to take action on several things, including the trade embargo, Chinese students, and American visitors to China. He also suggested that the Sino-American negotiation take place in either Moscow or New Delhi, which would give the Soviet Union or India more influence.[41] Meanwhile, Nehru sent a personal letter to Eisenhower; while pressing the Americans to respond to the Chinese gestures positively, he joined the British in suggesting that the negotiation with China include reducing tensions in addition to the practical problem of releasing American detainees.[42]

But the Americans would retreat no more. According to the State Department, the U.S. objective was getting back the American detainees and maintaining the ceasefire in the Taiwan Strait.[43] Instead of solving the Taiwan problem, the Americans just wanted to stabilize the situation. According to Dulles, negotiating with the Chinese was "the minimum needed to preserve [the] de facto cease-fire in [the] Formosa Straits."[44] Indeed, Robertson suggested to Dulles that Washington should prepare to raise renunciation of the use of force in the Taiwan Strait as "the best fall-back topic" that would give the United States "good ground for refusing to discuss other topics" that the Chinese would raise in the negotiation.[45]

The Chinese readily accepted the U.S. suggestion.[46] They were clear about the United States' intentions. According to the Chinese Foreign Ministry, the Americans agreed to talk because of diplomatic pressure. Washington's objective was limited to getting back American airmen and the other detainees, and it was not willing to discuss Taiwan with China. The United States kept the door open for higher level talks just to test the Chinese intentions and relax the tensions to break its isolation on the Taiwan issue. However, the Chinese calculated that they could still exploit the negotiation to push the Americans for further retreats: if the negotiation made progress, diplomatic pressure on the United States would increase. Meanwhile Chinese military pressure would increase after the Communist forces in the coastal area were further strengthened. Consequently, China might be able to force the United States to enter into higher level talks or to give up protection of the offshore islands. To strive for such a prospect, China would release eleven U.S. military personnel at the beginning of the negotiation to both eliminate any excuse for delay and intensify pressure on the Americans. In the negotiation, China would also strive to solve some practical problem to pave the way for a higher level of negotiation.[47]

In the process, the Chinese leaders sought Soviet coordination in its attendance of the Big Four summit in July. Zhou told the Soviet chargé J. Lomakin about his estimate of the U.S. intentions and China's plan. Because the Americans just used the ambassadorial talks to create the impression that the U.S. and China would negotiate over Taiwan to avoid this issue at the Geneva summit, Zhou suggested that the Soviets pressure Washington for a direct U.S.-China talk over Taiwan. He confided in the Soviet officials that China's objective was negotiation between the Chinese premier and the U.S. president. The Soviets endorsed the Chinese plan and suggested releasing some U.S. airmen before the summit in coordination.[48]

On the eve of the negotiation, Zhou made a last effort to recruit supporters. He informed the Indian ambassador in Beijing of China's decision to release more American pilots. While giving credit to the role the Indians had played on this issue, he expressed interest in a foreign minister meeting between the United States and China.[49] When Menon later complained that the Americans devalued the Indian role in bringing about the talk and let the British steal the thunder from India, Zhou reassured him that neither the British nor the UN played a significant role, and China had always attached importance to India's contribution.[50]

Finally, the ambassadorial talks started on August 1, 1955. On September 10, the two states reached an agreement: their civilians in each other's country had the right to return, and the United Kingdom and India would facilitate the return on behalf of the United States and China, respectively. The negotiation then deadlocked. China proposed holding a foreign minster meeting to discuss how to reduce tensions in the Taiwan area, but the Americans wanted all their citizens back first, as well as China's renunciation of the use of force in the Taiwan Strait. In the following two years, the meetings continued as a "dialogue of the deaf," with the two sides repeating their positions and refusing to make any concessions.[51]

The relationship between the United States and China from 1953 to 1956 was characterized by U.S. efforts to contain China and Beijing's struggles to break the containment. Washington viewed the PRC as its major enemy in Asia and tried to pressure and weaken China in the short run and to remove the Communist regime in the long run. Chinese leaders were worried about U.S. encirclement of China and strove to eliminate the U.S. menace.

To meet this challenge, leaders of both states adopted a strategy of isolating their enemy from its allies and potential supporters. Throughout the Eisenhower administration, U.S. officials had kept alive the idea of exploiting the divisions between China and the Soviet Union through pressure. However, realizing the limit of their strength and the priority of Europe, U.S. leaders relied on alliances and nuclear deterrence to contain the Communist regime rather than meeting the perceived Communist threat head on as the "wedge strategy" required, even in the face of China's military provocations.

Sensitive to differences within the Western camp, Chinese leaders consistently pursued a strategy of mobilizing U.S. allies and neutral states to pressure Washington to make concessions in order to reduce its threat to China. In Geneva, they exploited differences between the United States and the United Kingdom and France to neutralize Indochina and preclude a direct U.S. threat to China's southern flank. In the Taiwan Strait, Chinese leaders mobilized the United Kingdom and Asian states to push Washington to give up an MDT with GMD. In Bandung, they tried to unite China's Asian neighbors to develop a zone of peace that would exclude the United States from Southeast Asia. In the meantime, the Chinese were clear about the U.S. strategy to split the Sino-Soviet alliance. They in turn promoted unity with the Soviet Union and the DRV to put the pressure back on the United States.

Although U.S. leaders were aware of China's strategy of alienating them, they were less successful in meeting the challenge. Eisenhower's New Look stressed containing Communism through alliances and nuclear deterrence, but U.S. rhetoric about retaliating with atomic bombs frightened both neutral states and U.S. allies, who were worried about the destruction of a nuclear world war. This played right into the hands of the Chinese, and under diplomatic pressure from allies and neutral states, Washington retreated from its original positions. In Geneva, the Americans had to accept a peace settlement that China pursued and that the Americans had initially rejected. In the Taiwan Strait, they withdrew the commitment to the protection of the offshore islands and even pushed GMD to evacuate from them. During the Bandung Conference, the Americans were forced to enter official talks with Beijing.

The conciliatory actions on both sides were simply a different way to fight the enemy. The Americans had to demonstrate conciliation to reduce pressure from both the enemy and their friends, and the Chinese peace initiatives continued to press the United States, which the Americans correctly interpreted as peace offensives. Neither was in a position to change its own policy to improve relations. What Beijing meant by "reducing the tensions" was Washington giving up its hostility against and containment of China—on this basis, the two states could achieve "peaceful coexistence." Given these circumstances, the ambassadorial talks were doomed before they started.

China's active and realistic diplomacy in the mid-1950s resulted from several factors. First, it was part of the peace offensive the Soviet Union started in early 1953. Throughout the period, Chinese leaders collaborated closely with the Soviet Union. The Soviets aimed to expel the United States from Europe under the slogan of reducing tensions, and the Chinese leaders worked to eliminate the U.S. presence from its neighborhood in Asia using a similar strategy. Second, the Chinese Communist leaders inherited a long tradition of Chinese diplomacy. Playing off the Westerners against each other was a Chinese strategy that can be traced back to the beginning of its interactions with the West. In the Opium Wars, the Qing government attempted to exploit differences between Britain and the United States. In the late nineteenth century, Qing officials again tried to manipulate the United States against other imperialists over control of Manchuria and Ryukyu.[1] In the twentieth century, the GMD tried to play off the United Kingdom, France, and the United States against one an other in the 1920s. And the CCP leaders such as Mao and Zhang Wentian realized the importance of exploiting the disunity between the Westerners in 1940. In the Civil War, they put this into practice in their relations with the United Kingdom and the United States.[2] Third, developing a united front with potential sympathizers against the main enemy was credited by Mao as one of the "Three Magic Weapons" that ensured the CCP's victory over the GMD.[3] Forming an international united front against the United States was a natural refinement of this tactic. Finally, as the chief practitioner of the united front policy during China's Anti-Japanese War and the Civil War, Zhou's personal experiences and diplomatic skills contributed enormously to the conduct of the peace offensive. The period from 1953 to 1956 saw close cooperation between Mao and Zhou in diplomacy, which allowed Zhou to exert his capabilities to the utmost.

Throughout this period, Washington overestimated both China's capabilities and ambitions, and often mistook its long-term goal as its immediate objectives. America's initial reactions to China's initiatives were always intransigent, which strained relations with allies. Apparently, the Korean War had a deep psychological effect on the Americans. Throughout the 1950s, U.S. policymakers were obsessed with the idea that Communism was on the rise and that most of the Third World was susceptible to its expansion. China's performance in the Korean War led to the belief that Chinese Communist leaders ignored the value of human lives and would ruthlessly seek their objectives at any cost.[4] Because of these anxieties, Washington often inflated China's ambition. A typical example was the repeated exaggeration of China's aggression during the Taiwan Strait Crisis. The problem was compounded by the fact that the United States did not have diplomats in China after 1950, and the State Department lost most of its best China experts in the McCarthy witch hunt. Because their primary focus was on Europe and the Soviet threat, U.S. leaders were extraordinarily frustrated by

China's constant initiatives and provocations. After the Taiwan Strait Crisis, Washington saw China as more threatening than the Soviet Union, and the Americans became increasingly pessimistic about a Sino-Soviet split in the short run—ironically, this was just when differences between the Communists were developing.[5]

China's largely successful strategy of isolating the United States through diplomacy gradually gave way to a tit-for-tat confrontation. The year 1956 saw China's last efforts to mobilize pressure on the United States. In May, Zhou suggested direct talks with Dulles to discuss issues such as Taiwan. A month later, Zhou announced at the National People's Congress that China intended to liberate Taiwan peacefully. In early August, the Chinese government invited fifteen American news agencies to send journalists to visit China. All of these actions were aimed at pressuring Washington for more contacts between the two countries. At the ambassadorial talks, Chinese diplomats proposed to discuss the trade embargo, promotion of travel and cultural exchanges, and some cooperation on legal issues. In the Eighth National Congress of the CCP in September 1956, Mao expressed optimism about diplomacy with the Western countries. He announced that "our door is open. In twelve years, Britain, America, West Germany, and Japan will all want to do business with us."[6]

A turning point toward hardening diplomacy came in 1957. An indicator of this shifting policy was China's attitude toward the American journalists. When Washington finally allowed journalists to go to China, Beijing requested reciprocal treatment for Chinese journalists, which essentially refused entry to the Americans because the Chinese knew Washington was unwilling to grant visas to the Chinese journalists. In September 1957, Mao told Communist visitors to Beijing that China was not in a hurry to establish diplomatic relations with major Western states; instead, his focus was fighting against them.[7] In November, he stunned the world Communist leaders that met in Moscow to memorialize the fortieth anniversary of the Bolshevik Revolution by declaring that the strength of the Socialist camp was overwhelmingly superior to that of the Capitalists, and that he was not afraid of a nuclear war with the United States.[8]

The replacement of Zhou by Chen Yi as foreign minister in February 1958 indicated the official ending of China's pragmatism and the beginning of radical diplomacy. In June, Mao criticized the conservatism in China's conduct of diplomacy, and specifically the Chinese catering to the Americans in the ambassadorial talks. Mao told his new foreign minister that his decision to have diplomatic contacts with the United States was inconsistent with his usual ideas. Now he wanted to return to his initial thinking: China should fight against the United States instead of seeking to develop relations with it. After drawing Chen's attention to the fact that the Socialist strength was overwhelming the Capitalist power, Mao pushed Chen Yi to boost self-confidence in diplomacy and not be afraid of impasse: "It is to our advantage to be in an impasse with the United States. . . ."[9] Consequently, China accused the United States of stalling the ambassadorial talks and issued an ultimatum requesting Washington to resume the talks in fifteen days, which Washington ignored. After a careful review of China's diplomacy since 1949, as requested by Mao, the Chinese Foreign Ministry leaders concluded that China's diplomacy did have "a tendency toward conservatism and rightism," including "neglecting the necessary struggle in relations with the nationalist [neutral] countries, lacking clear-cut distinctions between socialism and nationalism, and maintaining a certain degree of wishful thinking in relations with imperialist countries." Based on this understanding, the Chinese Foreign Ministry planned to launch an all-out offensive targeting all types of countries: China's diplomacy should strive to "expose Yugoslavia and consolidate socialism; fight against the United States and bring down imperialism; and isolate Japan and win over the nationalist countries."[10]

Mao immediately put this idea into practice. In July, making use of a Soviet proposal for military cooperation that indeed benefited the Chinese, Mao exclaimed before a nervous Soviet ambassador that Moscow intended to control the Chinese military. He protested loudly against the Soviet's "big power chauvinism." When Khrushchev rushed to China to appease Mao, Beijing kept the Soviet leader in the dark about their plan to bomb Jinmen and initiate a new confrontation with the United States.[11] Shortly after Khrushchev left China, the PLA shelled the Jinmen Islands in late August, which started the Second Taiwan Strait Crisis. When confronting the United States directly, Mao challenged both the status of the Soviet leadership and its basic diplomatic guideline of seeking peaceful coexistence with the Western camp.[12] When the Americans agreed to resume the ambassadorial talks in response to the crisis, Mao was not interested in a compromise and took a hardline position: China would not discuss the other issues with the Americans unless it obtained a satisfied solution to the Taiwan issue.[13]

Several actions accounted for the radical turn of China in 1958. First of all, Mao harbored a mistaken confidence in the balance of power between the two camps. Successful completion of China's First Five-Year Plan, nationalization of the Chinese economy, and the preliminary modernization of the PLA gave Mao more confidence in China's strength. Second, the launch of the world's first satellite by the Soviets in 1957 indicated that perhaps the Soviet Union led the United States in science and technology, and that the balance of power between the two camps was tilting in the favor of the Socialist camp.[14]

Meanwhile, Khrushchev's de-Stalinization convinced Mao that the Soviet leader was not sophisticated enough to lead the Socialist camp. While willingly giving up the "sword of Stalin," Khrushchev's accusation of the great leader of the Communist camp sowed confusion among the Communists. Subsequent uprisings in Poland and Hungary later in 1956 proved that Mao himself was better qualified to lead the Communist world. The fact that the Soviets needed Chinese assistance in suppressing the protests and the rise of China's influence among the Communists after that further emboldened a confident Mao.[15]

Mao's observation of the relationship between the United States and the United Kingdom further goaded him. In 1957, during the Suez Crisis, Mao noticed that the two Western powers were virtually fighting among themselves. Apparently, Western unity was gone. Soon Mao concluded that the "enemies [were] deteriorating day by day, and we [were] prospering day by day."[16] Therefore, it was time to take an offensive against the imperialist powers. The Soviet's quest for peaceful coexistence with the West just indicated their fear of the Western camp—and hence it was no longer in a position to lead the Socialist states.

China's foreign policy became increasingly radical after 1958. It ultimately culminated in the rise of revolutionary diplomacy in the 1960s, which targeted both U.S. imperialism and Soviet revisionism while attempting to lead a world revolution in the Third World. This idealistic fervor, wishful thinking, and the blind adventurism of revolutionary diplomacy stood in contrast to the Bandung moment of the mid-1950s, which had featured a realistic assessment of China's strength vis-à-vis that of the United States and pragmatic diplomacy based on a sensitive perception of the Western camp and the rest of the world.

COUNTRIES THAT ESTABLISHED DIPLOMATIC RELATIONS WITH THE PRC BY 1957

ASIA

North Korea, October 6, 1949

Mongolia, October 16, 1949

DRV, January 18, 1950

India, April 1, 1950

Indonesia, April 13, 1950

Burma, June 8, 1950

Pakistan, May 21, 1951

Afghanistan, January 20, 1955

Nepal, August 1, 1955

EUROPE

Soviet Union, October 3, 1949

Bulgaria, October 4, 1949

Rumania, October 5, 1949

Hungary, October 6, 1949

Czechoslovakia, October 6, 1949

Poland, October 7, 1949

East Germany, October 27, 1949

Albania, November 23, 1949
Sweden, May 9, 1950
Denmark, May 11, 1950
Switzerland, September 14, 1950
Liechtenstein, September 14, 1950
Finland, October 28, 1950
Yugoslavia, January 2, 1955
Norway, October 5, 1954

AFRICA

Egypt, May 30, 1956
Syria, August 1, 1956
Yemen, September 24, 1956

NOTES

PROLOGUE

1. This book uses the PRC and China interchangeably to refer to the Communist government established by the CCP in 1949. It refers to the Republic of China (ROC) government as the GMD, which moved to Taiwan in 1949. Names of Chinese officials follow the Chinese naming order: family name first and then given name. Names of Chinese authors are spelled as they appear in their own publications.

2. Dwight D. Eisenhower, *The White House Years: Mandate for Change, 1953–1956* (Garden City, NY: Doubleday, 1963), 460.

3. U.S. Department of State, *Foreign Relations of the United States, 1952–54*, 14: 279 (hereafter cited as *FRUS* with appropriate year and volume numbers).

4. He Di, "The Evolution of the People's Republic of China's Policy Toward the Offshore Islands," in *The Great Powers in East Asia, 1953–1960*, ed. Warren I. Cohen and Akira Iriye (New York: Columbia University Press, 1990), 224–26; Gong Li, "Liangci Taiwan Haixia Weiji de Chengyin yu Zhongmei Zhijian de Jiaoliang," in *Cong Duishi Zouxiang Huanhe: Lengzhan Shiqi Zhongmei Guanxi zai Tantao* (From confrontation to détente: Reflections on Sino-American relations during the Cold War), ed. Jiang Changbin and Robert Ross (Beijing, China: Shijie Zhishi Chubanshe, 2000), 62; Zhang Baijia and Jia Qingguo, "Duikang zhong de Fangxiangpan, Huanchongqi he Tanceyi: Zhongmei Dashiji Huitan," in *Cong Duishi Zouxiang Huanhe: Lengzhan Shiqi Zhongmei Guanxi zai Tantao*, ed. Jiang Changbin and Robert Ross (Beijing, China: Shijie Zhishi Chubanshe, 2000), 171–78; Thomas E. Stolper, *China, Taiwan, and the Offshore Islands: Together with Some Implications for Outer Mongolia and Sino-Soviet Relations* (Armonk, NY: M. E. Sharpe, 1985); Allen Whiting, *China Crosses Yalu: The Decision to Enter the Korean War* (New York: Macmillan, 1960); and Qiang Zhai, *The Dragon, the Lion, and the Eagle: Chinese-British-American Relations, 1949–1958* (Kent, OH: The Kent State University Press, 1994).

5. Chen Jian, *Mao's China and the Cold War* (Chapel Hill: University of North Carolina Press, 2001).

6. Lorenz M. Lüthi, *The Sino-Soviet Split: Cold War in the Communist World* (Princeton, NJ: Princeton University Press, 2008).

7. Michael Sheng, "Mao and China's Relations with Superpowers in the 1950s: A New Look at the Taiwan Strait Crises and the Sino-Soviet Split," *Modern China* 34, no. 4 (October 2008): 477–507.

8. Roscoe Drummond and Gaston Coblentz, *Duel at the Brink: John Foster Dulles' Command of American Power* (Garden City, N.Y.: Doubleday, 1960); David Heller and Dean Heller, *John Foster Dulles: Soldier for Peace* (New York: Holt, Rinehart and Winston, 1960); Hans Morgenthau, "John Foster Dulles," in *An Uncertain Tradition: American Secretaries of State in the Twentieth Century*, ed. Norman Graebner (New York: McGraw-Hill, 1961), chap. 18; Townsend Hoopes, *The Devil and John Foster Dulles* (Boston: Little, Brown, 1973); and Norman Graebner, "Eisenhower and Communism: The Public Record of the 1950s," in *Reevaluating Eisenhower: American Foreign Policy in the Fifties*, ed. Richard A. Melanson and David Mayers (Chicago: University of Illinois Press, 1987), 67–87.

9. The discussion of Eisenhower revisionists draws on Stephen G. Rabe, "Eisenhower Revisionism: A Decade of Scholarship," in *Diplomatic History* 17, no. 1 (Winter 1993): 97–115; Richard H. Immerman, "Confessions of an Eisenhower Revisionist: An Agonizing Reappraisal," *Diplomatic History* 14, no. 3 (Summer 1990): 319–42; and Richard Melanson and David Mayers, preface in *Reevaluating Eisenhower: American Foreign Policy in the Fifties* (Chicago: University of Illinois Press, 1987), 1–10.

10. For Eisenhower's leadership style, see Richard Immerman, "Eisenhower and Dulles: Who Made the Decisions?" *Political Psychology* 1 (Autumn 1979): 21–38; Fred Greenstein, *The Hidden-Hand Presidency: Eisenhower as Leader* (New York: Basic, 1982); Anna Nelson, "The Top of the Policy Hill: President Eisenhower and the National Security Council," *Diplomatic History* 7 (Fall 1983): 307–28.

11. Robert Divine, *Eisenhower and the Cold War* (New York: Oxford University Press, 1981), 27–31; Stephen Ambrose, *Eisenhower: The President* (New York: Simon and Schuster, 1984), 97–99, 101–3, 104–7.

12. John Prados, *"The Sky Would Fall": Operation Vulture: The U.S. Bombing Mission in Indochina, 1954* (New York: Dial, 1983); Melanie Billings-Yun, *Decision Against War: Eisenhower and Dien Bien Phu, 1954* (New York: Columbia University Press, 1988); Llyod Gardner, *Approaching Vietnam: From World War II through Dien Bien Phu, 1941–1954* (New York: Norton, 1988); George C. Herring and Richard H. Immerman, "Eisenhower, Dulles, and Dien Bien Phu: 'The Day We Didn't Go to War' Revisited," *Journal of American History* 71 (September 1984): 343–63; Richard H. Immerman, "Between the Unattainable and the Unacceptable: Eisenhower and Dienbienphu," in *Reevaluating Eisenhower: American Foreign Policy in the Fifties* (Chicago: University of Illinois Press, 1987), 120–54; George C. Herring, " 'A Good Stout Effort': John Foster Dulles and the Indochina Crisis, 1954–1955," in *John Foster Dulles and the Diplomacy of the Cold War*, ed. Richard H. Immerman (Princeton, N.J.: Princeton University Press, 1990), 213–34; Gary R. Hess, "Redefining the American Position in Southeast Asia: The United States and the Geneva and the Manila Conferences," in *Dien Bien Phu and the Crisis of Franco-American Relations, 1954–1955*, ed. Lawrence S. Kaplan, Denise Artaud, and Mark R. Rubin (Wilmington, Del.: SR Books, 1989), 123–67.

13. Ambrose, *Eisenhower*, 212–55; Divine, *Eisenhower and the Cold War*, 55–66; Bennett Rushkoff, "Eisenhower, Dulles and the Quemoy–Matsu Crisis, 1954–1955," *Political Science Quarterly* 96, no. 3 (Fall 1981): 465–80; Leonard Gordon, "United States Opposition to the Use of Force in the Taiwan Strait, 1954–1962," *Journal of American History* 72, no. 3 (December 1985): 637–60.

14. Nancy Bernkopf Tucker, "Cold War Contacts: America and China, 1952–56," in *Sino-American Relations, 1945–1955: A Joint Reassessment of a Critical Decade*, ed. Harry Harding and Yuan Ming (Wilmington, Del.: Scholarly Resources, 1989), 238–66, and "John Foster Dulles and the Taiwan Roots of the 'Two Chinas' Policy," in *John Foster Dulles and the Diplomacy of the Cold War*, 235–62; Simei Qing, "The Eisenhower Administration and Changes in Western Embargo Policy Against China, 1954–1958," in *Great Powers in East Asia*, 121–42. See also Wang Jisi, "The Origins of America's 'Two China' Policy," in *Sino-American Relations*, 198–212; and Su-Ya Chang, "Reluctant Alliance: John Foster Dulles and the Making of the United States-Republic of China Mutual Defense Treaty of 1954," in *Chinese Yearbook of International Law and Affairs* 12 (1992–94): 126–71.

15. John Lewis Gaddis, "The American 'Wedge' Strategy, 1949–1955," in *Sino-American Relations*, 157–83, and in a longer version, in John Lewis Gaddis, *The Long Peace: Inquiries Into the History of the Cold War* (New York: Oxford University Press, 1987), 147–94; Gordon H. Chang, *Friends and Enemies: The United States, China, and the Soviet Union, 1948–1972* (Stanford, Calif.: Stanford University Press, 1990); David Allan Mayers, *Cracking the Monolith: U.S. Policy Against the Sino-Soviet Alliance* (Baton Rouge: Louisiana State University Press, 1986), and "Eisenhower and Communism: Later Findings," in *Reevaluating Eisenhower*, 88–119.

16. Shu Guang Zhang, *Economic Cold War: America's Embargo Against China and the Sino-Soviet Alliance, 1949–1963* (Washington, D.C.: Woodrow Wilson Center Press; Stanford, Calif.: Stanford University Press, 2001).

17. Robert Accinelli, *Crisis and Commitment: United States' Policy Toward Taiwan, 1950–1955* (Chapel Hill: University of North Carolina Press, 1996), x; Waldo Heinrichs, "Eisenhower and Sino-American Confrontation," in *Great Powers in East Asia*, 86–103; and Su-Ya Chang, "Taihai Weiji yu Meiguo dui Fangong Dalu Zhengce de Zhuanbian" (Taiwan Strait crises and U.S. policy toward GMD's "Restoration of the Mainland"), *Bulletin of the Institute of Modern History* 20 (June 1991): 369–41.

18. Gordon H. Chang, "To the Nuclear Brink: Eisenhower, Dulles, and the Quemoy-Mazsu Crisis," *International Security* 12, no. 4 (Spring 1986): 119.

19. Simei Qing, *From Allies to Enemies: Visions of Modernity, Identity, and U.S.-China Diplomacy, 1945–1960* (Cambridge, Mass.: Harvard University Press, 2007), 169–204.

20. Zhai, *The Dragon, the Lion, and the Eagle*.

21. Shu Guang Zhang, *Deterrence and Strategic Culture: Chinese-American Confrontations, 1949–1958* (Ithaca, N.Y.: Cornell University Press, 1992).

22. Qing, *From Allies to Enemies*.

23. Yafeng Xia, *Negotiating with the Enemy: U.S.-China Talks During the Cold War, 1949–1972* (Bloomington: Indiana University Press, 2006).

24. Meredith Oyen, *The Diplomacy of Immigration: Transnational Lives and the Making of U.S.–Chinese Relations in the Cold War* (Ithaca, N.Y.: Cornell University Press, 2015).

25. Gregg A. Brazinsky, *Winning the Third World: Sino-American Rivalry During the Cold War* (Chapel Hill: University of North Carolina Press, 2017).

26. Hsiao-Ting Lin, *Accidental State: Chiang Kai-shek, The United States, and the Making of Taiwan* (Cambridge, Mass.: Harvard University Press, 2016).

27. In addition to Michael Sheng's criticism of China's diplomacy, Chen Jian also points out the inconsistence between the militant policy in the Taiwan Strait and the quest for peaceful coexistence. See Chen, *Mao's China and the Cold War*, 168, 170, 173.

28. DRV Ministry of Foreign Affairs, "The Diplomatic Struggle as Part of the People's National Democratic Revolution (1945-1954), Volume Two," translated by Merle L. Pribbenow for the International Workshop, "Reconsidering the Geneva Conference: New Archival Evidence," held by the Cold War International History Project (CWIHP) of the Woodrow Wilson Center for Scholars, Washington, D.C., February 17-18, 2006. The author is indebted to Christopher Goscha for the procurement and the Woodrow Wilson Center for the publication of this document.

INTRODUCTION: SINO-AMERICAN RELATIONS AFTER THE KOREAN WAR

1. U.S. Department of State, *Foreign Relations of the United States (FRUS), 1952–54*, 14: 397. Charlton Ogburn was the regional planning adviser to the assistant secretary of state for Far Eastern affairs.

2. British Foreign Secretary Anthony Eden at the Bermuda Conference of the "Big Three," December 1953, cited in Chang, *Friends and Enemies*, 95.

3. *FRUS, 1952–54*, 13: 1440; NSC Meeting, April 29, 1954, Dwight D. Eisenhower Papers as President, 1953–61, Ann Whitmann File (hereafter AWF), NSC Series, box 5, DDEL.

4. Robert Jervis, "The Impact of the Korean War on the Cold War," *The Journal of Conflict Resolution* 24, no. 4 (December 1980): 574–76, 582–84. For works on the "lost chance" thesis, see Warren I. Cohen, "Acheson, His Advisers, and China, 1949–1950," in *Uncertain Years: Chinese-American Relations, 1947–1950*, ed. Dorothy Borg and Waldo Heinrichs (New York: Columbia University Press, 1980), 13–52; Nancy Bernkopf Tucker, *Patterns in the Dust: Chinese-American Relations and the Recognition Controversy, 1949–1950* (New York: Columbia University Press, 1983); David McLean, "American Nationalism, the China Myth, and the Truman Doctrine: The Question of Accommodation with Peking, 1949–50," *Diplomatic History* 10 (Fall 1986): 25–42; Thomas Christensen, "A 'Lost Chance' for What? Rethinking the Origins of the U.S.-China Confrontation," *Journal of American-East Asian Relations* 4 (Fall 1995): 249–78; Chen Jian, "The Myth of America's 'Lost Chance' in China: A Chinese Perspective in Light of New Evidence," *Diplomatic History* 21, no. 1 (Winter 1997): 77–86; and Michael Sheng, "The Triumph of Internationalism: CCP-Moscow Relations Before 1949," *Diplomatic History* 21, no. 1 (Winter 1997): 95–104.

5. *FRUS, 1952–54*, 14: 202. In early 1953, the British embassy in Washington reported to London that " 'Red China' is popularly regarded as worse than the Soviet Union. It is a recognized aggressor and a country with which the United States and its Allies are in practice at war, even though the war is limited to certain areas." Washington to Foreign Office (FO), February 7, 1953, FO 371/105261, NAUK; Peter Lowe, *Containing the Cold War in East Asia: British Policies Towards Japan, China and Korea, 1948–53* (New York: Manchester University Press, 1997), 143.

6. *FRUS, 1952–1954*, 14: 238.

7. *FRUS, 1952–1954*, 14: 279. The following analysis of the U.S. policy is primarily based on this document.

8. *FRUS, 1952–1954*, 13: 972.

9. For the origins of the defense perimeter strategy and the significance of Taiwan, see Gaddis, *The Long Peace*, 72–103.

10. *FRUS, 1952–1954*, 14: 227–29, 232–34, and 244–45.

11. *FRUS, 1952–1954*, 14: 175–79, and 279.

12. *FRUS, 1952–1954*, 2: 584.

13. *FRUS, 1952–54*, 14: 280–81

14. *FRUS, 1952–54*, 14: 304. For the U.S. "wedge strategy," see Gaddis, "The American 'Wedge' Strategy"; Chang, *Friends and Enemies*; and Mayers, *Cracking the Monolith*.

15. *FRUS, 1952–54*, 14, 281–82. For the Eisenhower administration's containment strategy, see John Lewis Gaddis, *Strategies of Containment: A Critical Appraisal of American National Security Policy During the Cold War* (New York: Oxford University Press, 2005), 125–61.

16. *FRUS, 1952–1954*, 13: 972–73.

17. *FRUS, 1952–1954*, 14: 308.

18. *FRUS, 1952–1954*, 2: 586.

19. *FRUS, 1952–1954*, 14: 306.

20. *FRUS, 1952–1954*, 2: 491–99, 579, 581.

21. *FRUS, 1952–1954*, 14: 306.

22. *Renmin Ribao (People's Daily)*, editorial, November 6, 1950.

23. "Enemy's frequent air invasion and harassment of coastal Shandong since the end of the Korean War," *Neibu Cankao* (Internal Reference, available in The Universities Service Center of the Chinese University of Hong Kong), August 19, 1953. See also "Statistics of intrusions into territorial air of the People's Republic of China by American aircraft from July 1950 to September 1954," Chinese Foreign Ministry Archives, Beijing (hereafter, CFMA), document no. 204-000148-04, 23–24. Unless indicated otherwise, English translation of Chinese sources from the CFMA and *Neibu Cankao* is by the author.

24. *Renmi Ribao*, August 16, 1953.

25. *Renmin Ribao*, August 13, 1953; "American strategists are planning to sow discord in Sino-Soviet relations," *Neibu Cankao*, March 16, 1953.

26. "U.S. imperialist aggression toward Taiwan," "Situation in Taiwan as told by insurgent personnel of Chiang bandit air force," "Changes of state of the enemy along coastal Fujian since 1953," in *Neibu Cankao*, October 19, 1953, and January 23 and 28, 1954.

27. Briefings in *Neibu Cankao*, November 4, 1952; April 22, July 18, September 17, October 12, and November 12, 1953.

28. *Renmin Ribao*, January 22, February 4 and 20, 1953; Zhongyang Wenxian Chubanshe, ed., *Jianguo Yilai Mao Zedong Wengao* (Mao Zedong's Manuscripts since the Foundation of the People's Republic of China) (hereafter, Mao Wengao), 3 (Beijing: Zhongyang Wenxian Chubanshe, 1989): 294, 331. See "The statistical table of the ships intercepted or plundered by the Chiang Kai-shek traitorous clique directed and supported by the U.S. aggressive clique off the China coast and on the high seas from September 1949 to October 1954," September 30, 1954, CFMA, 204-000148-04, 25–29.

29. "U.S. Imperialist Conspiracy of Holding a 'U.S.-Filipino Defense Meeting,'" November 4, 1952, CFMA, 105-00819-02, 39–41.

30. "The [British, American and French] Three Foreign Ministers Meeting and the Vietnam Issue," July 27, 1953, CFMA, 110-00234-04, 42–46.

31. *Renmin Ribao*, September 13, 1953; Zhang, *Deterrence and Strategic Culture*, 178.

32. *Renmin Ribao*, February 12, 14, 22, 23, 27, and 28, 1954.

33. "America is stepping up expanding Thailand military force," *Neibu Cankao*, November 16, 1953.

34. *Renmin Ribao*, January 18, February 20, and March 23, 1954.

35. "The Contradictions Between the French and Americans on War or Peace in Indochina After the Starting of the Dien Bien Phu Campaign," April 5, 1954, CFMA, 102-00159-02, 6–9.

36. *Remin Ribao*, January 14, 1953. Alice Langley Hsien, *Communist China's Strategy in the Nuclear Era* (Englewood Cliffs, N.J.: Prentice-Hall, Inc., 1962), 15–16; Zhang, *Deterrence and Strategic Culture*, 178.

37. *Renmin Ribao*, March 24, 30, 1954; *Survey of China Mainland Press* (SCMP), no. 755, February 26, 6–7; and no. 774, March 25, 1–2; and no. 775, March 26, 1–2. Goa was the Portuguese colony in India from the early sixteenth century to 1961; the Dutch colonized Western New Guinea in Indonesia from the mid-seventeenth century to 1963. Since their independence, India and Indonesia had fought for the return of the colonies.

38. Zhonghua Renmin Gongheguo Waijiaobu, Zhongyang Wenxian Yanjiushi, eds., *Mao Zedong Waijiao Wenxuan* (Mao Zedong's Selected Works on Diplomacy) (Beijing: Zhongyang Wenxian Chubanshe, 1994), 165. According to Chinese records, from July 1950 to September 1954, 8220 groups (32995 sorties) of U.S. aircrafts invaded China; and the U.S. airforce dropped over 230 human agents, 96 wireless sets, over a thousand guns, and 179,000 ammunitions into Chinese territory. See "Statistics of the invasion of U.S. airplane into China's airspace from 1950 to September 1954," and "Statistical table of agents, wireless sets, and arms air dropped into the interior of China by U.S.A.," September 30, 1954, CFMA, 204-00148-04, 23–24. *Renmin Ribao* published numerous protests against the U.S. invasion (for example, on January 7, 1954) and the statistics on October 11, 1954.

39. "Prime Minister Zhou Enlai's Report at the National Conference on Foreign Affairs of 1953," June 5, 1953, CFMA, 102-00110-01, 4–43; Li Ping and Ma Zhisun, et al. eds., *Zhou Enlai Nianpu, 1949–1976* (A Chronological Record of Zhou Enlai, 1949–1976), Vol. 1–3 (Beijing, China: Zhongyang Wenxian Chubanshe, 1997), 1: 305.

40. Emphasis added. Pang Xianzhi and Jin Chongji, et al., *Mao Zedong Zhuan, 1949–1976* (Biography of Mao Zedong, 1949–1976) (Beijing: Zhongyang Wenxian Chubanshe, 2003), 546–47; "Analysis of Eisenhower's Statement on December 26 by Our Embassy to the Soviet Union," December 30, 1953, CFMA, 102-00158-01, 14.

41. The latest works on the Soviet Peace Offensive include Vladslav M Zubok, *Soviet Intelligence and the Cold War: The "Small" Committee of Information, 1952–53*, CWIHP working paper 4; Geoffrey Roberts, "A Chance for Peace? The Soviet Campaign to End the Cold War, 1953–1955," CWIHP working paper 57; and Klaus Larres and Kenneth Osgood, eds., *The Cold War After Stalin's Death: A Missed Opportunity for Peace?* (Lanham, Md.: Rowman & Littlefield, 2006).

42. For the Soviet role in ending the Korean War, see Shen Zhihua, "Jieshu Chaoxian Zhanzheng: Zhongsu Lingdaoren de Zhengzhi Kaolu" (Ending the Korean War: political considerations of the Chinese and Soviet leaders), in *Lengzhan yu Zhongguo*, ed. Zhang Baijia and Niu Jun (The Cold War and China) (Beijing, China: Shijie Zhishi Chubanshe, 2002), 182–215; and Yang Kuisong, *Mao Zedong yu Mosike de*

Enen Yuanyuan (Love and Hate between Mao Zedong and Moscow) (Nanchang: Jiangxi Renmin Chubanshe, 2005), 415–18. For the Soviet perspective, see Kathryn Weathersby, "Stalin, Mao and the End of the Korean War," in *Brothers in Arms: The Rise and Fall of the Sino-Soviet Alliance, 1945–1963*, ed. Odd Arne Westad (Stanford, Calif: Stanford University Press, 1998), 90–116. For the armistice negotiation and the issue of POWs, see Rosemary Foot, *A Substitute for Victory: The Politics of Peacemaking at the Korean Armistice Talks* (New York: Cornell University Press, 1990).

43. For the Communist initiatives in 1953, see King Chen, *Vietnam and China, 1938–1954* (Princeton: Princeton University Press, 1969), 281.

44. *Pravda*, September 30, 1953, cited in Ilya Gaiduk, *Confronting Vietnam: Soviet Policy Toward the Indochina Conflict, 1954–1963* (Stanford, Calif.: Stanford University Press, 2003), 13; *Zhou Enlai Nianpu*, 1: 330–31, 333–36.

45. For the Soviet press reports about and the PRC's proposals for a peaceful settlement of the Indochina war, see DRV Ministry of Foreign Affairs, "The Diplomatic Struggle as Part of the People's National Democratic Revolution (1945–1954), Volume Two," 13, 14–15. This document was drafted in 1976, before the split of the Sino-Vietnamese alliance, and thus its description of the DRV's relations with the PRC was fairly objective. For the Soviet policy toward Indochina before Geneva, see Gaiduk, *Confronting Vietnam*, 1–14; and Mari Olsen, *Soviet-Vietnam Relations and the Role of China, 1949–1964* (New York: Rutledge, 2003), 13–27.

46. *Zhou Enlai Nianpu*, 1: 235–36.

47. For U.S. conflicts with Britain over India, see "U.S. Military Infiltration Into India," February 20, 1953, CFMA, 105-00247-02, 14–17; "U.S. Ambassador [Chester] Bowlers and U.S. Activities in India During His Tenure," February 26, 1953, CFMA, 105-00247-03, 19–33; "How Britain Had Reinforced Its Control of India Since 1952 and How the Contradictions Between Britain and the U.S. Had Intensified," April 1, 1953, CFMA, 105-00247-05, 40–44; "Report on Dulles's Visit to India," May 1953, CFMA, 105-00247-04, 35–38. For Chinese news reports about U.S.-UK conflict over Southeast Asia and the Near and Middle East, see *Renmin Ribao*, January 30, May 26, June 20, 1953.

48. For the Western opposition to the U.S. embargo on China, see "Bankruptcy of the U.S. Embargo Policy," September 30, 1952, CFMA, 110-00171-02, 22–33. For the French interests in trade with China, and their conflicts with the United States, see "The French and American Conflicts over 'Foreign Product Order,'" September 1 to 21, 1952, CFMA, 110-00186-05, and "Reply Regarding the French Trade Delegation," February 14, 1953, CFMA, 110-00212-01. For the French differences with the U.S. over Germany, see "Covert Struggles Between the U.S. and France," August 1952, CFMA, 110-00186-09, 90–94, and "Recent Internal Contradictions over the 'European Army,'" February 18, 1953, CFMA, 110-00234-09, 66–90. For the Japanese trade delegation to China, see *Zhou Enlai Nianpu*, 1: 226; and "Briefing of Sino-Japanese Meeting Regarding Trade Issues," March 4, 1953, CFMA, 105-00251-25, 83–88. For Chinese news reports about U.S. tensions with allies over trade, see *Renmin Ribao*, March 24, May 13, 25, 28, 31, June 7, July 8, August 31, September 8, 9, 20, November 11, 1953.

49. "Premier Zhou Enlai's Report at the National Conference on Foreign Affairs of 1953," June 5, 1953, CFMA, 102-00110-01, 4–43; *Zhou Enlai Nianpu*, 1: 305.

50. Zhihua Shen and Danhui Li, *After Leaning to One Side: China and Its Allies in the Cold War* (Washington, D.C.: Woodrow Wilson Center Press & Stanford: Stanford University Press, 2011), 13; Michael Share, "The Soviet Union, Hong Kong, and the

Cold War, 1945–1970," Cold War International History Project (CWIHP) working paper 41.

51. "American imperialism is sowing discord in Sino-Soviet relations," "U.S. new moves after Stalin's death," "U.S. journalists alienate Sino-Soviet leaders," "American strategists are making plans to drive a wedge between China and the Soviet Union," in *Neibu Cankao*, March 8, 9, and 16, 1953.

52. "British newspapers disapprove U.S. intensifying the Cold War against the Soviet Union," "British newspapers were anxious about U.S. policy toward the Far East," "United Press International sows discord in Sino-Soviet relations," in *Neibu Cankao*, March 10, 19, and August 18, 1953; *Renmin Ribao*, June 6, 7, and 16, 1953; January 8, 1954.

53. "Press Comments on the Bermuda Conference," December 10, 1953, CFMA, 110-00234-05, 47–50. Throughout February, *Renmin Ribao* focused on U.S. aggression in Indochina and tensions with France. See for example, *Renmin Ribao*, February 12, 14, 22, 23, 26, 1954.

1. NEUTRALIZING INDOCHINA

1. Zhongguo Waijiaobu, *Zhou Enlai Waijiao Huodong Dashiji* (Major Events in Zhou Enlai's Diplomatic Career) (Beijing, China: Shijie Zhishi Chubanshe, 1993), 58; Zhongguo Waijiaobu Danganguan, *1954 Nian Rineiwa Huiyi* (The Geneva Conference of 1954) (Beijing, China: Shijie Zhishi Chubanshe, 2006), 15–18; and Li Ping, Ma Zhisun, et al., *Zhou Enlai Nianpu, 1949–1976* (A Chronological Record of Zhou Enlai, 1949–1976), Vol. 1–3 (Beijing: Zhongyang Wenxian Chubanshe, 1997), 1: 3 60–61.

2. Minutes of Zhou's meeting with British Foreign Secretary Anthony Eden, July 17, 1954, in *1954 Nian Rineiwa Huiyi*, 246–51, translated in *CWIHP Bulletin*, Issue 16: 65–68.

3. The scholarly literature on China's policy has long stressed the significance of the Geneva Conference in boosting China's international status, but until recently scholars had not explored China's actions in depth. See Shu Guang Zhang, "Constructing 'Peaceful Coexistence': China's Diplomacy Toward the Geneva and Bandung Conferences, 1954–55," *Cold War History* 7, no. 4 (November 2007): 509–528; Chen Jian, "China and the Indochina Settlement at the Geneva Conference of 1954," in *The First Vietnam War: Colonial Conflict and Cold War Crisis*, ed. Mark Atwood Lawrence and Fredrik Logevall (Cambridge, Mass.: Harvard University Press, 2007), 240–62; and Qiang Zhai, "China and the Geneva Conference of 1954," *The China Quarterly*, no. 129 (March, 1992): 103–122.

4. "Transcript, Zhou Enlai's speech at a preparatory meeting by the Chinese delegation attending the Geneva Conference (excerpt)," February 17, 1954. The translation of the quotation is adapted from Chen's translation in the Wilson Center Cold War International History Project (CWIHP) Document Reader for the workshop on the Geneva Conference.

5. U.S. Department of State, *Foreign Relations of the United States (FRUS), 1952–54*, 16: 415.

6. Robert F. Randle, *Geneva 1954: The Settlement of the Indochinese War* (Princeton, N.J.: Princeton University Press, 1969), 48.

7. Vladislav Zubok, *Inside the Kremlin's Cold War: From Stalin to Khrushchev* (Cambridge, Mass: Harvard University Press, 1996), 155.

8. The Soviet proposal was published in *Pravda*, September 30, 1953; quoted in Ilya Gaiduk, *Confronting Vietnam: Soviet Policy Toward the Indochina Conflict, 1954–1963* (Stanford, Calif.: Stanford University Press, 2003), 13.

9. *Zhou Enlai Nianpu*, 1: 330–31, 333–36.

10. For the Soviet press reports about and China's proposals of a peaceful settlement of the Indochina war, see DRV Ministry of Foreign Affairs, "The Diplomatic Struggle as Part of the People's National Democratic Revolution (1945–1954), Volume Two," 13, 14–15 14–15. The available documents do not indicate whether or how the Soviet Union was involved in the Chinese proposal to the DRV. For the Soviet policy toward Indochina before Geneva, see Gaiduk, *Confronting Vietnam*, 1–14; and Mari Olsen, *Soviet-Vietnam Relations and the Role of China, 1949–1964* (New York: Routledge, 2003), 13–27.

11. *Mao Zedong Nianpu, 1949–1976* (A Chronological Record of Mao Zedong, 1949–1976), 6 vols., ed. Pang Xianzhi, Fen Hui, et. al. (Beijing, Zhongyang Wenxian Chubanshe, 2013), 2: 195; Pang Xianzhi and Jin Chongji, et al., *Mao Zedong Zhuan, 1949–1976* (Biography of Mao Zedong, 1949–1976) (Beijing, China: Zhongyang Wenxian Chubanshe, 2003), 552–53; Wen Zhuang, "Wo Suo Jingli de Rineiwa Huiyi" (The Geneva Conference as I Experienced) in *Dangshi Bolan* (General Review of the History of the Chinese Communist Party), December 2005, 18–23. Wen Zhuang, a Chinese advisor working in Vietnam, was the DRV delegation's interpreter during the Geneva Conference. The Chinese sources first reveal China's connection with Ho's proposal. On France's willingness to negotiate with the DRV, see "The Diplomatic Struggle," 6. For China's relations with the DRV after 1949, see Qiang Zhai, *China and the Vietnam Wars, 1950–1975* (Chapel Hill: University of North Carolina Press, 2000), 10–59.

12. "The Diplomatic Struggle," 16–17.

13. Unpaginated primary sources included in CWIHP Document Reader; *Renmin Ribao*, December 1, 1953.

14. Pierre Asselin, "The Democratic Republic of Vietnam and the 1954 Geneva Conference: A Revisionist Critique," *Cold War History* 11, no. 2 (May 2011): 161–63.

15. King Chen, *Vietnam and China, 1938–1954* (Princeton, N.J.: Princeton University Press, 1969), 282.

16. The Soviet strategy was so successful that Dulles had to admit: "If we had vetoed the resolution regarding Indochina, it would have probably cost us French membership in EDC [European Defense Community] as well as Indochina itself." See the transcription of his comments in *FRUS, 1952–54,* 13: 1080–81. For evaluation of the United States and its allies in Berlin, see Gaiduk, *Confronting Vietnam*, 17.

17. The Soviets provided the Chinese government with documents (ranging from January 23 to early March) about every development of the meeting in Berlin. See the list of documents provided in Chinese Foreign Ministry Archives (CFMA), Beijing, document no. 109-00396-01, especially 1–34.

18. Xiong Huayuan, *Zhou Enlai Chudeng Shijie Wutai* (Zhou Enlai's First Appearance on the World Stage) (Shenyang, China: Liaoning Renmin Chubanshe, 1999), 5–6.

19. *Zhou Enlai Nianpu*, 1: 355–58; "Preliminary Opinions on the Assessment of and Preparation for the Geneva Conference," March 2, 1954, CWIHP Document Reader; telegram from Zhou to Ho, March 11, 1954, CWIHP Document Reader; telegram from Chinese ambassador in Moscow to Beijing, March 6, 1954, as

quoted in Gaiduk, *Confronting Vietnam*, 17. The question of who first proposed the sixteenth parallel is not answered by the current documents. According to Chinese sources, Zhou first put forward the sixteenth parallel in his telegram to the DRV on March 2. See Xiong Huayuan and Liao Xinwen, *Zhou Enlai Zongli Shengya* (Zhou Enlai's Career as Premier) (Beijing, Renmin Chubanshe, 1997), 74–75. Gaiduk believed that as early as late January the Soviet diplomats had tested the French and British reactions to a partition along the sixteenth parallel, although he claimed that Soviet diplomats would not have done this without approvals from allies. See Gaiduk, *Confronting Vietnam*, 18. According to British sources, as early as late 1951, Chinese leaders had contemplated partition of Vietnam. See Nông Văn Dân, *Churchill, Eden and Indo-China, 1951–1955* (New York: Anthem Press, 2010), 54.

20. For the text of Dulles's remarks, see *Department of State Bulletin*, vol. 31, January 25, 1954, 107–10.

21. *New York Times*, March 30, 1954; *Department of State Bulletin*, April 12, 1954, 539–40.

22. *New York Times*, April 6, 1954.

23. *FRUS, 1952–54*, 13: 1280–81.

24. *New York Times*, April 17, 18, 1954; *FRUS, 1952–54*, 13: 1346–48.

25. "The French and British responses to U.S. clamor for 'United Action,'" April 16, 1954, CFMA, 102-00159-04, 14–17.

26. "America is stepping up expanding Thailand military force," in *Neibu Cankao*, November 16, 1953. After the Geneva Conference was decided, *Renmin Ribao* accused the United States of opposing negotiation and planning to expand the war on a daily basis. For example, see *Renmin Ribao*, March 4, 12, 14, 18, 19, 31, and April 3, 5, 9, 14, 18, 28, 1954.

27. "Premier Zhou Enlai's report on the national conference on foreign affairs of 1953," June 5, 1953, CFMA, 102-00110-01, 4–43.

28. "French attitude toward the Indochinese ceasefire negotiation as seen from the French parliament debate," March 9–13, 1954, CFMA, 102-00158-01, 71–3.

29. See "Latest development of the French and American contradictions on the issues of Indochinese ceasefire and 'European Army,'" March 15–20, 1954, CFMA, 102-00158-01, 75–79; "Our analysis of the French attitude toward the Vietnam problem," March 13, 1954, CFMA, 110-00258-08, 51–54; and "The American and French preparation for the Indochina issue to be discussed at the Geneva Conference," March 18, 1954, CFMA, 110-00258-04, 24–26.

30. Emphasis added. "Transcript, Zhou Enlai's speech at a preparatory meeting by the Chinese delegation attending the Geneva Conference (excerpt)," February 17, 1954. The translation of the quotation is adapted from Chen's translation in CWIHP Document Reader.

31. "Collection of documents on the British responses to the Indochina issue," March 25, 1954, CFMA, 110-00248-04, 16–21. For British policy toward the Geneva Conference, see Kevin Ruane, " 'Containing America': Aspects of British Foreign Policy and the Cold War in South-East Asia, 1951–54," in *Diplomacy & Statecraft* 7, no. 1 (March 1996): 141–74; Geoffrey Warner, "The Settlement of the Indochina War," in *The Foreign Policy of Churchill's Peacetime Administration, 1951–55*, ed. John W. Young (Leicester, UK: Leicester University Press, 1988), 233–59; and Matthew Jones, "Geneva Conference of 1954: New Perspectives and Evidence on British Policy

and Anglo-American Relations," presented at the Wilson Center workshop on the Geneva Conference, Washington, D.C., February 2006.

32. "The American and French preparation for the Indochina issue to be discussed at the Geneva Conference," March 18, 1954, CFMA, 110-00258-04, 24–26; *Renmin Ribao,* April 14, 1954.

33. *Mao Zedong Zhuan,* 555.

34. For China's position, see "Preliminary opinions on the peaceful solution of the Indochina problem prepared by Vietnam team of the Chinese delegation to the Geneva Conference," March 23, 1954, CFMA, 206-00057-03, 88–92; "Comprehensive proposal for the peaceful solution of the Indochina problem prepared by Vietnam team of the Chinese delegation to the Geneva Conference," March 24, 1954, CFMA, 206-00057-04, 99–100; "Proposal for restoring peace in Indochina," March 24, 1954, CFMA, 206-00057-05, 101–03; and "Draft proposal for the peaceful solution of the Indochina problem prepared by Vietnam team of the Chinese delegation to the Geneva Conference," March 1–31, 1954, CFMA, 206-00057-09, 195–202. For the Soviet position, see "Outline of directives on the issue of the restoration of peace in Indochina," March 17, 1954, included in the CWIHP Document Reader. For Chinese analysis of the DRV's positions and its difference with China, see "Table of proposals for the peaceful solution of the Indochina problem prepared by Vietnam team of the Chinese delegation to the Geneva Conference," March 1–31, 1954, CFMA, 206-00057-05, 143–58. This crucial document provides the most important information about the DRV leaders' considerations about the Geneva Conference at a series of politburo conferences held in preparation for the negotiation, and it is the only available document revealing the differences between China and the Vietnamese leadership. The message in this document is consistent with new Vietnamese documents, such as Vietnamese Ministry of Foreign Affairs, "The Diplomatic Struggle." The following analysis of the DRV's positions is primarily based on this document. See also Qian Jiang, *Zhou Enlai yu Rineiwa Huiyi* (Zhou Enlai and the Geneva Conference) (Beijing, China: Zhonggong Dangshi Chubanshe, 2005), 47–50. For the Chinese contact with the Soviets, see telegram from Zhang to Beijing, March 5, 1954, in *1954 Nian Rineiwa Huiyi,* 12–13; telegram from Zhang to Beijing, 6 March 1954, and Molotov's "Memorandum of Conversation with Zhang," 6 March 1954, both available in *CWIHP Bulletin,* Issue 16: 13–14, 86–88. For China's contact with the Vietnamese, see *Zhou Enlai Nianpu,* 1: 358. For the Soviet-Vietnamese contacts, see documents on March 5 and 31, 1954, CWIHP Document Reader; March 26, 1954, as quoted in Gaiduk, *Confronting Vietnam,* 17.

35. "Table of proposals for the peaceful solution of the Indochina problem prepared by the Vietnam team of the Chinese delegation to the Geneva Conference," March 1–31, 1954, CFMA, 206-00057-05, 143–58.

36. At this time, Chinese leaders had little idea about the history and geography of Indochina, as well as the situation in Laos and Cambodia, so they readily accepted the DRV's idea for an Indochinese Federation. See "Review of the work on the Geneva Conference (draft)," n.d., CFMA, 206-00019-01, 51.

37. See "Table of proposals for the peaceful solution of the Indochina problem prepared by the Vietnam team of the Chinese delegation to the Geneva Conference," March 1–31, 1954, CFMA, 206-00057-05, 143–58. For the evolution of the DRV's idea about a Federation of Indochina, see Christopher Goscha, "Geneva 1954 and

the 'de-internationalization' of the Vietnamese idea of Indochina" presented at the Wilson Center workshop on the Geneva Conference in February 2006.

38. For the DRV's reliance on China's assistance, see "The Diplomatic Struggle," 14. According to Qiang Zhai, "Until 1954, China bore full responsibility for guiding and support the Vietnamese revolution," in Zhai, "China and the Geneva Conference of 1954," 106.

39. According to Asselin, the DRV leaders "expected the Geneva talks to be difficult" and did "not harbour illusions that peace [would] come easily." See Asselin, "DRV and 1954 Geneva Conference," 166.

40. *Zhou Enlai Nianpu*, 1: 358; Zhongyang Wenxian Chubanshe, *Jianguo Yilai Mao Zedong Wengao* (Mao Zedong's Manuscripts since the Foundation of the People's Republic of China) (hereafter, Mao Wengao), (Beijing, China: Zhongyang Wenxian Chubanshe, 1989), 3: 480.

41. Olsen, *Soviet-Vietnam Relations and the Role of China*, 36; Qian, *Zhou Enlai yu Rineiwa Huiyi*, 67–69; *Mao Wengao*, 3: 474. The Chinese leaders also knew about the U.S. press prediction that China would not send troops to Indochina even if the United States increased assistance to France. "American *Business Week*'s misguided discussion of our attitude toward the Indochina issue," *Neibu Cankao*, April 7, 1954.

42. When meeting the North Korean delegation in Beijing on April 17, Zhou revealed that China would work against the United States' sabotage of Geneva and try to reach an agreement through diplomatic efforts. On the same day, Mao said he believed "it is possible that an armistice could happen in Vietnam," and in that case the Vietnamese artillery units, which were established and being trained in China, should be moved into Vietnam as soon as possible, lest an armistice prevented them from returning. *Mao Wengao*, 3: 480.

43. "Memorandum of Meeting between Soviet Ambassador Pavel Yudin and Mao," March 26, 1954, Soviet documents obtained by Shen Zhihua from Moscow (hereinafter cited SD with document number). For the Soviet perspective of the Communist meetings in Moscow, see Gaiduk, *Confronting Vietnam*, 22–24.

44. According to Goscha, the DRV leaders did not "over-emphasize the request that the Lao and Khmer resistance governments participate in the conference" in their talks with the Chinese and Soviets. Goscha, "Geneva 1954," 11.

45. "A comprehensive plan for Indochinese peace issue prepared by the Vietnam team of the Chinese delegation to the Geneva Conference," April 5, 1954, CFMA, 206-00055-04, 27–29. This Chinese document drafted during the Moscow meeting indicates that after the ceasefire, the two sides would adjust their territories "in a suitable way." This document is consistent with new Vietnamese sources, which clearly point out that the Communists failed to reach a consensus on this issue. See "The Diplomatic Struggle," 39. See also "Work summary of the Geneva Conference," undated document, CFMA, 206-00019-01, 13. This new evidence contradicts Gaiduk's argument that "during the negotiations in early April all principal questions relating to the Communist position at the forthcoming conference in Geneva were settled," and Olsen's argument that the Vietnamese agreed to divide Vietnam into two zones in the Communist meetings in Moscow. Gaiduk, *Confronting Vietnam*, 24; Olsen, *Soviet-Vietnam Relations and the Role of China*, 38.

46. On Soviet objectives in Geneva, see "Outline of directives on the issue of the restoration of peace in Indochina," March 17, 1954, in CWIHP Document Reader; and Qian, *Zhou Enlai yu Rineiwa Huiyi*, 63–65.

47. Olsen, *Soviet-Vietnam Relations and the Role of China*, 35.

48. Instructions by the Secretariat, April 7 and 10, 1954, CWIHP Document Reader. On his way to Geneva, Zhou once again met the Vietnamese leaders in Moscow. The Communists approved the Vietnamese "Opinions on the situation and our strategies and policies." See telegram from Zhou to Beijing about his meetings with the Communist leaders, April 23, 1954, CFMA, 206-00048-08, included in *1954 Nian Rineiwa Huiyi*, 18–19, and *CWIHP Bulletin*, Issue 16: 15. However, no Vietnamese document outlining these plans has turned up. Considering what happened later, the Vietnamese Communists apparently failed to come up with any concrete plans and just stated some general principles in it.

49. "Difficult situation facing France and the U.S. on the eve of the Geneva Conference," April 9, 1954, CFMA, 102-00159-03, 10–13.

50. Qian, *Zhou Enlai yu Rineiwa Huiyi*, 79–80; Li Lianqing, *She Zhan Rineiwa* (Verbal Warfare in Geneva) (Hong Kong, China: Cosmos Books, 1994), 15–18; *Renmin Ribao*, April 18, and 24, 1954.

51. *Zhou Enlai Waijiao Huodong Dashiji*, 58; *1954 Nian Rineiwa Huiyi*, 15–18; and *Zhou Enlai Nianpu*, 1: 60–61.

52. For the status of Hong Kong in U.S.-British relations during the 1950s, see Tracy Steel, "Hong Kong and the Cold War in the 1950s," in *Hong Kong in the Cold War*, ed. Priscilla Roberts and John M. Carroll (Hong Kong, China: Hong Kong University Press, 2016), 92–116; Chi-Kwan Mark, "A Reward for Good Behavior in the Cold War: Bargaining over the Defense of Hong Kong, 1949–1957," *The International History Review* 22, no. 4 (Dec., 2000): 837–61; Johannes R. Lombardo, "Eisenhower, the British and the Security of Hong Kong, 1953–60," *Diplomacy & Statecraft* 9, no. 3 (1998): 134–53; and Nancy Bernkopf Tucker, *Taiwan, Hong Kong, and the United States, 1945–1992: Uncertain Friendships* (New York: Twayne, 1994), 200–08.

53. As they expected, the discussion reached a deadlock three days after the conference because the United States did not want to solve the problem and Britain and France were not interested. See telegram from Zhou to Mao, Liu, and the CCP Central Committee, April 28, 1954, CWIHP Document Reader. Similarly, the Soviet leaders did not expect to solve the Korean problem, as Molotov had told Eden in Berlin. Gaiduk, *Confronting Vietnam*, 29.

54. Telegram from Zhou to Mao, April 26, 1954, *CWIHP Bulletin*, Issue 16: 15–16. The Soviets did not struggle for the attendance of the two "Resistance Governments" and were satisfied with the participation of the DRV delegation. For Molotov's efforts to invite the DRV and Western reactions to his proposal, see Gaiduk, *Confronting Vietnam*, 29–31. For the Communist plan about attendance of "Resistance Governments," see *1954 Nian Rineiwa Huiyi*, 120.

55. Telegram from Zhou, May 1, 1954, in *1954 Nian Rineiwa Huiyi*, 97; *CWIHP Bulletin*, Issue 16: 16–17. Telegram from Zhou to Beijing, May 3, 1954, in *1954 Nian Rineiwa Huiyi*, 402–07. "Telegram regarding setting up diplomatic relations with Britain," May 4, 1954, CFMA, 110-00023-04.

56. "British actions in the beginning period of the Geneva Conference," May 7, 1954, CFMA, 102-00159-07, 30–31; Telegram from Zhou to Mao, May 1, 1954, in *1954 Nian Rineiwa Huiyi*, 97; and "IV: Preliminary opinion on a peaceful solution to the Indochina problem," March 23, 1954, CFMA, 206-00057-03, 2.

57. As indicated earlier, the Communists had also attempted to let the delegations of the two "Resistance Governments" attend the conference independently but had to drop

the proposal in Geneva. For the Communist plan about attendance of "Resistance Governments," see *1954 Nian Rineiwa Huiyi*, 120. For Molotov's efforts to invite the DRV and the Western reactions, see Gaiduk, *Confronting Vietnam*, 29–31.

58. *1954 Nian Rineiwa Huiyi*, 122.

59. For details about the Franco-American secret talks, see chap. 2.

60. *1954 Nian Rineiwa Huiyi*, 259–60.

61. *1954 Nian Rineiwa Huiyi*, 261–63.

62. Anthony Eden, *Full Circle: The Memoirs of Sir Anthony Eden* (London: Cassell, 1960), 122.

63. "Minutes of the Meeting of Wang Jiaxiang, Pham Van Dong and Gromyko," May 15, 1954, CWIHP Document Reader. Meanwhile, the French stressed to the Chinese officials the significance of distinguishing Laos and Cambodia from Vietnam: the Vietnamese invasion of Laos and Cambodia would lead to a Southeast Asia bloc, which would put China in a disadvantageous position. For the minutes of the meeting between Chinese and French diplomats on May 18, 1954, see *1954 Nian Rineiwa Huiyi*, 259–60. For Zhou's report to Beijing about this issue on May 19, 1954, see *1954 Nian Rineiwa Huiyi*, 132.

64. "The Diplomatic Struggle," 40; and Gaiduk, *Confronting Vietnam*, 37.

65. 5 June 1954, CWIHP Document Reader; Qian, *Zhou Enlai yu Rineiwa Huiyi*, 263–64; Randle, *Geneva 1954*, 232.

66. For details, see chaps. 3 and 4.

67. Regarding the tensions in the Taiwan Strait and U.S. official visits to Taiwan, there are numerous briefings in the May 21, 22, 24, 25, 26, and 27 issues of *Neibu Cankao*. For Chinese Foreign Ministry analysis of U.S. efforts to conclude a Southeast Asia Defense Pact, see "U.S. actions in Southeast Asia after the liberation of Dien Bien Phu and the contradictions between the U.S. and Britain and France," May 28, 1954, CFMA, 102-000159-10, 42–44. See also, *Renmin Ribao*, May 26, 1954.

68. "The U.S. actions in the Southeast Asia after the liberation of Dien Bien Phu and the contradictions between the U.S. and Britain and France," May 28, 1954, CFMA, 102-000159-10, 42–44.

69. "The Diplomatic Struggle," 24.

70. Telegram from Zhou to Mao and others about the eighth restricted session, May 30, 1954, *CWIHP Bulletin*, Issue 16: 26; *Zhou Enlai Nianpu*, 1: 371–72; "The Diplomatic Struggle," 40; and Goscha, "Geneva 1954," 12–15. Zhou's telegram answers Gaiduk's question of what China did to convince the Vietnamese that partition served their interest. See Gaiduk, *Confronting Vietnam*, 38.

71. *1954 Nian Rineiwa Huiyi*, 268–70; and Minutes of Zhou's Meeting with Bidault, June 1, 1954, in *CWIHP Bulletin*, Issue 16: 28–30.

72. *1954 Nian Rineiwa Huiyi*, 271–76; and Minutes of Wang Bingnan's Meetings with Jean Chauvel and Jacques Guillermaz, June 5, 1954, in *CWIHP Bulletin*, Issue 16: 34–38.

73. *1954 Nian Rineiwa Huiyi*, 239.

74. *1954 Nian Rineiwa Huiyi*, 420–24.

75. "The Diplomatic Struggle," 40–41. The DRV made this decision under the pressure of U.S. intervention—coincidentally, just as the U.S. leaders decided to give up that option. See chap. 2.

76. Gaiduk, *Confronting Vietnam*, 37.

77. Goscha, "Geneva 1954," 19.

78. *FRUS*, 1952–54, 16: 899; Gaiduk, *Confronting Vietnam*, 36.

79. *1954 Nian Rineiwa Huiyi*, 165–66; June 10, 1954, CWIHP Document Reader.

80. *1954 Nian Rineiwa Huiyi*, 424–25.

81. *1954 Nian Rineiwa Huiyi*, 101–4. The negotiation on the Korean problem ended on June 16, without any result.

82. *Renmin Ribao*, June 9 and 10, 1954.

83. *Renmin Ribao*, June 5, 1954.

84. *Zhou Enlai Nianpu*,1: 380, 382.

85. "The Diplomatic Struggle," 41.

86. *1954 Nian Rineiwa Huiyi*, 166–67, 169, 240–41; and Minutes of Conversation between Zhang Wentian and [Harold] Caccia, June 15, 1954, CWIHP Document Reader.

87. *Zhou Enlai Waijiao Huodong Dashiji*, 66.

88. *1954 Nian Rineiwa Huiyi*, 170–72.

89. AVP RF, f. 06, op. 13a, p. 25, d. 8, ll., 29–33., as quoted by Gaiduk, *Confronting Vietnam*, 39.

90. *1954 Nian Rineiwa Huiyi*, 428–29.

91. *FRUS*, 1952–54, 16: 1189.

92. For Chinese Foreign Ministry analysis of the French politicians, see "Analysis of the French ruling group," January 29, 1954, CFMA, 110-00258-09, 56–57. For the Soviet contact with Mendès France's policy advisor, see MID USSR—Plans for discussions with Zhou and Ho, AVP RF, f. 022, op. 7b, pa. 106, d. 7, 23–26, quoted in Olsen, *Soviet-Vietnam Relations and the Role of China*, 34–35.

93. Emphasis added. *Zhou Enlai Nianpu*,1: 386; CWIHP Document Reader. On the DRV's considerations about Cambodia and Laos, see Goscha, "Geneva 1954," 18–24.

94. Asselin, "The Democratic Republic of Vietnamese and the Geneva Conference," 168. According to Edward Miller, the United States was not involved in Diem's appointment. See Miller, "Vison, Power, and Agency: The Ascent of Ngo Dinh Diem, 1945–1954," in *Making Sense of the Vietnam Wars: Local, National, and Transnational Perspectives*, ed. Mark Bradley and Marilyn Young (New York: Oxford University Press, 2008), 135–69.

95. *Mao Wengao*, 3: 509.

96. Goscha, "Geneva 1954," especially 30–34.

97. The Vietnamese saw the continuation of the conference against U.S. sabotage as a "victory of great significance," which exceeded "our original expectation." See "The Diplomatic Struggle," 30–31.

98. *Mao Wengao*, 3: 509.

99. *1954 Nian Rineiwa Huiyi*, 316–19; *Zhou Enlai Waijiao Huodong Dashiji*, 68; *Zhou Enlai Nianpu*,1: 389–90; CWIHP Document Reader; Goscha, "Geneva 1954," 21–22.

100. *Zhou Enlai Nianpu*, 1: 390; Gaiduk, *Confronting Vietnam*, 42.

101. *1954 Nian Rineiwa Huiyi*, 289–97; *CWIHP Bulletin*, Issue 16: 51–55.

102. *1954 Nian Rineiwa Huiyi*, 242; *CWIHP Bulletin*, Issue 16: 51.

103. *Renmin Ribao*, June 27, 1954; Eden, *Full Circle*, 131. The Pact of Locarno included a series of agreements between the two sides of WWI. It was initiated in Locarno, Switzerland, in October 1925 but signed in London in December. According to the

pact, the two former antagonistic sides mutually guaranteed each other's peace, and hence, "Locarno" or "the Spirit of Locarno" became synonymous with "compromise" or "a sense of goodwill."

104. "The U.S. attempts to form a 'Southeast Asian defense group'," June 30, 1954, CFMA, 105-00626-01, 1–12.

105. The goal of Zhou's visit to India has not been adequately discussed in the current literature. New sources from the CFMA show that his objective was to win over the Indians and build a zone of peace to exclude U.S. influence from Asia. See "About Concluding a Mutual Non-Aggression Treaty with Southeast Asian States," June 13, 1954, CFMA, 203-00005-06, 55–57; "Opinion About Concluding a Mutual Non-Aggression Treaty with Southeast Asian States," June 17, 1954, CFMA, 203-00005-06, 58–60; and "Goal and Plan for Premier Zhou Enlai's Visit to India," June 22, 1954, CFMA, 203-00005-01, 3–4. According to Goscha, the Indians were interested in the neutralization of Laos and Cambodia and were relieved when Zhou confirmed to Nehru that the two states were different from Vietnam and should become neutral states. See Goscha, "Geneva 1954," 24–25.

106. "Minutes of Zhou Enlai's meetings in his visit to India," June 25, 1954, CFMA, 203-00006-01; *Zhou Enlai Nianpu*, 1: 390–93. For the Indian records of Zhou's meetings with Nehru, see *The Selected Works of Jawaharlal Nehru*, ed. S. Gopal, et al. (New Delhi, India: Jawaharlal Nehru Memorial Fund; Distributed by Oxford University Press, 1999), 26: 366–98. For India's policy toward Indochina, see Gilles Boquérat, "India's Commitment to Peaceful Coexistence and the Settlement of the Indochina War," *Cold War History* 5, no. 2 (May 2005): 211–34.

107. "Summary of the issue of establishing Sino-British diplomacy," June 25, 1954, CFMA, 110-00023-18, 52; *Mao Zedong Zhuan*, 562–64; *Zhou Enlai Nianpu*, 1: 395; and *1954 Nian Rineiwa Huiyi*, 185.

108. Record of Conversation Between Soviet Chargé d'affaires in China Vaskov and Mao, July 5, 1954, AVP RF, f. 0100, op. 47, pa. 379, d. 7, 69–70; SD13016. See also Gaiduk, *Confronting Vietnam*, 43. The Chinese perception, however, was wrong. The British and American leaders reached a confidential seven-point agreement, which later served as the basis for the Western position in the Geneva negotiation. The essence of the agreement was integrity and independence for Laos and Cambodia, and division of Vietnam along the eighteenth parallel. But the agreement was not raised publicly at Eden's request. For the seven-point agreement, see Eden, *Full Circle*, 132–33, and "The Diplomatic Struggle," 34. Moreover, the British agreed to study concrete steps to be taken to establish the defense pact, and a joint study group started working quickly after the British visit. See *FRUS, 1952–54*, 13: 580–82 and *FRUS, 1952–54*, 16: 1254–55.

109. "Report on the so-called British Asian Locarno Plan," July 4, 1954, CFMA, 110-00244-03; *Renmin Ribao*, July 5, 1954.

110. Minutes of these important meetings are not found in the declassified documents, but the contents of the meetings are disclosed in Xiong, *Zhou Enlai Chudeng Shijie Wutai*, 139–44, Li, *Shezhan Rineiwa*, 335–36, *Zhou Enlai Nianpu*, 1: 394–95, and "The Diplomatic Struggle," 41, 54–55. For a detailed analysis of the meetings, see Chen, "China and the Indochina Settlement," 254–57.

111. "The Diplomatic Struggle," 35, 41–42; Asselin, "DRV and 1954 Geneva Conference," 169–70; and Goscha, "Geneva 1954," 28.

112. Ho's presentation is in Xiong, *Zhou Enlai Chudeng Shijie Wutai*, 143–44. English translation by Chen Jian is in "China and the Indochina Settlement," 257, and in CWIHP Document Reader.
113. Peking to Foreign Office (hereafter FO), July 8, 1954, FO 371/112076, NAUK; available in CWIHP Document Reader.
114. *Renmin Ribao*, July 11, 1954.
115. *Zhou Enlai Nianpu*, 1: 395–96.
116. Wang Bingnan, *Zhongmei Huitan Jiunian Huigu* (Reflections on the Nine-Year Sino-American Talks) (Beijing, China: Shijie Zhishi Chubanshe, 1985), 19–20; and *Mao Zedong Zhuan*, 560.
117. *1954 Nian Rineiwa Huiyi*, 185–86. The United States asked Britain to request that China set free some U.S. nationals detained in China, including a dozen U.S. airmen, whose planes were shot down on what China saw as reconnaissance trips in Manchuria. When the British approached China again in Geneva, Zhou suggested a direct meeting between Chinese and American officials. The two sides met four times, but the meetings were restricted to consulate affairs and did not bring about any results. For the consulate talks in Geneva, see Yafeng Xia, *Negotiating with the Enemy: U.S.-China Talks During the Cold War, 1949–1972* (Bloomington and Indianapolis: Indiana University Press, 2006), 77–79; and Su-Ya Chang, "Wengong Wuxia Xia de Tuisuo: Meiguo Jueding yu Zhonggong Juxing Dashiji Taipan de Guocheng Fenxi, 1954–1955" (Retreat before Verbal Attack and Military Threat: Analysis of US Decision to Hold Ambassadorial Talks with the Chinese Communists, 1954–1955), *Zhongyang Yanjiuyua Jingdaishi Yanjiusuo Jikan* 25 (June 1996): 384–92.
118. *1954 Nian Rineiwa Huiyi*, 231–32. For details about Zhou's meeting with the Soviet leaders, see Chen, "China and the Indochina Settlement," 258–59.
119. Li Kenong's report to Zhou on the progress of the Geneva Conference, July 12, 1954, in *Zhonggong Dangshi Ziliao* (Materials of the History of the Chinese Communist Party) issue of March 1999: 69; CWIHP Document Reader.
120. For the Chinese perception of the meeting in Paris, see *Remin Ribao*, July 15, 1954.
121. "Minutes of the meeting between Zhou Enlai and Pham Van Dong," July 12, 1954, CWIHP Document Reader. For detailed analysis of the meeting, see Chen, "China and the Indochina Settlement," 259–60.
122. Li Lianqing, *Lengnuan Suiyue: Yibosanzhe de Zhongsu Guanxi* (Warm and Cold Times: Ups and Downs in Sino-Soviet Relations) (Beijing, China: Shijie Zhishi Chubanshe, 1999), 226–27.
123. Li, *She Zhan Rineiwa*, 359–64; *1954 Nian Rineiwa Huiyi*, 305–9; and Minutes of Zhou's meeting with the French leader, July 13, 1954, in CWIHP Document Reader.
124. Gaiduk, *Confronting Vietnam*, 44.
125. Li, *She Zhan Rineiwa*, 364–69; *1954 Nian Rineiwa Huiyi*, 243–45; CWIHP Document Reader. The new sources first allow for a more sophisticated description of Zhou's diplomacy in the final stage of the Geneva Conference, especially Zhou's meetings with Laos and Cambodia, which best demonstrate both China's goal in Geneva and the tactics it used to achieve that goal.
126. For Zhou's meetings with the Cambodians and Laotians, see telegram from Zhou to Beijing, *1954 Nian Rineiwa Huiyi*, 320, 331; July 15, 1954, CWIHP Document Reader.

127. *FRUS, 1952–54*, 16: 1226, 1235–36, 1338, 1342.

128. *1954 Nian Rineiwa Huiyi*, 233–34; July 14, 1954, CWIHP Document Reader. *Renmin Ribao* reported that the negotiation was getting close to an agreement. *Renmin Ribao*, July 18, 1954.

129. Telegram from Zhou to Wei Guoqing, July 15, 1954, as quoted in *Zhou Enlai Nianpu*, 1: 399; and CWIHP Document Reader.

130. For the Soviet role in the last phase of the Geneva Conference, see Gaiduk, *Confronting Vietnam*, 45–53.

131. *Zhou Enlai Nianpu*, 1: 399; and "Record of a conversation with Chou En-lai and Pham Van Dong," July 16, 1954, in CWIHP Document Reader.

132. Goscha, "Geneva 1954," 28.

133. *Renmin Ribao*, July 8 and 19, 1954. However, the Chinese thought was incorrect. According to American documents, U.S. leaders were not considering an MDT with the GMD at this time, and Van Fleet's did not seek an MDT in his visit. See "Memorandum of Conversation between Wellington V. Koo and E. F. Drumright and Walter P. McConaughy," Records of the Bureau of Far Eastern Affairs Relating to Southeast Asia and the Geneva Conference, 1954, April–June 1954, box 14, RG 59, National Archives of the United States, College Park, Maryland (hereafter NAUS).

134. Some Chinese officials believed Van Fleet wanted to link the two military blocs in the North and South Pacific. See "Van Fleet's conspiracy in the Far East," July 17, 1954, CFMA, 206-00117-05, 101–2.

135. *Zhou Enlai Nianpu*, 1: 399–40; record of a conversation with Dong and Zhou, July 16, 1954, CWIHP Document Reader.

136. Record of a conversation with Dong and Zhou, July 16, 1954, CWIHP Document Reader.

137. "Mendès France cabinet and its domestic and foreign policy," July 17, 1954, CFMA, 206-00117-06, 103–5.

138. For Zhou's meeting with Eden, July 17, 1954, see *1954 Nian Rineiwa Huiyi*, 246–51; *CWIHP Bulletin*, Issue 16: 65–68. Eden's reassurances about SEATO did not seem to assuage Chinese leaders, who continued to believe the British wanted a Locarno-type pact.

139. *1954 Nian Rineiwa Huiyi*, 252–54. However, Eden played a dual game: he had privately reached an agreement with Smith that SEATO would cover these states, despite their exclusion from the membership. See Lloyd C. Gardner, *Approaching Vietnam: From World War II Through Dienbienphu, 1941–1954* (New York: Norton, 1988), 313.

140. *1954 Nian Rineiwa Huiyi*, 307–9; and Minutes of Zhou's meeting with Mendès France, July 17, 1954, in *CWIHP Bulletin*, Issue 16: 68–69. See also memorandum of conversation between Molotov, Zhou Enlai, and Pham Van Dong, July 17, 1954, AVP RF, f. 06, op. 13a, p. 25, d. 8, 1. 107, *CWIHP Bulletin*, Issue 16: 97–99.

141. *1954 Nian Rineiwa Huiyi*, 321–22.

142. *1954 Nian Rineiwa Huiyi*, 332–35.

143. Gaiduk, *Confronting Vietnam*, 47.

144. Gaiduk, *Confronting Vietnam*, 47.

145. *1954 Nian Rineiwa Huiyi*, 196–97; CWIHP Document Reader.

146. *1954 Nian Rineiwa Huiyi*, 310–12; 13–15; CWIHP Document Reader.

147. *1954 Nian Rineiwa Huiyi*, 252–58; *CWIHP Bulletin*, Issue 16: 77–78.
148. *1954 Nian Rineiwa Huiyi*, 322–38; *CWIHP Bulletin*, Issue 16: 80–83.
149. In addition to Zhou's combination of concessions and warnings, another important reason for the two states' agreement to neutralization was a change in U.S. policy. At this point, U.S. officials were convincing them to give up potential memberships in the Southeast Asian defense pact. See telegram: Smith-Kimny Meeting, July 18, 1954, in *FRUS, 1952–54*, 16: 1425–26.
150. *1954 Nian Rineiwa Huiyi*, 474–76. In private, Zhou believed letting the French stay was a wise way to keep the United States out.
151. *1954 Nian Rineiwa Huiyi*, 212; CWIHP Document Reader.
152. According to Olsen, "The Chinese performance during the Geneva Conference was decisive, not only in the eyes of the Western powers but also to the Soviets." See Olsen, *Soviet-Vietnam Relations and the Role of China*, 43–44.
153. To a great extent, the British misled the Chinese. According to Lloyd C. Gardner, the British public appearance was not consistent with the positions they privately reached with the Americans. Although British leaders were not able to convince the United States to take a conciliatory stance toward the Communists in their visit to Washington in late June, Churchill "portrayed the outcome of the Washington talks as a green light for pursuing a rapprochement with both Russia and China." While promising Zhou that Laos and Cambodia would not be included in any defense pact, Eden agreed with American delegates that SEATO should put under its protection the Indochinese associate states. Gardner, *Approaching Vietnam*, 307, 313. For the Chinese perception of conflicts between the Western states, see "Review of [our] participation in the Geneva Conference (draft)," March 1955, CFMA, 206-00019-01, 8–54.
154. For the division of labor among the Communists, see Gaiduk, *Confronting Vietnam*, 34; and Olsen, *Soviet-Vietnam Relations and the Role of China*, 28.
155. My perusal of the Chinese documents corroborates Gaiduk's analysis of the Soviet documents. See Gaiduk, *Confronting Vietnam*, 32. But it goes against Zhai's and Immerman's arguments about the conflicts between the Chinese and Soviet leaders. See Zhai, "China and the Geneva Conference of 1954"; and Richard Immerman, "The United States and the Geneva Conference of 1954: A New Look," *Diplomatic History* 14, no. 1 (January 1990).
156. For detailed analysis of the DRV leaders' need for the agreements, see Goscha, "Geneva 1954," 34–36, and Asselin, "The Democratic Republic of Vietnam and the Geneva Conference," 176–83.
157. Immediately after the conference, both the Vietnam delegation and Ho believed by securing peace the DRV won a "tremendous victory" through diplomacy; the VWP Central Committee concluded that the peaceful settlement of the Indochina problem "shattered the scheme of the American imperialists to prolong and expand war in Indochina." See "Diplomatic Struggle," 65, 67, and 69.
158. Chen, "China and the Indochina Settlement," 262.
159. Xiaoming Zhang, "Deng Xiaoping and China's Decision to go to war with Vietnam," *Journal of Cold War Studies* 12, no. 3 (Summer 2010), 3–29; James Mann, *About Face: A History of America's Curious Relationship with China, from Nixon to Clinton* (New York: Vintage Books, 2000), 26–154.

2. BETWEEN THE UNATTAINABLE AND THE UNACCEPTABLE

1. U.S. Department of State, *Foreign Relations of the United States (FRUS), 1952–54*, 16: 464. Bonsal was Director of Philippine and Southeast Asian Affairs of the State Department.

2. Brownjohn to Prime Minister, April 26, 1954, FO371/112057, National Archives of the United Kingdom, Kew, London (hereafter NAUK).

3. "Note sur la situation militaire en Indochine à la veille de la Conférence de Genève," 21 avril 1954, AN, F60 3038, dossier note sur la situation militaire en Indochine à la veille de la Conférence de Genève; cited in James David Anthony Waite, "The End of the First Indochina War: An International History," PhD diss., Ohio University, 2005, 242.

4. Eisenhower revisionists are mainly interested in Eisenhower's "decision against war" during the Dien Bien Phu crisis, and U.S. policy toward the Geneva negotiation was underexplored. Gary Hess and George Herring focus on Dulles's quest of "united action" with allies to deter the Communists and prepare for intervention, taking the negotiation as "holding action." See Gary Hess, "Redefining the American Position in Southeast Asia: The United States and the Geneva and Manila Conferences," in *Dien Bien Phu and the Crisis of Franco-American Relations, 1954–1955*, 123–67; and George Herring, " 'A Good Stout Effort': John Foster Dulles and the Indochina Crisis, 1954–1955," in *John Foster Dulles and the Diplomacy of the Cold War*, 213–33. A typical post revisionist work, Richard Immerman's "The United States and the Geneva Conference" examines Washington's perception of Sino-Soviet differences and explains why the Eisenhower administration failed to negotiate with the Communists, and thus laid the ground for the later Vietnam tragedy. There are more works studying U.S. relations with allies. See Lloyd Gardner, *Approaching Vietnam: From World War II Through Dienbienphu* (New York: Norton, 1989); Geoffrey Warner, "The Settlement of the Indochina War," in *The Foreign Policy of Churchill's Peacetime Administration, 1961–66*, ed. by John Young (Leicester, UK: Leicester University Press, 1988), 233–59; Kevin Ruane, " 'Containing America': Aspects of British Foreign Policy and the Cold War in South-East Asia, 1951–54," *Diplomacy & Statecraft* 7, no. 1 (March 1996): 141–74; Waite, "The End of the First Indochina War"; Lucia J. Rather, "The Geneva Conference of 1954: Problems in Allied Unity," PhD diss., University of North Carolina, 1994; and Matthew Jones, "The Geneva Conference of 1954: New Perspectives and Evidence on British Policy and Anglo-American Relations," presented at the international workshop on the Geneva Conference on Indochina, the Cold War International History Project, Woodrow Wilson International Center for Scholars, February 2006.

5. *FRUS, 1952–54*, 14: 358. See also *The Pentagon Papers* (Boston, Mass.: Beacon Press, 1971; Senator Gravel ed.), 1: 81–87; Richard Immeman, "The Prologue: Perceptions by the United States of Its Interests in Indochina," especially 7–13, in *Dien Bien Phu and the Crisis in Franco-American Relations*; Robert J. McMahon, *The Limits of Empire: The United States and Southeast Asia since World War II* (New York: Columbia University Press, 1999), 33–49, 59–63.

6. For the strategic status of Indochina, see Michael Schaller, "Securing the Great Crescent: Occupied Japan and the Origins of Containment in Southeast Asia," *Journal of American History* 69, no. 2 (September 1982): 392–414; George Herring, *America's Longest War: The United States and Vietnam, 1950–1975* (New York: McGraw-Hill 2002), 15–21.

7. Anita Inder Singh, *The Limits of British Influence: South Asia and the Anglo-American Relations, 1947–1956* (New York: St. Martin's Press, 1993), 158–59; Herring and Immerman, "Eisenhower, Dulles, and Dienbienphu," 344.

8. *FRUS, 1950,* 1: 234–92.

9. Herring, *America's Longest War,* 27.

10. *FRUS, 1952–54,* 12, part 1: 127–34; *Pentagon Papers,* 1: 384–90.

11. Dulles at the White House Conference for the Advertising Council, March 24, 1953; cited in Gurtov, *The Frist Vietnam Crisis: Chinese Communist Strategy and United States Involvement, 1953–1954* (New York: Columbia University Press, 1967), 27–28.

12. *New York Times,* August 5, 1953, 10; *FRUS, 1952–54,* 15: 1341–44. Some officials worried about Chinese intervention in Vietnam. An NSC document in January 1954 noticed that "the situation in Indochina today is almost identical to that existing in Korea during the second week of September 1950, the date of overt Chinese Communist participation. . . . With a simple change of place names, North Korea to Vietminh Army and minor variations to fit the situation, the reports, activities, and themes could be interchanged." But primarily, U.S. leaders believed China would not openly intervene in Indochina. See "Sino-Soviet Direction and Nature of the Indo-China Conflict," January 19, 1954, White House Office, National Security Council Staff Papers, 1948–61 (hereafter WHO-NSC), Operations Coordinating Board (OCB) Central File Series, box 37, Dwight D. Eisenhower Presidential Library (DDEL), Abilene, Kansas; "Probable Communist reactions to certain possible US courses of action in Indochina through 1954," December 18, 1953, Records of the Bureau of Intelligence and Research, Lot File No. 78 D394, box 3, Record Group 59, NAUS. See also Randle, *Geneva 1954,* 17; Herring, *America's Longest War,* 30–33; Gurtov, *First Vietnam Crisis,* 31; and Fredrik, *Embers of War: The Fall of An Empire and The Making of America's Vietnam* (New York: Random House, 2012), 345.

13. *FRUS, 1952–54,* 13: 971–76; *Pentagon Papers,* 1: 435–37.

14. *FRUS, 1952–54,* 13: 747.

15. "Evolution of Foreign Policy," Dulles speech to the Council of Foreign Relations, New York City, January 12, 1954. Department of State, *Press Release,* no. 81, January 12, 1954; *Department of State Bulletin,* January 25, 1954, 107–10. For evaluation of the strategy of massive retaliation, see John Lewis Gaddis, *Strategies of Containment: A Critical Reappraisal of Postwar American National Security Policy* (New York: Oxford University Press, 1982), 127–63.

16. *FRUS, 1952–54,* 8: 1168–69. See also *FRUS, 1952–54,* 8: 1157, 1166; and "Special Estimate for Secretary of State: Current Communist Tactics," April 24, 1953, Records of the Bureau of Intelligence and Research, Lot File No. 78 D394, box 3, RG 59, NAUS.

17. *FRUS, 1952–54,* 13: 971–76.

18. *FRUS, 1952–54,* 13: 929–31.

19. *FRUS, 1952–54,* 13: 1020–21; see also 796–97. Although the U.S. basic national security policy did not rule out the possibility of negotiating with Communists, Washington was only willing to talk to them from a position of strength. See Immerman, "The United States and the Geneva Conference," 45.

20. Cited in Francis Noland Dawson, "The 1954 Geneva Conference: Eisenhower's Indochina Policy," 39, PhD diss., West Virginia University, 1985. For the French policy toward the Geneva Conference, see Pierre Grosser, "Untying the Knots: France and the Geneva Conference," in *Dien Bien Phu and the Crisis in Franco-American*

Relations, 1954–1955, ed. Lawrence Kaplan, Denise Artaud, and Mark Rubin (Wilmington, Del.: Scholarly Resources, 1990), 29–48.

21. *FRUS, 1952–54*, 13: 656–66; 706–9; 736–37. James Cable, *The Geneva Conference of 1954 on Indochina* (Basingstoke, UK: Macmillan, 1986), 21.

22. For the French reaction to Ho's initiative and their interest in the five-power conference, see Logevall, *Embers of War*, 397–99; 349–52 and 402; and Gardner, *Approaching Vietnam*, 141, 156, 160–62.

23. Nông Văn Dân, *Churchill, Eden and Indo-China, 1951–1955* (New York: Anthem, 2010), 81–90; Young, "Churchill, the Russians and the Western Alliance," 889–912; and Rosemary Foot, "Search for a Modus Vivendi: Anglo-American Relations and China Policy," in *Great Powers in East Asia*, 143–63. For the UK–U.S. differences, see Ruane, " 'Containing America' "; and "Anthony Eden, British Diplomacy and the Origins of the Geneva Conference of 1954," in *Historical Journal 37*, 1 (1994): 153–72.

24. Gardner, *Approaching Vietnam*, 160. For interpretation of the Bermuda Conference, see J. W. Young, "Churchill, the Russians and the Western Alliance: The Three-Power Conference at Bermuda, December 1953," *English Historical Review* 101, no. 401 (October 1986): 889–912.

25. *FRUS, 1952–54*, 13: 1057, 1080–81; *FRUS, 1952–54*, 7: 1205; "RC's Summary of Principal Points Made by the President in Talking with Republican Leaders, May 3, 1954," Dulles Papers, Subject Series, box 9, DDEL. Immerman, "The United States and the Geneva Conference," 49–50. For the importance of EDC and the leverage the French enjoyed in its relations with the United States, see *Pentagon Papers*, 1: 54, 75–81. For interpretation of the EDC, see Brian R. Duchin, "The 'Agonizing Reappraisal': Eisenhower, Dulles, and the European Defense Community," *Diplomatic History* 16, no. 2 (Spring 1992), 201–21; Ruane, "Containing America," 159–60; "Anthony Eden and Geneva 1954," 169; and Cable, *The Indochina Conference of 1954*, 42–43. For detailed analysis of the U.S.-Franco-British relations and the Berlin meeting, see Kevin Ruane, "Anthony Eden, British Diplomacy and the Origins of the Geneva Conference of 1954," 153–72.

26. U.S. Delegation (Berlin) to Department of State (DOS), January 26, 1954, 396.1-BE/1-2654, NAUS; cited in Rather, "The Geneva Conference of 1954," 81.

27. *FRUS, 1952–54*, 7: 890–92, 1205, 1046; "Far Eastern Aspects of the Berlin Conference," January 15, 1954, Records of the Bureau of the Far Eastern Affairs Relating to the Southeast Asia and the Geneva Conference (hereafter FE Records on Geneva), box 2, RG 59, NAUS.

28. *FRUS, 1952–54*, 16: 417–24; "Possible Problems vis-à-vis France in Connection to the Geneva Conference," March 8, 1954, FE Records on Geneva, box 13, RG 59, NAUS. U.S. officials learned from a Soviet diplomat in early March that the Communists wanted a partition at the sixteenth parallel. See *Pentagon Papers*, 1: 134.

29. *FRUS, 1952–54*, 14: 389. See also "U.S. position to be taken at Geneva—Chinese Communist commentary on Indochina," April 15, 1954, FE Records on Geneva, box 13, RG 59, NAUS.

30. *FRUS, 1952–54*, 16: 464. See also "China newspaper article listing reasons for U.S. agreeing to the Geneva Conference at Berlin," March 13, 1954, FE Records on Geneva, box 13, RG 59, NAUS; "Preparation for the Geneva Conference: recommendation for establishing additional working group on Communist China," March 15, 1954, General Subject File Relating to the People's Republic of China, 1954–61 (hereafter PRC File), box 24, RG 59, NAUS.

31. Dulles, to Eisenhower, February 1, 1954, AWF, Dulles-Herter Series, box 1, DDEL.

32. *FRUS, 1952–54*, 14: 391–93. Immerman, "The United States and the Geneva Conference," 52–54.

33. *FRUS, 1952–54*, 14: 397–99; "Preparation for the Geneva Conference: recommendation for establishing additional working group on Communist China," March 15, 1954, PRC File, box 24, RG 59, NAUS. See also *FRUS, 1952–54*, 16: 476; *FRUS, 1952–54*, 13: 1109–16, 1174.

34. *FRUS, 1952–54*, 16: 427–28, 448–51, and 472–479; *FRUS, 1952–54*, 13: 1093, 1174. See also *From Pearl Harbor to Vietnam: The Memoirs of Admiral Arthur W. Radford*, ed. Stephen Jurika Jr. (Stanford, Calif.: Hoover Institution Press, 1980), 388–93.

35. *FRUS, 1952–54*, 16: 441–42; *FRUS, 1952–54*, 13: 1109–16. For U.S.-French collaboration in Indochina and the Origins of the Navarre Plan, see Herring, *America's Longest War*, 24–33.

36. *FRUS, 1952–54*, 14: 396, 400, 407; *FRUS, 1952–54, 13*: 1150.

37. *FRUS, 1952–54*, 16: 427–28, 449, 475–76; *FRUS, 1952–54*, 14: 398; *FRUS, 1952–54*, 13: 1174. For the "holding action" diplomacy, see Gary R. Hess, "Redefining the American Position in Southeast Asia: The United States and the Geneva and Manila Conferences," in *Dien Bien Phu and the Crisis of Franco-American Relations*, 123–48.

38. *FRUS, 1952–54*, 13: 1280–81. For the full record of the news conference, see *Public Papers of the Presidents of the United States: Dwight D. Eisenhower, 1954* (Washington, D.C.: Governmental Printing Office, 1959–1964), 381–90.

39. DOS to Paris, March 30, Geneva Conference Indochina Phase: U.S. Position with French, FE Records on Geneva, box 13, RG 59, NAUS. The United States' negative attitude toward the conference was so obvious that the French press accused the United States of trying to "postpone or call off Geneva Conference on any possible pretext." *FRUS, 1952–54*, 16: 466, 470–71, 484; *FRUS, 1952–54*, 13: 1206.

40. *FRUS, 1952–54*, 13: 1283–84. See also *FRUS, 1952–54*, 13: 947–54, 1145–46, 1237, 1273, 1299; U.S. reaction to Chinese Communist introduction of air power in Indochina, April 9, 1954, FE Records on Geneva, box 13, RG 59, NAUS; *Pentagon Papers*, 1: 88–104.

41. *FRUS, 1952–54*, 13: 1206, 1214–18, 1224, 1236, 1242, 1253–54. For analysis of Dulles and Eisenhower's speeches, see Logevall, *Embers of War*, 461–63.

42. *FRUS, 1952–54*, 14: 396–97; *FRUS, 1952–54*, 13: 1280–81; *FRUS, 1952–54*, 16: 487; *Department of State Bulletin*, April 12, 1954, 539–42.

43. *Pentagon Papers*, 1: 108–09. For more details about Dulles's quest for united action in response to Dien Bien Phu, see Herring and Immerman, "Eisenhower, Dulles, and Dienbienphu"; and Hall "Anglo-US Relations in the Formation of SEATO," *Stanford Journal of East Asian Affairs* 50, no. 1 (Winter 2005), 116–121.

44. "Note sur la situation militaire en Indochine à la veille de la Conférence de Genève," 21 avril 1954, AN, F60 3038, dossier note sur la situation militaire en Indochine à la veille de la Conférence de Genève; cited in Waite, "End of the First Indochina War," 242. See also *FRUS, 1952–54*, 13: 1304; Paris to FO, April 7, 1954, FO371/112050, NAUK; Rather, "The Geneva Conference of 1954," 127. For the French perspective about relations with the United States over Dien Bien Phu, see Laurent Cesari, "The French Military and U.S. Participation in the Indochina War"; and Laurent Cesari and Jacques de Folin, "Military Necessity, Political Impossibility: The French Viewpoint on Operation Vautour," in *Dien Bien Phu and the Crisis of Franco-American Relations*, 49–54, 105–20.

45. *FRUS, 1952–54*, 13: 1236–38, 1352–54, 1358; *FRUS, 1952–54*, 16: 440; Herring, " 'A Good Stout Effort,'" 218. For the original French position, see *FRUS, 1952–54*, 16: 436, 445–46; "Possible Problems vis-à-vis France in Connection to the Geneva Conference," March 8, 1954, FE Records on Geneva, box 13, RG 59, NAUS.

46. *FRUS, 1952–54*, 16: 557, 581–83; memorandum, April 9, 1954, FO371/112051; Gardner, *Approaching Vietnam*, 218. For the visit of General Paul Ely, Chairman of French Chiefs of Staff, to Washington seeking U.S. assistance, see *FRUS, 1952–54*, 13: 1133–34, 1137–45, 1158–60; Radford, *From Pearl Harbor to Vietnam*, 390–92; *Pentagon Papers*, 1: 97–98, 455–60.

47. Cable, *The Geneva Conference of 1954*, 18–19; Warner, "The Settlement of Indochina War," 235–36. The British indifference to Indochina was best indicated by a remark made by Churchill—"I have lived 78 years without hearing of bloody places like Cambodia." Cited in Cable, *The Geneva Conference of 1954*, 1.

48. *FRUS, 1952–54*, 16: 804–05; Peking to FO, no. 334, October 19, 1953, and January 12, 1954, no. 9, in *British Documents on Foreign Affairs: Reports and Papers from the Foreign Office*, Part V, Series E, 4: 88–90, and 6: 12 (Bethesda, Md.: LexisNexis, 2005).

49. Brownjohn to Prime Minister, April 26, 1954, FO371/112057, NAUK. See also *FRUS, 1952–54*, 6: 1030–32; *FRUS, 1952–54*, 16: 558; *FRUS, 1952–54*, 13: 1416–17; Eisenhower, *Mandate for Change*, 346–47. For British anxiety about the U.S. nuclear policy, see Jones, "Geneva Conference of 1954." The United States tested its first hydrogen bomb in November 1952. The Soviet Union had its test in August 1953. From March through mid-May 1954, the United States held a series of tests (code-named Operation Castle) in the Marshalls Islands in the Pacific to prove the feasibility of deployable hydrogen bombs. The whole world was shocked by both the destruction and contamination of this new weapon. Dulles's efforts for united action happened during this period.

50. "Draft Policy towards Indochina," March 16, 1954, FO371/112048, NAUK; Joint Intelligence Committee, "PTI", March 31/April 1, 1954, FO371/112050, NAUK; Cable, minute, February 23, 1954, FO371/112047, NAUK; Allen to Scott, February 24, 1954, FO371/112047, NAUK.

51. The French originally proposed the "leopard skin" zones, which left all the major urban centers in French hands, but in private, they acknowledged that a partition was more realistic. "Memorandum of Conversation: French Military Briefing—Indochina," May 11, 1954, Executive Secretariat Conference Files, 1949–1963, box 49, RG 59, NAUS; Philippe Devillers and Jean Lacouture, *End of a War: Indochina, 1954* (New York: Praeger, 1969), 206–7.

52. *FRUS, 1952–54*, 13: 1214–17; Scott, "Record of Interview at State Department," April 2, 1954, FO371/112050, NAUK; Washington to FO, April 2, 1954, FO371/112049, NAUK; memo of the meeting, April 2, 1954, FE Records on Geneva, box 13, RG 59, NAUS. British Foreign Office started to consider a partition to end the Indochina war in March and the suggestion was approved by Eden on April 1. See "Draft Policy towards Indochina," March 16, 1954, FO371/112048, NAUK; Malcolm MacDonald to FO, March 18, 1954, FO371/112048; Joint Intelligence Committee, "PTI", March 31/April 1, 1954, FO371/112050, NAUK.

53. Dulles to Washington, May 3, 1954, cited in Waite, "The End of the First Indochina War," 223.

54. *FRUS, 1952–54*, 16: 604–05, 640–41; *Public Papers of the Presidents of the United States: Dwight D, Eisenhower, 1954*, 427–38.

55. *FRUS, 1952–54*, 13: 1044–46; *FRUS, 1952–54*, 16: 445, 458–60; Rumbold to FO, March 16, 1954, FO371/112048, March 26, 1954, FO371/112049, NAUK; Paris to DOS, February 13, 1954, 751G.5/2-1354, RG 59, NAUS; "Intelligence Report: Probable French Position on Indochina at Geneva (NIE 6)," March 26, 1954, Miscellaneous Lot Files, 1944–59, Intelligence Bureau, Office of the Director, Lot 58D528, box 65, RG 59, NAUS; "U.S. Position at Geneva," FE Records on Geneva, box 13, RG 59, NAUS.

56. Eden to Churchill, May 22, 1954, PREM 11/649, NAUK; Waite, "The End of the Indochina War," 175–76.

57. *FRUS, 1952–54*, 16: 485, and also 488; Geneva Conference Indochina Phase: U.S. Position with French, April 5, 1954, FE Records on Geneva, box 13, RG 59, NAUS.

58. Gardner, *Approaching Vietnam*, 222.

59. *FRUS, 1952–54*, 13: 1231–35. For Australia's role during the Geneva Conference, see Gregory James Pemberton, "Australia, the United States, and the Indochina Crisis of 1954," *Diplomatic History 13*, no. 1 (Winter 1989): 45–66.

60. *FRUS, 1952–54*, 13: 1287. Before his trip, Dulles was already warned that the United Action was "hardly likely" to get support. Telegram, April 7, 1954, *FRUS, 1952–54*, 13: 1282–83. For Dulles's travel to Europe, see *Pentagon Papers*, 1: 101–03; Eisenhower, *Mandate for Change*, 348–49.

61. *FRUS, 1952–54*, 13: 1311–13, 1319–23; Eden, *Full Circle*, 106–111. Warner, "The Settlement of Indochina War," 242, 245.

62. *FRUS, 1952–54*, 16: 533–34, 537; *FRUS, 1952–54*, 13: 1349–50, 1474, 1482.

63. *FRUS, 1952–54*, 13: 1290–92, 1327–40; *FRUS, 1952–54*, 16: 517–20, 524–25, 532–34; "Tripartite meeting in Paris on Indochina," April 16, 1954, FO371/112055, NAUK; Dulles memo of conversation with Bidault, April 14, 1954, AWF, Dulles-Herter Series, box 2, DDEL; *Pentagon Papers*, 1: 103.

64. Eden to FO, April 26, 1954, FO371/112056, NAUK; *FRUS, 1952–54*, 16: 553–57, 570–71; *FRUS, 1952–54*, 13: 1374–75. For the meetings between the three foreign ministers in Paris and then in Geneva on the eve of the negotiation, see *FRUS, 1952–54*, 16: 544–48; 550–52, 575–77, 648–49; *FRUS, 1952–54*, 13: 1361–63, 1386–96; Eden to Churchill, Pairs to FO, April 24, 1954, FO371/112055, FO371/112056, NAUK; Shuckburgh minute, April 25, 1954, FO371/112056, NAUK; FO to Canada, April 28, 1954, FO371/112056, NAUK; Eden to FO, May 2, 1954, FO371/112058, NAUK; Dulles to DOS, April 22, 23, 24, 25, 1954, AWF, Dulles-Herter Series, box 2, DDEL; *Pentagon Papers*, 1: 104–06, 477–82; Eden, *Full Circle*, 111–24.

65. *FRUS, 1952–54*, 13: 1423; *FRUS, 1952–54*, 16: 698.

66. *FRUS, 1952–54*, 13: 1404–05. Arthur Radford supported air strikes to save Dien Bien Phu, and Dulles thought of using the U.S. Air Force and Navy to restrain China from supporting the DRV. See *FRUS, 1952–54*, 13: 1198–99, 1200–02, note 3. For a U.S. military estimate of using the atomic bomb to eliminate the DRV from Dien Bien Phu, see *FRUS, 1952–54*, 13: 1270–72. For detailed discussion, see Herring and Immerman, "Eisenhower, Dulles, and Dienbienphu: 'The Day We Didn't Go to War' Revisited," *Journal of American History* 71 (September 1984): 343–63.

67. *FRUS, 1952–54*, 13: 1250–65, 1369–70, 1376–77, 1440–41; *FRUS, 1952–54*, 16: 575–76, 605–07.

68. *FRUS, 1952–54*, 13: 1430, 1431–45; *FRUS, 1952–54*, 16: 605, 640.

69. *FRUS, 1952–54*, 16: 507–10, 530, 631–35, 690.

70. *FRUS, 1952–54*, 13: 1290–92; *FRUS, 1952–54*, 16: 689–90.; U.S. Delegation to DOS, May 4, 1954, 396.1 GE/5-454, NAUS; UK Delegation to FO, May 5, 1954, FO371/112059, NAUK.

71. Chinese newspaper article listing reasons for U.S. agreeing to the Geneva Conference at Berlin, March 13, 1954, FE Records on Geneva, box 13, RG 59, NAUS; and PRC File, box 24, RG 59, NAUS. For the American responses to the British and French positions on the Dien Bien Phu crisis in late April, see Eisenhower Diary, April 27, 1954, and Eisenhower to Hazlett, April 27, 1954, AWF, Diary Series, "April 1954," DDEL.

72. *FRUS, 1952–54*, 16: 466; Paris to FO, April 7, 1954, FO371/112050; May 3, 1954, FO371/112058, NAUK.

73. *FRUS, 1952–54*, 13: 1449; *FRUS, 1952–54*, 16: 589; Dean memo about meeting with Spender regarding Chinese Communist Commentary on Indochina, April 9, 1954, FE Records on Geneva, box 13, RG59, NAUS.

74. *FRUS, 1952–54*, 16: 619.

75. *FRUS, 1952–54*, 16: 446.

76. *FRUS, 1952–54*, 16: 579–80; Dulles to DOS, April 30, 1954, Dulles Papers, Chronological Series, "May 1954 (5)," DDEL; and U. Alexis Johnson, *The Right Hand of Power* (Englewood Cliffs, N.J.: Prentice-Hall, 1984), 220. For interpretation of U.S. perception of Sino-Soviet differences, see Immerman, "The United States and the Geneva."

77. *FRUS, 1952–54*, 14: 401–7, 408–12; Dulles to DOS, April 30, 1954, Dulles Papers, Chronological Series, "May 1954 (5)," DDEL.

78. For the DRV's proposal and the U.S. perception, see *Pentagon Papers*, 1: 118–21. Eden also judged that the DRV wanted to "grab the whole of Indochina including Laos and Cambodia." See Eden's telegram regarding his meeting with Zhou, May 20, 1954, FO371/112067, NAUK.

79. *FRUS, 1952–54*, 13: 1505, 1519. For U.S. military estimates of the DRV's movements, see Memo of conversation: situation in Indochina and possible defense arrangements in SEA, FE Records on Geneva, box 14, RG 59, NAUS.

80. Joint State-CIA Estimate on Communist Intentions regarding Indochinese phase of Conference—Memo to Heath from Cooper and Yager, May 10, 1954, FE Records on Geneva, box 14, RG 59, NAUS. U.S. officials noticed the uncompromising tone of China's propaganda and believed it indicated that the Chinese would not take any moves in the direction of moderation. See memo, Martin for Robertson: Comments on Molotov's May 14 speech, May 20, 1954, Lot71D68, PRC File, 1954–61, box 24, RG 59, NAUS.

81. *FRUS, 1952–54*, 16: 699–700, 730–31, 744.

82. *FRUS, 1952–54*, 16: 583–84. Originally, Dulles proposed the UN as supervisor, but he had to give it up later because the French feared that the question of their colonies in Africa would be raised, and Dulles also came to realize that getting the UN involved would inevitably lead to discussion about the PRC's membership in the United Nations.

83. Geneva to FO, May 13, 1954, FO371/112066, NAUK; Eden to FO, May 22, 1954, FO371/111863, and PREM 11/649, NAUK.

84. *FRUS, 1952–54*, 16: 645–46; see also 672–76, 681–85.

85. *FRUS, 1952–54*, 16: 564, 731–32, 778–79, 779–80, 787–88, 807; *FRUS, 1952–54*, 13: 1509, 1516.

86. *FRUS, 1952–54*, 13: 1532–33, 1590–92, 1606–07; *FRUS, 1952–54*, 16: 727–28.

87. *FRUS, 1952–54*, 16: 775, 792, 799, 837–38; Cable, *The Geneva Conference*, 70. For the British approach towards SEATO, see Geoffrey Warner, "From Geneva to Manila: British Policy Toward Indochina and SEATO, May–September 1954," in *Dien Bien Phu and the Crisis of Franco-American Relations*, 149–67.

88. *FRUS, 1952–54*, 16: 728–29, 762; *FRUS, 1952–54*, 13: 1516, 1522–25, 1526–28, 1542.

89. The conditions for U.S. intervention included an invitation from the Indochinese governments; independence to Laos, Cambodia, and Vietnam; UN approval; a joint effort of some other nations in the area; and the French guarantee that it would continue to fight. *Pentagon Papers*, 1: 124.

90. Eden to FO, May 17, 1954, Colville to Stark, May 17, 1954, FO371/112067; Rather, "Geneva Conference of 1954," 298; Waite, "End of First Indochina War," 331–32.

91. *FRUS, 1952–54*, 13: 1601–2, 1643–44, 1689–90. See also *Pentagon Papers*, 1: 122–30, 135–36.

92. *FRUS, 1952–54*, 13: 1676, 1576, and 1571, 1588, 1604. See also *FRUS, 1952–54*, 16: 1056, 1100–01.

93. *FRUS, 1952–54*, 16: 815, 834–35, 836, 869, 943, 1023; *New York Times*, May 18, 1954.

94. *Public Papers of the Presidents of the United States: Dwight D, Eisenhower, 1954*, 497.

95. *FRUS, 1952–54*, 13: 1534–35, 1581, 1583–84, 1591–92, 1620; *FRUS, 1952–54*, 16: 1067–69; *FRUS, 1952–54*, 14: 434, 444. For the tensions in the Taiwan Strait in May 1954, see chaps. 3 and 4.

96. *FRUS, 1952–54*, 16: 865; *FRUS, 1952–54*, 13: 1584, 1586–90, 1594; *Pentagon Papers*, 1: 136–37; Dawson, "The 1954 Geneva Conference," 123–24.

97. *FRUS, 1952–54*, 16: 1051, 1066. Immerman, "The United States and the Geneva Conference," 57–60.

98. *FRUS, 1952–54*, 16: 944, 1057; *FRUS, 1952–54*, 13: 1597–98, 1653, 1655–57, 1660; *FRUS, 1952–54*, 14: 425–27, 428–30, 433–34; NIE 35-3-54, submitted by CIA on May 25, cited in Dawson, "1954 Geneva Conference," 129. See also excerpts of the NIE on Communist capabilities in Indochina, Yager and Cooper to Heath, June 3, 1954, FE Records on Geneva, box 14, RG 59, NAUS; Martin memo for Robertson on Molotov's May 14 speech, May 29, 1954, PRC Files, box, 24, RG 59, NAUS.

99. *FRUS, 1952–54*, 14: 438–43. The Americans were correct: Beijing was actually using the detained Americans as tools in their relations with the United States, as shown in chap. 1. For the meetings between Chinese and American diplomats, see *FRUS, 1952–54*, 14: 462–80.

100. *FRUS, 1952–54*, 16: 1055.

101. "Overt Chinese aggression in Southeast Asia," memo of conversation between Dulles and Australian, New Zealand ambassadors, June 4, 1954, FE Records on Geneva, box 14, RG 59, NAUS.

102. *FRUS, 1952–54*, 16: 1068–69; DOS Press Release, no. 309, June 8, 1954; *Department of State Bulletin*, June 21, 1954, 947–49; Randle, *Geneva 1954*, 255.

103. *FRUS, 1952–54*, 16: 992, 1013–14; Eden to FO regarding his meeting with Smith and Molotov, June 12, 1954, FO371/112071, NAUK.

104. *FRUS, 1952–54*, 13: 1659.

105. *FRUS, 1952–54*, 16: 876, 919–20, 1030, 1056, 1058, 1103–05.

106. *FRUS, 1952–54*, 16: 1051–54, 1059–60.
107. UK Delegation to FO, June 12, 1954, FO371/112071, NAUK; Reading to FO, June 7, 1954, FO371/112069, NAUK; *FRUS, 1952–54*, 16: 1066–67, 1069, 1083–85,1132–34; Drumright memo about meeting with Scott regarding Far East problems, June 3, 1954, FE Records on Geneva, box 14, RG 59, NAUS.
108. *FRUS, 1952–54*, 16: 1125, 1130, 1134, 1142, 1146–47; Randle, *Geneva 1954*, 262.
109. Cable, *Geneva Conference of 1954*, 97–98.
110. *FRUS, 1952–54*, 16: 1169, 1228.
111. *FRUS, 1952–54*, 16: 1169, 1170–71, 1173–74, 1190; Paris to SOS regarding Zhou's meeting with Mendès France, June 24, 1954, AWF, Dulles-Herter Series, box 1, DDEL. Eden to FO, June 16, 1954, FO371/112074; UK Delegation to FO, June 16, 1954, FO371/112073.
112. *FRUS, 1952–54*, 12: 563; "Soviet Capabilities and Main Lines of Policy through Mid-1959," Yager and Cooper memo to Heath, June 9, 1954, FE Records on Geneva, box 14, RG 59, NAUS; "Recent Developments in Communist China," June 10, 1954, Miscellaneous Lot Files, 1944–59, Intelligence Bureau, Office of the Director, 1950–59, Lot 58D528, box 65, RG 59, NAUS.
113. *FRUS, 1952–54*, 16: 1224, 1228; *FRUS, 1952–54*, 13: 1732; "Soviet Capabilities and Main Lines of Policy through Mid-1959," Yager and Cooper memo to Heath, June 9, 1954, FE Records on Geneva, box 14, RG 59, NAUS.
114. Eden to FO, June 16, 1954, FO371/112074, NAUK; UK Delegation to FO, no. 747 and 751, June 16, 1954, FO371/112073, NAUK; Eden to FO, June 18 and July 13, 1954, FO 371/112073, and FO371/112077, NAUK.
115. Eden to FO, regarding meetings with Zhou, June 16, 18, and 19, 1954, FO371/112073, NAUK; Eden to FO, regarding meeting with Bidault, June 17, 1954, FO371/112073, NAUK; Reading to FO, June 22, 1954, and account of the French note regarding Mendès France meeting with Zhou, June 23, 1954, FO371/112074, NAUK; Paris to FO, regarding meeting between Mendès France and Zhou, June 24, 1954, FO371/112075, NAUK; *Pentagon Papers*, 1: 138.
116. Geneva to FO, July 1, 1954, FO371/112076, NAUK; *FRUS, 1952–54*, 16: 1248–49, and 1253; *FRUS, 1952–54*, 13: 1751–52.
117. *FRUS, 1952–54*, 16: 1228–29. The French actually deliberately kept the United States in the dark. See Geneva to FO, June 25, 1954, FO371/112075, NAUK.
118. For Eden's thoughts about a Locarno Pact in Asia, see Nông Văn Dân, *Churchill, Eden and Indo-China*, 152, 157–58; Cable, *Geneva Conference of 1954*, 108–111; and Randle, *Geneva 1954*, 292–95.
119. *FRUS, 1952–54*, 13: 1700–01, 1705–09, 1745; *Pentagon Papers*, 1: 121–22; "Probable Developments in Indochina (up to July 15, 1954)," Cooper and Yager memo to Heath, June 16, 1954, FE Records on Geneva, box 14, RG 59, NAUS.
120. *FRUS, 1952–54*, 16: 1226–27; *FRUS, 1952–54*, 12: 554–63; Eden to FO, June 9, 1954, FO371/112070, NAUK. "ANZUS Action in the Event of Overt Chinese Aggression in Indochina," June 11, 1954, FE Records on Geneva, box 14, RG 59, NAUS.
121. *FRUS, 1952–54*, 13: 1670, 1687–89, 1689–90, 1712, 1714–17, 1742–43; *FRUS, 1952–54*, 16: 1374, 1391; Dulles to Paris, June 14, 1954, Dulles Papers, Subject Series, box 9, DDEL; *Public Papers of the Presidents*, no. 138, June 10, 1954; *Department of State Bulletin*, no. 30, June 21, 1954, 947–49.
122. *FRUS, 1952–54*, 12: 554–63; *FRUS, 1952–54*, 16: 1283–86; *FRUS, 1952–54*, 13: 1748–51; "ANZUS Action in the Event of Overt Chinese Aggression in Indochina," June 11,

1954, and "The Choice of U.S. Policy in Indochina," June 23, 1954, FE Records on Geneva, box 14, RG 59, NAUS.

123. *FRUS, 1952–54*, 16: 1056; DOS to U.S. Delegation, June 18, 1954, 396.1 GE/6-1854, NAUS; Rather, *Geneva Conference of 1954*, 388; Logevall, *Embers of War*, 570–75.

124. *FRUS, 1952–54*, 16: 1249–51.

125. Kirkpatrick to Brownjohn, May 18, 1954, FO371/112067, NAUK. For British diplomatic reports about the tensions between the United States and the United Kingdom, see Washington to FO, May 17, 1954, FO371/112066; May 19, 1954, FO371/112067; Makins to Eden, May 21, 1954, FO371/111869, NAUK.

126. *FRUS, 1952–54*, 13: 1757–58; *Pentagon Papers*, 1: 141–46; Eden, *Full Circle*, 147–50. For U.S. positions before the British visit, see "The Choice of U.S. Policy in Indochina," June 23, 1954, FE Records on Geneva, box 14, RG 59, NAUS.

127. Nông Văn Dân, *Churchill, Eden and Indo-China*, 152; for U.S. Congressional opposition to Locarno, see House Committee on Foreign Affairs to President, June 24, 1954, Dulles papers, Subject Series, box 9, DDEL.

128. *FRUS, 1952–54*, 16: 1254–55. Paris wanted its allies to warn the Communists in their statement that the situation would deteriorate if no agreement was reached in Geneva. FO to Saigon, June 29, 1954, FO371/112075, NAUK.

129. Paris to FO, June 28, 1954, FO371/112076, and June 30, 1954, FO371/112075, NAUK.

130. *FRUS, 1952–54*, 13: 1775; 1780–81; *FRUS, 1952–54*, 14: 486–88; *FRUS, 1952–54*, 16: 1253.

131. *FRUS, 1952–54*, 13: 1781, 1788, 1791–92, 1801–03, 1807–10, 1813–16; *FRUS, 1952–54*, 16: 1256, 1271, 1294, 1309–10.

132. *FRUS, 1952–54*, 16: 1302, 1305; *FRUS, 1952–54*, 13: 1794–95; Paris to FO, July 14, 1954, FO371/112077, NAUK.

133. *FRUS, 1952–54*, 13: 1797, 1802, 1819–26; *FRUS, 1952–54*, 16: 1333–34; *Pentagon Papers*, 1: 149–53.

134. Paris to DOS, July 14, 1954, AWF, Dulles-Herter Series, box 1, DDEL.

135. *FRUS, 1952–54*, 16: 1359–63, 1381; Eden to FO through G. Jebb, July 14, 1954, FO371/112077, NAUK.

136. Immerman, "The United States and Geneva Conference of 1954," 63.

137. *FRUS, 1952–54*, 16: 1267, 1278–80; *FRUS, 1952–54*, 13: 1769–70; Geneva to FO, July 9, 1954, FO371/112077, NAUK.

138. *FRUS, 1952–54*, 16: 1280–82.

139. *FRUS, 1952–54*, 16: 1346–47, 1350–52, 1368–69; "Account of the French Note," June 23, 1954, FO371/112015.

140. Dulles's meeting with Congress members, July 16, 1954, Dawson, "1954 Geneva Conference," 219–20.

141. *FRUS, 1952–54*, 16: 1420–21, 1437, 1449, 1466; telegrams regarding Eden's meetings with Zhou on July 13, 17, and 18, 1954, FO371/112077, FO371/112078, FO371/112079, and FO371/112080, NAUK; Eden to FO regarding meeting with Mendès France about the latter's meeting with Zhou, July 18, 1954, FO371/112079, NAUK.

142. At the beginning of the last phase of the negotiation, the DRV requested almost half of the Laos territory for regrouping and demanded a coalition government in Laos. Zhou demanded that Cambodia not join the Southeast Asia pact, allow U.S. military bases, or accept U.S. military instructors. And Molotov was firm on the date for election in Vietnam. *FRUS, 1952–54*, 16: 1405, 1420–21.

143. *FRUS, 1952–54*, 13: 1844.

144. *FRUS, 1952–54*, 13: 1848–50; *FRUS, 1952–54*, 16: 1428–30, 1454.

145. *FRUS, 1952–54*, 13: 1802, 1851–53; *FRUS, 1952–54*, 16: 1436, 1454. For the British dissatisfaction and Eden's meeting with Mendès France about this, see Eden to FO, July 19, 1954, FO371/112080, NAUK.

146. *FRUS, 1952–54*, 16: 1175, 1207–08, 1213–15, 1226, 1228, 1231–32, 1234–36, 1338–39, 1342, 1350, 1449–50; *FRUS, 1952–54*, 13: 1742–43, 1792–93. For the importance of Cambodia for the United States, see Kenton J. Clymer, "Cambodia: The View from the United States, 1945–1954," *The Journal of American–East Asian Relations* 6, nos. 2–3 (Summer–Fall 1997), 91–124.

147. *FRUS, 1952–54*, 13: 1805–06; *FRUS, 1952–54*, 16: 1338–39; *Pentagon Papers*, 1: 154–55.

148. *FRUS, 1952–54*, 16: 1425–26. Meanwhile, Smith blamed Eden for telling Molotov that the allies were not planning to include Laos and Cambodia in the security pact. See *FRUS, 1952–54*, 16: 1429. According to Chinese sources, Eden made the promise to Molotov after he obtained Smith's agreement; see chap. 1.

149. *FRUS, 1952–54*, 16: 1378–81, 1405, 1420, 1449–50, 1468–69; *Pentagon Papers*, 1: 156–57. The French might also have contributed to the Laotian retreat. According to Eden, Mendès France opposed Dulles's suggestion of the United States providing Laos with weapons and economic aid when the three foreign ministers met in Paris. There is no further document showing whether the French pressured the Laotians to give up the idea of requesting U.S. weapons, but given their influence on Laos and their eagerness for a settlement, it was highly likely that they pressured the Laotians. See Eden (Paris) to FO through G. Jebb, July 14, 1954, FO371/112077, NAUK.

150. *Pentagon Papers*, declassified by NAUS in 2011, section 3.3, from B-9 to B-16. *http://www.archives.gov/research/pentagon-papers/*, accessed May 18, 2017. The French had feared that Washington would support the SV objecting to the agreement they reached with the Vietminh. See Frank Robert to Selwyn Lloyd, June 18, 1954, FO371/112076, NAUK.

151. *FRUS, 1952–54*, 16: 1503, 1550–51.

152. "Note on Relations with the United States, China and the Colombo Powers," August 8, 1954, FO371/111852, NAUK; Jones, "Geneva Conference of 1954," 34–35.

3. PREVENTING THE MUTUAL DEFENSE TREATY

1. *Mao Zedong Wenji* (Collection of Mao Zedong's Works) (Beijing, China: Renmin Chubanshe, 1999), 6: 333.

2. "Zhou Enlai's Report on Foreign Affairs," August 12, 1954, Fujian Provincial Archives, 101-5-542.

3. Michael Sheng sees a "dictatorial and impulsive" Mao carrying out an "erratic policy" with neither long-term strategy nor short-term plan. See Michael M. Sheng, "Mao and China's Relations with the Superpowers in the 1950s: A New Look at the Taiwan Strait Crises and the Sino-Soviet Split," *Modern China* 34, no. 4 (October 2008): 477–87. Chen Jian, however, sees China's actions in the Taiwan Strait as part of Mao Zedong's policy to create diplomatic momentum to mobilize Chinese people for his domestic program. Chen, *Mao's China and the Cold War* (Chapel Hill: University of North Carolina Press, 2001), 167–70. Unlike Chen and Sheng,

most existing works argue that China initiated the confrontation to prevent a U.S.-GMD military alliance. See Gordon H. Chang and He Di, "The Absence of War in the U.S.-China Confrontation over Quemoy and Matsu in 1954–1955: Contingency, Luck, Deterrence?," *American Historical Review* 95, no. 5 (December 1993): 1500–24; Qiang Zhai, *The Dragon, the Lion & the Eagle: Chinese-British-American Relations, 1949–1958* (Kent, Ohio: Kent State University Press, 1994), 153–77; and Shu Guang Zhang, *Deterrence and Strategic Culture: Chinese-American Confrontations, 1948–1958* (Ithaca, N.Y.: Cornell University Press, 1992), 189–224.

4. For details of Beijing's propaganda campaign, see Thomas E. Stolper, *China, Taiwan, and the Offshore Islands: Together with Some Implications for Outer Mongolia and Sino-Soviet Relations* (Armonk, N.Y.: M. E. Shape, 1985), 34–38; Chang and He, "The Absence of War," 1509. Most existing works see the bombing of Jinmen Island in September as the beginning of the crisis.

5. *Renmin Ribao*, July 23, 1954.

6. See, for example, articles in *Renmin Ribao*, July 24, 28, 31; August 1, 3, 8, 13, 15, 20.

7. *Important Documents concerning the Question of Taiwan* (Peking: Foreign Languages Press, 1955), 109–26, 127–32; *Zhou Enlai Nianpu, 1949–1976*, Vol. 1–3 (A chronological record of Zhou Enlai, 1949–1976), eds. Li Ping and Ma Zhisun, et al. (Beijing, China: Zhongyang Wenxian Chubanshe, 1997), 1: 406.

8. Chinese Communist leaders prepared for but did not get a chance to discuss the Taiwan issue at the Geneva Conference. See *Mao Wengao*, 3: 480; *Mao Zedong Zhuan*, 555; and "Speech script on Sino-American relations," undated document prepared for the Geneva Conference, April 17, 1954, Chinese Foreign Ministry Archives (CFMA), 206-00053-03, 26–39.

9. Chinese Foreign Ministry outward telegram: "Van Fleet's Conspiratorial Acts in the Far East," July 17, 1954, CFMA, 206-00117-05, 101–2; *Renmin Ribao*, July 8, 19, 21, 1954. However, although the Chinese worry was reasonable, their estimate of both the U.S. need for an MDT and the objectives of Van Fleet's visits to Taiwan was incorrect. See chap. 4.

10. *Renmin Ribao*, July 9, 31, August 8, 1954.

11. Emphasis added. "The CCP Central Committee Telegram to Zhou Enlai Concerning Policies and Measures in the Struggle against the United States and Chiang (Kai-shek) after the Geneva Conference," July 27, 1954, CFMA, 206-00048-11, 1–4. The English translation is adapted from Chen Jian's translation in CWIHP Document Reader. This new document for the first time discloses Chinese leaders' considerations behind the propaganda. For Chinese press articles about the MDT, see *Renmin Ribao*, May 24, June 13 and 17, August 8, 20, 29; Xin Hua She (New China News Agency), May 18, July 30, 31, August 20, 30.

12. This is clearly shown in a CCP Central Committee instruction on the "Liberate Taiwan Campaign" issued on July 24: "At present, the direct target of our military struggle is Chiang Kai-shek and his cohorts in Taiwan. The United States should not be treated as our direct target. We should confine the conflicts with the United States to the diplomatic arena only." CCP Central Publicity Department and the Political Department of the Central Military Commission, "Guanyu Taiwan Wenti de Junshi Baodao de Zhishi," July 24, 1954; cited in Chang and He, "The Absence of War," 1510. This document also points out that the nature of the Communist attacks on GMD forces in the Taiwan Strait was different from previous actions, which were military moves aiming to capture islands.

13. "The CCP Central Committee Telegram to Zhou Enlai Concerning Policies and Measures in the Struggle against the United States and Chiang (Kai-shek) after the Geneva Conference," July 27, 1954, CFMA, 206-00048-11, 1–3; Chen Jian, *Mao's China and the Cold War*, 167–70.

14. "Development of the US efforts to whipping together a 'Southeast Asia Defense Group,' " June 30, 1954, CFMA, 105-00626-01, 1–12; "Situation in Indonesia," *Neibu Cankao*, July 15, 1954; *Zhou Enlai Nianpu*, 1: 392; "Responses of Southeast Asian states to US opposition to our entry into the UN," July 24, 1954, CFMA, 102-000159-13, 55–58; and "Zhou Enlai's Report on Foreign Affairs (excerpts)," August 12, 1954, Fujian Provincial Archives, 101-5-542. The Chinese perception was correct. According to British diplomats, U.S. relations with Asian states "worsened by her recent conduct of foreign policy" after the Geneva Conference, while the British influence in Southeast Asia was enhanced. See MacDonald, Notes on relations with U.S., China and Colombo Powers, August 13, 1954, and Dodds-Parker, Visit to Southeast Asia by Dodds-Parker, October 6, 1954; both in *British Documents on Foreign Affairs: Reports and Papers from the Foreign Office*, Part V, Series E, 7 (Bethesda, Md.: Lexis-Nexis, 2005): 508–9, 510–12.

15. Although in July Eden told Zhou in Geneva that the British no longer pursued a Locarno Pact, Chinese leaders somehow still believed the British did not give up the idea. See "Zhou Enlai's report on foreign affairs (excerpts)," August 12, 1954, Fujian Provincial Archives, 101-5-542. Most probably the Chinese leaders were misled by Churchill's remarks in Washington about peaceful coexistence with the Communists. Interestingly, the GMD government also believed the British wanted to pursue a Locarno Pact with the Communists. See documents about Churchill-Eisenhower meetings, June 28–30, 1954, GMD Foreign Ministry Archives, Institute of Modern History, Academia Sinica, Taipei (hereafter, ROCFMA), document no. 713.2; *Zhongyang Ribao* (Central Daily Newspaper), June 30, 1954, from GMD History Archive, Taipei (hereafter, GMDHA); and *Chiang Kai-shek Diaries*, Hoover Institution, Stanford University (hereafter CKS Diaries), entry June 30, 1954.

16. "Minutes of provincial committee meeting on 'The Issue of Liberating Taiwan,' " August 13, 1954, Fujian Provincial Archives, 101-1-384. For British records of GMD plundering vessels, see Tamsui to Foreign Office (FO), December 11, 1954, FO371/112059, National Archives of the United Kingdom (NAUK). According to the Chinese record, the GMD "committed 111 acts of interception, plunder and shelling and strafing against 67 merchant ships along the China coast and on the high seas. Of these, 86 were against 43 British ships, 15 against 14 Panamanian Vessels." See statistics table of the ships intercepted or plundered by the GMD from September 1949 to October 1954, September 30, 1954, CFMA, 204-00148-04, 25–29. For U.S.-UK differences over trade with China and the GMD blockade, see Bruce A. Elleman, *High Seas Buffer: The Taiwan Patrol Force, 1950–1979* (New Port: R.I.; Naval War College Press, 2012), 45–57.

17. "Report about British economy achieving obvious recovery," July 16, 1954, CFMA, 206-00117-04.

18. "Zhou Enlai's Report on Foreign Affairs (excerpts)," August 12, 1954, Fujian Provincial Archives, 101-5-542. For Chinese news reports about allied opposition to U.S. retaliation of the PLA air force, *Renmin Ribao*, July 28, August 1, 1954.

19. As early as July 7, Mao had come to this conclusion based on Zhou Enlai's report about his experience in Geneva. *Zhou Enlai Nianpu,* 1: 395–96; *Mao Zedong Wenji,* 332–33; *Mao Zedong Zhuan,* 562–64.
20. While Eisenhower revisionists focus on U.S. efforts to split Sino-Soviet alliance, the existing interpretations of Chinese diplomacy stress differences between the Communists during the crisis, but newly available sources prove that the Soviet Union and China indeed cooperated closely throughout the crisis.
21. "Zhou Enlai's Telegram to the CCP Central Committee Concerning Van Fleet's Trip to Taiwan," July 11, 1954, CFMA, 206-00048-10, 1.
22. David J. Dallin, *Soviet Foreign Policy After Stalin* (New York: J. B. Lippincott Company, 1961), 155–65; Li Lianqing, *Lengnuan Suiyue: Yibosanzhe de Zhongsu Guanxi* (Cold and Warm Times: The Ups and Downs in Sino-Soviet Relations) (Beijing, China: Shijie Zhishi Chubanshe, 1999), 230. According to Dallin, after Geneva, Moscow believed "perhaps the onset of the disintegration of the Western alliance was beginning."
23. Memorandum of conversation between Malenkov and Zhou Enlai, July 29, 1054, AVPRF f. 06, o. 13a, d. 25, ll. 8; in *CWIHP Bulletin,* Issue 16: 102–3; see also *Zhou Enlai Nianpu,* 1: 405.
24. Humphrey Trevelyan, *Living with the Communists: China, 1953–5, Soviet Union, 1962–5* (Boston: Gambit, 1971), 111.
25. *Mao Wengao,* 3: 516; "The CCP Central Committee Telegram to Zhou Concerning Policies and Measures in the Struggle against the United States and Chiang (Kai-shek) after the Geneva Conference," July 27, 1954, CFMA, 206-00048-11, 3.
26. "Regarding approval of the British Labour Party's Visit to China," May 9, 1954, CFMA, 110-00026-03; "Regarding the British Labour Party's Visit to China," May 11, 1954. CFMA, 110-00026-03, 7–8. For the British sources, see Tom Buchanan, *East Wind: China and the British Left, 1925–1976* (New York: Oxford University Press, 2012), 149. The available sources, however, fail to show if Beijing finally paid the trip for the Labourites. For the origins of the visit, see "Telegrams requesting instruction and reply regarding the British Labour Party's plan to send a delegation to China," January 5, 1954, CFMA, 110-00026-01; *New York Times,* May 27, 1953, 3.
27. "Regarding Press Publication of Important News such as the British Labour Party's Visit to China and the Geneva Conference," June 9, 1954, CFMA, 110-00026-08; *Zhou Enlai Nianpu,* 1: 373. For the Labour Party's criticism of U.S. policy toward China, *Renmin Ribao,* July 18, 1954.
28. "Concerning the propaganda guideline and plan for the British Labour Party's visit," undated document, CFMA, 110-00127-04, 5–6; "Zhou Enlai's Report on Foreign Affairs (excerpt)," August 12, 1954, Fujian Provincial Archives, 101-5-542; Zhou Enlai, *Zhou Enlai Waijiao Wenxuan* (Selected Diplomatic Works of Zhou Enlai) (Beijing, China: Zhongyang Wenxian Chubanshe, 1990), 79–86.
29. Peking to FO, September 2, 1954, *British Documents on Foreign Affairs: Part V, Series E,* 6: 57–58.
30. *Zhou Enlai Nianpu,* 1: 372–73.
31. "Excerpts of Zhou Enlai's talk with the British Labour Party delegation," August 15, 1954, CFMA, 110-00027-05, 1–10; *Zhou Enlai Nianpu,* 1: 408–9.
32. *Mao Zedong Zhuan,* 567. See also Peking to FO, August 16, 1954, FO371/110247, NAUK.

33. Emphasis added. Memo: "Labour Party Delegation Visit to China," August 27, 1954, FO371/110248, NAUK.

34. Peking to FO, September 2, 1954, in *British Documents on Foreign Affairs*, Part V, Series E, 6: 57–58.

35. Trevelyan, *Living with the Communists*, 119, 131–32; Peking to FO, August 16, 25, and September 2, *British Documents on Foreign Affairs*, Part V, Series E, 6: 56–58; FO minutes, May 21, August 5, 1954; Copenhagen to FO, June 14, 1954, FO371/112047, NAUK.

36. Brussel to FO, June 4, 1954, FO371/110247. The Chinese perception of UK-U.S. relations was obviously misled by their limited diplomatic experience. When the Burmese prime minister U Nu visited China in December after the MDT had been concluded, he frankly told the Chinese "it was absurd to suppose that the United Kingdom would suddenly desert its close relationship with the United States." And in private Nu told the British that "the Chinese were much too prone to jump to conclusions about United Kingdom policies and states on the basis of newspaper reports." See Telegram regarding Visit to China by U Nu, Gore-Booth, no. 301, December 22, 1954, in *British Documents on Foreign Affairs:* Part V, Series E, 6: 94–96. U.S. officials, nevertheless, got the British signal, see chap. 4.

37. Trevelyan believed the Chinese "may well consider the visit to have been a successful experiment." Peking to FO, September 2, 1954, *British Documents on Foreign Affairs:* Part V, Series E, 6: 58.

38. "British press responses to the Labour Party's visit to China," August 18, 1954, CFMA, 110-00241-18, 57–59.

39. Analysis of British press reports of the Labour Party's visit, August 18–25, CFMA, 110-00241-13, 52–59.

40. Telegram regarding responses to the Labour Party's visit, August 29, 1954, CFMA, 110-00241-13, 60–61. The Communist Party of Great Britain provided important information for Beijing's policymaking but declassified Chinese documents on this are rare. For English works on the PRC's relations with the Communist Party of Great Britain, see Buchanan, *East Wind*, especially 142–78. For Labour members attacking U.S. policy on Taiwan in the parliament, see *Renmin Ribao*, September 17, 1954.

41. "Regarding the key points on intelligence collecting after the Labour Party's visit to China," September 2, 1954, CFMA, 110-00234-02, 51–53.

42. "Responses from different parties on the Taiwan issue after the publication of Zhou's report on foreign affairs and multi-party joint statement," August 28, 1954, CFMA, 102-00171-03, 8–13; "Foreign press coverage of the Taiwan issue," August 31, 1954, CFMA, 102-00171-02, 5–7. Beijing may also attribute the U.S. change of policy to allied pressure. *Renmin Ribao* reported that U.S. State Department declared in mid-August that SEATO would be established in early September. However, Britain and France opposed establishing a military alliance, and London also refused to include Taiwan in the coverage of the organization. *Renmin Ribao*, August 17, 28, 1954.

43. In contrast, Jinmen was a safe target: there were no U.S. forces in the Jinmen area and the U.S. Navy was reported to have eliminated the possibility of protecting it. See "Foreign press coverage of the Taiwan issue," August 31, 1954, CFMA, 102-00171-02, 5–7; *Mao Zedong Zhuan*, 581–86; *Mao Wengao*, 3: 533; Xu Yan, *Jinmen zhi Zhan* (The Wars over Jinmen) (Beijing, China: Zhongguo Guangbo Dianshi Chubanshe, 1992), 175; and Liu Tong, *Kua Hai zhi Zhan—Jinmeng, Hainan, Yijiangshan* (The Cross-Sea Wars: Jinmen, Hainan, Yijiangshan) (Beijing: Sanlian Shudian, 2010), 448.

44. "Responses to our shelling of the Jinmen Islands," September 7, 1954, CFMA, 102-00171-01, 1–4.

45. "British Labour Party and the Conservative Party government's attitude toward and remarks about the status of Taiwan," September 13, 1954, CFMA, 110-00244-01, 19.

46. "Southeast Asian and Northern European states' responses to our proposal to liberate Taiwan," September 21, 1954, CFMA, 102-00159-15, 65–67.

47. The GMD air raids of the coastal area, which lasted until late September, caused great anxiety among the Chinese people and influenced industrial and agricultural production as well as normal life. This worked against the Communist leaders' intention to mobilize people for construction. For this reason, they needed to take more actions to ease people's anxiety. For impact of the air raids, see "Confusions among the masses in coastal Fujian after our military's bombardment of Jinmen," "Frequent air harassments of Xiamen by the enemy after our bombardment of Jinmen," "Continuous raids of our towns in coastal Fujian by the enemy's air force and navy," *Neibu Cankao*, September 14, 21, and 22.

48. "SEATO and different states' responses to and attitudes toward it," October 1, 1954, CFMA, 102-000626-02, 85.

49. Liu Tong, *Kua Hai zhi Zhan*, 448; Dai Chaowu, *Didui yu Weiji de Niandai: 1954–1958 Nian de Zhongmei Guanxi* (Years of Hostility and Crises: U.S.-China Relations, 1954–1958) (Beijing, China: Shehui Kexue Chubanshe, 2003), 130. This fact further proves that the shelling of Jinmen was essentially a diplomatic move, not the beginning of an assault on Jinmen, let alone Taiwan.

50. Stolpler, *China, Taiwan, and the Offshore Islands*, 42.

51. The Chinese Communist leaders were also busy with the First Chinese People's Congress, which was top on their agenda for the year and lasted from September 15 to 28.

52. For the Chinese knowledge about recent American speculations about the Sino-Soviet differences, see "American *United Press* tries to distort Soviet peace policy and dares discuss Sino-Soviet relations," "United Press International sows discord in Sino-Soviet relations making use of the visit of Soviet government delegation to China," *Neibu Cankao*, August 11 and October 5, 1954.

53. *Zhou Enlai Nianpu*, 1: 418; *Renmin Ribao*, October 11, 18, 1954. For Soviet policy toward China in this period, see Dallin, *Soviet Foreign Policy After Stalin*, 222–32.

54. *Renmin Ribao*, October 12, 1954.

55. Khrushchev's name was not included in the initial plan. See "Resolution concerning related measures to be taken for celebrating the fifth anniversary of the PRC," August 1954, SD08096.

56. Shi Zhe, *Zai Lishi Juren Shenbian: Shi Zhe Huiyilu* (On the Side of the Historical Giants: Shi Zhe's Memoir) (Beijing, China: Zhongyang Wenxian Chubanshe, 1991), 572–73; for the Soviet assistance to China's nuclear program, see Shen Zhihua, "Yuanzhu yu Xianzhi: Sulian yu Zhongguo de Hewuqi Yanzhi, 1949–1960" (Assistance and Restriction—The Soviet Union and China's research on the nuclear weapons, 1949–1960), www.shenzhihua.net/zhongsu31.htm, accessed June 10, 2005; and John Wilson Lewis and Xue Litai, *China Builds the Bomb* (Stanford, Calif.: Stanford University Press, 1988), 11–46.

57. *Renmin Ribao*, August 17, 1954; АВПРФ, ф.0100, оп.47, п.383, д.40, л.4–5; АВПРФ, ф.0100, оп.47, п.383, д.40, л.10–19; АВПРФ, ф.0100, оп.47, п.383, д.40, л.10–19, from SD 08096, 08097, 08101, and 08098; Shi, *Zai Lishi Juren Shenbian*, 270–1.

58. "Excerpts of Nehru's remarks on foreign affairs," October 31, 1954, CFMA, 204-00142-03, 40–43.

59. "Responses on the Taiwan issue after the publication of Premier Zhou's report on foreign affairs and our multi-party joint declaration," August 28, 1954, CFMA, 102-00171-02, 8–13.

60. "Zhou Enlai's Report on Foreign Affairs before the Visit of Nehru," October 18, 1954, Fujian Provincial Archives, 101-5-542, 11–21; *Zhou Enlai Nianpu*, 1: 419–20.

61. *Zhou Enlai Nianpu*, 1: 420–21.

62. *Mao Zedong Waijiao Wenxuan*, 163–76; "Excerpts of Nehru's talks with Chairman Mao Zedong and Premier Zhou Enlai," November 7, 1954, CFMA, 204-00148-02, 4–14. Before Nehru's arrival, *Renmin Ribao* published detailed statistics about U.S. aggression. See *Renmin Ribao*, October 11, 1954.

63. *Selected Works of Nehru*, 26: 34.

64. "Nehru's remarks about the Taiwan issue," October 29, 1954, *Neibu Cankao*; "Nehru's remarks on foreign policy," October 31, 1954, CFMA, 204-00142-03, 41–59.

65. Memo of Soviet diplomat Dobrynin's talk with Washington Bureau Chief of *Christian Science Monitor*, October 21, 1954, SD10219. But no document indicates if the Soviets shared this information with the Chinese. According to British sources, the Chinese perception was basically correct. The visit did leave a good impression on Nehru and raised U.S. displeasure. See Washington to FO, "Mr. Nehru's Visit to Peking," October 15, 1954; CRO minute: "Mr. Nehru's Impression of China," November 4, 1954; High Commissioner in India to CRO, November 2, 1954; CRO minute: "Mr. Nehru's Visit to China," November 26, 1954; all in FO371/110226, NAUK.

66. For more details about Nehru's involvement in the UN initiative, see chap. 4.

67. "Zhou Enlai's Report on Foreign Affairs before the Visit of Nehru," October 18, 1954, Fujian Provincial Archives, 101-5-542, 11–21; *Zhou Enlai Nianpu*, 1: 419–20; "Zhou's Political Report at the First People's Congress," http://news.xinhuanet.com/ziliao/2004-10/11/content_2075930.htm, accessed December 10, 2011.

68. Even after the British participated in SEATO, Chinese Communist officials still believed Britain wanted to carry out the Locarno Pact in Asia. According to Chinese officials, although Britain gave up the idea "temporarily" in late July, it resumed pursuit of the policy when Asian countries such as India refused to join SEATO. See "Preliminary analysis of the Southeast Asian collective defense pact," September 9, 1954, CFMA, 105-00626-03, 13–17. However, British documents did not indicate the British took the Locarno Pact seriously. Moreover, the Chinese leaders were also unaware that at this point the United States and United Kingdom were preparing to take the Taiwan issue to the UN Security Council, and the British agreed to the U.S. plan to conclude the MDT with the GMD to make sure the UN resolution would be successful. See chap. 4. For analysis of the ANZUS, see Thomas Robb and David Gill, "The ANZUS Treaty during the Cold War: A Reinterpretation of U.S. Policy in Southwest Pacific," *Journal of Cold War Studies* 17, no. 4 (Fall 2015): 109–57.

69. FO minute "Quemoy and Formosa" November 18, 1954, FO371/110238, NAUK.

70. For China's efforts to induce Britain with trade, see Shu Guang Zhang, *Beijing's Economic Statecraft During the Cold War, 1949–1991* (Washington, D.C.: Woodrow Wilson Center Press; Baltimore: John Hopkins University Press, 2014), 52–3.

71. Trevelyan, *Living with the Communists*, 166–67. For the Sino-British Trade Committee, see FO guidance telegram, July 14, 1954, and Trevelyan's telegram regarding the visit of Sino-British Trade Committee delegation to China in November–December 1954, December 21, 1954, in *British Documents on Foreign Affairs*: Part V, Series E, 6: 92–93.

72. FO minute "Quemoy and Formosa," November 18, 1954, FO371/110238, NAUK. The Chinese judgment was accurate. On October 14, Dulles sent a letter to Chiang, informing him of the decision to have an MDT. The negotiation started on November 2 and was completed on November 23. See chap. 4.

73. See *Renmin Ribao*, November 11, 19, 29, 1954.

74. *Renmin Ribao*, November 25, 1954. For the issue of U.S. pilots, see Trevelyan, *Living with the Communists*, 151–56. For Chinese sources, see "Documents concerning American Espionages," CFMA, 111-00053-01, 02, and 03. As early as July, Mao decided to use U.S. nationals in China as a diplomatic tool, which led to Sino-American consulate meetings in Geneva. See *Mao Zedong Wenji*, 6: 332–33.

75. Jiang Ying, "50 Niandai Mao Zedong Waijiao Sixiang Shulun," in *Cong Duishi Zouxiang Huanhe: Lengzhan Shiqi de Zhongmei Guanxi* (From Confrontation to Détente: Sino-American Relations during the Cold War), eds. Jiang Changbing, Robert Ross (Beijing, China: Shijie Zhishi Chubanshe, 2000), 587–88; Xu, *Jinmen zhi Zhan*, 180. The PLA had long prepared to attack Dachen and Yijiangshan. As early as January 1954, the PLA leaders decided to take the offshore islands following an order from north to south, and from small to bigger ones. In May, the PLA captured the Dongji Islands. In July, the PLA wanted to bomb Dachen and Yijiangshan, but Mao stopped the action in order to avoid a conflict with the U.S. forces in the area. In late August, the PLA decided to take Yijiangshan before Dachen. From November 1 to 4, preparatory bombing on Dachen and Yijiangshan started and on November 14, the PLA sank a GMD major destroyer. Liu Tong, *Kua Hai zhi Zhan*, 433, 446–47, 460–61.

76. *Zhou Enlai Nianpu*, 1: 430; *Renmin Ribao*, December 3, 5, 9, 1954.

77. *Renmin Ribao*, December 13, 17, 1954.

78. Liu Tong, *Kua Hai zhi Zhan*, 465.

79. "British response to U.S.-Chiang Agreement," December 6, 1954, CFMA, 110-00276-01, 1–5.

80. "British response to U.S.-Chiang Agreement," December 6, 1954, CFMA, 110-00276-01, 1–5; "A comprehensive analysis of British responses to Premier's [Zhou] statement on December 8," December 13, 1954, CFMA, 110-00276-01, 6–9; "British deputy secretary of state Nutting talked about the Taiwan issue on U.S. TV programs," December 14, 1954, CFMA, 110-00276-02.

81. "Zhou Enlai's political report on the first plenary conference of the second Chinese People's Political Consultative Conference," *Renmin Ribao*, December 21, 1954; *Zhou Enlai Nianpu*, 1: 433–4.

82. "Statistics of U.S. fighters' invasion of our air space from 1950 to September 1954," September 30, 1954, CFMA, 204-00148-04, 23–29.

83. *Zhou Enlai Nianpu*, 1: 428–29; *Zhou Enlai Waijiao Huodong Dashiji* (Chronicle of Major Events in Zhou Enlai's Diplomatic Career). ed. the PRC Foreign Ministry (Beijing, China: Shijie Zhishi Chubanshe, 1993), 93–94; *Mao Zedong Zhuan*, 576–80.

84. "Burmese press response to U Nu's visit to China," December 12, 1954, CFMA, 102-000159-19, 89–91. Indeed, China's diplomacy on Burma was so successful that it caused the British diplomats to worry that U Nu "have leaned over excessively in

the direction of the Communist point of view." See telegrams regarding U Nu's visit to China, from Gore-Booth, December 22, 1954, and Trevelyan, December 22, 1954; both in *British Documents on Foreign Affairs: Part V, Series E*, 6: 94–96, 97–98.

85. "Existing problems in Coastal Fujian's struggle against the enemy," "Responses of the masses in Fuzhou and Xiamen to U.S.-Chiang 'Mutual Defense Treaty'," *Neibu Cankao*, December 30, 1954.

86. For the PLA's plan to attack Yijiangshan, see Jiang Ying, "50 Niandai Mao Zedong Waijiao Sixiang Shulun," 587–88; Xu, *Jinmen zhi Zhan*, 180. According to Chang and He, after studying the MDT, Chinese leaders concluded it did not cover the offshore islands. See Chang and He, "The Absence of War," 1513.

87. *Mao Wengao*, 3: 518; 4: 23, 25; Liu Tong, *Kua Hai zhi Zhan*, 481.

88. *FRUS, 1955–1957*, 2: 111–12. There was no evidence that the Soviets forwarded this message to the Chinese, but Mao's decision to stop attacking Dachen most probably did not result from this signal, because throughout the crisis, the PLA never took military actions against the GMD forces if there were U.S. forces around. In this sense, the confrontation in the Taiwan Strait was never out of the control of the Communist leaders, as Shu Guang Zhang argues. See Zhang, *Deterrence and Strategic Culture*, 189–90.

89. *FRUS, 1955–57*, 2: 162–63.

90. For Sino-Soviet coordination on this, see memos of Lomakin's meetings with Zhou, January 29 and 30 1955, АВПРФ, ф.0100, оп.48, п.394, д.10, л.185-187, 188–89; SD09933, SD09934.

91. Memorandum of Zhou Enlai's meeting with Soviet diplomat, February 2, 1955, АВПРФ, ф.0100, оп.48, п.394, д.10, л.203–6; SD09935. This new source first reveals the Chinese collaboration with the Soviet Union and gives more significance to the conciliation in February.

92. Existing works argue that the Soviet Union, not China, attempted to mobilize Asian states at this point. For example, G. H. Jansen argues [the Soviet inclusion of Colombo states in the proposal] "indicates how quickly Russian diplomacy played up to and sought to use this new Asian grouping, for which Mr. Dulles had only ill-concealed contempt." See G. H. Jansen, *Afro-Asia and Non-Alignment* (London: Faber and Faber, 1966), 183.

93. *Zhou Enlai Waijiao Wenxuan*, 107.

94. *Zhou Enlai Waijiao Huodong Dashiji*, 100.

95. *Zhou Enlai Nianpu*, 1: 442–43.

96. Memorandum of Yudin and Mao Zedong's meeting, January 8, 1955, АВПРФ, ф.0100, оп.48, п.393, д.9, л.24–30; SD09844, and Paul Wingrove, "Mao's Conversation with the Soviet Ambassador, 1953–1955," CWIHP, working paper #36.

97. Emphasis added. *Zhou Enlai Waijiao Huodong Dashiji*, 95.

98. Nehru told the press that the GMD's harassment of the mainland produced an "uncomfortable and unpleasant situation." See "Nehru's Remarks Concerning Foreign Policy," October 31, 1954, CFMA, 204-00142-03, 45. For Chinese analysis of the Southeast Asian responses to the bombing of Jinmen, see "Southeast Asian and North European States' Responses to Our Declaration to Liberate Taiwan," September 21, 1954, CFMA, 102-000159-15, 65–67.

99. See *Selected Works of Nehru*, 27: 32–40, 105, 116.

100. Telegram from Chinese Embassy in Indonesia, February 2, 1955, CFMA, 105-00173-12, 1.

101. Shijie Zhishi Chubanshe, ed., *Zhongmei Guanxishi Ziliao Huibian* (*Collection of Documents on Sino-American Relations*) (Beijing, China: Shijie Zhishi Chubanshe, 1957), 2: 2168, 2177.

102. "Excerpts of Charge d'affaires Huan Xiang's Talk with Nehru," February 1, 1955, CFMA, 105-00058-04, 6–8. For Nehru's concerns about the Taiwan Strait in early February, 1955, see *Selected Works of Nehru*, 28: 158–67.

103. Telegram from Soviet Embassy to Molotov, February 8, 1955, АВПРФ, ф.0100, оп.48, п.394, д.10, л.222–23; SD09937.

104. *Selected Works of Nehru*, 28: 167–72; telegram from Soviet Embassy to Molotov, February 8, 1955, АВПРФ, ф.0100, оп.48, п.394, д.10, л.222-223; SD09937; "The Ceylonese and Indian High Commissioners' Visit Regarding the Commonwealth Conference's discussion of the Taiwan Issue," February 5, 1955, CFMA, 110-00276-06, 37.

105. *Zhou Enlai Waijiao Huodong Dashiji*, 100.

106. Memorandum of conversation between Lomakin and Zhang Hanfu, February 6, 1955, АВПРФ, ф.0100, оп.48, п.394, д.10, л.215–19; SD09936.

107. "Reply to Nehru's talk with chargé Huan," February 6, 1955, CFMA, 105-00058-05, 1–2.

108. Chinese diplomats had a very interesting analysis of the causes of Nehru's shifting position. According to the Chinese chargé in London, Nehru was influenced by three factors: 1) the British, especially the last Viceroy of India, Louis Mountbatten, had strong influence with on Nehru, because Nehru was Ms. Mountbatten's "old lover" and still infatuated with her. 2) The Indian Communists had the upper hand in the election in India's Andhra, and the National Congress was frightened by the Communists, and hence Nehru's attitude toward Communists changed. 3) The United States had made efforts to attract India: it sold India ten tons of heavy water and promised to help with India's construction of atomic power plants. See "Nehru's attitude on the Taiwan Issue Changed significantly After the Commonwealth Premiers' Conference," February 17, 1955, CFMA, 110-00276-06, 45–46. See also Lomakin's telegram to Molotov, February 8, 1955, АВПРФ, ф.0100, оп.48, п.394, д.10, л.222-223; SD09937; memo of Lomakin's meeting with Zhou, February 8, 1955, АВПРФ, ф.0100, оп.48, п.394, д.10, л.233–34; SD09940.

109. Telegrams between Chinese Foreign Ministry and Yuan and Huan, February 23, 1955, CFMA, 110-00276-04, and 110-00276-06; memorandum of conversation between Lomakin and Zhang Hanfu, February 23, 1955, АВПРФ, ф.0100, оп.48, п.394, д.10, л.271–76; SD09941; telegram regarding India-Soviet contact over the Taiwan issue, February 22, 1955, CFMA, 105-00058-12, 27–29.

110. *Zhou Enlai Waijiao Huodong Dashiji*, 102.

111. "India Press Response of Asia-African Conference before February 5," February 5, 1955, CFMA, 207-00002-02, 54–55; "Excerpts of Vice Minister Zhang Hanfu's Meeting with Indonesian Ambassador," February 16, 1955, CFMA, 207-00003-05, 56–59. U Nu sent the Chinese message to Dulles when the latter visited Burma in late February. See Evelyn Colbert, *Southeast Asia in International Politics, 1941–1956* (Ithaca, N.Y.: Cornell University Press, 1977), 320–21.

112. "Summary of British Press Coverage and Our Embassy's Analysis of the Bang-kok Conference," February 28, 1955, CFMA, 105-00173-13, 65–67; "Increase of U.S. Activities in Indonesia to Sabotage the Asia-African Conference," March 7, 1955, CFMA, 207-00002-02, 57–58; and "U.S. Actions toward Indonesia before the Asia-African Conference," March 25, 1955, CFMA, 207-00002-04, 136–39.

113. Memorandum of Zhou's conversation with Lomakin, February 2, 1955, АВПРФ, ф.0100, оп.48, п.394, д.10, л.203–6; SD09935. This was exactly what Chinese lead-ers did when India mediated between the United States and China in May. See memorandum of Zhou's conversation with Soviet diplomat, May 21, 1955, АВПРФ, ф.0100, оп.48, п.394, д.11, л.125–34; SD09943.

114. Memorandum of conversation between Lomakin and Zhang Hanfu, February 23, 1955, АВПРФ, ф.0100, оп.48, п.394, д.10, л.271–76; SD 09941.

115. "Comments on Eden's statement in the Parliament," January 27, 1955, CFMA, 110-00276-06, 51–52; and Chinese telegram regarding the conclusion of the Common-wealth Premiers' meeting, February 9, 1955, CFMA, 110-00276-06, 43–44.

116. Chang and He, "The Absence of War," 1515–17; Liu, *Kuahai zhi Zhan*, 507–10.

117. The U.S. government did not protest or retaliate; instead, it declared that the fight-ers "drifted off course." Apparently, Washington wanted to avoid a confrontation. See Liu, *Kua Hai zhi Zhan*, 508.

118. The CCP Central Committee, "U.S. interference in the question of our liberation of Taiwan," February 21, 1954; and "Guangyu Zhou Enlai Tongzhi he Yingguo Zhu-woguo Daiban Trevelyan Tanhua Neirong," February 28, 1954; cited in Chang and He, "The Absence of War," 1516.

119. For Chinese knowledge of Dulles's threat to use nuclear weapons to stop China from invading Taiwan, see *Renmin Ribao*, March 6, 1955. Most of the current lit-erature argues that Chinese concern about the nuclear threat led to their shift to its conciliation in Bandung. Yet they often neglect the Chinese conciliation in Febru-ary, which happened before the U.S. leaders threatened to use atomic bombs in March. China's public petition against the use of atomic bombs in January, which some works cite as evidence of China's fear of U.S. nuclear threats, turned out to be part of a joint diplomatic offensive launched by the Soviet Union to protest NATO's adoption of nuclear deterrence in the fall of 1954. See "Directive Concerning Car-rying out a Nationwide Campaign to Enlist Signatures for the Petition against the Use of Atomic Weapons," February 19, 1955, CFMA, 102-00214-02, 35–36. For a description of China's anti-nuclear propaganda, see Stolper, *China, Taiwan, and the Offshore Islands*, 98–99. For the new NATO nuclear policy, see Matthew Jones, "Targeting China: U.S. Nuclear Planning and 'Massive Retaliation' in East Asia, 1953–1955," *Journal of Cold War Studies* 10, no. 4 (Fall 2008): 40. For China's chang-ing perception of the U.S. nuclear threat in 1954–55, see Alice Langley Hsien, *Com-munist China's Strategy in the Nuclear Era* (Englewood Cliffs, N.J.: Prentice-Hall, 1962), 15–49.

120. Zhonggong Jiangsushen Dangshi Yanjiushi, ed., *Su Yu Nianpu* (A Chronological Record of Su Yu) (Beijing, China: Dangdai Zhongguo Chubanshe, 2006), 567; *Mao Wengao*, 5: 51; Liu, *Kua Hai zhi Zhan*, 510.

121. Mao Zedong, "Concluding remarks at the National Conference of the CCP," March 31, 1954, in *The Writings of Mao Zedong, 1949–1976*, eds. Michael Y. M. Kau and John K. Leung (New York: M. E. Sharpe, 1986), 540; and "Outlines of the concluding

speech at the National Congress of the CCP," March 31, 1954, *Mao Wengao*, 5: 72; English translation is from Zhang, *Deterrence and Strategic Culture*, 221; Liu, *Kua Hai zhi Zhan*, 512.
122. See chap. 4.
123. Memorandum of conversation between Lomakin and Zhang Hanfu, February 23, 1955, АВПРФ, ф.0100, оп.48, п.394, д.10, л.271–176; SD09941. Liu Shaoqi, Mao's successor apparent, assured the Soviets that China would not attack such islands as Jinmen and Mazu, given the limited capabilities of the PLA. Li Danhui, ed., *Beijing yu Mosike: Cong Lianmeng Zouxiang Duikang* (Beijing and Moscow: From Alliance to Confrontation) (Guilin: Guangxi Shifan Daxue Chubanshe, 2002), 248.
124. *Zhou Enlai Nianpu*, 1: 445.
125. *FRUS, 1952–54*, 14: 1005, 1062; *FRUS, 1955–57*, 2: 25. For the process of U.S. policy-making, see Robert Accinelli, *Crisis and Commitment: United States Policy Toward Taiwan, 1950–1955* (Chapel Hill: University of North Carolina Press, 1996), 180–82; Su-Ya Chang, "Taihai Weiji Qian Meiguo dui Waidao de Zhengce" (U.S. policy toward the offshore islands before the Taiwan Strait Crisis), *Zhongyang Yanjiuyua Jingdaishi Yanjiusuo Jikan* (Bulletin of the Institute of Modern History, Academia Sinica), 23 (June 1994): 322–28.

4. "A HORRIBLE DILEMMA"

1. Commonwealth Relations Office (CRO) to High Commissioners, August 31, 1954, FO371/110257, National Archives of the United Kingdom (NAUK).
2. U.S. Department of State, *Foreign Relations of the United States (FRUS), 1952–54*, 14: 567.
3. *FRUS, 1955–57*, 2: 202–3.
4. The conventional interpretation stresses Dulles's militant response during the Taiwan Strait Crisis. See David Heller and Dean Heller, *John Foster Dulles: Soldier for Peace* (New York: Holt, Rinehart and Winston, 1960), chap. 9; Townsend Hoopes, *The Devil and John Foster Dulles* (Boston: Little, Brown, 1973), chap. 17. Eisenhower revisionists commend the president's restraint and flexibility, which successfully prevented a war with China. See Leonard Gordon, "United States Opposition to Use of Force in the Taiwan Strait 1954–1962," *Journal of American History* 72, no. 3 (December 1985): 637–60; Robert Divine, *Eisenhower and the Cold War* (New York: Oxford University Press, 1981), 55–66; Stephen Ambrose, *Eisenhower: The President* (New York: Simon and Schuster, 1984), 212–15; Rushkoff Bennett, "Eisenhower, Dulles and the Quemoy-Matsu Crisis, 1954–1955," *Political Science Quarterly* 96 (Fall 1981): 465–80 Post-revisionists criticize Eisenhower's policy as inconsistent and crisis driven. See Robert Accinelli, *Crisis and Commitment: United States Policy Toward Taiwan, 1950–1955* (Chapel Hill: University of North Carolina Press, 1996); H. W. Brands, "Testing Massive Retaliation: Credibility and Crisis Management in the Taiwan Strait," *International Security* 12, no. 4 (Spring 1988): 124–51; Gordon Chang, "To the Nuclear Brink: Eisenhower, Dulles, and the Quemoy-Mazsu Crisis," *International Security* 12, no. 4 (Spring 1986): 96–123; Gordon Chang and Di He, "The Absence of War in the U.S.-China Confrontation over Quemoy and Matsu in 1954–1955," *American Historical Review* 98 (December 1993): 1500–24;

and the series of articles by Su-Ya Chang: "Taihai Weiji Qian Měiguo dui Waidao de Zhengce" " (U.S. Policy toward the Offshore Islands before the Taiwan Strait Crisis). *Zhongyang Yanjiuyua Jingdaishi Yanjiusuo Jikan* 23 (June 1994): 295–330; "Taihai Weiji yu Meiguo Dui 'Fangong Dalu' Zhengce the Zhuanbian" (The Taiwan Strait Crisis and the Shifting US Policy toward [GMD's] "Restoring the Mainland" Policy), *Zhongyang Yanjiuyuan Jingdaishi Yanjiusuo Jikan* 36 (December 2001): 231–97; "Anlihui Tinghuo An: Meiguo Yingfu Diyici Taihai Weiji Celur zhi Yi" (Oracle: US Response to the Taiwan Strait Crisis, I), *Zhongyang Yanjiuyuan Jingdaishi Yanjiusuo Jikan* 22, no. 2 (June 1993): 61–106; "Jinma Chejun: Meiguo Yingfu Dierci Taihai Weiji Celue zhi Er" (Evacuating Jinmen and Mazu: US Response to the Taiwan Strait Crisis, II), *Zhongyang Yanjiuyuan Jingdaishi Yanjiusuo Jikan* 24, no. 1 (June 1995): 413–72; and "Reluctance Alliance: John Foster Dulles and the Making of the United States–Republic of China Mutual Defense Treaty of 1954," in *Chinese Yearbook of International Laws and Affairs* 12 (1992–1994): 126–71.

5. Dwight D. Eisenhower, *The White House Years: Mandate for Change, 1953–1956* (Garden City, N.Y.: Doubleday, 1963), 463; and *FRUS, 1952–54*, 14: 619.

6. *FRUS, 1952–54*, 14: 529.

7. *FRUS, 1952–54*, 14: 518–19. Meanwhile, in Taiwan, Chiang believed the Communist propaganda aimed to deter the United States from concluding the MDT and increasing assistance to the GMD. He predicted that the Communists would intensify their peace offensive to further isolate the United States. See Chiang Kai-shek Diaries, Hoover Institution, Stanford University (CKS Diaries), entries July 26 and 31, 1954.

8. *FRUS, 1952–54*, 14: 392–94, 412–14, 415–16, 418, 425–26. For the PLA capture of Dongji, see Liu Tong, *Kuai Hai zhi Zhan—Jinmeng, Hainan, Yijiangshan* (The Cross-Sea Wars: Jinmen, Hainan, Yijiangshan) (Beijing, China: Sanlian Shudian, 2010), 428–32.

9. *FRUS, 1952–54*, 14: 433–34.

10. *FRUS, 1952–54*, 12: 666–81; Herring, " 'A Good Stout Effort," 213–33.

11. Makins to FO, no. 388, August 3, 1954, in *British Documents on Foreign Affairs: Reports and Papers from the Foreign Office*, Part V, Series E, 7 (Bethesda, Md.: Lexis-Nexis, 2005): 120–25.

12. *FRUS, 1952–54*, 16: 1503.

13. *FRUS, 1952–54*, 16: 1550–51, 1552–62.

14. U.S. preoccupation with Indochina was demonstrated by the fact that post-Geneva Indochina remained the most important subject of the NSC meetings throughout August 1954. For the establishment of SEATO, see Dingman, "John Foster Dulles and the Creation of the South-East Asia Treaty Organization in 1954," *The International History Review*, XI, 3 (August 1989): 457–77; Hall "Anglo-US Relations in the Formation of SEATO," 121–32; and George Herring, " 'A Good Stout Effort': John Foster Dulles and the Indochina Crisis, 1954–1955," in *John Foster Dulles and the Diplomacy of the Cold War*, ed. Richard Immerman, 213–33, (Princeton, N.J.: Princeton University Press, 1990).

15. *FRUS, 1952–54*, 14: 505, 507–12.

16. For the American knowledge of the Chinese propaganda, see *Survey of China Mainland Press* (SCMP), 1953–1956 (compiled and translated by American Consulate General in Hong Kong) Springfield, Va.: Reproduced by National Technical Information Service, no. 855 (July 24 to 26), 858 (July 29), and 860 (July 31 to August 2).

17. *FRUS, 1952–54*, 14: 518–19.

18. *FRUS, 1952–54*, 14: 537.

19. *FRUS, 1952–54*, 14: 542–43.

20. *CKS Diaries*, entries August 18 and 19, 1954.

21. *FRUS, 1952–54*, 14: 562, footnote 1; President's News Conference, August 17, 1954, *Public Papers of the Presidents of the United States: Dwight D. Eisenhower (1953–1958)* (Washington, D.C.: Governmental Printing Office, 1959–1964), 1954, 719; Washington to FO, August 19, 1954, FO371/110257, NAUK.

22. For the evolution of U.S. policy toward these islands, see Chang, "Taihai Weiji Qian Meiguo dui Waidao de Zhengce," 295–311.

23. *FRUS, 1952–54*, 14: 49–50; Appu K. Soman, *Double-Edged Sword: Nuclear Diplomacy in Unequal Conflicts: The United States and China, 1950–1958* (Westport, Conn.: Praeger, 2000), 119.

24. Liu, *Kua Hai zhi Zhan*, 330–43, 422; Stephen Hartnett, "Avoiding 'A Chain Reaction of Disaster': A Reappraisal of the Eisenhower White House's Handling of the 1954–1955 Quemoy Crisis," *Presidential Studies Quarterly* 48, no. 4 (December 2018): 773–74.

25. Liu, *Kua Hai zhi Zhan*, 419.

26. *FRUS, 1952–54*, 14: 144–45, 193; Chang, "Taihai Weiji Qian Meiguo dui Waidao de Zhengce," 298–99, 301–3.

27. For the process of the conflicts, see Liu, *Kua Hai zhi Zhan*, 422–43.

28. *FRUS, 1952–54*, 14: 428–30. For details about U.S. responses to the tensions in May 1954, see Accinelli, *Crisis and Commitment*, 148–50; Chang, "Taihai Weiji Qian Meiguo dui Waidao de Zhengce," 304–5.

29. *FRUS, 1952–54*, 14: 226–28, 235–36, 339–40; Chang, "Taihai Weiji Qian Meiguo dui Waidao de Zhengce," 301.

30. *FRUS, 1952–54*, 14: 308, see also 133–35, 240–41.

31. *FRUS, 1952–54*, 14: 537–38, 611, 615, 618. Robert Accinelli, "Eisenhower, Congress, and the 1954–55 Offshore Island Crisis," *Presidential Studies Quarterly* 20, no. 2 (Spring 1990): 331.

32. *FRUS, 1952–54*, 14: 543.

33. *FRUS, 1952–54*, 14: 554; CRO outgoing telegram, August 31, 1954, FO371/110257, NAUK.

34. For a detailed description of the GMD's efforts, see Chang, "Reluctant Alliance," 139–50; and Hsiao-Ting Lin, *Accidental State: Chiang Kai-shek, The United States, and the Making of Taiwan* (Cambridge, Mass.: Harvard University Press, 2016), 223–27. For Chiang's simultaneous quest for a multilateral regional alliance, see Chang, "Reluctant Alliance," 128–39; and Hao Chen, "Resisting Bandung? Taiwan's Struggle for 'Representational Legitimacy' in the Rise of the Asian Peoples' Anti-Communist League, 1954–57," in *The International History Review*, https://www .tandfonline.com/doi/full/10.1080/07075332.2020.1762239?scroll=top&needAccess=true, published online on May 6, 2020 (accessed May 18, 2020).

35. Koo first proposed the MDT to the new Eisenhower administration in March 1953. See Gu Weijun (Wellington Koo), *Gu Weijun Hui Yi Lu* (Wellington Koo Memoirs), 11 (Beijing: Zhonghua Book Company, 1983): 181–82. The GMD provided a draft treaty in December 1953. See Chang, "Reluctance Alliance," 141–42. Soon Chiang sent a letter to Eisenhower requesting an MDT. See Correspondence between

Presidents Chiang and Eisenhower, April to July 1954, ROCFMA, document no. 412.4/0085. For records of Chiang's talks with Van Fleet and Wilson from April to June 1954, see ROCFMA, 412.22/1248, and 412.22/1249; Chiang Kai-shek Presidential Documents, 002080106034007-16, Academia Historica.

36. *FRUS, 1952–54*, 14: 490–91. Chiang first made the promise in February 1953, after the U.S. declaration to "unleash" the GMD. See Su-Ya Chang, "Unleashing Chiang Kai-shek? Eisenhower and the Policy of Indecision Toward Taiwan, 1953," *Zhongyang Yanjiuyua Jingdaishi Yanjiusuo Jikan* (Bulletin of the Institute of Modern History, Academia Sinica) 20 (June 1991): 369–401.

37. Chang, "Reluctant Alliance," 148; Stolper, *China, Taiwan and the Offshore Islands: Together with Some Implications for Outer Mongolia and Sino-Soviet Relations* (Armonk, N.Y.: M. E. Shape, 1985), 25–26; and Accinelli, *Crisis and Commitment*, 144–55. For example, *Zhongyang Ribao* (Central Daily) reported on July 5, 1954, that Van Fleet believed the MDT was necessary, from Guomindang History Archive (GMDHA), Taipei.

38. *New York Times*, June 30, 1954; Townsend Hoopes, *The Devil and John Foster Dulles* (Boston, Mass.: Little, Brown, 1973), 263–64.

39. Stolper, *China, Taiwan and the Offshore Islands*, 19. For Truman's policy toward East Asia and the evolution of the idea of building a "defense perimeter," see Gaddis, "Drawing Lines." This paragraph draws on Su-Ya Chang, "Reluctant Alliance," 133–39.

40. *FRUS, 1952–54*, 14: 493; Chang, "Reluctant Alliance," 133, 137.

41. "Reluctant Alliance," 138.

42. *FRUS, 1952–54*, 14: 913.

43. The EDC was at the top of the U.S. leaders' agenda. Ironically, the French Parliament vetoed the plan on August 30, 1954, despite all the U.S. enticements and pressures, although it was the French themselves who initiated the plan. For details about the EDC, see Frank Costigliola, *France and the United States: The Cold Alliance Since World War II* (New York: Twayne, 1992), 90–104; and Brian R. Cuchin, "The 'Agonizing Reappraisal': Eisenhower, Dulles, and the European Defense Community," *Diplomatic History* 16, no. 2 (Spring 1992), 201–21.

44. *FRUS, 1952–54*, 14: 399–401. For details about Dulles's considerations, see Accinelli, *Crisis and Commitment*, 144–45; Chang, "Reluctant Alliance," 141–45.

45. Conference with the president, May 23, 1954, Dulles Papers, White House Memorandum Series, box 1, Dwight D. Eisenhower Presidential Library (DDEL); cited in Shuang Guang Zhang, *Deterrence and Strategic Culture: Chinese–American Confrontations, 1949–1958* (Ithaca, NY: Cornell University Press, 1992), 204.

46. Chang, "Reluctant Alliance," 148. In Taiwan, Chiang believed both Eisenhower and Dulles declared that they would sign an MDT with the GMD and also increase assistance to Taiwan. See *CKS Dairies*, entry July 31, 1954.

47. *FRUS, 1952–54*, 14: 548–50; 555. Accinelli believed that Dulles "had drawn perceptibly nearer to approval of a treaty before he departed for Manila." See Accinelli, *Crisis and Commitment*, 146. But according to Su-Ya Chang, Dulles did not have a decision before the PLA bombed Jinmen. See Chang, "Reluctant Alliance," 149–50.

48. *Gu Weijun Hui Yi Lu*, 11: 308–9; *FRUS, 1952–54*, 14: 572–73, 614, 624–27; Washington to FO, September 7, 1954, FO371/110231, NAUK; "Discussion at the 214th Meeting of the National Security Council, Sunday, September 12, 1954," AWF, NSC Series, box 6, DDEL. Dulles's actual talk with Chiang lasted five hours.

49. For interpretation of the British policy toward the crisis, see Michael Dockrill, "Britain and the First Chinese Off-Shore Islands Crisis, 1954–55," in *British Foreign Policy, 1949–1956*, eds. Michael Dockrill and John Young (London: Macmillan, 1989), 173–96, and Qiang Zhai, *The Dragon, the Lion and the Eagle: Chinese-British-American Relations, 1949–1958* (Kent, Ohio: Kent State University Press, 1994), 153–77. The current works have concentrated on the British role after the bombardment of Jinmen and do not examine their perceptions of China's propaganda and the Labour Party's visit.

50. Peking to FO, July 24, 1954, FO371/110257, NAUK. In Taiwan, Chiang believed the Communist propaganda aimed to deter the United States from concluding the MDT and increasing assistance to the GMD. He predicted that the Communist peace offensive would be intensified to further isolate the United States. See *CKS Diaries*, entries July 26 and 31,1954.

51. Peking to FO, August 26, 1954, FO371/110257; see also Peking to FO, August 17 and 18, 1954, FO371/110216, NAUK.

52. FO minute, attached to "Future of Formosa, brief for Lord Reading," September 2, 1954, FO371/110257, NAUK.

53. Peking to FO, September 2, 1954, *British Documents on Foreign Affairs*, Part V, Series E, 6: 57–58.

54. FO minute, "Invasion of Formosa," August 25, 1954, FO371/110257, NAUK; "Future of Formosa, brief for Lord Reading," September 2, 1954, FO371/110257, NAUK; FO to Washington, August 30, 1954, FO371/110257, NAUK.

55. FO minute, August 16, 1954, FO371/110216, NAUK.

56. FO minute, June 22, 1954, FO371/110222, NAUK. A comprehensive and accurate analysis of China's foreign policy after Geneva in late August is Trevelyan's telegram to FO, August 31, 1954, FO371/110216, NAUK.

57. FO minute: Position regarding Formosa, August 20, 1954; FO to Washington, August 30, 1954, FO371/110257, NAUK.

58. "British Labour Party Delegation's Visit to China," August 27, 1954, attached memorandum, September 7, 1954, CA Records, box 45, RG 59, NAUS; Peking to FO, August 25, 1954, PREM 11/697, NAUK. On September 3, *New York Times* published the Labour delegation head Attlee's talk in Hong Kong, which indicated China wanted the Labour Party to convince the United States to withdraw from the off-shore islands. From September 7 on, the newspaper started a seven-day series of reports about the Labour visit. See *Gu Weijun Hui Yi Lu*, 11: 322; and *CKS Diaries*, entries September 4 and 26, 1954.

59. FO minute: Position regarding Formosa, August 20, 1954, FO371/110257, NAUK.

60. *FRUS, 1952–54*, 14: 548. See also Scott to FO, August 25, 1954, FO371/110257, NAUK; FO minute, August 25, 1954, FO371/110257, NAUK.

61. *FRUS, 1952–54*, 14: 567.

62. *FRUS, 1952–54*, 14: 522–24, 545–47.

63. Washington to FO, August 25, 1954, FO371/110257, NAUK.

64. *CKS Diaries*, entries June 1 and 2, 1954.

65. *FRUS, 1952–54*, 14: 537–39.

66. Record of the NSC meeting discussion is in *FRUS, 1952–54*, 14: 526–40.

67. Chang and He, "The Absence of War," 1505.

68. *FRUS, 1952–54*, 14: 556–57, 561–63, 563–71, 571; Eisenhower, *Mandate for Change*, 459, 462–63.

69. *FRUS, 1952–54*, 14: 563–71, 595–97.

70. Anderson to Eisenhower, September 3, 1954, AWF, Dulles-Herter Series, box 3, DDEL.

71. *FRUS, 1952–54*, 14: 596.

72. *FRUS, 1952–54*, 14: 573, note 3; *New York Times*, September 3, 1954, page 1; *Gu Weijun Hui Yi Lu*, 11: 322.

73. *FRUS, 1952–54*, 14: 571. At his meeting with Dulles, Chiang did not even discuss the bombing. For Dulles' meeting with Chiang, see *Gu Weijun Hui Yi Lu*, 11: 308–9; "Discussion at the 214th Meeting of the National Security Council, Sunday, September 12, 1954," AWF, NSC Series, box 6, DDEL. In private, Chiang believed that the CCP bombed Jinmen in order to push the United States through the United Kingdom to withdraw the Seventh Fleet from Taiwan. See *CKS Diaries*, entry September 4, 1954. GMD leaders concluded on September 6 that the action was part of Communist efforts to isolate the United States and split the Western alliance, so it was more political than military, although it may lead to a military conflict. See Record of the 139th Meeting of the Standing Committee of the 7th Central Committee, September 6, 1954, vol. 7.3/11, GMDHA.

74. *FRUS, 1952–54*, 14: 584–85.

75. *FRUS, 1952–54*, 14: 572.

76. The only exception was chief of staff for the U.S. Army, General Matthew Ridgway, who believed the offshore islands were not essential to Taiwan and did not deserve protection. Eisenhower, *Mandate for Change*, 463; *FRUS, 1952–54*, 14: 598–610.

77. *FRUS, 1952–54*, 14: 616.

78. *FRUS, 1952–54*, 14: 611.

79. *FRUS, 1952–54*, 14: 616; for the full discussion at NSC, see: 613–24.

80. *FRUS, 1952–54*, 14: 612. See also Eisenhower, *Mandate for Change*, 463–64. For detailed interpretation of the decision-making process, see Chang, "Taihai Weiji Qian Meiguo dui Waidao de Zhengce," 311–17; "Anlihui Tinghuo An," 66–73; and Accinelli, *Crisis and Commitment*, 158–62. Chiang, still in the dark, believed the Americans had decided to protect the offshore islands but were not willing to publicize the decision in order to have freedom of action. See *CKS Diaries*, entries September 18 and 26, 1954.

81. *FRUS, 1952–54*, 14: 650–51; FO minutes, September 16, 1954, FO371/110231, NAUK. For the Dulles-Eden meeting on September 17, 1954, and British considerations about the MDT, see record of the meeting and the minute by Allen "Formosa and Quemoy," September 18, 1954, FO371/110231, NAUK; Accinelli, *Crisis and Commitment*, 166. For interactions between allies over the UN move, see Scott Kaufman, "Operation Oracle: The United States, Great Britain, New Zealand, and the Offshore Islands Crisis of 1954–55," *The Journal of Imperial and Commonwealth History* 32, no. 3 (September 2004): 106–24.

82. By this time, U.S. officials believed the Communist goal was Dachen, and the PLA shelled Jinmen to distract attention. See *FRUS, 1952–54*, 14: 659. A CIA estimate on September 8 said the PLA was not preparing for an invasion of Jinmen. See "The Chinese Offshore Islands," a "top secret" copy for the president prepared by the CIA, September 8, 1954, AWF, International Series, box 9, DDEL; Hartnett, "Avoiding 'A Chain Reaction of Disaster,' " 777.

83. Record of the meeting, September 18, 1954, FO371/110231, NAUK.

84. Scott to FO, January 9, 1954; Eden to FO, June 14, 1954, FO371/110222, NAUK.

85. Nancy Bernkopf Tucker, "John Foster Dulles and the Taiwan Roots of the 'Two Chinas' Policy," in *John Foster Dulles and the Diplomacy of the Cold War*, ed. Richard Immerman (Princeton, N.J.: Princeton University Press, 1990), 255.

86. *FRUS, 1952–54*, 14: 664.

87. *FRUS, 1952–54*, 14: 661–62.

88. *FRUS, 1952–54*, 14: 667–69. A *Washington Post* article on September 19 analyzed that China was using the Taiwan issue to isolate the United States. See *Gu Weijun Hui Yi Lu*, 11: 319.

89. *FRUS, 1952–54*, 14: 653–55, 663–64, 676.

90. *FRUS, 1952–54*, 14: 701–5, 710–13, 716–20, 724–28. For the British documents regarding Oracle, see Dixon to FO, September 30, FO371/110231; Eden to Makins, October 7 and 8, 1954, FO371/110232; and Dixon to Eden, October 8, 1954, FO371/110233, NAUK. For discussions about Oracle, see Washington to FO, October 18 and 19, 1954, FO371/110235, NAUK. On October 15, Chiang got Dulles' letter that the MDT was determined but would not be declared before Oracle. *CKS Diaries*, entry October 15, 1954.

91. *FRUS, 1952–54*, 14: 682–83, 693, 706–7, and 708. and "Memo, Robertson to Dulles re Mutual Security Treaty with the Government of the Republic of China," October 2, 1954, 794a.5MSP/10-254, RG 59, NAUS. For detailed discuss of the decision, see Chang, "Reluctant Alliance," 150–58; Accinelli, *Crisis and Commitment*, 167–68.

92. *FRUS, 1952–54*, 14: 728–53.

93. Chang, "Anlihui Tinghuo An," 76–78.

94. Washington to FO, October 19, 1954, FO371/110235, NAUK.

95. CRO outward telegram, October 16, 1954, FO371/110235, NAUK; *FRUS, 1952–54*, 14: 757–61.

96. Telegrams between Washington and FO, October 15, 1954, FO371/110234; UN delegation to FO, October 15, 1954, FO371/110234; Allen to FO, October 19, 1954, FO371/110235, NAUK; Eden to FO, October 19 and 21, 1954, FO371/110235; Colonial Office to High Commissioners, October 26, 1954, FO371/112035, NAUK. Su-Ya Chang argues that Dulles developed this idea after the decision was already made to justify the treaty with the GMD. See Chang, "Reluctant Alliance," 156–57. See also Accinelli, *Crisis and Commitment*, 169–70.

97. Telegrams between FO and Washington, October 15, 1954, FO371/110234, NAUK; Washington to FO, October 18, 1954, FO371/110235, NAUK.

98. UN delegation to FO, October 15, 1954, FO371/110234, NAUK; Washington to FO, October 15, 1954, FO371/110234, NAUK. British chargé Trevelyan, however, did not think the Chinese would accept Oracle and warned about the negative impact to Sino-British relations. See Trevelyan to FO, September 25, 1954, FO371/110231, and October 29, 1954, FO371/110236. See also Chang, "Anlihui Tinghuo An," 79–80.

99. The GMD also observed the PRC-Soviet collaboration carefully and interpreted it as a Communist effort to divide the Western alliance and remove the Seventh Fleet from the Taiwan Strait. See *Gu Weijun Hui Yi Lu*, 11: 352–54; *CKS Diaries*, entry October 12, 1954.

100. *FRUS, 1952–54*, 14: 674.

101. *FRUS, 1952–54*, 14: 690.

102. *FRUS, 1952–54*, 14: 715–16, 720–21; "Discussion at the 217th Meeting of the National Security Council, Thursday, October 14, 1954," AWF, NSC Series, box 6, DDEL.

103. *FRUS, 1952–54*, 14: 706–7.

104. *FRUS, 1952–54*, 14: 765–67.

105. *FRUS, 1952–54*, 14: 777.

106. *FRUS, 1952–54*, 14: 802.

107. *FRUS, 1952–54*, 14: 831.

108. *FRUS, 1952–54*, 14: 551, 842. For Nehru's message to Eden about his visit to China, see Nehru, "Note on Visit to China and Indo-China," November 14, 1954, FO371/115018, NAUK; "Discussion at the 217th Meeting of the National Security Council, Thursday, October 14, 1954," AWF, NSC Series, box 6, DDEL.

109. *FRUS, 1952–54*, 14: 823–26, 866; New York to FO, October 14, 1954, and High Commissioner in India to CRO, October 15, 1954, FO371/110232, NAUK; and Peking to FO, October 21, 1954, FO 371/112035, NAUK. For communication between the United States and Britain on Nehru's visit to China, see Eden to Makins, October 29, 1954, and Makins to FO, November 1, 1954, FO371/112036, NAUK.

110. Peking to FO, October 21, 1954, FO371/110235, NAUK; *FRUS, 1952–54*, 14: 893–95. For more discussion about Nehru's visit to Beijing, see chap. 5.

111. For the NSC discussion on November 2, see *FRUS, 1952–54*, 14: 827–39.

112. *FRUS, 1952–54*, 14: 840–42.

113. For the process of the negotiation, see Accinelli, *Crisis and Commitment*, 174–76; Chang, "Reluctant Alliance," 158–69; and Lin, *Accidental State*, 232–34.

114. *FRUS, 1952–54*, 14: 842–51, 855–65, 870–80, 887–92, 895–911. Soman argues that the U.S. military opposed formally excluding the coastal islands, which would demonstrate further softening of the U.S. position. See Soman, *Double-Edged Sword*, 128.

115. *FRUS, 1952–54*, 14: 823–24, note 2, 830; FO to Washington, November 29, 1954, FO371/110238, NAUK.

116. *FRUS, 1952–54*, 14: 880–81, 919–20; Minute by Crowe, regarding Quemoy and Formosa, November 13, 1954, FO371/110238, NAUK; Eden to Dixon, November 13, 1954; telegrams, FO to Makins, November 19, 1954, FO371/110238, NAUK; and FO to Makins, about meeting with the Chinese chargé in London, November 18, 1954, 793.00/11-2054, RG 59, NAUS.

117. *FRUS, 1952–54*, 14: 962–66, 989–93, 1001–03, 1035; Makins to FO, and Notes for Cabinet by the Far Eastern Department of FO, November 23, 1954; Eden to Makins, November 24, 1954, FO371/112038, NAUK.

118. Indeed, U.S. leaders knew a few of them were real spies. See *FRUS, 1952–54*, 14: 950–51, 977–78. For U.S. perception of Beijing's changing attitude toward Britain, see "Discussion at the 228th National Security Council meeting, December 9, 1954," AWF, NSC Series, box 6, DDEL. Chiang interpreted the CCP's action as an effort to deter the U.S. from concluding MDT. See *CKS Diaries*, entry November 27, 1954.

119. *FRUS, 1952–54*, 14: 956–57; Eisenhower, *Mandate for Change*, 465. Accinelli, *Crisis and Commitment*, 177–78; and Su-Ya Chang, "Wengong Wuxia Xia de Tuisuo: Meiguo Jueding yu Zhonggong Juxing Dashiji Taipan de Guocheng Fenxi, 1954–1955" (Retreat before Verbal Attack and Military Threat: Analysis of U.S. Decision to Hold Ambassadorial Talks with the Chinese Communists, 1954–1955), *Zhongyang Yanjiuyua Jingdaishi Yanjiusuo Jikan* 25 (June 1996): 393–94.

120. *FRUS, 1952–54*, 14: 1003, 1016–17, 1049–50.

121. Chang, "Wengong Wuxia," 397–99. For British analysis of the U.S. reactions, see Makins to FO, January 26, 1955, FO371/115026, NAUK.

122. *FRUS, 1952–54*, 14: 1004–6; *FRUS, 1955–57*, 2: 50–52. See "Discussion at the 232nd Meeting of the National Security Council, Thursday, January 21, 1954," AWF, NSC Series, box 6, DDEL. In late September, the CIA concluded that the Chinese target was Dachen and Jinmen was a diversionary attack. In early October, it concluded the PLA would soon have the strength to attack any of the islands. See *FRUS, 1952–54*, 14: 659, 689.

123. *FRUS, 1955–57*, 2: 137.

124. Washington to FO, January 29, 1955, FO371/115029; *FRUS, 1955–57*, 2: 136

125. *FRUS, 1955–57*, 2: 41–44, 69–82; New York to FO, February 4, 1954, FO371/115032, NAUK; Eisenhower, *Mandate for Change*, 466–67. For the GMD's request for help and the U.S. decision to evacuate from the offshore islands, see Chang, "Jinma Chejun," 418–21; Accinelli, *Crisis and Commitment*, 187–89.

126. *FRUS, 1955–57*, 2: 82; Dulles memo to Eisenhower, January 20, 1955, AWF, Dulles-Herter Series, box 1, DDEL. See also "Discussion at the 232nd Meeting of the National Security Council, Thursday, January 21, 1954," AWF, NSC Series, box 6, DDEL.

127. *FRUS, 1955–57*, 2: 130–32; FO to New York, January 21, 1955, FO371/115024, NAUK.

128. *FRUS, 1955–57*, 2: 86–89, 91–92; telegrams between Washington and FO, January 19, 20 and 21, 1955, FO371/115023, and FO371/115024, NAUK; Makins to Dulles, January 21, 1955, 793.00/1-2155, RG 59, NAUS; telegrams between Eden and Makins, January 29 and February 1, 1955; Churchill to Eisenhower, January 29, 1955, FO371/115029, NAUK.

129. *FRUS, 1955–57*, 2: 96–99. In private, Eisenhower believed the United States should not fight for the offshore islands. See "Discussion at the 229th Meeting of the National Security Council, Tuesday, December 21, 1954," AWF, NSC Series, box 6, DDEL.

130. Washington to FO, January 21, 1955, FO371/115024, NAUK. However, Accinelli argues that the British misunderstood the U.S. position, and the resolution actually gave the president "unequivocal authority to take military action as needed throughout the Taiwan area." See Accinelli, *Crisis and Commitment*, 191–92.

131. *FRUS, 1955–57*, 2: 217, note 2; Moscow to FO, February 4, 1954, FO371/115032, NAUK. The British diplomat believed that the Soviets "intend[ed] it seriously and not as a propaganda move," but it was "clear enough" that the United States would oppose it.

132. *FRUS, 1955–57*, 2: 217–18; see also 210–12.

133. *FRUS, 1955–57*, 2: 239. For the British response to the Soviets after they consulted with the United States, see FO to Moscow, February 8, 1955, FO371/115035, NAUK; "Formosa-Soviet Proposals," February 12, 1955, FO371/115032, NAUK. For the Indians' response, see FO to Washington, February 10, 1955, FO371/115035, and Moscow to FO, March 7 and 9, 1955, FO370/115041, and FO371/115042, NAUK.

134. *FRUS, 1952–1954*, 14: 940–41; Chang, "Wengong Wuxia," 392–93, 401–3.

135. *FRUS, 1955–57*, 2: 237, 244; Eden to Moscow, February 8, 1955, FO371/115035, NAUK; Chang, "Wengong Wuxia," 404.

136. *FRUS, 1955–57*, 2: 177–78. For U.S. officials' meeting with Molotov, see telegrams from Berlin to Secretary of State (SOS), January 30 and February 1, 1955, AWF, Dulles-Herter Series, box 1, DDEL.

137. *FRUS, 1955–57*, 2: 199.

138. *FRUS, 1955–57*, 2: 202–3.

139. Washington to FO, February 4, 1955, FO371/115032, NAUK; Eisenhower, *Mandate for Change*, 469; "Discussion at the 235th Meeting of the National Security Council, Thursday, February 3, 1954," AWF, NSC Series, box 6, DDEL.

140. Chiang had also resisted Oracle but finally abstained from voting in the Security Council, after the U.S. officials threatened that if they vetoed they would "make a great mistake." *FRUS, 1955–57*, 2: 38–46, 106–10, 124, 152–57.

141. *FRUS, 1955–57*, 2: 220–22; *CKS Diaries*, entry January 28, 1955. For the process of evacuation from Dachen, see Bruce A. Elleman, *High Seas Buffer: The Taiwan Patrol Force, 1950–1979* (New Port, R.I.: Naval War College Press, 2012), 63–66.

142. *FRUS, 1955–57*, 2: 213–14, 218–19, 244–47, 265; telegrams between Washington and FO, March 9, 12, 14, 16, 1955, FO370/115042, NAUK; Makins to Eisenhower, February 4, 1955, AWF, Dulles-Herter Series, box 1, DDEL. The GMD believed the Commonwealth conference decided to push it to give up the coastal islands and sought a ceasefire with the Communists; on this basis, both the Communists and the GMD could enter the UN. Chiang was furious at this "unreasonable and unfaithful" proposal. See *CKS Diaries*, entry February 1, 1955; and *Gu Weijun Hui Yi Lu*, 12, 160.

143. *FRUS, 1955–57*, 2: 270–73; Eisenhower, *Mandate for Change*, 470–74; *CKS Diaries*, entries February 17–18, and 23, 1955.

144. *FRUS, 1955–57*, 2: 281, note 5; Washington to FO, February 14–17, 1955, FO371/115036, FO371/115037, and FO371/115039, NAUK.

145. *FRUS, 1955–57*, 2: 234–38, 244–47; New York to FO, February 17, 1955, FO371/115037, NAUK.

146. *FRUS, 1955–57*, 2: 307–12; Eisenhower, *Mandate for Change*, 474–75; Bangkok to FO, February 25, 1955, FO371/115040, NAUK; FO to Kuala Lumpur, March 1, 1955, FO371/115041, NAUK. Eden may have been encouraged by a message from the Canadian foreign secretary about his meeting with Dulles on February 16: Dulles promised the United States would push the GMD for an eventual withdrawal from the coastal islands, although at present, it would help it if the Chinese Communists attacked. CRO outward telegram, February 28, 1955, FO371/115040, NAUK; Bangkok to SOS, February 25, 1955, AWF, Dulles-Herter Series, Box 1, DDEL.

147. Soman argues that "Dulles was obviously not playing straight with Eden" by withholding the fact that the U.S. commitment to Jinmen and Mazu was still valid. Soman, *Double-Edged Sword*, 134.

148. For Trevelyan's report about Zhou criticizing Britain for following the United States, see Peking to FO, February 25, 1955, FO371/115040, NAUK. For the British reports about Beijing's press attacks on Britain, see Peking to FO, February 5, 1954, 1955, FO371/115032, and February 25, 1955, FO371/115040, NAUK.

149. For the text of Zhou's reply, see Peking to FO, March 1, 1955, FO371/115040, NAUK. For Eden's response, see FO to Peking, March 7, 1955, FO371/115040, NAUK. For Trevelyan's meetings with Zhou, see Peking to FO, March 1, 1955, FO371/115040, and February 28, 1955, FO371/115040. For other contacts between Trevelyan and Zhou, see Peking to FO, February 25 and 26, 1955, FO371/115040, and March 4 and 7, 1955, FO371/115041, NAUK.

150. *Renmin Ribao* editorial, March 7, 1955.

151. *FRUS, 1955–57*, 2: 307–10, 319–20, 334, 339–43, 345–50, 352–53, 357.

152. GMD ambassador in Washington Gu Weijun was impressed by the war scare in late February. See *Gu Weijun Hui Yi Lu*, 12: 222.

153. *FRUS, 1955–57*, 2: 308, 341 footnote 4, 347; Vientiane to SOS, February 27, 1955, AWF, Dulles-Herter Series, box 1, DDEL.

154. *FRUS, 1955–57*, 2: 320–28; *CKS Diaries*, entries March 1 and 3, 1955. Still, Dulles publicly suggested the United States might take actions to the mainland in its defense of Taiwan and Penghu islands. See Hartnett, "Avoiding 'A Chain Reaction of Disaster'," 789. Indeed, it was Dulles's threat to China after he returned to the United States that made Chiang feel a war in Asia was imminent. See *CKS Diaries*, entries March 8 and 10, 1955.

155. *FRUS, 1955–57*, 2: 340.

156. Eisenhower, *Mandate for Change*, 476.

157. *FRUS, 1955–57*, 2: 336–37.

158. *FRUS, 1955–57*, 2: 345–50. For the military plan, see Chang "To the Nuclear Brink," 97–98; Matthew Jones, "Targeting China: U.S. Nuclear Planning and 'Massive Retaliation' in East Asia, 1953–1955," *Journal of Cold War Studies* 10, no. 4 (Fall 2008): 50–65; Brands, "Testing Massive Retaliation," 141; Soman, *Double-Edged Sword*, 139, 149–53.

159. *CKS Diaries*, entries March 8 to 12, 1955; *Gu Weijun Hui Yi Lu*, 12: 254–56; 258–61.

160. *New York Times*, March 16, 17, and 18, 1955; Eisenhower, *Mandate for Change*, 477–78.

161. Chang "To the Nuclear Brink," 97.

162. *FRUS, 1955–57*, 2: 360. After the EDC failed in August 1954, the Treaty of Brussels was amended to accept West Germany and Italy into the Western Union Defense Organization, which was renamed the Western European Union. A *New York Times* editorial on April 1 warned that U.S. allies opposed protecting the islands. If the United States went to war with China, it would not get any ally. See *Gu Weijun Hui Yi Lu*, 12: 258–61, 273. For the U.S. anti-war sentiment, see Su-Ya Chang, "Jinma Chejun," 458–59.

163. Emphasis added. Peking to FO, February 5, 1955, PREM 11/867, NAUK; cited in Elleman, *High Seas Buffer*, 40.

164. *FRUS, 1955–57*, 2: 360; Eisenhower, *Mandate for Change*, 478–80.

165. *FRUS, 1955–57*, 2: 364–66, 372–74, 397–98, 416–17; New York to FO, March 24, 1955, FO371/115043, NAUK; Eisenhower, *Mandate for Change*, 475. In July 1954, the British suspected that Beijing was promoting a pan-Asian non aggression pact. See telegrams between Washington and FO, July 1, 9, 14, 1954, FO371/111869, NAUK, and telegrams, Eden to Makins, March 12, 1955, FO371/115042, NAUK.

166. *FRUS, 1955–57*, 2: 374–75; Peking to FO, February 4, 1955, FO371/115032; Singapore to FO, March 2, 1955, FO371/115041; and FO to Washington, March 24, FO371/115043, NAUK.

167. *FRUS, 1955–57*, 2: 368–71, 384, 477–78; High Commissioner in Canada to CRO, March 23, 1955, FO371/115043; FO to Washington, March 28, 1955, FO371/115043, NAUK.

168. *FRUS, 1955–57*, 2: 392–93.

169. *FRUS, 1955–57*, 2: 444–45, 453–55.

170. *FRUS, 1955–57*, 2: 300–2, 305, 315, 354; Memorandum, Eisenhower to Dulles, April 5, 1955, Dulles Papers, Subject Series, box 9, DDEL; Washington to FO, April 7, 1955,

FO371/115045, NAUK. Su-Ya Chang argues that in mid-February, Eisenhower and Dulles had already thought about evacuating the islands in their efforts to defuse the crisis. See Chang, "Jinma Chejun," 448–51.

171. Emphasis added. *FRUS, 1955–57*, 2: 444–45, 450–51.

172. *FRUS, 1955–57*, 2: 440.

173. *FRUS, 1955–57*, 2: 445–50.

174. *FRUS, 1955–57*, 2: 473–75, 479–89.

175. *FRUS, 1955–57*, 2: 465–66, 471–73, 475–76.

176. *FRUS, 1955–57*, 2: 491–93. Memo, conversation between Eisenhower and Hoover, April 21, Dulles Papers, Subject Series, box 9, DDEL.

177. *FRUS, 1955–57*, 2: 493–95, 503, 504, 505–06. For a detailed discussion of the blockade, see Chang, "To the Nuclear Brink," 96–122; Accinelli, *Crisis & Commitment*, 222–26.

178. *FRUS, 1955–57*, 2: 510–17; Eisenhower, *Mandate for Change*, 481–82; Robertson to Secretary, April 25, 1955, AWF, International Series, box 9, DDEL. In private, Chiang cursed Radford as a trustless "rascal." *CKS Diaries*, entry April 27, 1955.

179. Accinelli, "Eisenhower, Congress, and the 1954–55 Offshore Island Crisis," 341.

180. For Beijing's military objective, see Chang and He, "The Absence of War," 1514; Yafeng Xia, *Negotiating with the Enemy: U.S.-China Talks During the Cold War, 1949–1972* (Bloomington: Indiana University Press, 2006), 82, note 20; Liu, *Kua Hai zhi Zhan*, 448–49.

181. Eisenhower, *Mandate for Change*, 459–60.

182. For a nuanced analysis of the whole process, see Chang, "Jinma Chejun."

183. Eisenhower, *Mandate for Change*, 483.

184. Chang, "To the Nuclear Brink."

5. FORMULATING A ZONE OF PEACE

1. "Opinion about Concluding a Mutual Non-Aggression Treaty with Southeast Asian States," June 17, 1954, Chinese Foreign Ministry Archives (CFMA), 203-00005-06, 58–60.

2. *Zhou Enlai Nianpu, 1949–1976*, Vol. 1–3 (A chronological record of Zhou Enlai, 1949–1976), ed. Li Ping and Ma Zhisun, et al. (Beijing, China: Zhongyang Wenxian Chubanshe, 1997) 1: 393; "Minutes of Premier Zhou's Second Meeting with Premier U Nu," June 29, 1954, CFMA, 203-00007-03, 46–57.

3. The twenty-nine states were Afghanistan, Cambodia, China, Egypt, Ethiopia, Gold Coast, Iran, Iraq, Japan, Jordan, Laos, Lebanon, Liberia, Libya, Nepal, Philippines, Saudi Arabia, Sudan, Syria, Thailand, Turkey, DRV, SV, Yemen, and the five Colombo Powers: Burma, Ceylon, India, Indonesia, and Pakistan.

4. For the Colombo meeting, see G. H. Jansen, *Afro-Asia and Non-Alignment* (London: Faber and Faber, 1966), 143–68; Jamie Mackie, *Bandung 1955: Non-Alignment and Afro-Asian Solidarity* (Singapore: Editions Didier Millet, 2005), 54. For the Chinese perception, see "About the meeting of the Five Asian Premiers," April 30, 1954, CMFA, 102-00159-06, 25–28. For the Colombo Powers and the Bandung Conference, see Cindy Ewing, "The Colombo Powers: Crafting Diplomacy in the Third World and Launching Afro-Asia at Bandung," *Cold War History* 19, no. 1 (Spring 2019): 1–19.

5. Telegrams about the Bogor Conference from Chinese Embassy in Indonesia, December 31, 1954 and January 6, 1955, CFMA, 207-00002-04, 94–95, 100–102; "Behaviors of the Five Premiers at the Bogor Conference," *Neibu Cankao*, February 1, 1955. See also Jansen, *Afro-Asia and Non-Alignment*, 169–81.

6. See for example, telegram about the Bogor Conference from the Chinese Embassy in Indonesia, December 29, 1954, 207-00002-04, 92; and "Procedure of the Bogor Conference of Premiers of Five Southeast Asian States and their attitudes towards Chinese participation of the Afro-Asian Conference," December 29, 1954, CFMA, 102-00159-21, 99–102.

7. Traditional works stress the significance of the PRC entering the world stage and Zhou's contribution to the "Bandung Spirit," but they do not examine China's policy per se. See Xue Mouhong, et al., *Dangdai Zhongguo Waijiao* (Contemporary Chinese Diplomacy) (Beijing, China: Zhongguo Shehui Kexue Chubanshe, 1990), 81–94; and Pei Jianzhang, et al., *Zhonghua Renmin Gongheguo Waijiaoshi, 1949–56* (History of the Diplomacy of the People's Republic of China) (Beijing, China: Shijie Zhishi Chubanshe, 1994), 231–55. For the latest works, see Shu Guang Zhang, "Constructing 'Peaceful Coexistence': China's Diplomacy Toward the Geneva and Bandung Conferences, 1954–55," *The Cold War History* 7, no. 4 (2007): 509–28; and Chen Jian, "Bridging Revolution and Decolonization: The 'Bandung Discourse' in China's Early Cold War Experience," *The Chinese Historical Review* 15, no. 2 (2008): 207–41.

8. Chinese newspapers at the time were full of the government rhetoric about building a zone of peace against the United States. For early works arguing China aimed to build a zone of peace in Asia, see David A. Wilson, "China, Thailand and the Spirit of Bandung" (Part I and II), *The China Quarterly*, no. 30 (1967): 149–69, and no. 31 (1967): 96–127; Kuo-kang Shao, "Chou En-lai's Diplomatic Approach to Non-Aligned States in Asia: 1953–60," *The China Quarterly*, no. 78 (1979): 324–38, and "Zhou Enlai's Diplomacy and the Neutralization of Indo-China, 1954–55," *The China Quarterly*, no. 107 (1986): 483–504.

9. *Renmin Ribao*, April 21, 24, 1954; *The Selected Works of Jawaharlal Nehru*, 25–27. S. Gopal, et al. (New Delhi, India: Jawaharlal Nehru Memorial Fund. Distributed by Oxford University Press, 1999–2001), 25: 442–43. For India's policy toward Indochina, see Gilles Boquérat, "India's Commitment to Peaceful Coexistence and the Settlement of the Indochina War," *Cold War History* 5, no. 2 (May 2005): 211–34.

10. Also known as "Panchsheel" or "Pancha Shilla," these principles include mutual respect for sovereignty and territorial integrity, mutual non aggression, mutual non interference in each other's internal affairs, equality and mutual benefit, and peaceful coexistence. It was first proposed by Zhou in late December 1953, when India and China negotiated over India's trade relations with Tibet.

11. "About the Five Asian Premiers' Meeting," April 30, 1954, CFMA, 102-00159-06, 25–28. *Selected Works of Nehru*, 25: 426. Boquérat, "India's Commitment to Peaceful Coexistence," 218–20; Jansen, *Afro-Asia and Non-Alignment*, 143–68.

12. "Responses of India, Indonesia, Burma and Britain to U.S. Active Quest for Southeast Asian Collective Defense Organization," June 5, 1954, CFMA, 102-00159-11, 1–3; and "Southeast Asian Collective Defense Treaty and Attitudes and Responses to It from Different States," October 1, 1954, CFMA, 105-00626-02, 44.

13. "Nehru's Remarks Concerning Foreign Policy," October 31, 1954, CFMA, 204-00142-03, 43; *Selected Works of Nehru*, 25: 438.

14. "Report from Chinese Embassy in the Soviet Union regarding the British so-called Asian Locarno Plan," July 4, 1954, CFMA, 110-00244-03. The Chinese perception was basically correct. According to G. H. Jansen, the British "utilized the possibility of gaining Asian support as a brake on Mr. Dulles," and the Colombo meeting was part of their efforts. See Jansen, *Afro-Asia and Non-Alignment*, 151.

15. The English translation is from *Survey of China Mainland Press (SCMP)*, no. 807 (May 13, 1954): 2.

16. "About Concluding a Mutual Non-Aggression Treaty with Southeast Asian States," June 13, 1954, CFMA, 203-00005-06, 55–57. These recently declassified telegrams between Zhou and Beijing first reveal China's motives.

17. "Opinion about Concluding a Mutual Non-Aggression Treaty with Southeast Asian States," June 17, 1954, CFMA, 203-00005-06, 58–60.

18. Foreign Ministry telegram to Yuan Zhongxian, June 20, and 22–25, 1954, CFMA, 203-00005-02; "Goal and Plan for Premier Zhou Enlai's Visit to India," June 22, 1954, CFMA, 203-00005-01, 3–4; *Zhou Enlai Waijiao Huodong Dashiji* (Chronicle of Major Events in Zhou Enlai's Diplomatic Career), ed. PRC Foreign Ministry (Beijing, China: Shijie Zhishi Chubanshe, 1993), 62.

19. For Nehru's message to Chinese leaders and Chinese Foreign Ministry's policy recommendation, see "Nehru's Request for Our Support to U Nu Sent to Vice Foreign Minister Zhang Hanfu via the Indian Ambassador," May 16, 1954, CFMA, 105-00044-01, 11–15.

20. "Draft Treaty of Safeguarding Peace in Asia," June 23, 1954, CFMA, 203-00005-07, 63–65.

21. "Minutes of Zhou Enlai's talks during his visit to India," June 25, 1954, CFMA, 203-00159-12, 1–56; *Zhou Enlai Nianpu*, 1: 390–93. Nehru was clear about China's concern and Zhou's aim for a zone of peace in Asia. See *Selected Works of Nehru*, 26: 354–55. In private, however, Nehru told U Nu and Ali Sastroamidjojo that a bilateral statement was the most one could expect at this stage; a non aggression pact between them would "appear as a kind of ganging up" and raise the suspicion of the United States. Sastroamidjojo concurred after he learned that the United States would see a non aggression pact as an agreement against the "free world." See Nehru's telegrams to Ali Sastroamidjoji on June 12, and U Nu on June 27, 1954, *Selected Works of Nehru*, 26: 351, 407–10.

22. Mackie, *Bandung 1955*, 62. The two prime ministers' remarks about Bandung are available in *Selected Works of Nehru*, 26: 383–90. For the Indian records of Zhou's five meetings with Nehru, see *Selected Works of Nehru*, 26: 366–98.

23. *Zhou Enlai Nianpu*, 1: 393–94; "Minutes of Prime Minister Zhou's First Meeting with Prime Minister U Nu," June 28, 1954, CFMA, 203-00007-02, 37–45; and "Minutes of Prime Minister Zhou's Second Meeting with Prime Minister U Nu," June 29, 1954, CFMA, 203-00007-03, 46–57.

24. The Chinese knew the Burmese condition that in order to have good relations with Burma, China must stop supporting the Burmese communists. See telegram to the Foreign Ministry, CFMA, 102-00158-01, 23–24.

25. For Nehru's message to Chinese leaders and Chinese Foreign Ministry's policy recommendation, see "Nehru's Request for Our Support to U Nu Sent to Vice Foreign Minister Zhang Hanfu via the Indian Ambassador," May 16, 1954, CFMA, 105-00044-01, 11–14. For Chinese leaders' consideration about the statement, see "About

Concluding Treaty of Non-aggression with Southeast Asian States," June 13, 1954, CFMA, 203-00005-06, 1–3.

26. Mao first put forward the intermediate zone theory in 1946. It deemed that the intermediate zone between the United States and the Soviet Union in Asia, Africa, and Europe would determine the future of the world, and China should support these peoples' efforts for national independence and form a united front against the United States. When the Soviet Union put forward the two camps theory in 1947, which denied the existence of neutral forces between the two camps, Mao gave up his theory. In 1948, Mao publicly denied the existence of a "third road." In 1949, Mao declared "leaning to the Soviet side" as one of the three diplomatic principles of the new People's Republic of China. For detailed analysis of the evolution of the theory, see Chen Jian, "Bridging Evolution and Decolonization: The 'Bandung Discourse' in China's Early Cold War Experience," *The Chinese Historical Review* 15, no. 2 (2008): 211–33.

27. *Mao Zedong Wenji*, 1–8 (Collection of Mao Zedong's works). (Beijing, China: Renmin Chubanshe, 1999), 6: 332–33; and *Mao Zedong Zhuan, 1949–1976* (A biography of Mao Zedong, 1949–1976), ed. Pang Xianzhi and Jin Chongji (Beijing, China: Zhongyang Wenxian Chubanshe, 2003), 562–64; *Zhou Enlai Nianpu*, 1: 395. The Chinese leaders had previously viewed these neutral states as "running dogs" of the Capitalist states, under the influence of the two camps theory. By now, they came to realize that they were neutral between the Capitalists and Socialists—and hence the intermediate zone. This shift indicated that the Communist worldview had become more sophisticated after their experiences in the Korean War and the Geneva Conference.

28. Shen Zhihua, "Mao Zedong yu Dongfang Qingbaoju: Yazhou Geming Lingdaoquan de Zhuanyi" (Mao Zedong and the Eastern Information Bureau: The Transfer of Leadership in Asian Revolution), *Journal of East China Normal University*, no. 6 (2011): 27–37. See also Yang Kuisong, "Liushi Nianqian de 'Zhongguo Daolu' " ('The Chinese Road' of Sixty Years Ago), in *Tongzhou Gongjin*, Issue 1 (2010): 30–33.

29. For Southeast Asian states' perception of the Chinese threat during the Cold War, see Ang Cheng Guan, "Southeast Asian Perceptions of the Domino Theory," in *Connecting Histories: Decolonization and the Cold War in Southeast Asia, 1945–1962*, ed. Christopher E. Goscha and Christian F. Ostermann (Washington, D.C.: Woodrow Wilson Center Press; Stanford, Calif.: Stanford University Press, 2009), 301–34.

30. For example, see "American United Press spreads rumors about Burmese Communist leaders' visit to China," "Foreign press discusses Communist new strategy in Southeast Asia," and "United Press International spreads slanders about China holding senior official conference to make plans for expansion in Southeast Asia," in *Neibu Cankao*, January 3, 9, and 15, 1954.

31. "Nehru's Request for Our Support to U Nu Sent to Vice Foreign Minister Zhang Hanfu via the Indian Ambassador," May 16, 1954, CFMA, 105-00044-01, 11–14; "About Concluding Treaty of Non-aggression with Southeast Asian States," June 13, 1954, CFMA, 203-00005-06, 1–3. The CCP had little influence on the Indian Communist Party in the 1950s. See Bhabani Sen Gupta, "China and Indian Communism," *The China Quarterly*, no. 50 (April–June, 1972): 272–94.

32. Pei, *Zhonghua Renmin Gongheguo Waijiaoshi*, 117, 124, and 178; and David Wilson, "China, Thailand and the Spirit of Bandung (Part I)," *The China Quarterly*, no. 30 (June 1967): 150. For an overview of China's policy toward overseas Chinese in the

1950s, see Stephen Fitzgerald, "China and Overseas Chinese: Perceptions and Policies," *The China Quarterly*, no. 44 (October–December, 1970): 1–37.

33. The Common Program, adopted in 1949 as the temporary constitution of the PRC, stipulated that the PRC "shall do its utmost to protect the proper rights and interests of Chinese residents abroad." The PRC government had since committed itself to the "lawful rights and interests" of the overseas Chinese. Wilson, "China, Thailand and the Spirit of Bandung (Part I)," 155.

34. For Chinese Foreign Ministry's response to the Indonesian request, see "Plan for Our Negotiation with the Indonesian Government on the Issue of Dual Citizenship (draft)," July 6, 1954, CFMA, 118-00778-04, 106–111.

35. Xue, *Dangdai Zhongguo Waijiao*, 179–86; John W. Garver, *Protracted Contest: Sino-Indian Rivalry in the Twentieth Century* (Seattle: University of Washington Press, 2001), 32–109; Neville Maxwell, *India's China War* (New Delhi, India: Natraj Publishers, 2015), 1–87; and "China and India: The Un-Negotiated Dispute," *The China Quarterly*, no. 43 (July–September, 1990): 414–29.

36. For Sino-Burmese border negotiation, see Xue, *Dangdai Zhongguo Waijiao*, 145–47; David I. Steinberg and Hong Wei Fan, *Modern China-Myanmar Relations: Dilemmas of Mutual Dependence* (Copenhagen, Denmark: NIAS Press, 2012), 56–70; Shao, "Chou En-lai's Diplomatic Approach," 332–38; and Shen-Yu Dai, "Peking and Rangoon," *The China Quarterly*, no. 5 (January–March, 1961): 131–44.

37. The Chinese government categorized India as a Southeast Asian state in the 1950s.

38. Jansen, *Afro-Asia and Non-Alignment*, 118, 131, and 170, 195; and Sarvepalli Gopal, *Jawaharlal Nehru: A Biography* (Cambridge, Mass.: Harvard University Press, 1979), 2: 195. For Nehru's idea about the zone of peace, see Sisir Gupta, *India and Regional Integration in Asia* (New York: Asia Publishing, 1964), 48–51.

39. Xue, *Dangdai Zhongguo Waijiao*, 174.

40. "The Agreement between Pakistan and Turkey and Struggles between the U.S., and UK and India," February 28, 1954, CFMA, 102-00158-01, 58–60; "U.S. Actions after the Conclusion of Turkey-Pakistan Agreement," March 19, 1954, CFMA, 102-00158-01, 97–98; "India's Response to the Military Treaty between the U.S. and Pakistan," April 17, 1954, CFMA, 105-00247-06, 1–4.

41. "Nehru's Remarks Concerning Foreign Policy," October 31, 1954, CFMA, 204-00142-03, 1–18. For details about the Indian response to the alliance, see H. W. Brands, *India and the United States: The Cold Peace* (Boston: Twayne, 1990), 75–77; and Robert J. McMahon, *The Cold War on the Periphery: The United States, India, and Pakistan* (New York: Columbia University Press, 1994), 172–73. For India-American relations in this period, see Brands, *India and the United States*, 70–89; McMahon, *Cold War on the Periphery*, 80–231; and Charles H. Heimsath, "Indo-American Relations," *Journal of International Affairs* 6, no. 2 (Spring 1952): 151–62.

42. For Burma's relations with China in the 1950s, see Steinberg and Fan, *Modern China-Myanmar Relations*, 3–70; and Dai, "Peking and Rangoo." For Burma's relations with the U.S. in the 1950s, see Robert McMahon, *The Limits of Empire: The United States and Southeast Asia Since World War II* (New York: Columbia University Press, 1999), 51–54, and 98–101.

43. Burma and the United States signed an economic cooperation agreement in September 1950, and the United States had provided assistance according to it. For the GMD forces in Burma, see Victor S. Kaufman, "Trouble in the Golden Triangle:

The United States, Taiwan and the 93rd Nationalist Division," in *The China Quarterly*, no. 166 (June 2001): 440–56; Nancy Bernkopf Tucker, "John Foster Dulles and the Taiwan Roots of the 'Two Chinas' Policy," in *John Foster Dulles and the Diplomacy of the Cold War*, ed. Richard H. Immerman (Princeton, N.J.: Princeton University Press, 1992), 244–51; and Steinberg and Fan, *Modern China-Myanmar Relations*, 46–55. For the U.S. efforts to push the GMD to withdraw from Burma, see Chiang Kai-shek Presidential Documents, no. 062090103007217, 062090103007219, 062090103007233, 062090103007244, Academia Historica. These documents range from September to November 1953.

44. Evelyn Colbert, *Southeast Asia in International Politics, 1941–1956* (Ithaca, N.Y.: Cornell University Press, 1977), 316–17; and Jansen, *Afro-Asia and Non-Alignment*, 124–25.

45. Telegrams to the Foreign Ministry about the economic problems facing Burma, and the U.S. pressure on its trade with China, December 8, 1954, CFMA, 105-00272-01, 1–3; December 10, 1954, CFMA, 105-00272-02, 1–3; and January 20, 1954, CFMA, 102-00158-01, 37–38; Pei, *Zhonghua Renmin Gongheguo Waijiaoshi*, 128. Steinberg and Fan, *Modern China-Myanmar Relations*, 38–39; and Dai, "Peking and Rangoo," 135–37.

46. For U.S.-Indonesian relations from 1950 to 1954, see McMahon, *Limits of Empire*, 49–51. For Indonesia's relations with China in the 1950s, see Lea E. Williams, "Sino-Indonesian Diplomacy: A Study of Revolutionary International Politics," *The China Quarterly*, no. 11 (July–September, 1962): 184–99.

47. "The United States and Chiang Kai-shek the traitor collaborate in a conspiracy to overthrow the Indonesian government," *Neibu Cankao*, November 24, 1954. The Indonesian ambassador told Zhou that the GMD's intervention in the Indonesian internal affairs was approved by the United States. See "Excerpts of the Minutes of the Prime Minister's Meeting with the Indonesian Ambassador A. Mononutu," February 28, 1955, CFMA, 207-00003-02, 28. This accusation was partly confirmed by GMD sources. Chiang in his diaries recorded his meetings with Indonesian anti-Communist guerrilla leaders to discuss "cooperation." See *CKS Diaries*, March 18, 1955.

48. "Responses to the Asia-African Conference," November 15, 1954, CFMA, 207-00002-04, 109–11; Pei, *Zhonghua Renmin Gongheguo Waijiaoshi*, 111.

49. This was an estimate the CIA made a year before. See McMahon, *Limits of Empire*, 51.

50. John Lionel Kotelawala, *An Asian Prime Minister's Story* (London, UK: G. G. Harrap, 1956), 140 and 184; Jansen, *Afro-Asia and Non-Alignment*, 125.

51. Despite their frequent meetings as Colombo Powers, the Ceylonese could not afford the price Burma charged on the rice it sold. See William Howard Wriggins, *Ceylon: Dilemmas of a New Nation* (Princeton, N.J.: Princeton University Press, 1960), 427. The author is indebted to Cindy Ewing for recommending this book.

52. *Zhou Enlai Nianpu*, 1: 261–62, 415–16. For the Ceylonese perspective on trade with China, see Kotelawala, *An Asian Prime Minister's Story*, 127–29, 138–39, 144.

53. "Ceylonese trade delegation head Si Ke Xiulai Keliya responds to Sino-Ceylonese trade," *Neibu Cankao*, November 25, 1954.

54. This was the first step toward METO (Middle East Treaty Organization, or Baghdad Pact) established in February 1955, including Britain, Iran, Iraq, Pakistan, Turkey, and with the U.S. as adjunct. It was renamed CENTO (Central Treaty Organization) in 1959.

55. *Renmin Ribao*, May 24, 1954. For the U.S.-Pakistani alliance, see McMahon, *Cold War on the Periphery*, 155–88, 194; Brands, *India and the United States*, 70–89.

56. "Southeast Asian Collective Defense Treaty and Attitudes and Responses to It from Different States," October 1954, CFMA, 105-00626-02, 56.

57. Pei, *Zhonghua Renmin Gongheguo Waijiaoshi*, 134.

58. "Southeast Asian Collective Defense Treaty and Attitudes and Responses to It from Different States," October 1954, CFMA, 105-00626-02, 23, 46; and *Renmin Ribao*, May 15, September 14, 1954. Ang Cheng Guan, *Southeast Asia's Cold War: An Interpretative History* (Honolulu: University of Hawai'i Press, 2018), 76; McMahon, *Cold War on the Periphery*, 215.

59. "About the Asia-African Conference," September 4, 1954, CFMA, 207-00085-19, 150–52.

60. For the British attempts to recruit Colombo Powers into SEATO, see Boquérat, "India's commitment to peaceful coexistence," 224–25.

61. "Southeast Asian Collective Defense Treaty and Attitudes and Responses to It from Different States," October 1, 1954, CFMA, 105-00626-02, 82.

62. "Nehru's Remarks Concerning Foreign Policy," October 31, 1954, CFMA, 204-00142-03, 13–14; "Southeast Asian Collective Defense Treaty and Attitudes and Responses to It from Different States," October 1, 1954, CFMA, 105-00626-02, 23, 47, and 49.

63. "The Foreign Ministry's Directive Concerning the National Day Celebration," September 5, 1954, CFMA, 102-00114-02, 2–5.

64. Pei, *Zhonghua Renmin Gongheguo Waijiaoshi*, 125.

65. "Summary of Our Negotiation with Indonesia on Dual Nationality Issue," February 4, 1955, CFMA, 118-00779-04, 37–40. Meanwhile, Zhou also pushed Indonesian visitors to work with China to realize the zone of peace idea. See *Zhou Enlai Nianpu*, 1: 416–17.

66. "Zhou Enlai's Report on China's Diplomacy before Nehru's Visit to China," October 18, 1954, Fujian Provincial Archives, 101-5-542, 11–21. *Zhou Enlai Nianpu* includes an excerpt of Zhou's talk, but the new source reveals China's considerations in detail. See *Zhou Enlai Nianpu*, 1: 419–20.

67. *Selected Works of Nehru*, 27: 6–38. *Zhou Enlai Nianpu*, 1: 420–21; Zhonghua Renmin Gongheguo Waijiaobu and Zhongyang Wenxian Yanjiushi eds., *Mao Zedong Waijiao Wenxuan* (Selected Diplomatic Papers of Mao Zedong) (Beijing, 1994), 163–76; *Mao Zedong Wenji*, 6: 361–73; and "Excerpts of Nehru's Meetings with Mao Zedong and Zhou Enlai," November 7, 1954, CFMA, 204-00148-02, 4–14.

68. Mary Keynes believed that Chinese leaders successfully convinced Nehru of China's "good intentions" and the value of the Bandung Conference. See Mary Keynes, "The Bandung Conference," *International Relations* 1 (October 1957): 362.

69. "Indian and Burmese Press Comments on Nehru's Visit to China," November 19, 1954, CFMA, 102-00258-05, 27–29.

70. "Press Response of India, Burma, Indonesia, Pakistan, and Nepal to Nehru's Visit of China," November 3, 1954, CFMA, 102-00159-17, 74–78; memo of Soviet diplomat Dobrynin's talk with Washington bureau chief of *Christian Science Monitor*, October 21, 1954, SD10219.

71. "Nehru's remarks about the Taiwan issue," *Neibu Cankao*, October 29, 1954.

72. *Mao Zedong Zhuan*, 575–80. Wilson, "China, Thailand and the Spirit of Bandung" (Part I and II); Kornphanat Tungkeunkunt and Kanya Phuphakdi, "Blood Is Thicker

Than Water: A History of the Diplomatic Discourse 'China and Thailand Are Brothers,' " *Asian Perspective 42* (2018): 597–621.

73. *Mao Zedong Wenji*, 6: 374–83; and *Zhou Enlai Waijiao Huodong Dashiji*, 93–94. By this time, Chinese leaders were still uncertain if China could be invited to Bandung, as indicated by the Foreign Ministry telegram to Huang Zhen, Chinese Ambassador to Indonesia, December 9, 1954, *in Zhongguo Daibiaotuan Chuxi 1955 Nian Yafei Huiyi* (Chinese Delegation Attending the Bandung Conference of 1955; hereafter *1955 Nian Yafei Huiyi*), ed. *Zhonghua Renmin Gongheguo Waijiaobu Dang'an'guan* (Beijing, China: Shijie Zhishi Chubanshe, 2007), 13.

74. *People's China*, January 1, 1955, Supplement, 3; Steinberg and Fan, *Modern China-Myanmar Relations*, 35–38.

75. "Intelligence Report (Intelligence Estimate Number 70): The Conference of Afro-Asian States: Probable Issues and Outcome (with appendixes)," prepared by the Office of Intelligence Research, January 21, 1955 (hereafter Intelligence Report 70), Miscellaneous Lot Files, 1944–1959, Intelligence Bureau, Office of the Director, 1950–1959 (Lot58D528), box 65, RG 59, NAUS; also available in Department of State Central Decimal File, 1955–59, box 2668, RG 59, NAUS (hereafter Box 2668, NAUS).

76. Jansen, *Afro-Asia and Non-Alignment*, 169–81, and Roseland Bulganin, *The Bandung Connection—The Asia-Africa Conference in Bandung in 1955* (Singapore: Gunning Aging, 1981), 17–39. For the British pressure, see *Selected Works of Nehru*, 27: 106.

77. Jansen, *Afro-Asian and Non-Alignment*, 174–76.

78. "About Bogor Meeting," December 31, 1954, CFMA, 207-00002-04, 94–95. For the objectives of the conference spelled out in the communique, see Ang, *Southeast Asia's Cold War*, 79.

79. Chinese Embassy in Switzerland telegram regarding the British, French and American responses to China's invitation to the Bandung Conference, January 10, 1955, CFMA, 207-00002-06, 159–61.

80. "Preliminary Work Plan Draft for Attending Asia-African Conference," January 16, 1955, CFMA, 207-00004-03, 22–25.

81. *Zhou Enlai Nianpu*, 1: 442–43.

82. Telegram regarding Pakistani press comments on the Bangkok Conference, March 3, 1955, CFMA, 105-00173-13, 54–55.

83. "Situation Report on the Bangkok Conference," March 5, 1955, CFMA, 105-00173-10, 33–36.

84. "Situation Report on the Bangkok Conference," February 23, 1955, CFMA, 105-00173-09, 28–32.

85. "Indian Press Response to the Bangkok Conference Communique," March 2, 1955, CFMA, 105-00173-13, 46–47.

86. Telegram from Chinese Embassy in Switzerland about the U.S., UK and French attitudes toward China's participation in Bandung Conference, January 10, 1955, CFMA, 207-00002-06, 159–161.

87. "About the Issue of Asian-African Conference," and "About the Asian-African Conference," December 15 and 18, 1954, CFMA, 207-00085-16, 128–136, 144–148.

88. "Report concerning the issue of the Asia-African Conference," January 21, 1955, CFMA, 207-00002-04, 146–47; "U.S. actions towards Indonesia before the Asian-African Conference," March 25, 1955, CFMA, 207-00002-04, 136–39; "Indonesia's response to the Asia-African Conference," April 3, 1955, CFMA, 207-00002-04, 140–43.

89. "The U.S. has recently worked hard in India to ruin the Asia-African Conference," March 7, 1955, CFMA, 207-00002-02, 57–59; "Summary of excerpts of telegrams concerning the Asian-African Conference," March 31, 1955, CFMA, 207-00004-07, 63–71; "Nehru's attitude on the Taiwan issue changed significantly after the Commonwealth Premiers' conference," February 17, 1955, CFMA, 110-00276-06, 45–46.

90. "Trade Plan for Attending the Asia-African Conference (draft)," March 12, 1955, Chinese Foreign Trade Department document, CFMA, 207-00070-03, 86–94; "Summary of excerpts of telegrams concerning the Asian-African Conference," March 31, 1955, CFMA, 207-00004-07, 63–71.

91. Chinese officials believed Britain also wanted to moderate U.S. infiltration into its traditional sphere of influence in Asia. See "Report of British situation, II," January 11, 1955, CFMA, 110-00275-01, 6–8; and "Preliminary British official response to the Asian-African Conference," February 1, 1955, CFMA, 110-00248-03, 22–26. As the following chapter shows, the Chinese perception of U.S. actions was very accurate.

92. "Plan for Attending Asia-African Conference," April 5, 1955, CFMA, 207-00004-01, 1–15.

93. "India's Preparation for the Bandung Conference," March 8, 1955, CFMA, 207-00064-09, 13–15. For what Nehru told Chinese leaders about Bandung when he visited China, see *Selected Works of Nehru*, 27: 20.

94. "Summary of excerpts of telegrams concerning the Asian-African Conference," March 31, 1955, CFMA, 207-00004-07, 63–71. For the Indonesians' attempts to "neutralize" U.S. worries about the Bandung Conference, see Abdulgani, *The Bandung Connection*, 40–48.

95. "Issues of and opinion about the Asia-African Conference," March 1954, CFMA, 207-00004-06, 59–62; "Plan for Attending Asia-African Conference," April 5, 1955, CFMA, 207-00004-01, 1–15. It is interesting to compare the Communist categorization of attendees with that of the United States, the United Kingdom, and the GMD. See chap. 6, and "Record of the 187th Meeting of the Standing Committee of the 7th Central Committee: Study of Responses to Asia-African Conference," April 20, 1955, vol. 7.3/16, GMDHA.

96. Memo of Lomakin's talk with Zhou, February 2, 1955, АВПРФ, ф.0100, оп.48, п.394, д.10, л.203–6; SD09935; "Plan for Attending Asia-African Conference," April 5, 1955, CFMA, 207-00004-01, 5.

97. "Trade Plan for Attending the Asia-African Conference (draft)," March 12, 1955, Chinese Foreign Trade Department document, CFMA, 207-00070-03, 86–94. The Chinese Foreign Ministry also prepared detailed plans for carrying out cultural activities and social events in Bandung to impress the participants. See "Preliminary Plan for Cultural and Friendly Activities to Be Held When Attending the Bandung Conference," March 30, 1955, CFMA, 207-00004-04, 26–31; and "Work Plan for the Social and Communicative Team (draft)," March 30, 1955, CFMA, 207-00004-04, 36–38. For secondary work on China's cultural diplomacy, see Emily Wilcox, "Performing Bandung: China's Dance Diplomacy with India, Indonesia, and Burma, 1953–1962," *Inter-Asia Cultural Studies* 18, no. 4 (2017): 518–39.

98. "Zhang Hanfu's Report on his meetings with [Burmese ambassador] U Hlao Maung, [Indonesian ambassador] Arnold Mononutu, and [Indian ambassador] N. *Raghavan*," March 29, 1955, CFMA 207–Y0004, in *1955 Nian Yafei Huiyi*, 32–33. "Plan for Attending Asia-African Conference," April 5, 1955, CFMA, 207-00004-01, 6.

However, Chinese leaders finally decided to put off the release as a consequence of the "Kashmir Princess Incident" the GMD produced, which killed eleven Chinese delegates. Zhou's talk with Nehru regarding releasing U.S. pilots on April 23, 1955 is seen in *Selected Works of Nehru*, 28: 179. For the "Kashmir Princess Incident," see Steve Tsang, "Target Zhou Enlai: The 'Kashmir Princess' Incident of 1955," *The China Quarterly* 139 (1994): 766–82; and Wendell L. Minnick, "Target Zhou Enlai: Was America's CIA Working with Taiwan Agents to Kill Chinese Premier?" *The Far Eastern Economic Review*, July 13, 1995, 54–55. Declassified Chinese government documents about this incident are included in *1955 Nian Yafei Huiyi*, 144–260.

99. *Zhou Enlai Nianpu*, 1: 463–64; "Excerpts of the Talk between Zhou Enlai, Nehru and U Nu," April 16, 1955, and two attachments concerning Nehru's plan for conference agenda and discussion topics, April 17, 1954, CFMA, 207-00015-01, 1–13. The Chinese Foreign Ministry prepared a separate document about diplomacy toward Burma, which provided a comprehensive analysis of relations with the latter. See "A guideline for solving some practical problems in the present Sino-Burmese relations," April 5, 1954, CFMA, 207-00004-02, 18–21.

100. "Experts' Opinions on the Asia-African Conference," April 6, 1955, CFMA, 207-00004-10, 84–87.

101. For the process of the conference, see Jansen, *Afro-Asia and Non-Alignment*, 96–163, and Abdulgani, *The Bandung Connection*, 182–226.

102. At Nehru's request, the heads of the delegations agreed on the procedure before the conference started. Seven items were on the agenda: economic cooperation, cultural cooperation, national independence, human rights and self-determination, promotion of world peace and cooperation, weapons of mass destruction, and universality of UN membership.

103. For Zhou's speech, see Abdulgani, *The Bandung Connection*, 104–7; *1955 Nian Yafei Huiyi*, 52–77.

104. George McTurnan Kahin, *The Asian-African Conference, Bandung, Indonesia, April 1955* (Ithaca, N.Y.: Cornell University Press, 1956), 19–20; Abdulgani, *The Bandung Connection*, 117–18.

105. Zhou was well clear about the risk of this ambiguity. See Zhou's telegram to the CCP Central Committee, April 26, 1955, CFMA, 207-00063-10, 20–21; "Excerpts of the Foreign Ministry Party Committee's Expanded Conference," May 9, 1955, CFMA, 207-00004-05, 46–52. Later Zhou had to restate his explanation in China's People's Congress on May 13, 1955. See *1955 Nian Yafei Huiyi*, 109–119.

106. Abdulgani, *The Bandung Connection*, 147.

107. *1955 Nian Yafei Huiyi*, 75; Djakarta to SOS, 670.901/4-2355, Box 2669, NAUS.

108. Those states that had known China's initiative in February understood Zhou did not do anything new. See Nehru's telegram to Eden, April 29, 1955, *Selected Works of Nehru*, 28: 138. C. T. Crowe memo for Prime Minister, April 24, 1954; Peking to FO, April 25, 1954, FO371/115047.

109. A. Doak Barnett, *Chou En-Lai at Bandung: Chinese Communist Diplomacy at the Asia-African Conference: A Report from A. Doak Barnett* (New York: American Universities Field Staff, 1955), 14.

110. "The Significance of the Bandung Conference for Southeast Asia," Intelligence Report No. 6925, June 16, 1955, Lot File 86D232; Entry (AI) 5518, box 2, NAUS.

111. Abdulgani, *The Bandung Connection*, 147–48.

112. For the text of the communique, see Abdulgani, *The Bandung Connection*, 181–90.

113. For the discussion of the liaison office and the second conference, see *Selected Works of Nehru*, 27: 124.

114. Barnett, *Chou En-Lai at Bandung*, 11.

115. Gopal, *Jawaharlal Nehru*, 2: 243. Geoffrey Barraclough and Rachel F. Wall, *Survey of International Affairs, 1955–56* (New York: Oxford University Press, 1960), 62. For Thailand's relations with China, see Tungkeunkunt and Phuphakdi, "Blood Is Thicker Than Water," 604–5.

116. "Minutes of Zhou Enlai's Meeting with Lebanon Ambassador to the U.S. during the Bandung Conference," CFMA, 207-00015-02, 16; *Zhou Enlai Waijiao Huodong Dashiji*, 106–8.

117. Barraclough and Wall, *Survey of International Affairs, 1955–56*, 60. According to Ang Cheng Guan, the Thai prime minister felt the need to establish a working relationship with it. Prince Wan, the foreign minister, was concerned about overreliance on the United States and wanted to know Zhou. In Bandung, after a private dinner Zhou offered, Prince Wan felt Zhou was "an extraordinarily charming man, and a natural diplomat: astute, patient, unfailingly courteous . . . not anything like a communist bandit." Ang, *Southeast Asia's Cold War*, 81, 83. For Sino-Thai relations in the 1950s, see Wilson, "China, Thailand and the Spirit of Bandung (Part I) and (Part II)."

118. For Zhou's meeting with the Japanese in Bandung, see Kweku Ampiah, *Political and Moral Imperatives of the Bandung Conference: The Reactions of the U.S., UK and Japan* (Folkestone, Kent, UK: Global Oriental, 2007), 186–88. For the U.S. response to Japanese participation, see Ampiah, *Political and Moral Imperatives of the Bandung Conference*, 88–102. For the U.S. perceptions of Japan's relations with China in the 1950s, see Sayuri Shimizu, "Perennial Anxiety: Japan-U.S. Controversy over Recognition of the PRC, 1952–1958," *The Journal of American-East Asian Relations* 4, no. 3 (Fall 1995): 223–48.

119. "Foreign Diplomatic Missions' Comments on the Bandung Conference," April 28, 1955, CFMA, 207-00002-02.

120. *Zhou Enlai Nianpu*, 1: 476–77, and "Excerpts of the Foreign Ministry Party Committee's Expanded Conference," May 9, 1955, CFMA, 207-00004-05, 46–52.

121. "Draft Plan for Promoting China's Relations with Asian and African Countries," July 16, 1955, CFMA, 207-00086-01, 1–7.

122. "Excerpts of the Foreign Ministry Party Committee's Expanded Conference," May 9, 1955, CFMA, 207-00004-05, 46–52.

123. *Mao Zedong Zhuan*, 593–94.

124. Xue, *Dangdai Zhongguo Waijiao*, 134–42.

6. A BLESSING IN DISGUISE?

1. Editorial Note, *Foreign Relations of the United States (FRUS), 1955–57*, 21: 30. U.S. Department of State (Washington, D.C.: Governmental Printing Office).

2. *FRUS, 1955–57*, 21: 82.

3. Untitled document, late December 1954, Records of the Office of Chinese Affairs Numerical Files, 1949–55 (CA Records) box 47, RG 59, National Archives, College Park, Maryland (NAUS).

4. Cary Fraser, "An American Dilemma: Race and Realpolitik in the American Response to the Bandung Conference, 1955," in *Window on Freedom: Race, Civil Rights, and Foreign Affairs, 1945–1988*, ed. Brenda Gayle Plummer (Chapel Hill: University of North Carolina Press, 2003), 129. Most of the existing works focus either on race or the impact of the Third World to the Cold War. See Matthew Jones, "A 'Segregated' Asia: Race, the Bandung Conference, and Pan-Asians Fears in American Thought and Policy, 1954–1955," *Diplomatic History* 29, no. 5 (November 2005): 841–67; Fraser, "An American Dilemma," in *Window on Freedom*, 115–40; Jason Parker, "Cold War II: The Eisenhower Administration, the Bandung Conference, and the Reperiodization of the Postwar Era," *Diplomatic History* 30, no. 5 (November 2006): 867–92; and "Small Victory, Missed Chance: The Eisenhower Administration, the Bandung Conference, and the Turning of the Cold War," in *The Eisenhower Administration, the Third World, and the Globalization of the Cold War*, ed. Kathryn C. Statler and Andrew L. Johns (Lanham, Md.: Rowman and Littlefield, 2006), 153–74; and Kweku Ampiah, *The Political and Moral Imperatives of the Bandung Conference of 1955: The Reactions of the U.S., UK and Japan* (Folkstone, Kent, UK: Global Oriental Let., 2007), chap. 2. For contemporary work on the Bandung Conference, see George McTurnan Kahin, *The Asian-African Conference: Bandung, Indonesia, April 1955* (Ithaca, N.Y.: Cornell University Press, 1955). For works by witnesses of the conference, see Barnett, *Chou En-Lai at Bandung*; and Richard Wright, *The Color Curtain: A Report on the Bandung Conference* (New York: World, 1956). The general secretary of the conference Roeslan Abdulgani also published his memory of the conference, and the English translation is *The Bandung Connection: The Asia-Africa Conference in Bandung in 1955* (Singapore: Gunung Agung, 1981).

5. For U.S. observations of and attempts to influence the Colombo meeting through Pakistan, see Bureau of Far East Asian Affairs memos "Chinese Communist Endorsement of 'Asia for Asians,' " May 1, 1954; and "Meeting of Asian Primer Ministers at Colombo," May 25, 1954 CA Records, box 47, RG 59, NAUS; and *FRUS, 1952–54*, 13: 1344–45; *FRUS, 1952–54*, 14: 499–501. For British observation of China's relations with Colombo Powers, see telegrams, Peking to FO, September 13, September 23, and October 4, 1954, FO371/110251, National Archives, Kew, London (NAUK). For secondary works about the American perception of the Colombo conference and China's diplomacy, see Boquérat, "India's commitment to peaceful coexistence," 218; and Gregg Brazinsky, *Winning the Third World: Sino-American Rivalry During the Cold War* (Chapel Hill: University of North Carolina Press, 2017), 80. For an overview of the American attitude toward neutralism, see Cecil V. Crabb Jr., "The United States and the Neutralists: A Decade in Perspective," *The Annals of the American Academy of Political and Social Science* 362 (Summer 1965): 92–101.

6. *FRUS, 1952–54*, 14: 518.

7. *FRUS, 1955–57*, 21: 3; memorandum of telephone call, Dulles and Robertson, December 31, 1954, Dulles Papers, Telephone Call Series, box 3, Dwight D. Eisenhower Presidential Library (DDEL).

8. Circular telegram to chiefs of mission, January 7, 1955, 670.901/1-755, in Department of State Central Decimal File, 1955-59, box 2668, RG 59, NAUS (hereafter Box 2668, NAUS).

9. Memorandum, McConaughy to Robertson: Communist China and the Bandung Conference, January 4, 1955, 670.901/1-455, Box 2668, NAUS.

10. *FRUS, 1955–57*, 21: 3–4.

11. *FRUS, 1955–57*, 21: 2–3; Circular telegram, February 25, 1955, 670.901/2-2555, Box 2668, NAUS.

12. For the State Department's initial analysis of the Bandung Conference, see "The Question of the Afro-Asian Conference," late December 1954, CA Records, box 47, RG 59, NAUS; and Cuming to SOS, January 2, 1955, 670.901/1-255, Box 2668, NAUS.

13. *FRUS, 1955–57*, 21: 2.

14. Paris to SOS, January 12, 1955, 670.901/1-1255, Box 2668, NAUS.

15. Untitled report, Operations Coordinating Board (OCB), January 12, 1955, White House Office, National Security Council Staff Papers, 1948–61 (WHO-NSC), Executive Secretary's Subject File Series, box 58, DDEL.

16. *FRUS, 1955–57*, 21: 3.

17. "The Question of the Afro-Asian Conference," December 30, 1954, CA Records, box 47, NAUS.

18. Memorandum, conversation on Afro-Asian Conference at the State Secretary's Office, January 7, 1955, 671.901/1-755, Box 2668, NAUS. Note: the quoted sentence was deleted when the meeting was later published. See *FRUS, 1955–57*, 21: 4.

19. Circular telegram, January 7, 1955, 670.901/1-755, Box 2668, NAUS; *FRUS, 1955–57*, 21: 3–4.

20. Memorandum, conversation on Afro-Asian Conference at the State Secretary's Office, January 7, 1955, 671.901/1-755, Box 2668, NAUS; *The Selected Works of Jawaharlal Nehru*, 25–27. S. Gopal et al. (New Delhi, India: Jawaharlal Nehru Memorial Fund. Distributed by Oxford University Press, 1999–2001), 27: 106, note 2. For the U.S. analysis of the Arab states, see "Intelligence Report (Intelligence Estimate Number 70): The Conference of Afro-Asian States: Probable Issues and Outcome (with appendixes)," 46–47, prepared by the Office of Intelligence Research, January 21, 1955, Miscellaneous Lot Files, 1944–1959, Intelligence Bureau, Office of the Director, 1950–1959 (Lot58D528), box 65, RG 59, NAUS; also available in Box 2668, NAUS (hereafter Intelligence Report 70). For interpretation of U.S. relations with Egypt from 1952 to 1956, see H. W. Brands, *The Specter of Neutralism: The United States and the Emergence of the Third World, 1947–1960* (New York: Columbia University Press, 1989), 223–62.

21. Eric D. Pullin, "The Bandung Conference: Ideological conflict and the limitations of U.S. propaganda," in *Neutrality and Neutralism in the Global Cold War: Between or Within the Blocs?*, ed. Sondra Bott, Jussi Hanhimaki, Janick Marina Schaufelbuehl, and Marc Wyss (London: Routledge, 2016), 55–56; Memorandum, conversation on Afro-Asian Conference at the State Secretary's Office, January 7, 1955, 671.901/1-755, Box 2668, NAUS. This sentence was also deleted in *FRUS*. See *FRUS, 1955–57*, 21: 4.

22. Washington to FO, January 8, 1955, FO371/116975, NAUK; SOS to London, January 8, 1954, 670.901/1-855, Box 2668, NAUS. For Arab states in Bandung, see Georgiana G. Stevens, "Arab Neutralism and Bandung," *Middle East Journal* 11, no. 2 (Spring 1957): 139–52. According to Stevens, Nehru played a decisive role convincing the Egyptians to attend the conference.

23. For Britain and the Bandung Conference, see Nicholas Tarling, "Ah-Ah: Britain and the Bandung Conference of 1955," *Journal of Southeast Asian Studies* 23, no. I (March 1992): 74–111; Ampiah, *The Political and Moral Imperatives of the Bandung Conference of 1955*, chapter 3: 118–65.

24. *FRUS, 1955–57*, 21: 5; Memo of a meeting, January 10, 1955, 670.901/1-1055, Box 2668, NAUS; "Afro-Asian Conference," memo, Sebald to MacArthur, January 5, 1955, 670.901/1-555, Box 2668, NAUS.

25. FO to Addis Ababa, saving other diplomatic institutions, October 21, 1954, "Proposed Afro-Asian Conference," October 15, 1955, and Paterson minute "Afro-Asian Conference," October 19, 1954, in FO371/111930, NAUK.

26. Memorandum, conversation with Menon, December 10, 1954, FO371/111930, NAUK; Tarling, "Britain and the Bandung Conference," 81; for detailed analysis of the British efforts to prevent the conference and subsequent shift of policy, see 79–83.

27. *Selected Works of Nehru*, 27: 106; Sarvepalli Gopal, *Jawaharlal Nehru: A Biography* (Cambridge, Mass.: Harvard University Press, 1979), 232–33; Anita Inder Singh, *The Limits of British Influence: South Asia and the Anglo-American Relations, 1947–1956* (New York: St. Martin, 1993), 182.

28. "Afro-Asian Conference," minute by Paterson, January 4, 1955, FO371/116975, NAUK; FO to Washington, January 11, 1955, FO371/116975, NAUK; and "Afro-Asian Conference," FO memo on British position for use of the foreign secretary at the Cabinet meeting, January 12, 1955, FO371/116976, NAUK.

29. Paris to Washington, January 12, 1955, 670.901/1-1255, Box 2668, NAUS; FO minute "Attitude of United Kingdom, United States, and France toward the Afro-Asian Conference," February 2, 1955, FO371/116978, NAUK.

30. Memo, conversation on Afro-Asian Conference, January 19, 1955, 670.901/1-1955, Box 2668, NAUS. For Australia and the Bandung Conference, see David Walker, "Nervous Outsiders: Australia and the 1955 Asia-Africa Conference in Bandung," in *Australian Historical Studies*, 36, no. 125 (January 2005): 40–59.

31. "Analysis of the Communist Tactics to Use Asia-African Conference to Conduct Diplomacy," April 16, 1955, Vice President Chen Cheng Documents, no. 00801060200010002, Academia Historica. For the U.S. knowledge of the GMD attitude, see Taipei to DOS, January 7, 1955, 670.901/1-755, Box 2668, NAUS. For the GMD's response to the conference, see Hao Chen, "Resisting Bandung? Taiwan's Struggle for 'Representational Legitimacy' in the Rise of the Asian People's Anti-Communist League, 1954–57." *The International History Review* (May 2020): 7–8.

32. Telegrams from Djakarta, January 3, 1955, 670.901/1-355, Karachi, January 5, 1955, 670.901/1-555, Colombo, January 4, 1955, 670.901/1-455, Rangoon, January 3, 1955, 670.901/1-355, Ankara, January 13, 1955, 670.901/1-1355; all in Box 2668, NAUS.

33. Intelligence Report 70, 6. For an estimate of Japan's attitude toward the conference, see Intelligence Report 70, 28–30. For an interpretation of Japan's participation in the conference, see Ampiah, *Political and Moral Imperatives of the Bandung Conference*, 4: 166–202.

34. Intelligence Report 70, 2, 6, 20.

35. Ankara to SOS, January 13, 1955, 670.901/1-1355, Box 2668, NAUS.

36. Intelligence Report, No. 6797, "The Chinese Communist Position at the Afro–Asian Conference," January 20, 19551, WHO-NSC, OCB Central File Series, box 85, DDEL.

37. Circular telegram to certain diplomatic missions, January 25, 1955, 670.901/1-2555, Box 2668, NAUS; *FRUS, 1955–57*, 21: 23.

38. Intelligence Report 70, 17; New Delhi to SOS, January 28, 1955, 670.901/1-2855, Box 2668, NAUS.

39. *FRUS 1955–57*, 21: 51; "Exposing the Nature of the Afro-Asian Conference," memorandum for the executive officer, January 21, 1955, WHO-NSC, OCB Central File Series, box 85, DDEL; Jackson to Rockefeller, January 11, 1955, C. D. Jackson Papers, box 91, DDEL; Parker, "Small Victory, Missed Chance," 158; Fraser, "An American Dilemma," 127.

40. *FRUS, 1955–57*, 21: 29.

41. Circular telegram to certain diplomatic missions, February 25, 1955, 670.901/2-2555, Box 2668, NAUS; *FRUS, 1955–57*, 21: 50–54.

42. Washington to FO, January 27, 1955, FO371/116976, NAUK; memo to the UK and France for coordination, March 18, 1955, 670.901/3-1855, Box 2668, NAUS; *FRUS, 1955–57*, 21: 63–66. The GMD officials also noticed the shift of U.S. policy toward Bandung. See "Analysis of the Communist Tactics to Use Asia-African Conference to Conduct Diplomacy," April 16, 1955, and "Prospect of the Asia-African Conference," April 19, 1955, Vice President Chen Cheng Documents, no. 0080106020010002 and 0080106020010004, Academia Historica.

43. The British policy was best summarized in "Afro-Asian Conference," a memo the British Embassy in Washington provided to the U.S. State Department, March 18, 1955, 670.901/3-1855, Box 2668, NAUS. See also J. E. Cable minute "Afro-Asian Conference," March 3, 1955, and "Evidence on Afro-Asian Conference," March 2, 1955, FO371/116978, NAUK; "U.S. recommendations on attitude to adopt towards Afro-Asian Conference," February 16, 1955, FO371/116976, NAUK; circular telegram to certain diplomatic missions, February 25, 1955, 670.901/2-2555, Box 2668, NAUS, and *FRUS, 1955–57*, 21: 50–54; and "Guidance on Afro-Asian Conference sent by State Department to U.S. missions in countries concerned," February 26, 1955, FO371/116977, NAUK. For detailed analysis of the British role, see Tarling, "Britain and the Bandung Conference," 95–101.

44. *FRUS, 1955–57*, 21: 30.

45. *FRUS, 1955–57*, 21: 62.

46. *FRUS, 1955–57*, 21: 29. For a detailed analysis of the conference participants, see Intelligence Report 70, 17.

47. Memorandum, Landon to Staats, March 17, 1955, WHO-NSC, OCB Central File Series, box 85, DDEL. Among the numerous background papers are circular telegram 509 on March 5, regarding nuclear moratorium, disarmament, and peaceful use of atomic energy, 670.901/3-755; circular telegram 563 on March 24, on possible resolutions calling for recognition of Two Chinas (to be introduced by Japan), 670.901/3-2455; circular telegrams on April 2, "Obstacles to trade with Soviet bloc," "The Kremlin's forgotten Asian Empire," and "U.S. record on peaceful use of atomic energy," 670.901/4-255; and State to Embassies, March 3, 1955, 670.901/3-355; all in Box 2668, NAUS.

48. For U.S. relations with the Philippines in the 1950s, see Robert McMahon, *The Limits of Empire: The United States and Southeast Asia Since World War II* (New York: Columbia University Press, 1999), 56–59, 90–95.

49. For analysis of attitude of the Filipino leaders toward the conference and China, see Intelligence Report 70, 33–34; telegram, Manila to SOS, January 6, 1955, 670/901/1-655, Box 2668, NAUS.

50. Memo by Lacy, February 9, 1955, 670.901/2-955; "View of General Romulo on Afro-Asian Conference and Pacific Pact," 670.901/1-355, Box 2668, RG 59, NAUS. For

interpretation of Romulo's role, see Lisandro E. Claudio, "The Anti-Communist Third World: Carlos Romulo and the Other Bandung," in *Southeast Asian Studies* 4, no. 1 (April 2015), 125–56.

51. "Call on the Secretary by ambassador Carlos Romulo on Feb. 17," February 17, 1955, 670.901/2-1755, Box 2668, NAUS.

52. Memo of telephone conversation with Romulo on the Bandung Conference, February 21, 1955, 670.901/2-2155, Box 2668, NAUS.

53. *FRUS, 1955–57,* 21: 31–32.

54. Telegram to U.S. embassies, March 3, 1955, 670.901/3-355, Box 2668, NAUS.

55. Fraser, "An American Dilemma," 128. For analysis of Turkey's attitude toward the conference, see Intelligence Report 70, 47.

56. Gürol Baba and Senem Ertan, "Turkey at the Bandung Conference: A fully-aligned among the non-aligned," http://web.isanet.org/Web/Conferences/AP%20Hong%20Kong%202016/Archive/64185d87-7a01-44f1-acbc-1566b192398f.pdf (accessed August 18, 2017).

57. For analysis of Pakistan's attitude toward the conference, see Intelligence Report 70, 41–42. For the U.S. relations with Pakistan from 1953 to 1957, see H. W. Brands, *India and the United States: The Cold Peace* (Boston: Twayne, 1990), 70–89; and Robert McMahon, *The Cold War on the Periphery: The United States, India, and Pakistan.* (New York: Columbia University Press, 1994.), 155–231.

58. Karachi to DOS, about the Pakistani proposals for conduct of Bandung Conference, March 22, 1955, 670.901/3-2255, Box 2668, NAUS; Karachi to SOS, April 12, 1955, 670.901/4-1255, Department of State Central Decimal File, 1955–59, Box 2669, RG 59, NAUS (hereafter Box 2669, NAUS).

59. Karachi to DOS, January 7, 1955, 670.901/1-755, Box 2668, NAUS.

60. Karachi to DOS, January 6, 1955, 670.901/1-655; Karachi to DOS, January 7, 1955, 670.901/1-755; DOS to U.S. embassies, March 3, 1955, 670.901/3-355, Box 2668, NAUS. Ampiah, *The Political and Moral Imperatives of the Bandung Conference of 1955,* 70–71.

61. For details of the British efforts, see Tarling, "Britain and the Bandung Conference," 97, 99–100. For U.S. knowledge of the British diplomacy in Colombo, see Colombo to the SOS, April 7, 1955, 670.701/4-755, Box 2668, NAUS.

62. Colombo to SOS, January 3 and 4, 1955, 670.901/1-355, 670.901/1-455, Box 2668, NAUS.

63. Colombo to SOS, March 25, 1955, 670.901/3-2555, Box 2668, NAUS; Colombo to SOS, April 9, 1955, 671.901/4-955, Box 2669, NAUS; High Commissioner in Ceylon to the CRO, April 15, 1955, FO371/116981, NAUK.

64. Colombo to DOS: "Discussions with Ceylonese Officials on the Asian-African Conference to be held at Bandung, Indonesia in April, 1955," April 7, 1955, 670.901/4-755, Box 2668, NAUS.

65. Intelligence Report 70, 43; for analysis of Ceylon's attitude toward the conference and China, see 42–43.

66. Colombo to the SOS, April 7, 1955, 670.701/4-755, Box 2668, NAUS.

67. Rangoon to SOS, February 28, 1955, 670.901/2-2855, Box 2668, NAUS. For an estimate of Burma's attitude toward the conference in late January, see Intelligence Report 70, 21–23.

68. New Delhi to SOS, March 31, 1955, 670.901/3-3155, Box 2669, NAUS. For an estimate of India's attitude toward the conference in late January, see Intelligence Report 70, 39–41.

69. Intelligence Report 70, 8–10.
70. *FRUS, 55–57*, 2: 385, 393, 399.
71. *FRUS, 55–57*, 2: 465–66.
72. Emphasis added. *FRUS, 1955–57*, 21: 80; memo of conversation, April 7, 1955, 670.901/4-755, Box 2669, NAUS. For a British record of the meeting, see telegrams, Makins to FO, April 8, 1955, FO371/115045, NAUK.
73. *FRUS, 1955–57*, 21: 81. The British were also aware of U.S. efforts to influence the conference. See Makins to FO, April 9, 1955, FO371/115045/693, NAUK.
74. *FRUS, 1955–57*, 2: 466–67.
75. Makins to Macmillan, April 14, 1954, FO371/115048, NAUK.
76. "Probability of Chinese Communist attack on Quemoy and Matsu," note by the Joint Intelligence Committee for the Minister of Defense, March 29, 1955, FO371/115045, NAUK; and Washington to FO, April 19, 1955, FO371/115047, NAUK.
77. FO to Ankara, April 11, 1955, 670.901/4-1155, Box 2669, NAUS.
78. CRO telegram to High Commissioners, April 15, 1955, FO371/115046, NAUK; and CRO outward telegram, April 22, 1955, FO371/115047, NAUK.
79. Memo of Dulles's meeting with Romulo, April 14, 1955, 670.901/4-1455, Box 2669, NAUS.
80. Memo of Henry Villard's meeting with Malik, April 6, 1955, 670.901/4-655, Box 2668, NAUS.
81. *FRUS, 1955–57*, 21: 82–84.
82. Emphasis added. "Intelligence Note: Probable Communist Position at the Bandung Conference," Armstrong memo to SOS, April 15, 1955, 670.901/4-1555, Box 2669, NAUS.
83. "Status Report on Asian-African Conference," Staats to Villard, March 28, 1955, and attached agenda item 3, "Approval of Minutes of March 23 OCB Meeting," WHO-NSC, OCB Central File Series, box 85, DDEL; circular telegram, April 2, 1955, 670.901/4-255, Box 2668, NAUS.
84. *FRUS, 1955–57*, 21: 77. For the U.S. efforts to spread information to influence the conference, see Pullin, "The Bandung Conference," 58–62; and Jones, "A 'Segregated' Asia," 858–59. However, the Americans were probably not involved in the Kashmir Princess Incident the GMD produced, although the CIA did have a separate but aborted plan to assassinate Zhou in Bandung. See Steve Tsang, "Target Zhou Enlai: The 'Kashmir Princess' Incident of 1955," *The China Quarterly* 139 (1994): 766–82. For the CIA's attempt, see Wendell L. Minnick, "Target Zhou Enlai: Was America's CIA working with Taiwan agents to kill Chinese premier?" *The Far Eastern Economic Review*, July 13, 1995, 54–55.
85. Memorandum: "Discussion at the 244th Meeting of the National Security Council, Thursday, April 7, 1955," April 8, 1955, AWF, NSC series, box 6, DDEL; Washington to FO, April 16, 1955, FO371/115046, NAUK.
86. Brands, *India and the United States*, 83.
87. Press Release, Dulles (via Hagerty), April 27, 1955, AWF, Dulles-Herter Series, box 5, DDEL; *Department of State Bulletin*, May 2, 1955, 727–28. The State Department confirmed to the British that Dulles's statement aimed at the Bandung Conference. See Washington to FO, April 19, 1955, FO371/115047, NAUK.
88. For the text of the statement, see *FRUS, 1955–57*, 2: 507–8, note 2; DOS to Taipei, April 23, 1955, 670.901/4-2355, Box 2669, NAUS. For the State Department deliberations

leading to the statement, see Sebald to Dulles: "Developments Over Week End Relating to Chou En-lai's Negotiation Proposal," April 25, 1955, 670.901/4-2555, Box 2669, NAUS.

89. John Lionel Kotelawala, *An Asian Prime Minister's Story* (London: G. G. Harrap, 1956), 185; *FRUS, 1955–57*, 2: 508, 525.

90. G. H. Jansen, *Afro-Asia and Non-Alignment* (London, UK: Faber and Faber, 1966), 218.

91. *FRUS, 1955–57*, 21: 105.

92. Washington to FO, April 30, 1955, FO371/115049, NAUK.

93. Washington to FO, April 24 and 26, 1955, FO371/115047 and FO371/115049, NAUK.

94. Crowe minute for the prime minister, "Formosa: Chou En-lai's speech at Bandung," April 24, 1955, FO371/115047, NAUK; Peking to FO, April 24, 1955, FO371/115047; and April 26, FO371/115048, NAUK.

95. CRO to High Commissioners, April 23, 1955, FO371/115047, NAUK.

96. FO to Washington, April 26, 1955, FO371/115048, NAUK.

97. "Australia: Comments Concerning Bandung Conference," May 31, 1955, 670.901/5-3155, Department of State Central Decimal File, 1955–59, Box 2670, RG 59, NAUS (hereafter Box 2670, NAUS).

98. British survey of Chinese press coverage of Dulles's press conference and responses from around the world, May 4, 1955, FO371/115048, NAUK.

99. Leonard A. Kusnitz, *Public Opinion and Foreign Policy: America's China Policy, 1949–1979* (Westport, Conn.: Greenwood Press, 1984), 73.

100. Washington to FO, April 13, 1955, FO371/115046, NAUK.

101. Washington to FO, April 25, 1955, FO371/115048, NAUK.

102. Washington to FO, April 26, 1955, FO371/115048, NAUK.

103. Dulles later told Eisenhower that George gave him a lot of pressure. See Gordon Chang, *Friends and Enemies: The United States, China and the Soviet Union, 1948–1972* (Stanford, Calif: Stanford University Press, 1990), 163; and Qiang Zhai, "Crisis and Confrontation: Chinese-American Relations During the Eisenhower Administration," *The Journal of American-East Asian Relations* 9, no. 3/4 (Fall–Winter 2000): 235.

104. A report from the British Embassy in Washington on U.S. press responses to Dulles's statement accurately summarized the reasons for the U.S. change of policy. See Washington to FO, April 27, 1955, FO371/115049, NAUK.

105. For the text of Dulles's statement, see Department of State Press Release "Hopeful Development in Europe and Asia," Dulles Papers, duplicate correspondence, box 89, Seeley G. Mudd Manuscript Library, Princeton University; Editorial Note, *FRUS, 1955–57*, 2: 519–20. Su-Ya Chang argues that Dulles actually surrendered to the Chinese request. For Dulles's justification of the agreement to negotiate with China, see Su-Ya Chang, "Wengong Wuxia Xia de Tuisuo: Meiguo Jueding yu Zhonggong Juxing Dashiji Taipan de Guocheng Fenxi, 1954–1955" (Retreat before Verbal Attack and Military Threat: Analysis of U.S. Decision to Hold Ambassadorial Talks with the Chinese Communists, 1954–1955), *Zhongyang Yanjiuyua Jingdaishi Yanjiusuo Jikan* 25 (June 1996): 409–10, 510–17.

106. Washington to FO, April 28, 1955, FO371/115049, NAUK.

107. CRO to High Commissioners, April 27, 1955, FO371/115048, NAUK.

108. FO to Peking, April 27, 1955, FO371/115048, NAUK.

109. CRO outward telegram, April 27, 1955, FO371/115048, NAUK; telegrams, CRO to High Commissioners in Canada, New Zealand, Australia, India, and Pakistan, April 27, 1955, FO371/115049, NAUK.

110. High Commissioner in Australia to CRO, April 27, 1955, FO371/115049, NAUK; Allen minute "Formosa Straits," April 28, 1955, FO371/114059, NAUK; High Commissioner in Australia to CRO, April 29, 1955, FO371/115049, NAUK.

111. Record of Cabinet meeting, April 29, 1954, AWF, Cabinet Series, box 5, DDEL.

112. *FRUS, 1955–57*, 21: 91–92; "Preliminary Evaluation of Results of Asian-African Conference," May 25, 1955, 670.901/5-255, Box 2670, NAUS; and report attached to Memo, Staats to OCB, May 12, 1955, WHO-NSC, OCB Central File Series, box 86, DDEL.

113. "Preliminary Evaluation of Results of Afro-Asian Conference Circular telegram from State," May 2, 1955, 670.901/5-255, Box 2670, NAUS; telegrams of thanks to representatives of the Philippines, Iraq, Pakistan and Ceylon, who denounced Soviet colonialism at the Afro-Asian Conference in Bandung, April 22, 1955, 670.901/4-2255, Box 2669, NAUS; record of conversation, May 24, 1955, 670.901/5-2455, Box 2670, NAUS; and *FRUS, 1955–57*, 21: 94–98, 103–5.

114. Itty Abraham, "From Bandung to NAM: Non-alignment and Indian Foreign Policy, 1947–65," *Commonwealth & Comparative Politics* 46, no. 2 (April 2008): 205.

115. "Evaluation of Afro-Asian Conference," memo, McNair to Craig, May 13, 1955, WHO-NSC, OCB Central File Series, box 86, DDEL; British assessment of the Bandung Conference, May 26, 1955, 670.901/5-2655, Box 2670, NAUS; Australia: Comments on the Bandung Conference, May 26, 1955, 670.901/5-3155, Box 2670, NAUS; Intelligence Report, No. 6925, June 16, 1955, Lot File 86D232, Entry (AI) 5518, box 2, NAUS; High Commissioner in Karachi to FO, April 28, 1955, FO371/115049, NAUK; High Commissioner in Colombo to CRO, May 2, 1955, FO371/115049, NAUK; *FRUS, 1955–57*, 21: 103–5; and Singh, *The Limits of British Influence*, 184.

116. *FRUS, 1955–57*, 21: 104.

117. *FRUS, 1955–57*, 21: 95–96.

118. The Lebanese ambassador Charles Malik accurately judged that China had not intended to ask the conference to support its attack on Taiwan. But he did not seem to convince Dulles when they met in May after the conference. See *FRUS, 1955–57*, 21: 97.

119. "Results of the Bandung Conference: A Preliminary Analysis," OIR No. 6903, April 27, 1955;"Bandung Conference of April 1955," memorandum for the Operations Coordinating Board, May 12, 1955; and memorandum, McNair to Craig, "Evaluation of Afro-Asian Conference," May 13, 1955, WHO-NSC, OCB Central File Series, box 86, DDEL.

120. Eisenhower agreed with Dulles's suggestion to start negotiation with the Chinese in a brief conversation on April 25, see *FRUS, 1955–57*, 2: 517. This is the only source available about the decision-making. U.S. leaders probably did not have any serious discussion when they decided to talk to the Chinese. The British diplomats, who maintained close communication with Dulles around this time, did not report any such discussions. Indeed, the U.S. shift of policy was so surprising that the British ambassador Roger Makins believed Dulles improvised the position during the press conference, probably out of the frustration that the U.S. failed to convince Chiang to withdraw from the offshore islands. See Scott to FO, April 25, 26, 1955, FO371/115048, NAUK. For the British record of Dulles's press conference, see Scott to FO, April 27, 1955, FO371/115048, NAUK.

121. *FRUS, 1955–57*, 2: 668, 672, 675.

CONCLUSION: THE AMBASSADORIAL TALKS

1. *Foreign Relations of the United States (FRUS) 1955–1957*, 2: 601. U.S. Department of State (Washington, D.C.: Governmental Printing Office).

2. *FRUS, 1955–57*, 2: 659.

3. *FRUS, 1955–57*, 2: 532.

4. Washington to FO, May 5, 1955, FO371/115049, NAUK.

5. *FRUS, 1955–57*, 2: 539; Washington to FO, May 3, 1955, FO371/115049, NAUK.

6. *FRUS, 1955–57*, 2: 535–36.

7. *FRUS, 1955–57*, 2: 545–49, 557–58.

8. *FRUS, 1955–57*, 2: 560.

9. *FRUS, 1955–57*, 2: 572–74.

10. Washington to FO, April 30, 1955, FO371/115049, NAUK.

11. *FRUS, 1955–57*, 2: 554–57.

12. Washington to FO, May 3, 6, 1955, FO371/115050, NAUK; *FRUS, 1955–57*, 2: 534–35.

13. Robert Accinelli, "Eisenhower, Congress, and the 1954–55 Offshore Island Crisis," *Presidential Studies Quarterly* 20, no. 1 (Winter 1990): 342; U. Alexis Johnson, *The Right Hand of Power* (Englewood Cliffs, N.J.: Prentice-Hall, 1984), 234.

14. *FRUS, 1955–57*, 2: 543–45.

15. *FRUS, 1955–57*, 2: 557–58.

16. "Reply to U.S. Request for Meetings," May 17, 1955, CFMA, 111-00064-08, 3. For the beginning of the consular talks in Geneva, see Yafeng Xia, *Negotiating with the Enemy: U.S.-China Talks During the Cold War, 1949–1972* (Bloomington: Indiana University Press, 2006), 78–81; Su-Ya Chang, "Wengong Wuxia Xia de Tuisuo: Meiguo Jueding yu Zhonggong Juxing Dashiji Taipan de Guocheng Fenxi, 1954–1955" (Retreat before Verbal Attack and Military Threat: Analysis of U.S. Decision to Hold Ambassadorial Talks with the Chinese Communists, 1954–1955). *Zhongyang Yanjiuyua Jingdaishi Yanjiusuo Jikan* 25 (June 1996): 384–92.

17. "Report of Chinese Embassy in Switzerland about Western European press response to Premier Zhou's talk," April 28, 1955, CFMA, 207-00002-08, 164–65.

18. "British Response to Premier Zhou's Statement on Taiwan," April 30, 1955, CFMA, 110-00276-06, 67–69.

19. *Mao Zedong Zhuan, 1949–1976* (A Biography of Mao Zedong, 1949–1976), eds. Pang Xianzhi and Jin Chongji (Beijing, China: Zhongyang Wenxian Chubanshe, 2003), 593–94; *Mao ZeDong Waijiao Wenxuan* (Selected Mao Zedong's Works on Diplomacy), eds. Zhonghua Renmin Gongheguo Waijiaobu and Zhongyang Wenxian Yanjiushi (Beijing, China: Zhongyang Wenxian Chubanshe, 1994), 203–4.

20. *Zhou Enali Waijiao Huodong Dashiji* (Chronicle of Major Events in Zhou Enlai's Diplomatic Career), ed. PRC Foreign Ministry (Beijing, China: Shijie Zhishi Chubanshe, 1993), 110–11; *Zhou Enlai Nianpu, 1949–1976*, Vol. 1–3 (A Chronological Record of Zhou Enlai, 1949–1976), eds. Li Ping and Ma Zhisun, et al. (Beijing, China: Zhongyang Wenxian Chubanshe, 1997), 1: 478, 483; *Mao Zedong Waijiao Wenxuan*, 208–13; *Mao Zedong Zhuan*, 595–96; "Excerpts of Premier Zhou's First Meeting with Indonesian Premier," May 27, 1955, CFMA, 204-00014-02, 12–23; "Excerpts of Premier Zhou's Second Meeting with Indonesian Premier," May 28, 1955, CFMA 204-00014-03, 25–35; and "Excerpts of Premier Zhou's Third Meeting with Indonesian Premier," May 29, 1955, CFMA 204-00014-04, 37–46.

21. *Zhou Enlai Nianpu*, 1: 477; *Zhou Enlai Waijiao Huodong Dashiji*, 110–11; *FRUS, 1955–57*, 2: 562; Peking to FO, May 9, 1955, FO371/115050, NAUK.

22. "Excerpts of Premier Zhou's Meeting with Trevelyan," May 26, 1955, CFMA, 207-00010-16, 61–65; *FRUS, 1955–57*, 2: 581–83.

23. Memo of Mao's Talk with Yudin, May 25, 1955, АВПРФ, ф.0100, оп.48, п.393, д.9, л.107-112; SD13019. For Americans sources on Menon's meetings with Chinese leaders, see *FRUS, 1955–57*, 2: 576–78. For what Menon told the British before his departure for China, see memorandum about a meeting between British Consul in Madras and Menon, May 6, 1955, FO 371/115050, NAUK.

24. For U.S. policy toward Chinese students and scholars, see Yelong Han, "An Untold Story: American Policy Toward Chinese Students in the United States, 1949–1955," *The Journal of American-East Asian Relations* 1 (Spring 1993): 77–99.

25. *Zhou Enali Nianpu*, 1: 478–79; *Zhou Enali Waijiao Huodong Dashiji*, 111–12; "Record of Comrade Qiao Guanhua's Talk with Menon," May 13, 1955, CFMA, 105-00056-09, 79–81; "Record of Assistant Minister Qiao Guanhua's Talk with Menon," May 17, 1955, CFMA, 105-00056-10, 85–86; "Memo of Zhou Enlai's Talk with Lomakin," May 21, 1955, АВПРФ, ф.0100, оп.48, п.394, д.11, л.125-134; SD09943.

26. "Report of Premier Zhou Enlai on the Afro-Asian Conference at the Fifteenth Enlarged Conference of the Standing Committee of the National People's Congress," cited in Xia, *Negotiating with the Enemy*, 84–85.

27. "About the Issue of Deporting Four American Airmen," May 28–29, 1955, CFMA, 110-00064-09, 1–5.

28. Memo of Mao's Talk with Yudin, May 25, 1955, АВПРФ, ф.0100, оп.48, п.393, д.9, л.107-112; SD13019.

29. "Materials Premier Zhou Sent to Ambassador Yudin," May 27, 1955, CFMA, 207-00018-01, 1–4.

30. *FRUS, 1955–57*, 2: 682, 591–93, 619–22.

31. *FRUS, 1955–57*, 2: 595–602, 603–04.

32. *FRUS, 1955–57*, 2: 626; for Menon's talks with the Americans, see 622–26, 629–37.

33. *FRUS, 1955–57*, 2: 605, 631.

34. *FRUS, 1955–57*, 2: 591.

35. *FRUS, 1955–57*, 2: 616–18.

36. *FRUS, 1955–57*, 2: 640–41, note 2.

37. *FRUS, 1955–57*, 2: 610–11.

38. *FRUS, 1955–57*, 2: 640–41, note 2.

39. *FRUS, 1955–57*, 2: 601, 605, 627–28.

40. *FRUS, 1955–57*, 2: 629–30, 637–39, 640–41, 643–44.

41. *FRUS, 1955–57*, 2: 631–37.

42. *FRUS, 1955–57*, 2: 641–42, 644–45, 663.

43. *FRUS, 1955–57*, 2: 685–87.

44. *FRUS, 1955–57*, 2: 659.

45. *FRUS, 1955–57*, 2: 649.

46. "Premier Zhou's Telegram to Menon about Sino-American Relations and Chinese Nationals and Students in the U.S.," July 14, 1955, CFMA, 105-00061-03, 12–16; "About U.S. Government Suggestion to Change the Geneva Meeting to the Ambassadorial Level," July 15, 1955, CFMA, 111-00061-01, 2–3; *Zhou Enlai Nianpu*, 1: 493–94.

47. "Directive about Sino-American Ambassadorial Talks in Geneva," July 30, 1955, CFMA, 111-00009-01, 1–8; "Plan for Sino-American Talk," July 30, 1955, CFMA, 111-00009-02, 1–9. For Chinese knowledge about the British pressure on the U.S., see "British Views of and Attitude toward Sino-American Talks in Geneva," August 10, 1955, CFMA, 111-00276-06, 38–40.

48. Memos of Zhou's meeting with Lomakin, July 15, 1955, АВПРФ, ф.0100, оп.48, п.394, д.11, л.274-276; and July 18, 1955, АВПРФ, ф.0100, оп.48, п.394, д.11, л.291-292; SD09897, and SD09892; "Reply to Soviet Communist Party Central Committee about the Four-Power Summit," 1955 (exact date not indicated), CFMA, 111-00065-02, 8–9.

49. "Foreign Minister's Telegram to Wang Bingnan Regarding Releasing Text of Sino-American Talk and News Article," July 31, 1955, CFMA, 111-00014-04, 18–31; *Zhou Enlai Nianpu*, 1: 495–96.

50. "Excerpts of Ambassador Yuan's Talk with Menon," August 14, 1955, CFMA, 105-00058-16, 67–72; "Reply Regarding Entertaining Menon and Excerpts of Talk with Him," August 20, 1955, CFMA, 105-00058-17, 57–59. Washington chose to let the UK release the decision to start the talks to deliberately downplay the importance of India.

51. Xia, *Negotiating with the Enemy*, 89–105; Steven Goldstein, "Dialogue of the Deaf? The Sino-American Ambassadorial Level Talks, 1955–70," in *Re-examining the Cold War—U.S.-China Diplomacy, 1954–1973*, eds., Robert Ross and Jiang Changbin (Cambridge, Mass.: Harvard University Asia Center, 2002), 200–38, especially 209–19.

EPILOGUE

1. See Michael H. Hunt, *The Making of a Special Relationship: The United States and China to 1914* (New York: Columbia University Press, 1983).

2. Qiang Zhai, *The Dragon, the Lion & the Eagle: Chinese-British-American Relations, 1949–1958* (Kent, Ohio: Kent State University Press, 1994), 14–16.

3. The other two "Magic Weapons" are party building and armed struggle.

4. Rosemary Foot, "The Eisenhower Administration's Fear of Empowering the Chinese," *Political Science Quarterly* 111, no. 3 (Autumn 1996): 505–21; Robert J. McMahon, "The Illusion of Vulnerability: American Reassessments of the Soviet Threat, 1955–1956," *The International History Review* 18, no. 3 (1996): 591–619.

5. *FRUS, 1955–57*, 14: 534; *FRUS, 1955–57*, 3: 292; *FRUS, 1955–57*, 21: 98–103. Norman Graebner, "Eisenhower and Communism: The Public Record of the 1950s," in *Reevaluating Eisenhower*, ed. Richard Melanson and David Mayers (Chicago: University of Illinois Press, 1987), 82–83; Gordon Chang, *Friends and Enemies: The United States, China and the Soviet Union, 1948–1972* (Stanford, Calif: Stanford University Press, 1990), 131, 144, 150, 175–82; John Gaddis, "The Unexpected John Foster Dulles: Nuclear Weapons, Communism, and the Russians," in *John Foster Dulles and the Diplomacy of the Cold War*, ed. Richard H. Immerman (Princeton, N.J.: Princeton University Press, 1989), 63–64, 71; Ronald W. Pruessen, "Over the Volcano: The United States and the Taiwan Strait Crisis, 1954–1955," in *Re-examining the Cold War: U.S.-China Diplomacy, 1954–1973*, ed. Robert S. Ross and Jiang Changbin (Cambridge, Mass.: Harvard University Press, 2001), 81–82.

6. He Di, "The Most Respected Enemy: Mao Zedong's Perception of the United States," in *Toward a History of Chinese Communist Foreign Relations, 1920s-1960s: Personalities and Interpretative Approaches*, ed. Michael H. Hunt and Niu Jun (Washington, D.C.: Woodrow Wilson Center Asia Program, 1995), 40.

7. *Mao Zedong Waijiao Wenxuan* (Selected Mao Zedong's Works on Diplomacy), ed. Zhonghua Renmin Gongheguo Waijiaobu and Zhongyang Wenxian Yanjiushi (Beijing, China: Zhongyang Wenxian Chubanshe, 1994), 288; Yafeng Xia, *Negotiaiting with the Enemy: U.S.-China Talks During the Cold War, 1949-1972* (Bloomington: Indiana University Press, 2006), 97.

8. For the Communist Moscow conference of 1957, see Zhihua Shen and Yafeng Xia, *Mao and the Sino-Soviet Partnership, 1945-1959* (New York: Lexington, 2015), 241-82.

9. Xia, *Negotiating with the Enemy*, 97.

10. The quote is from Chen Xiaolu, "Chen Yi and China's Diplomacy," in *Toward a History of Chinese Communist Foreign Relations*, 91-92. See also He Di, "Most Respected Enemy," 43; Chen Jian, *Mao's China and the Cold War* (Chapel Hill: University of North Carolina Press, 2001), 72-73; and Xia, *Negotiating with the Enemy*, 97.

11. Chen, *Mao's China and the Cold War*, 73-78.

12. Chen, *Mao's China and the Cold War*, 163-204; Sheng, "Mao and China's Relations with the Superpowers in the 1950s"; Shen Zhihua, "1958 Nian Paoji Jinmen qian Zhongguo Shifou Gaozhi Sulian?: Jiantan Lengzhanshi Yanjiu Zhong Shiliao de Jiedu yu Liyong" (Did China Inform the Soviet Union before It bombed Jinmen in 1958?: About Use and Interpretation of Cold War History Sources), http://www.people.com.cn/GB/198221/198974/199957/12798861.html, accessed March 18, 2019.

13. Chen, "Chen Yi and China's Diplomacy," 93; He, "Most Respected Enemy," 46.

14. Chen, "Chen Yi and China's Diplomacy," 93.

15. For Chinese responses to the Soviet Twentieth Party Congress and involvement in the Poland and Hungarian crises, see Zhihua Shen and Yafeng Xia, *Mao and the Sino-Soviet Partnership, 1945-1959*, 133-205; Chen, *Mao's China and the Cold War*, 64-71.

16. He, "Most Respected Enemy," 42.

BIBLIOGRAPHY

ARCHIVES

Chinese

Chinese Foreign Ministry Archives (CFMA), Beijing
  Declassified diplomatic records from 1949 to 1960
The GMD sources, Taipei
  President Chiang Kai-shek and Vice President Chen Cheng Documents (Academia Historica)
  Foreign Ministry documents (Institute of Modern History, Academia Sinica)
  GMD documents from the 1950s (The Guomingdang History Archive)
The Hoover Institution, Stanford University, California
  Chiang Kai-shek Diaries
Universities Service Centre for China Studies, Chinese University of Hong Kong, Hong Kong
  Neibu Cankao (Internal Reference), 1950–1956.

American

Dwight D. Eisenhower Library, Abilene, Kansas
  John Foster Dulles Papers
  Dwight D. Eisenhower Papers
  White House Central Files
Seeley G. Mudd Manuscript Library, Princeton University, New Jersey
  John Foster Dulles Papers
National Archives, College Park, Maryland (NAUS)
  Record Group 59: Department of State documents
  Record 273: National Security Council records

British

National Archives, Kew, London (NAUK)
  Cabinet Office records
  Commonwealth Office records
  Dominion Office records
  Foreign Office records
  Prime Minister's Office records

Soviet Union

Shen Zhihua's Personal Archives on Sino-Soviet Relations (SD)
Cold War International History Project, translated documents and related bulletins

Vietnamese

DRV Ministry of Foreign Affairs, "The Diplomatic Struggle as Part of the People's National Democratic Revolution (1945–1954), Volume Two," 1976. Acquired by Christopher Goscha and translated by Merle L. Pribbenow for the international workshop: "Reconsidering the Geneva Conference: New Archival Evidence," held by CWIHP of the Woodrow Wilson International Center for Scholars, February 17–18, 2006, Washington, D.C.
To supplement the Vietnamese source, Chinese Foreign Ministry Archives have a number of reports about the Vietnamese Workers' Party Politburo meetings, including:
"Preliminary opinions on the peaceful solution of the Indochina problem prepared by Vietnam team of the Chinese delegation to the Geneva Conference," March 23, 1954, CFMA, 206-00057-03.
"Comprehensive proposal for the peaceful solution of the Indochina problem prepared by Vietnam team of the Chinese delegation to the Geneva Conference," March 24, 1954, CFMA, 206-00057-04.
"Draft proposal for the peaceful solution of the Indochina problem prepared by Vietnam team of the Chinese delegation to the Geneva Conference," March 1–31, 1954, CFMA, 206-00057-09.
"Table of proposals for the peaceful solution of the Indochina problem prepared by Vietnam team of the Chinese delegation to the Geneva Conference," March 1–31, 1954, CFMA, 206-00057-05.

PUBLISHED DOCUMENTS

China

1954 Nian Rineiwa Huiyi (The Geneva Conference of 1954), ed. Zhongguo Waijiaobu Danganguan. Beijing: Shijie Zhishi Chubanshe, 2006.
Important Documents Concerning the Question of Taiwan. Peking, China: Foreign Languages Press, 1955.

Jianguo Yilai Liu Shaoqi Wengao (Liu Shaoqi's manuscripts since the foundation of the PRC), 1–7. Beijing: Zhongyang Wenxian Chubanshe, 2005–2008.

Jianguo Yilai Mao Zedong Wengao (Mao Zedong's manuscripts since the foundation of the PRC), 1–13. Beijing: Zhongyang Wenxian Chubanshe, 1990–1992.

Mao Zedong Nianpu, 1949–1976 (A chronological record of Mao Zedong, 1949–1976). Pang Xianzhi, Fen Hu, et al. Beijing: Zhongyang Wenxian Chubanshe, 2013.

Mao ZeDong Waijiao Wenxuan (Selected works of Mao Zedong on diplomacy), ed. Zhonghua Renmin Gongheguo Waijiaobu and Zhongyang Wenxian Yanjiushi. Beijing: Zhongyang Wenxian Chubanshe, 1994.

Mao Zedong Wenji, 1–8 (Collection of Mao Zedong's works). Beijing: Renmin Chubanshe, 1999.

Mao Zedong Zhuan, 1949–1976 (A biography of Mao Zedong, 1949–1976), ed. Pang Xianzhi and Jin Chongji. Beijing: Zhongyang Wenxian Chubanshe, 2003.

Peng Dehuai Nianpu (A Chronological Record of Peng Dehuai). Beijing: Renmin Chubanshe, 1998.

Su Yu Nianpu (A chronological record of Su Yu). ed. Zhonggong Jiansu Shenwei Lishi Yanjiushi. Beijing: Dangdai Zhongguo Chubanshe, 2006.

Taiwan Wenti Wenjian Huibian (A collection of materials concerning the Taiwan issue). Beijing: Shijie Zhishi Chubanshe, 1957.

Zhonggong Zhongyang Wenjian Huibian: 1954 Nian (A collection of the Chinese Communist Party Central Committee documents: 1954). Beijing: Shijie Zhishi Chubanshe, 1956.

Zhongguo Daibiaotuan Chuxi 1955 Nian Yafei Huiyi (China's participation of the Asian-African Conference of 1955). ed. Zhongguo Waijiaobu Danganguan. Beijing: Shijie Zhishi Chubanshe, 2007.

Zhonghua Renmin Gongheguo Duiwai Guanxi Wenjianji, 1 (1949–1950) and 2 (1951–1953) (A collection of documents of foreign relations of the PRC). Beijing: Shijie Zhishi Chubanshee, 1957, 1958.

Zhongmei Guanxishi Ziliao Huibian (Collection of documents on Sino-American relations). ed. Shijie Zhishi Chubanshe. Beijing: Shijie Zhishi Chubanshe, 1957.

Zongtong Jianggong Dashi Changbian Chugao (Draft of documents on President Chiang Kai-shek's career), Vol 12–13. Ed. Qing Xiaoyi. Taipei, Taiwan: Zhongzheng Wenjiao Jijinhui, 2005–2008.

Zhou Enlai Nianpu, 1949–1976, Vol 3. (A chronological record of Zhou Enlai, 1949–1976). Ed. Li Ping and Ma Zhisun. Beijing: Zhongyang Wenxian Chubanshe, 1997.

Zhou Enlai Waijiao Huodong Dashiji (Chronicle of Major Events in Zhou Enlai's Diplomatic Career). ed. the PRC Foreign Ministry. Beijing: Shijie Zhishi Chubanshe, 1993.

Zhou Enlai Waijiao Wenxuan (Selected works of Zhou Enlai's on diplomacy). Beijing, China: Zhongyang Wenxian Chubanshe, 1990.

Zhou Enlai Xuanji (Selected works of Zhou Enlai). Beijing: Renmin Chubanshe, 1984.

United States

Department of State Bulletin, 1953–55. Washington, D.C.: Office of Public Communication.

Foreign Relations of the United States, 1952–1954, 7, 12, 13, 14, 15, and 16; 1955–1957, 2, 3, 19, and 21. U.S. Department of State. Washington, D.C.: Governmental Printing Office.

Public Papers of the Presidents of the United States: Dwight D. Eisenhower (1953–1958). Washington, D.C.: Governmental Printing Office, 1959–1964.

Survey of China Mainland Press (SCMP), 1953–1956 (compiled and translated by American Consulate General in Hong Kong). Springfield, Va.: Reproduced by National Technical Information Service.

The Pentagon Papers (Senator Gravel edition). Boston: Beacon, 1971.

The Pentagon Papers. Newly declassified complete version by National Archives. Online access at: http://www.archives.gov/research/pentagon-papers/

Tracking the Dragon: National Intelligence Estimates on China During the Era of Mao, 1948–1976, ed. John K. Allen, John Carver, and Tom Elmore. Washington, D.C.: Government Printing Office, 2004.

United Kingdom

British Documents on Foreign Affairs: Reports and Papers from the Foreign Office, Part 5, Series E, Vols. 4–7. Bethesda, Md.: LexisNexis, 2005.

India

The Selected Works of Jawaharlal Nehru, 25–27. Ed. S. Gopal, et al. New Delhi: Jawaharlal Nehru Memorial Fund (Distributed by Oxford University Press), 1999–2001.

NEWSPAPERS

New York Times, 1953–1955.

Renmin Ribao (People's Daily), 1950–1956.

BOOKS AND ARTICLES

Abdulgani, Roeslan. *The Bandung Connection: The Asia-Africa Conference in Bandung in 1955.* trans. Molly Bondan. Singapore: Gunung Agung, 1981.

Abraham, Itty. "From Bandung to NAM: Non-alignment and Indian Foreign Policy, 1947–65." *Commonwealth & Comparative Politics* 46, no. 2 (April 2008): 195–219.

Accinelli, Robert. *Crisis and Commitment: United States Policy Toward Taiwan, 1950–1955.* Chapel Hill: University of North Carolina Press, 1996.

——. "Eisenhower, Congress, and the 1954–55 Offshore Island Crisis." *Presidential Studies Quarterly* 20, no. 1 (Winter 1990): 329–48.

Adie, W. A. C. "China, Russia, and the Third World." *The China Quarterly* 11 (September 1962): 200–13.

Ambrose, Stephen E. *Eisenhower: The President.* New York: Simon and Shuster, 1984.

Ambrose, Stephen E. and Gunter Bischof, eds. *Eisenhower: A Century Assessment.* Baton Rouge: Louisiana State University Press, 1995.

Ampiah, Kweku. *The Political and Moral Imperatives of the Bandung Conference of 1955: The Reactions of the U.S., UK and Japan.* Folkestone, Kent, UK: Global Oriental, 2007.

Anderson, David L. "J. Lawton Collins, John Foster Dulles, and the Eisenhower Administration's 'Point of No Return' in Vietnam." *Diplomatic History* 12 (Spring 1988): 127–47.

——. *Trapped by Success: The Eisenhower Administration and Vietnam, 1953–61*. New York: Columbia University Press, 1991.

Ang, Cheng Guang. *Southeast Asia's Cold War: An Interpretative History*. Honolulu: University of Hawai'i Press, 2018.

——. "The Domino Theory Revisited: The Southeast Asia Perspective." *War & Society* 19, no. 1 (May 2001): 109–30.

——. *Vietnamese Communists' Relations with China and the Second Indochina Conflict, 1956–1962*. London: McFarland, 1997.

Arnold, James R. *The First Domino: Eisenhower, the Military, and America's Intervention in Vietnam*. New York: Morrow, 1991.

Asselin, Pierre. "Choosing Peace: Hanoi and the Geneva Agreement on Vietnam, 1954–1955." *Journal of Cold War Studies* 9, no. 2 (Spring 2007): 95–126.

——. "The Democratic Republic of Vietnam and the 1954 Geneva Conference: A Revisionist Critique." *Cold War History* 11, no. 2 (2011): 155–95.

Baba, Gürol, and Senem Ertan. "Turkey at the Bandung Conference: A fully-aligned among the non-aligned," http://web.isanet.org/Web/Conferences/AP%20Hong%20Kong%202016/Archive/64185d87-7a01-44f1-acbc-1566b192398f.pdf (accessed August 18, 2017).

Bachrack, Stanley D. *The Committee of One Million: "China Lobby" Politics, 1953–1971*. New York: Columbia University Press, 1976.

Barnett, A. Doak. *Chou En-Lai at Bandung: Chinese Communist Diplomacy at the Asia-African Conference, A Report from A. Doak Barnett*. New York: American Universities Field Staff, 1955.

Bennett, Rushkoff C. "Eisenhower, Dulles and the Quemoy-Matsu Crisis, 1954–1955." *Political Science Quarterly* 96 (Fall 1981): 465–80.

Billings-Yun, Melanie. *Decision against War: Eisenhower and Dien Bien Phu, 1954*. New York: Columbia University Press, 1988.

Bo Yibo. *Ruogan Zhongda Juece yu Shijian de Huiyi* (Reflections on Major Policymaking Decisions and Events). Beijing, China: Zhongyang Dangxiao Chubanshe, 1991.

Boone, A. "The Foreign Trade of China." *The China Quarterly*, no. 11 (September 1962): 169–83.

Boquérat, Gilles. "India's Commitment to Peaceful Coexistence and the Settlement of the Indochina War." *Cold War History* 5, no. 2 (May 2005): 211–34.

Borg, Dorothy, and Waldo Heinrichs, ed. *Uncertain Years: Chinese-American Relations, 1947–1950*. New York: Columbia University Press, 1980.

Bowie, Robert, and Richard Immerman. *Waging Peace: Eisenhower's Strategy for National Security*. New York: Oxford University Press, 1998.

Boyle, Peter G., ed. *The Churchill-Eisenhower Correspondence, 1953–1955*. Chapel Hill: University of North Carolina Press, 1990.

Brands, H. W. *India and the United States: The Cold Peace*. Boston: Twayne, 1990.

——. "Testing Massive Retaliation: Credibility and Crisis Management in the Taiwan Strait." *International Security* 12, no. 4 (Spring 1988): 124–51.

——. *The Specter of Neutralism: The United States and the Emergence of the Third World, 1947–1960*. New York: Columbia University Press, 1989.

Brazinsky, Gregg A. *Winning the Third World: Sino-American Rivalry During the Cold War*. Chapel Hill: University of North Carolina Press, 2017.

Bridgham, Philip, Arthur Cohen, and Leonard Jaffe. "Mao's Road and Sino-Soviet Relations: A View from Washington, 1953." *The China Quarterly*, no. 52 (December 1972): 670–98.

Brown, MacAlister. "The Indochinese Federation Idea: Learning from History." In *Postwar Indochina: Old Enemies and New Allies*, ed Joseph J. Zasloff, 77–101. Washington, D.C.: Center for the Study of Foreign Affairs, Foreign Service Institute, U.S. Department of State, 1988.

Bulganin, Roseland. *The Bandung Connection—The Asia-Africa Conference in Bandung in 1955*. Singapore: Gunning Aging, 1981.

Buzzanco, Robert. "Prologue to Tragedy: U.S. Military Opposition to Intervention in Vietnam, 1950–1954." *Diplomatic History* 17, no. 2 (Spring 1993): 201–22.

Cable, James. *The Geneva Conference of 1954 on Indochina*. London: Macmillan, 1986.

Cai, Jiahe. *Shuangchong de Ezhi: Aisenhaoweier Zhengfu de Dongya Zhengce* (Double Containment: Eisenhower Administration's Policy toward East Asia). Nanjing, China: Nanjing Daxue Chubanse, 1999.

Casey, Richard Gardiner. *Australian Foreign Minister: The Diaries of R. G. Casey, 1951–60*. ed. T. B. Millar. London: Collins, 1972.

Chang, Gordon H. *Friends and Enemies: The United States, China and the Soviet Union, 1948–1972*. Stanford, Calif: Stanford University Press, 1990.

——. "To the Nuclear Brink: Eisenhower, Dulles, and the Quemoy-Mazsu Crisis." *International Security* 12, no. 4 (Spring 1986): 96–123.

Chang, Gordon H. and He Di, "The Absence of War in the U.S.-China Confrontation over Quemoy and Matsu in 1954–1955." *American Historical Review* 98 (December 1993): 1500–24.

Chang, Su-Ya. "1950 Niandai Meiguo Tuitai Juece Moshi Fenxi" (Analysis of the Model of U.S. Policy toward Taiwan in the 1950s). *Zhongyang Yanjiuyua Jingdaishi Yanjiusuo Jikan, Academia Sinica* 40 (June 2003): 1–54.

——. "Anlihui Tinghuo An: Meiguo Yingfu Diyici Taihai Weiji Celue zhi Yi" (UN Security Council Ceasefire Act: U.S. Response to the First Taiwan Strait Crisis, I). *Zhongyang Yanjiuyuan Jingdaishi Yanjiusuo Jikan* (Bulletin of the Institute of Modern History) 22 (June 1993): 61–106.

——. "Jinma Chejun: Meiguo Yingfu Diyici Taihai Weiji Celue zhi Er" (Withdrawal from Jinmen and Mazu: U.S. Response to the First Taiwan Strait Crisis, II). *Zhongyang Yanjiuyuan Jingdaishi Yanjiusuo Jikan* 24 (June 1995): 413–72.

——. "Lanqin Dashi yu 1950 Niandai de Meiguo Tuitai Zhengce" (Ambassador Rankin and U.S. Policy toward Taiwan in the 1950s). *Oumei Yanjiu* (The Journal of European and American Studies) 28, no. 1 (March 1998): 193–262.

——. "Reluctant Alliance: John Foster Dulles and the Making of the United States—Republic of China Mutual Defense Treaty of 1954." *Chinese Yearbook of Internationals Law and Affairs* 12 (1992–1994): 126–71.

——. "Taihai Weiji Qian Meiguo dui Waidao de Zhengce" (U.S. Policy toward the Offshore Islands before the Taiwan Strait Crisis). *Zhongyang Yanjiuyua Jingdaishi Yanjiusuo Jikan* 23 (June 1994): 295–330.

——. "Taihai Weiji yu Meiguo dui 'Fangong Dalu' Zhengce the Zhuanbian" (Taiwan Strait Crises and U.S. Policy toward the [KMT] Policy of "Restoring the Mainland"). *Zhongyang Yanjiuyuan Jingdaishi Yanjiusuo Jikan* 36 (December 2001): 231–97.

——. "Unleashing Chiang Kai-shek? Eisenhower and the Policy of Indecision Toward Taiwan, 1953." *Zhongyang Yanjiuyua Jingdaishi Yanjiusuo Jikan, Academia Sinica* 20 (June 1991): 369–401.

——. "Wengong Wuxia Xia de Tuisuo: Meiguo Jueding yu Zhonggong Juxing Dashiji Taipan de Guocheng Fenxi, 1954–1955" (Retreat before Verbal Attack and Military Threat: Analysis of U.S. Decision to Hold Ambassadorial Talks with the Chinese Communists, 1954–1955). *Zhongyang Yanjiuyua Jingdaishi Yanjiusuo Jikan* 25 (June 1996): 379–424.

Chen, Hao, "Resisting Bandung? Taiwan's Struggle for 'Representational Legitimacy' in the Rise of the Asian People's Anti-Communist League, 1954–57." *The International History Review* (May 2020): 1–21. doi: 10.1080/07075332.2020.1762239

Chen, Jian. "Bridging Revolution and Decolonization: The 'Bandung Discourse' in China's Early Cold War Experience." *The Chinese Historical Review* 15, no. 2 (2008): 207–41.

——. "China and the Indochina Settlement at the Geneva Conference of 1954." In *The First Vietnam War: Colonial Conflict and Cold War Crisis*, ed. Mark Atwood Lawrence and Fredrick Logevall, 240–62. Cambridge, Mass.: Harvard University Press, 2007.

——. *China's Road to the Korean War: The Making of the Sino-American Confrontation*. New York: Columbia University Press, 1996.

——. *Mao's China and the Cold War*. Chapel Hill: University of North Carolina Press, 2001.

——. "The Myth of America's 'Lost Chance' in China: A Chinese Perspective in Light of New Evidence." *Diplomatic History* 21, no. 1 (Winter 1997): 77–86.

Chen, King. *Vietnam and China, 1938–1954*. Princeton, N.J.: Princeton University Press, 1969.

Christensen, Thomas. "A 'Lost Chance' for What? Rethinking the Origins of the U.S.-China Confrontation." *The Journal of American-East Asian Relations* 4 (Fall 1995): 249–78.

——. *Useful Adversaries: Grand Strategy, Domestic Mobilization, and Sino-American Conflict, 1947–1958*. Princeton, N.J.: Princeton University Press, 1996.

——. *Worse Than a Monolith: Alliance Politics and Problems of Coercive Diplomacy in Asia*. Princeton, N.J.: Princeton University Press, 2011.

Claudio, Lisandro E. "The Anti-Communist Third World: Carlos Romulo and the Other Bandung." *Southeast Asian Studies* 4, no. 1 (April 2015), 125–56.

Clymer, Kenton J. "Cambodia: The View from the United States, 1945–1954." *The Journal of American-East Asian Relations* 6, no. 2/3 (Summer–Fall, 1997): 91–124.

Cohen, Warren I. "Acheson, His Advisers, and China, 1949–1950." In *Uncertain Years: Chinese-American Relations, 1947–1950*, ed. Dorothy Brog and Waldo Heinrichs, 3–52. New York: Columbia University Press, 1980.

——. *America's Response to China: A History of Sino-American Relations*. New York: Columbia University Press, 2010.

——. "Symposium: Rethinking the Lost Chance in China." *Diplomatic History* 21 (Winter 1997): 71–116.

Cohen, Warren I., and Akira Iriye, eds. *The Great Power in East Asia, 1953–1960*. New York: Columbia University Press, 1990.

Colbert, Evelyn. *Southeast Asia in International Politics, 1941–1956*. Ithaca, N.Y.: Cornell University Press, 1977.

Combs, Arthur. "The Path Not Taken: The British Alternative to U.S. Policy in Vietnam, 1954–1956." *Diplomatic History* 1 (Winter 1995): 33–57.

Costigliola, Frank. *France and the United States: The Cold Alliance Since World War II.* New York: Twayne, 1992.

Crabb, Cecil V., Jr. "The United States and the Neutralists: A Decade in Perspective." *The Annals of the American Academy of Political and Social Science* 362 (Summer 1965): 92–101.

Creswell, Michael. "With a Little Help from Our Friends: How France Secured an Anglo-American Continental Commitment, 1945–54." *Cold War History* 3, no. 1 (October 2002):1–28.

Dai, Bing. "Daguo dui 1954 Nian Rineiwa Huiyi de Taidu" (Attitudes of the Great Powers toward the Geneva Conference of 1954). *Shixue Jikan* (Bulletin of Historical Studies), Issue 5 (2007): 66–71.

——. "Rineiwa Huiyi yu Laowo, Jianpuzhai de Zhongli" (The Geneva Conference and the Neutralization of Laos and Cambodia). *Shehui Kexue Yanjiu* (The Journal of Social Science Study), 2 (2008): 51–56.

Dai, Chaowu. *Didui yu Weiji de Niandai: 1954–1958 Nian de Zhongmei Guanxi* (Years of Hostility and Crises: Sino-American Relations, 1954–1958). Beijng, China: Shehui Kexue Wenxian Chubanshe, 2003.

——. "The Impact of the Bombardment of Jinmen in 1958 Upon Sino-Soviet Relations," Parallel History Project on NATO and the Warsaw Pact, The Cold War History of Sino-Soviet Relations. June 2005. http://www.php.isn.ethz.ch/lory1.ethz.ch/publications/areastudies/documents/sinosov/Ch aowu.pdf, accessed March 18, 2019.

Dai, Shen-Yu. "Peking and Rangoon." *The China Quarterly*, no. 5 (March 1961): 131–44.

——. "Peking, Katmandu and New Delhi." *The China Quarterly*, no. 16 (December 1963): 86–98.

Dallin, David J. *Soviet Foreign Policy after Stalin.* New York: J. B. Lippincott, 1961

Dân, Nông Văn. *Churchill, Eden and Indo-China, 1951–1955.* New York: Anthem, 2010.

Dawson, Francis Noland. "The 1954 Geneva Conference: Eisenhower's Indochina Policy." PhD diss., West Virginia University, 1985.

Devillers, Philippe, and Jean Lacouture. *End of A War: Indochina, 1954.* trans. Alexander Lievan and Adam Roberts. New York: Praeger, 1969.

Dingman, Roger, "John Foster Dulles and the Creation of the South-East Asia Treaty Organization in 1954." *International History Review* 2 (August 1989): 457–77.

Divine, Robert. *Eisenhower and the Cold War.* New York: Oxford University Press, 1981.

Dockrill, Michael. "Britain and the First Chinese Off-Shore Islands Crisis, 1954–55." In *British Foreign Policy, 1949–1956*, ed Michael Dockrill and John Young, 173–96. London: Macmillan, 1989.

Drummond, Roscoe, and Gaston Coblentz. *Duel at the Brink: John Foster Dulles: Commander of American Power.* Garden City, N.Y.: Doubleday, 1960.

Duchin, Brian R. "The 'Agonizing Reappraisal': Eisenhower, Dulles, and the European Defense Community." *Diplomatic History* 16, no. 2 (Spring 1992), 201–21.

Duiker, William J. *Ho Chi Minh: A Life.* New York: Hyperion, 2000.

Dulles, Foster Rhea. *American Policy Toward Communist China, 1949–1969.* New York: Thomas Y. Crowell, 1972.

Eden, Anthony. *Full Circle: The Memories of Anthony Eden.* London: Cassell, 1960.

Eisenhower, Dwight D. *The White House Years: Mandate for Change, 1953–1956*. Garden City, N.Y.: Doubleday, 1963.

Elleman, Bruce. *High Seas Buffer: The Taiwan Patrol Force, 1950–1979*. New Port, R.I.: Naval War College Press, 2012.

Ewing, Cindy. "The Colombo Powers: Crafting Diplomacy in the Third World and Launching Afro-Asia at Bandung." *Cold War History* 19, no. 1 (Spring 2019): 1–19.

Fall, Bernard B. *Hell of a Very Small Place: The Siege of Dien Bien Phu*. Philadelphia: Lippincott, 1967.

Ferrell, Robert, ed. *The Eisenhower Diaries*. New York: W.W. Norton, 1981.

——. *Viet-Nam Witness, 1953–1966*. New York: Praeger, 1966.

Fitzgerald, Stephen. "China and the Overseas Chinese: Perceptions and Policies." *The China Quarterly*, no. 44 (October–December 1970): 1–37.

Foot, Rosemary. *A Substitute for Victory: The Politics of Peacemaking at the Korean Armistice Talks*. New York: Cornell University Press, 1990.

——. "The Eisenhower Administration's Fear of Empowering the Chinese." *Political Science Quarterly* 111, no. 3 (Autumn 1996): 505–21.

——. *The Practice of Power: U.S. Relations with China since 1949*. Oxford: Oxford University Press, 1995.

——. "Search for a Modus Vivendi: Anglo-American Relations and China Policy." In *The Great Powers in East Asia*, ed. Warren Cohen and Akira Iriye, 143–63. New York: Columbia University Press, 1990.

Forland, Tor Egil. "Selling Firearms to the Indians: Eisenhower's Export Control Policy, 1953–54." *Diplomatic History* 15 (Spring 1991): 221–44.

Fraser, Cary. "An American Dilemma; Race and Realpolitik in the American Response to the Bandung Conference, 1955." In *Window on Freedom: Race, Civil Rights, and Foreign Affairs, 1945–1988*, ed. Brenda Gayle Plummer, 115–40. Chapel Hill: North Carolina University Press, 2003.

——. "Understanding American Policy Towards the Decolonization of European Empires, 1945–64." *Diplomacy & Statecraft* 3, no. 1 (1992): 105–25.

Friedman, Jeremy Scott. "Reliving Revolution: The Sino-Soviet Split, The 'Third World,' and the Fate of the Left." PhD diss., Princeton University, 2011.

Gaddis, John. *Strategies of Containment: A Critical Reappraisal of Postwar American National Security Policy During the Cold War*. New York: Oxford University Press, 1982.

——. "The American 'Wedge' Strategy, 1949–1955." In *Sino-American Relations, 1945–1955: A Joint Reassessment of a Critical Decade*, ed. Harry Harding and Yuan Ming, 157–83. Wilmington, Del.: Scholarly Resources, 1989.

——. *The Landscape of History: How Historians Map the Past*. New York: Oxford University Press, 2002.

——. *The Long Peace: Inquiries Into the History of the Cold War*. New York: Oxford University Press, 1987.

——. "The Unexpected John Foster Dulles: Nuclear Weapons, Communism, and the Russians." In *John Foster Dulles and the Diplomacy of the Cold War*, ed. Richard H. Immerman, 47–77. Princeton, N.J.: Princeton University Press, 1989.

Gaiduk, Ilya V. *Confronting Vietnam: Soviet Policy Toward the Indochina Conflict, 1954–1963*. Stanford, Calif.: Stanford University Press, 2003.

Gao, Wenqian. *Wannian Zhou Enlai* (Zhou Enlai in His Late Years). Hong Kong, China: Mirror, 2003.

Gardner, Lloyd C. *Approaching Vietnam: From World War II Through Dienbienphu.* New York: W. W. Norton, 1988.

——. *"Poisoned Apples*: John Foster Dulles and the 'Peace Offensive.' " In *The Cold War after Stalin's Death: A Missed Opportunity for Peace?*, ed. Klaus Larres and Kenneth Osgood, 73–94. New York: Rowman and Littlefield, 2006.

Garver, John W. "Polemics, Paradigms, Responsibility, and the Origins of the U.S.-PRC Confrontation in the 1950s." *Journal of American-East Asian Relations* 3 (Spring 1994): 1–34.

——. *Protracted Contest: Sino-Indian Rivalry in the Twentieth Century.* Seattle: University of Washington Press, 2001.

George, Alexander, and Richard Smoke. *Deterrence in American Foreign Policy.* New York: Columbia University Press, 1971.

Gobarev, Viktor. "Soviet Policy Toward China: Developing Nuclear Weapons, 1949–69." *Journal of Slavic Military Studies* 12, no. 4 (December 1999): 1–53.

Gopal, Sarvepalli. *Jawaharlal Nehru: A Biography.* Cambridge, Mass.: Harvard University Press, 1979.

Gordon, Leonard. "United States Opposition to the Use of Force in the Taiwan Strait, 1954–1962." *Journal of American History* 72, no. 3 (December 1985): 637–60.

Goscha, Christopher. "Decolonization, Cold War & Diplomatic Failure." Unpublished article Goscha provided the author.

——. "Geneva 1954 and the 'De-internationalization' of the Vietnamese Idea of Indochina," presented at the international workshop on the Geneva Conference, held by Cold War International History Project of the Woodrow Wilson Center, February 17–18, 2006.

——. "The Revolutionary Laos of the Democratic Republic of Vietnam: The Making of a Transnational 'Pathet Lao Solution' (1954–1956)." Unpublished article Goscha provided the author.

Graebner, Norman, ed. *An Uncertain Tradition: American Secretaries of State in the Twentieth Century.* New York: McGraw-Hill, 1961.

——. "Eisenhower and Communism: The Public Record of the 1950s." In *Reevaluating Eisenhower*, ed Richard Melanson and David Mayers, 67–87. Chicago: University of Illinois Press, 1987.

Greene, Daniel P. O'C. "John Foster Dulles and the End of the Franco-American Entente in Indochina." *Diplomatic History* 16, no. 4 (October 1992): 551–72.

Greenstein, Fred I. *The Hidden-Hand Presidency: Eisenhower as Leader.* New York: Basic Books, 1982.

Greenwood, Sean. *Britain and the Cold War, 1945–1991.* New York: St. Martin, 2000.

Gu, Weijun. *Gu Weijun Hui Yi Lu* (Memoir of Wellington Koo), 7–12. Beijing, China: Zhonghua Shuju, 1988–94.

Gupta, Bhabani Sen. "China and Indian Communism." *The China Quarterly* 50 (April–June 1972): 272–94.

Gupta, Sisir. *India and Regional Integration in Asia.* New York: Asia Publishing, 1964.

Gurtov, Melvin. *China and Southeast Asia: The Politics of Survival.* Lexington, Mass.: Heath Lexington, 1972.

——. *The First Vietnam Crisis: Chinese Communist Strategy and United States Involvements, 1953–1954*. New York: Columbia University Press, 1968.

——. "The Taiwan Strait Crisis Revisited: Politics and Foreign Policy in Chinese Motives." *Modern China* 2 (January 1976): 49–103.

Hagerty, James C. *The Diary of James C. Hagerty: Eisenhower in Mid-Course, 1954–1955*. Bloomington: Indiana University Press, 1983.

Hall, Andrew. "Anglo-U.S. Relations in the Formation of SEATO." *Stanford Journal of East Asian Affairs* 5, no. 1 (Winter 2005), 113–32.

Han, Yelong. "An Untold Story: American Policy Toward Chinese Students in the United States, 1949–1955." *Journal of American-East Asian Relations* 1 (Spring 1993): 77–99.

Harding, Harry, and Yuan Ming, eds. *Sino-American Relations, 1945–55: A Joint Reassessment of a Critical Decade*. Wilmington, Del.: Scholarly Resources, 1989.

Hartnett, Stephen J. "Avoiding 'A Chain Reaction of Disaster': A Reappraisal of the Eisenhower White House's Handling of the 1954–1955 Quemoy Crisis." *Presidential Studies Quarterly* 48, no. 4 (December 2018): 768–803.

Hasegawa, Tsuyoshi, ed. *The Cold War in East Asia, 1945–1991*. Washington, D.C.: Woodrow Wilson Center Press, 2011.

He, Di. "The Evolution of the People's Republic of China's Policy Toward the Offshore Islands." In *The Great Powers in East Asia, 1953–1960*, ed. Warren Cohen and Akira Iriye, 224–26. New York: Columbia University Press, 1990.

——. " 'The Last Campaign to Unify China': The CCP's Unmaterialized Plan to Liberate Taiwan, 1949–50." *Chinese Historians* 5, no. 1 (Spring 1992): 1–16.

——. "The Most Respected Enemy: Mao Zedong's Perception of the United States." *The China Quarterly* 137 (March 1994): 144–58.

Heimsath, Charles. "Indo-American relations." *Journal of International Affairs* 6, no. 2 (Spring 1952): 151–162.

Heinrichs, Waldo. "Eisenhower and Sino-American Confrontation." In *The Great Powers in East Asia, 1953–1960*, ed. Warren Cohen and Akira Iriye, 224–26. New York: Columbia University Press, 1990.

Heller, David, and Dean Heller. *John Foster Dulles: Soldier for Peace*. New York: Holt, Rinehart and Winston, 1960.

Herring, George C. " 'A Good Stout Effort': John Foster Dulles and the Indochina Crisis, 1954–1955." In *John Foster Dulles and the Diplomacy of the Cold War*, ed. Richard Immerman, 213–33. Princeton, N.J.: Princeton University Press, 1990.

——. *America's Longest War: The United States and Vietnam, 1950–1975*. New York: McGraw-Hill, 2002

Herring, George C., and Richard Immerman. "Eisenhower, Dulles, and Dienbienphu: 'The Day We Didn't Go to War' Revisited." *Journal of American History* 71 (September 1984): 343–63.

Hess, Gary. "Redefining the American Position in Southeast Asia: The United States and the Geneva and Manila Conferences." In *Dien Bien Phu and the Crisis of Franco-American Relations, 1954–1955*, ed. Lawrence Kaplan, Denise Artaud, and Mark Rubin, 123–48. Wilmington, Del.: Scholarly Resources, 1990.

Hoopes, Townsend. *The Devil and John Foster Dulles*. Boston: Little, Brown, 1973.

Hsieh, Alice Langley. *Communist China's Strategy in the Nuclear Era*. Englewood Cliffs, N.J.: Prentice-Hall, 1962.

Hu, Qiaomu. *Hu Qiaomu Huiyi Mao Zedong* (Hu Qiaomu's Recollections of Mao Zedong). Beijing, China: Renmin Chubanshe, 1994.

Huei, Pang Yang. "The Four Faces of Bandung: Detainees, Soldiers, Revolutionaries and Statesmen." *Journal of Contemporary Asia* 39, no. 1 (February 2009): 63–86.

Hughes, Phillip. "Division and Discord: British Policy, Indochina, and the Origins of the Vietnam War, 1954–56." *The Journal of Imperial and Commonwealth History* 28, Issue 3 (2000): 94–112.

Hunt, Michael. *The Genesis of Chinese Communist Foreign Policy.* New York: Columbia University Press, 1996.

———. *The Making of a Special Relationship: The United States and China to 1914.* New York: Columbia University Press, 1985.

Hunt, Michael, and Niu Jun. *Toward a History of Chinese Communist Foreign Relations, 1920s–1960s: Personalities and Interpretative Approaches.* Washington, D.C.: Woodrow Wilson Center Asia Program, 1995.

Immerman, Richard H. "Between the Unobtainable and the Unacceptable: Eisenhower and Dienbienphu." In *Reevaluating Eisenhower: American Foreign Policy in the Fifties,* ed. Richard Melanson and David Mayers, 120–154. Urbana: University of Illinois Press, 1988.

———. "Confessions of an Eisenhower Revisionist: An Agonizing Reappraisal." *Diplomatic History* 14 (Summer 1990): 319–42.

———. "Eisenhower and Dulles: Who Made the Decisions?" *Political Psychology* I (Autumn 1979): 21–38.

———, ed. *John Foster Dulles and the Diplomacy of the Cold War.* Princeton, N.J.: Princeton University Press, 1989.

———. *John Foster Dulles: Piety, Pragmatism, and Power in U.S. Foreign Policy.* Wilmington, Del.: Scholarly Resources, 1999.

———. "The Prologue: Perceptions by the United States of Its Interests in Indochina." In *Dien Bien Phu and the Crisis in Franco-American Relations, 1954–55,* ed. Lawrence S. Kaplan, Denise Artaud, and Mark R. Rubin. Wilmington, Del.: Scholarly Resources, 1990.

———. "The United States and the Geneva Conference of 1954: A New Look." *Diplomatic History* 14 (Winter 1990): 43–66.

Jansen, G. H. *Afro-Asia and Non-Alignment.* London: Faber and Faber, 1966.

Jervis, Robert. *Perception and Misperception in International Politics.* Princeton, N.J.: Princeton University Press, 1976.

———. "The Impact of the Korean War on the Cold War." *The Journal of Conflict Resolution* 24, no. 4 (December 1980): 574–76, 582–84.

Jia, Qingguo, "Unmaterialized Rapprochement: Sino-American Relations in the Mid-1950s." PhD diss., Cornell University, 1988.

———. *Wei Shixian de Hejie* (Unmaterialized Rapprochement). Beijing, China: Wenyi Chubanshe, 1998.

Jiang, Changbin, and Robert Ross, eds. *Cong Duishi Zouxiang Huanhe: Lengzhan Shiqi Zhongmei Guanxi zai Tantao* (From Confrontation to Détente: Review of Sino-American Relations during the Cold War). Beijing, China: Shijie Zhishi Chubanshe, 2000.

———. *Re-examining the Cold War: U.S.-China Diplomacy, 1954–1973.* Cambridge, Mass.: Harvard University Press, 2001.

Jiang, Ying, "50 Niandai Mao Zedong Waijiao Sixiang Shulun." In *Cong Duishi Zouxiang Huanhe: Lengzhan Shiqi Zhongmei Guanxi zai Tantao* (From Confrontation to Détente: Review of Sino-American Relations during the Cold War), ed. Jiang Changbing and Robert Ross, 257–96. Beijing, China: Shijie Zhishi Chubanshe, 2000.

Jin, Guangyao. "Gu Weijun yu Mei Tai Guanyu Yanhai Daoyu de Jiaoshe, 1954 Nian 12 Yue-1955 Nian 2 Yue" (Wellington Koo and the Interactions between the U.S. and Taiwan on the Offshore Islands, Dec. 1954–Feb. 1955). *Shixue Yuekan* (Monthly Journal of History Studies) 6, 2005.

Johnson, Alexis. *The Right Hand of Power.* Englewood Cliffs, N.J.: Prentice-Hall, 1984.

Johnson, Andrew M. "Mr. Slessor Goes to Washington: The Influence of the British Global Strategy Paper on the Eisenhower New Look." *Diplomatic History* 22, no. 3 (Summer 1998): 361–98.

Jones, Matthew. "A 'Segregated' Asia?: Race, the Bandung Conference, and Pan-Asianist Fears in American Thought and Policy, 1954–1955." *Diplomatic History* 29, no. 5 (November 2005): 841–68.

——. *After Hiroshima: The United States, Race and Nuclear Weapons in Asia, 1945–1965.* Cambridge, UK: Cambridge University Press, 2012.

——. "Targeting China: U.S. Nuclear Planning and 'Massive Retaliation' in East Asia, 1953–1955." *Journal of Cold War Studies* 10, no. 4 (Fall 2008): 37–65.

——. "The Geneva Conference of 1954: New Perspectives and Evidence on British Policy and Anglo-American Relations," presented at the international workshop on the Geneva Conference on Indochina, sponsored by the Cold War International History Project, Woodrow Wilson International Center for Scholars, February 2006.

Jurika, Stephen Jr., ed. *From Pearl Harbor to Vietnam: The Memoirs of Admiral Arthur W. Radford.* Stanford, Calif.: Hoover Institution, 1980.

Kahin, George McTurnan. *The Asian-African Conference, Bandung, Indonesia, April 1955.* Ithaca, N.Y.: Cornell University Press, 1956.

Kalicki, Jan H. *The Pattern of Sino-American Crises: Political-Military Interactions in the 1950s.* London: Cambridge University Press, 1975.

Kaplan, Lawrence, Denise Artaud, and Mark Robin, eds. *Dien Bien Phu and the Crisis of Franco-American Relations, 1954–1955.* Wilmington, Del.: Scholarly Resources, 1990.

Kau, Michael Y. M., and John K. Leung, eds. *The Writings of Mao Zedong, 1949–1976.* New York: M. E. Sharpe, 1986.

Kaufman, Victor S. "Argument and Accord: Anglo-American Policies Toward China, 1948–1972." PhD diss., Ohio University, 1998.

——. *Confronting Communism: U.S. and British Policies Toward China.* Columbia: University of Missouri Press, 2001.

——. "Operation Oracle: The United States, Great Britain, New Zealand, and the Offshore Islands Crisis of 1954–55." *The Journal of Imperial and Commonwealth History* 32, no. 3 (September 2004): 106–24.

——. "Trouble in the Golden Triangle: The United States, Taiwan and the 93rd Nationalist Division." *The China Quarterly* 166 (June 2001): 440–56.

Keynes, Mary. "The Bandung Conference." *International Relations* 1 (October 1957): 362–76.

Khan, Sulmaan Wasif. "Cold War Co-operation: New Chinese Evidence on Jawaharlal Nehru's 1954 Visit to Beijing." *Cold War History* 11, no. 2 (May 2011): 197–222.

Khrushchev, Nikita S. *Khrushchev Remembers.* Boston: Little, Brown, 1970.

———. *Khrushchev Remembers: The Glasnost Tapes*. Boston: Little, Brown, 1990.

Kolko, Gabriel. *Anatomy of a War: Vietnam, the United States, and the Modern Historical Experience*. New York: Pantheon, 1985.

Kotelawala, John Lionel. *An Asian Prime Minister's Story*. London: G. G. Harrap, 1956.

Kusnitz, Leonard A. *Public Opinion and Foreign Policy: America's China Policy, 1949–1979*. Westport, Conn.: Greenwood Press, 1984.

LaFeber, Walter. *America, Russia, and the Cold War, 1945–1996*. New York: McGraw-Hill, 1997.

———. *The American Age*. New York: Norton, 1989.

Larres, Klaus. "Eisenhower and the First Forty Days After Stalin's Death: The Incompatibility of Détente and Political Warfare." *Diplomacy & Statecraft* 6 (July 1995): 431–69.

Larres, Klaus, and Kenneth Osgood, eds. *Cold War After Stalin's Death: A Missed Opportunity for Peace?* Lanham, Md.: Rowman and Littlefield, 2006.

Lawrence, Mark Atwood, and Fredrik Logevall, eds. *The First Vietnam War: Colonial Conflict and Cold War Crisis*. Cambridge, Mass.: Harvard University Press, 2007.

Leab, Daniel J. "Canned Crisis: U.S. Magazines, Quemoy and the Matsus." *Journalism Quarterly* 44 (1967): 340–44.

Leffler, Melvyn P. *For the Soul of Mankind: The United States, the Soviet Union, and the Cold War*. New York: Hill and Wang, 2007.

Levine, Steven. "Mao Tse-tung and the Issue of Accommodation with the United States, 1948–1950." In *Uncertain Years: Chinese-American Relations, 1947–1950*, ed. Dorothy Borg and Waldo Heinrichs, 185–233. New York: Columbia University Press, 1980.

Levine, Steven, and Alexander V. Pantsov. *Mao: The Real Story*. New York: Simon and Shuster, 2012.

Lewis, John W., and Xue Litai. *China Builds the Bomb*. Stanford, Calif.: Stanford University Press, 1988.

Li, Danhui, ed., *Beijing yu Mosike: Cong Lianmeng Zouxiang Duikang* (Beijing and Moscow: From Alliance to Confrontation). Guilin, China: Guangxi Shifan Daxue Chubanshe, 2002.

———. "Guanyu 1950–1970 Niandai Zhongyue Guanxi de Jige Wenti: Jianping Lisun Tan Zhongyue Guanxi de Wenjian" (Several Issues in Sino-Vietnamese Relations, 1950–1970: Brief Comments on the Document of Le Duan's Remarks about Vietnam-Chinese Relations). Available at: www.shenzhihua.net, accessed June 10, 2005.

———. "Tongzhi Jia Xiongdi: 1950 Niandai Zhongsu Bianjie Guanxi" (Comrades Plus Brothers: Sino-Soviet Border Relations in the 1950s). *Research of the Cold War International History Studies* 1. Shanghai, China: Huadong Shida Chubanshe, 2004.

Li, Guangmin. "Zhou Enlai yu Gaoqi Dazhizhu Wanlong Huiwu Shuping" (Review of the meeting between Zhou Enlai and Tatsunosuke Takasaki in Bandung). *Dang de Wenxian* (Party Literature) 1 (2003): 63–68.

Li, Lianqing. *Da Waijiaojia Zhou Enlai* (Zhou Enlai the Great Diplomat), 6 Vols. Hong Kong, China: Taidi Tushu, Ltd., 1994.

———. *Lengnuan Suiyue: Yibosanzhe de Zhongsu Guanxi* (Cold and Warm Times: The Ups and Downs in Sino-Soviet Relations). Beijing, China: Shijie Zhishi Chubanshe, 1999.

Li, Xiaobing. *Building Ho's Army: Chinese Military Assistance to North Vietnam*. Lexington: University Press of Kentucky, 2019.

Li, Xiaobing and Li Hongshan, eds. *China and the United States: A New Cold War History*. Lanham, Md.: University Press of America, 1998.

Li, Zhisui. *Mao Zedong Siren Yisheng Huiyilu* (The Memoirs of Mao Zedong's Private Physician). Taipei, Taiwan: Shibao Wenhua Chubanshe, 1994.

Lin, Hsiao-Ting. *Accidental State: Chiang Kai-shek, The United States, and the Making of Taiwan*. Cambridge, Mass.: Harvard University Press, 2016.

Liu, Lianfen. "1955 Nian Yafei Huiyi yu Zhongtai Guanxi de Youxian Huanhe" (The 1955 Asia-African Conference and the Limited Détente of the Sino-Thai Relations). *Dangdai Zhongguoshi Yanjiu* (Journal of Contemporary Chinese History Studies) 3 (2008): 60–67.

Liu, Tong, *Kua Hai zhi Zhan—Jinmeng, Hainan, Yijiangshan* (The Cross-Sea Wars: Jinmen, Hainan, Yijiangshan). Beijing, China: Sanlian Shudian, 2010.

Liu, Xiao. *Chushi Sulian Banian* (Eight-year Ambassadorship in the Soviet Union). Beijing, China: Zhonggong Dangshi Ziliao Chubanshe, 1986.

Liu, Xiaoyuan. *To the End of Revolution: The Chinese Communist Party and Tibet, 1949–1959*. New York: Columbia University Press, 2020.

Logevall, Federik. *Embers of War: The Fall of an Empire and the Making of America's Vietnam*. New York: Random House, 2012.

Lombardo, Johannes R. "Eisenhower, the British and the Security of Hong Kong, 1953–60." *Diplomacy & Statecraft* 9, no. 3 (November 1998): 134–53.

Lowe, Peter. *Containing the Cold War in East Asia: British Policies Toward Japan, China, and Korea, 1948–53*. New York: Manchester University Press, 1997.

Lu, Xun. "The American Cold War in Hong Kong, 1949–1960: Intelligence and Propaganda." In *Hong Kong in the Cold War*, ed. Priscilla Roberts and John M. Carroll, 117–40. Hong Kong, China: Hong Kong University Press, 2016.

Lüthi, Lorenz M. *The Sino-Soviet Split: Cold War in the Communist World*. Princeton, N.J.: Princeton University Press, 2008.

Lyon, Peter. *Eisenhower: Portrait of the Hero*. Boston: Little, Brown, 1974.

Ma, Liping. "Wanlong Huiyi yu Zhongai Jianjiao" (The Bandung Conference and the Establishment of Diplomatic Relations between China and Egypt). *Alabo Shijie* (The Arab World) 3 (2000): 14–17.

Mackie, Jamie. *Bandung 1955: Non-Alignment and Afro-Asian Solidarity*. Singapore: Editions Didier Millet, 2005.

Mann, James. *About Face: A History of America's Curious Relationship with China, from Nixon to Clinton*. New York: Vintage, 2000.

Mark, Chi-Kwan. "A Reward for Good Behavior in the Cold War: Bargaining over the Defense of Hong Kong, 1949–1957." *The International History Review* 22, no. 4 (December 2000): 837–61.

——. *China and the World Since 1945: An International History*. Abingdon, UK: Routledge, 2011.

Marks, Fredrick W, III. *Power and Peace: The Diplomacy of John Foster Dulles*. Westport, Conn.: Praeger, 1993.

Mastny, Vojtech. "The Soviet Union's Partnership with India." *Journal of Cold War Studies* 12, no. 3 (Summer 2010): 50–90.

Maswell, Neville. "China and India: The Un-Negotiated Dispute." *The China Quarterly* 43 (September 1970): 47–80.

——. *India's China War*. New Delhi, India: Natraj Publishers in Association with Wildlife Protection Society of India, 2015.

Mayers, David Allan. *Cracking the Monolith: U.S. Policy Against the Sino-Soviet Alliance*. Baton Rouge: Louisiana State University Press, 1986.

McIntyre, W. David. *Background to the ANZUS Pact: Policymaking, Strategy, and Diplomacy, 1945–55*. New York: St. Martin, 1995.

McLean, David. "American Nationalism, the China Myth, and the Truman Doctrine: The Question of Accommodation with Peking, 1949–50." *Diplomatic History* 10 (Fall 1986): 25–42.

McMahon, Robert J. "Eisenhower and Third World Nationalism: A Critique of the Revisionists." *Political Science Quarterly* 101 (1986): 453–73.

——. *The Cold War in the Third World*. New York: Oxford University Press, 2013.

——. *The Cold War on the Periphery: The United States, India, and Pakistan*. New York: Columbia University Press, 1994.

——. "The Illusion of Vulnerability: American Reassessments of the Soviet Threat, 1955–1956." *The International History Review* 18, no. 3 (1996): 591–619.

——. *The Limits of Empire: The United States and Southeast Asia Since World War* II. New York: Columbia University Press, 1999.

Melanson, Richard, and David Mayers, eds. *Reevaluating Eisenhower: American Foreign Policy in the Fifties*. Urbana: University of Illinois Press, 1987.

Menon, K. P. S. *The Flying Troika: Extracts from a Diary by K. P. S. Menon, India's Ambassador to Russia, 1952–61*. London: Oxford University Press, 1963.

Millet, Allan R. "Dwight D. Eisenhower and the Korean War: Cautionary Tale and Hopeful Precedent." *The Journal of American-East Asian Relations* 10, no. 3/4 (Fall–Winter 2001): 155–174.

Minnick, Wendell L. "Target Zhou Enlai: Was America's CIA Working with Taiwan Agents to Kill Chinese Premier?" *The Far Eastern Economic Review*, July 13, 1995, 54–55.

Nation, Craig. *Black Earth Red Star: A History of Soviet Security Policy 1917–1991*. Ithaca, N.Y.: Cornell University Press, 1992.

Nelson, Anna. "The Top of the Policy Hill: President Eisenhower and the National Security Council." *Diplomatic History* 7 (Fall 1983): 307–28.

Nguyen, Lien-Hang T. *Hanoi's War: An International History of the War for Peace in Vietnam*. Chapel Hill: University of North Carolina Press, 2012.

Nie, Rongzhen. *Nie Rongzhen Huiyilu* (The Memoirs of Nie Rongzhen). Beijing, China: Jiefangjun Chubanshe, 1986.

Niu, Dayong, and Shen Zhihua, eds. *Lengzhan yu Zhongguo de Zhoubian Guanxi* (The Cold War and China's Relations with Its Neighbors). Beijing, China: Shijie Zhishi Chubanshe, 2004.

Niu, Jun. *Cong Yan'an Zouxiang Shijie: Zhongguo Gongchandang Duiwai Guanxi de Qiyuan* (From Yan'an to the World: Origins of the Chinese Communist Foreign Relations). Fuzhou, China: Fujian Renmin Chubanshe, 1992.

Niu, Jun, and Zhang Baijia, eds. *Lengzhan yu Zhongguo* (Cold War and China). Beijing, China: Shijie Zhishi Chubanshe, 2002.

Olsen, Mari. *Soviet-Vietnam Relations and the Role of China, 1949–64*. New York: Routledge, 2006.

Osgood, Kenneth. "The Perils of Coexistence: Peace and Propaganda in Eisenhower's Foreign Policy." In *The Cold War After Stalin's Death: A Missed Opportunity for*

Peace?, ed. Kenneth Osgood and Klaus Larres, 40–42. Lanham, Md.: Rowman and Littlefield, Harvard Cold War Series, 2006.

——. *Total Cold War: Eisenhower's Secret Propaganda Battle at Home and Abroad*. Lawrence: University Press of Kansas, 2006.

Painter, David S. *The Cold War: An International History (The Making of the Contemporary World)*. New York: Routledge, 1999.

Painter, David S., and Sally G. Irvine. *The Geneva Conference of 1954: Indochina*. Washington, D.C.: Distributed by the Institute for the Study of Diplomacy, School of Foreign Service, Georgetown University, 1988.

Parker, Jason. "Cold War II: The Eisenhower Administration, the Bandung Conference, and the Reperiodization of the Postwar Era." *Diplomatic History* 30 (November 2006): 867–92.

—— "Small Victory, Missed Chance: The Eisenhower Administration, the Bandung Conference, and the Turning of the Cold War." In *The Eisenhower Administration, the Third World, and the Globalization of the Cold War*, ed. Kathryn C. Statler and Andrew L. Johns, 153–74. Lanham, Md.: Rowman and Littlefield, 2006.

Pei, Jianzhang. *Zhonghua Renmin Gongheguo Waijiaoshi, 1949–56* (A History of the Diplomacy of the People's Republic of China). Beijing, China: Shijie Zhishi Chubanshe, 1994.

Pemberton, Gregory James. "Australia, the United States, and the Indochina Crisis of 1954." *Diplomatic History* 13, no. 1 (Winter 1989): 45–66.

Prados, John. *The Sky Would Fall: Operation Vulture: The U.S. Bombing Mission in Indochina 1954*. New York: Dial, 1983.

Pullin, Eric D. "The Bandung Conference: Ideological Conflict and the Limitations of U.S. Propaganda." In *Neutrality and Neutralism in the Global Cold War: Between or Within the Blocs?*, ed. Sondra Bott, Jussi Hanhimaki, Janick Marina Schaufelbuehl, and Marc Wyss, 52–71. London: Routledge, 2016.

Qian, Jiang. *Zhou Enlai yu Rineiwa Huiyi* [Zhou Enlai and the Geneva Conference]. Beijing, China: Renmin Chubanshe, 2005.

Qing, Simei, *From Allies to Enemies: Visions of Modernity, Identity, and U.S.-China Diplomacy, 1945–1960*. Cambridge, Mass.: Harvard University Press, 2007.

——. "The Eisenhower Administration and Changes in Western Embargo Policy Against China, 1954–1958." In *The Great Powers in East Asia, 1953–1960*, ed. Warren Cohen and Akira Iriye, 121–42. New York: Columbia University Press, 1990.

Qu, Xin. *Zhongguo Waijiao 50 Nian* [Chinese Diplomacy in the Past Fifty Years]. Nanjing, China: Jiangsu Renmin Chubanshe, 2000.

Randle, Robert F. *Geneva 1954: The Settlement of the Indochinese War*. Princeton, N.J.: Princeton University Press, 1969.

Rankin, Karl L. *China Assignment*. Seattle: University of Washington Press, 1964.

Rather, Lucia J. "The Geneva Conference of 1954: Problems in Allied Unity." PhD diss., University of North Carolina, 1994.

Ren, Donglai, "Cong 'Liangda Zhenyin' Lilun dao 'Heping Gongchu Wuxian Yuanze': Zhongguo dui Minzuzhuyi Guojia Kanfa he Zhengce de Yanbian" (From 'Two Camps' Theory to 'Five Principles of Peaceful Coexistence': Evolution of China's Perception and Policy toward Nationalist Countries). *Taipingyang Xuebao* 4 (2000): 87–94.

Robb, Thomas K., and David James Gill. "The ANZUS Treaty During the Cold War: A Reinterpretation of U.S. Diplomacy in the Southwest Pacific." *Journal of Cold War Studies* 17, no. 4 (Fall 2015): 109–157.

Roberts, Geoffrey. "A Chance for Peace? The Soviet Campaign to End the Cold War, 1953–1955." Cold War International History Project, working paper #57. December 2008.

——. *The Soviet Union in World Politics: Coexistence, Revolution and Cold War, 1945–1991*. London: Routledge, 1999.

Roberts, Priscilla, ed. *Behind the Bamboo Curtain: China, Vietnam, and the World Beyond Asia*. Washington, D.C.: Woodrow Wilson Center, 2006.

Roberts, Priscilla, and John M. Carroll. *Hong Kong in the Cold War*. Hong Kong, China: Hong Kong University Press, 2016.

Romula, Carlos P. *The Meaning of Bandung*. Chapel Hill: University of North Carolina Press, 1955.

Ross, Robert S. and Jiang Changbing, eds. *Re-examining the Cold War: U.S.-China Diplomacy, 1954–1973*. Cambridge, Mass.: Harvard University Press, 2001.

Ruane, Kevin. "Anthony Eden, British Diplomacy and the Origins of the Geneva Conference of 1954." *The Historical Journal*, 37, no. 1 (1994): 153–72.

——. " 'Containing America': Aspects of British Foreign Policy and the Cold War in South-East Asia, 1951–54." *Diplomacy & Statecraft* 7, no. 1 (March 1996): 141–74.

——. "Eden, the Foreign Office, and the War in Indo-China, October 1951 to July 1954." PhD diss., University of Kent at Canterbury (United Kingdom), 1991.

——. "Refusing to Pay the Price: British Foreign Policy and the Pursuit of Victory in Vietnam, 1952–4." *The English Historical Review* 110, no. 435 (February 1995): 70–92.

Rushkoff, Bennett. "Eisenhower, Dulles and the Quemoy-Matsu Crisis, 1954–1955." *Political Science Quarterly* 96, no. 3 (Fall 1981): 465–80.

Rust, William J. *Before the Quagmire: American Intervention in Laos, 1954–1961*. Lexington: University Press of Kentucky, 2012.

——. *Eisenhower & Cambodia: Diplomacy, Covert Action, and the Origins of the Second Indochina War*. Lexington: University Press of Kentucky, 2016.

Schaller, Michael. *The United States and China: Into the Twenty-First Century*. New York: Oxford University Press, 2016.

——. "Securing the Great Crescent: Occupied Japan and the Origins of Containment in Southeast Asia." *The Journal of American History* 69, no. 2 (September 1982): 392–414.

Selverstone, Marc Jay. " 'All Roads Lead to Moscow': The United States, Great Britain, and the Communist Monolith." PhD diss., Ohio University, 2000.

Setzekorn, Eric. "Eisenhower's Mutual Security Program: Taiwan as a Strategic Bargain." *Journal of American-East Asian Relations* 23 (2016): 33–55.

Shao, Kuo-kang. "Chou En-lai's Diplomatic Approach to Non-Aligned States in Asia: 1953–60." *The China Quarterly*, no. 78 (1979): 324–38.

——. *Zhou Enlai and the Foundations of Chinese Foreign Policy*. New York: St. Martin, 1996.

——. "Zhou Enlai's Diplomacy and the Neutralization of Indo-China, 1954–55." *The China Quarterly*, no. 107 (1986): 483–504.

Share, Michael. "The Soviet Union, Hong Kong, and the Cold War, 1945–1970," CWIHP working paper 41.

Shimizu, Sayuri. "Perennial Anxiety: Japan-U.S. Controversy over Recognition of the PRC, 1952–1958." *The Journal of American-East Asian Relations* 4, no. 3 (Fall 1995): 223–248.

Shen, Zhihua. "1958 Nian Paoji Jinmen qian Zhongguo Shifou Gaozhi Sulian?: Jiantan Lengzhanshi Yanjiu Zhong Shiliao de Jiedu yu Liyong" (Did China Inform the Soviet Union before It bombed Jinmen in 1958?: About Use and Interpretation of Cold War History Sources), http://www.people.com.cn/GB/198221/198974/199957/12798861.html, accessed March 18, 2019.

——. "Jieshu Chaoxian Zhanzheng: Zhongsu Lingdaoren de Zhengzhi Kaolu" (Ending the Korean War: Political Considerations of the Chinese and Soviet Leaders). In *Lengzhan yu Zhongguo* (The Cold War and China), ed. Zhang Baijia and Niu Jun, 182–215. Beijing, China: Shijie Zhishi Chubanshe, 2002.

——. *Mao Zedong, Sidalin yu Chaoxian Zhanzheng* (Mao Zedong, Stalin, and the Korean War). Guangzhou, China: Guangdong Renmin Chubanshe, 2004.

——. *Sulian Zhuanjia zai Zhongguo, 1948–1960* (Soviet Experts in China, 1948–1960). Beijing, China: Xinhua Chubanshe, 2009.

——. "Yuanzhu yu Xianzhi: Sulian yu Zhongguo de Hewuqi Yanzhi, 1949–1960" (Assistance and Restriction—The Soviet Union and China's research on the nuclear weapons, 1949–1960). *Lishi Yanjiu* (Historical Research) 3 (2004): 110–31.

——, ed. *Zhongsu Guanxi Shigang* (Historical Outline of Sino-Soviet Relations). Beijing, China: Xinhua Chubanshe, 2008.

Shen, Zhihua, and Li Danhui. *After Leaning to One Side: China and Its Allies in the Cold War*. Washington, D.C.: Woodrow Wilson Center Press; Stanford. Calif.: Stanford University Press, 2011.

Shen, Zhihua, and Yafeng Xia. "Between Aid and Restriction: The Soviet Union's Changing Policies on China's Nuclear Weapons Program, 1954–1960," *Asian Perspective* 36 (2012): 95–122.

——. "Leadership Transfer in Asian Revolution: Mao and the Asian Cominform." *Cold War History* 14, no. 2 (2014): 195–213.

——. *Mao and the Sino-Soviet Partnership, 1945–1959*. New York: Lexington, 2015.

Sheng, Michael M. "Mao and China's Relations with the Superpowers in the 1950s: A New Look at the Taiwan Strait Crises and the Sino-Soviet Split." *Modern China* 34, no. 4 (October 2008): 477–507.

——. "The Triumph of Internationalism: CCP-Moscow Relations Before 1949." *Diplomatic History* 21, no. 1 (Winter 1997): 95–104.

Shi, Zhe. *Zai Lishi Juren Shenbian: Shi Zhe Huiyilu* (On the Side of Historical Giants: Shi Zhe's Memoirs). Beijing, China: Zhongyang Wenxian Chubanshe, 1991.

Shimizu, Sayuri. "Perennial Anxiety: Japan-U.S. Controversy over Recognition of the PRC, 1952–1958." *The Journal of American-East Asian Relations* 4, no. 3 (Fall 1995): 223–48.

Shuckburgh, Evelyn. *Descent to Suez, Diaries 1951–56*. London: Weidenfeld and Nicolson, 1986.

Singh, Anita Inder. *The Limits of British Influence: South Asia and the Anglo-American Relations, 1947–1956*. New York: St. Martin, 1993.

Soman, Appu K. *Double-Edged Sword: Nuclear Diplomacy in Unequal Conflicts: The United States and China, 1950–1958*. Westport, Conn.: Praeger, 2000.

Stapleton, Bradford Ian. "The Korea Syndrome: An Examination of War-Weariness Theory." *Journal of Cold War Studies* 17, no. 3 (Summer 2015): 36–81.

Statler, Kathryn C., and Andrew L. Johns, eds. *The Eisenhower Administration, the Third World, and the Globalization of the Cold War*. Lanham, Md.: Rowman and Littlefield, 2006.

Steel, Tracy. "Hong Kong and the Cold War in the 1950s." In *Hong Kong in the Cold War*, ed. Priscilla Roberts and John M. Carroll, 92–116. Hong Kong, China: Hong Kong University Press, 2016.

Steinberg, David I, and Hongwei Fan. *Modern China-Myanmar Relations: Dilemmas of Mutual Dependence*. Copenhagen, Denmark: Nordic Institute of Asian Studies Press, 2012.

Stevens, Georgiana. "Arab Neutralism and Bandung." *Middle East Journal* 11, no. 2 (Spring, 1967): 139–52.

Stolper, Thomas. *China, Taiwan, and the Offshore Islands: Together with Some Implications for Outer Mongolia and Sino-Soviet Relations*. Armonk, N.Y.: M. E. Shape, 1985.

Su, Ge. *Meiguo Duihua Zhengce yu Taiwan Wenti* (U.S. Policy toward China and the Taiwan Issue). Beijing, China: Shijie Zhishi Chubanshe, 1998.

Sutter, Robert G. *China-Watch: Sino-American Reconciliation*. Baltimore, Md.: Johns Hopkins University Press, 1978.

Swaine, Michael, and Zhang Tuosheng, eds. *Managing Sino-American Crises*. Washington, D.C.: Carnegie Endowment for International Peace, 2006.

Tan, See Seng, and Amitav Acharya, eds. *Bandung Revisited: The Legacy of the 1955 Asian-African Conference for International Order*. Singapore: Nus Press, 2008.

Tang, James Tuck-Hong. *Britain's Encounter with Revolutionary China, 1949–54*. New York: St. Martin, 1992.

Tao, Wenzhao. *Zhongmei Guanxi Shi, 1949–1972* (A History of Sino-American Relations, 1949–1972). Shanghai, China: Shanghai Renmin Chubanshe, 1999.

Tarling, Nicolas. " 'Ah-Ah': Britain and the Bandung Conference of 1955." *Journal of Southeast Asian Studies* 23, no. I (March 1992): 74–112.

Taylor, Jay. *The Generalissimo: Chiang Kai-shek and the Struggle for Modern China*. Cambridge, Mass.: Harvard University Press, 2009.

Thayer, Carlyle A. *War by Other Means: National Liberation and Revolution in Vietnam, 1954–60*. Sydney, Australia: Allen and Unwin, 1989.

Trevelyan, Humphrey. *Living with the Communists: China, 1953–5, Soviet Union, 1962–5*. Boston: Gambit, 1971.

Tsang, Steve. "Target Zhou Enlai: The 'Kashmir Princess' Incident of 1955." *China Quarterly* 139 (September 1994): 766–82.

——. *The Cold War's Odd Couple: The Unintended Partnership Between the Republic of China and the UK, 1950–1958*. New York: I. B. Tauris, 2006.

Tucker, Nancy Bernkopf. "Cold War Contacts: America and China, 1952–56." In *Sino-American Relations, 1945–55: A Joint Reassessment of a Critical Decade*, ed. Harry Harding and Yuan Ming, 238–66. Wilmington, Del.: Scholarly Resources Inc., 1989.

——. "John Foster Dulles and the Taiwan Roots of the Two Chinas Policy." In *John Foster Dulles and the Diplomacy of the Cold War*, ed. Richard Immerman, 235–62. Princeton, N.J.: Princeton University Press, 1990.

——. *Patterns in the Dust: Chinese-American Relations and the Recognition Controversy, 1949–1950*. New York: Columbia University Press, 1983.

——. *Taiwan, Hong Kong, and the United States, 1945–1992: Uncertain Friendships*. New York: Twayne Publishers, 1994.

——. *The China Threat: Memories, Myths, and Realities in the 1950s*. New York: Columbia University Press, 2012.

Waite, James David Anthony. "The End of the First Indochina War: An International History." PhD diss., Ohio University, 2005.

Walker, David. "Nervous Outsiders: Australia and the 1955 Asia-Africa Conference in Bandung." *Australian Historical Studies* 36, no. 125 (January 2005): 40–59.

Wang, Bingnan. *Zhongmei Huitan Jiunian Huigu* (Recollections on the Nine-year Sino-American Talks). Beijing, China: Shijie Zhishi Chubanshe, 1985.

Wang, Dong. "Quarrelling Brothers: New Chinese Archives and a Reappraisal of the Sino-Soviet Split, 1959–1962." CWIHP working paper #49.

Wang, Jisi. "The Origins of America's 'Two China' Policy." In *Sino-American Relations, 1945–55: A Joint Reassessment of a Critical Decade*, ed. Harry Harding and Yuan Ming, 198–212. Wilmington, Del.: Scholarly Resources Inc., 1989.

Wang, Yazhi. "Huigu yu Sikao: 1950 Niandai Zhongsu Junshi Guanxi Ruogan Wenti I (part 1)" (Reflections on the Sino-Soviet Military Relations in the 1950s I [part 1]). *Guoji Zhengzhi Yanjiu* (Studies of International Politics) no. 4 (2003): 54–59.

——. "Huigu yu Sikao: 1950 Niandai Zhongsu Junshi Guanxi Ruogan Wenti I (part 2)" (Reflections on the Sino-Soviet Military Relations in the 1950s I [part 2]). *Guoji Zhengzhi Yanjiu* (Studies of International Politics) no. 1 (2004): 87–92.

——. "Huigu yu Sikao: 1950 Niandai Zhongsu Junshi Guanxi Ruogan Wenti II (part 1)" (Reflections on the Sino-Soviet Military Relations in the 1950s II [part 1]). *Guoji Zhengzhi Yanjiu* (Studies of International Politics) no. 2 (2004): 114–23.

——. "Huigu yu Sikao: 1950 Niandai Zhongsu Junshi Guanxi Ruogan Wenti II (part 2)" (Reflections on the Sino-Soviet Military Relations in the 1950s II [part 2]). *Guoji Zhengzhi Yanjiu* (Studies of International Politics) no. 3 (2004): 55–64.

——. "Huigu yu Sikao: 1950 Niandai Zhongsu Junshi Guanxi Ruogan Wenti II (part 3)" (Reflections on the Sino-Soviet Military Relations in the 1950s II [part 3]). *Guoji Zhengzhi Yanjiu* (Studies of International Politics) no. 4 (2004): 114–21.

——. "Huigu yu Sikao: 1950 Niandai Zhongsu Junshi Guanxi Ruogan Wenti III"(Reflections on the Sino-Soviet Military Relations in the 1950s III). *Guoji Zhengzhi Yanjiu* (Studies of International Politics) no. 1 (2005): 106–25.

——. "Xin Zhongguo Chengli Chuqi Sulian yu Zhongguo de Jundui Zhuangbei: 1950 Niandai Zhongsu Junshi Guanxi Ruogan Wenti IV" (The Soviet Union and the Chinese Military Equipment in the Early Years After the Founding of PRC: Reflections on the Sino-Soviet Military Relations in the 1950s IV). *Guoji Zhengzhi Yanjiu* (Studies of International Politics) no. 3 (2004): 30–55.

Warner, Geoffrey. "From Geneva to Manila: British Policy Toward Indochina and SEATO, May-September 1954." In *Dien Bien Phu and the Crisis of Franco-American Relations, 1954–1955*, ed. Lawrence Kaplan, Denise Artaud, and Mark Robin, 149–67. Wilmington, Del.: Scholarly Resources, 1990.

——. "The Settlement of the Indochina War." In *The Foreign Policy of Churchill's Peacetime Administration, 1961–66*, ed. John Young, 233–59. Leicester, UK: Leicester University Press, 1988.

Watry, David, M. *Diplomacy at the Brink: Eisenhower, Churchill and Eden in the Cold War*. Baton Rouge: Louisiana State University Press, 2014.

Weathersby, Kathryn. "Stalin, Mao and the End of the Korean War." In *Brothers in Arms: The Rise and Fall of the Sino-Soviet Alliance, 1945–1963*, ed. Odd Arne Westad, 90–116. Stanford, Calif.: Stanford University Press, 1998.

Wei, Zongyou. "Lun Rineiwa Huiyi hou Meiguo yu Jianpuzhai Guanxi de Yanbian, 1954–1960" (Evolution of the Relations between the U.S. and Cambodia, 1954–1960). *Dongnanya Yanjiu* (Journal of Southeast Asian Studies) 2 (2006): 35–41.

Wen, Zhuang. "Wo Suo Jingli de Rineiwa Huiyi" (The Geneva Conference as I experienced). *Dangshi Bolan* (General Review of the History of the Chinese Communist Party) (December 2005): 18–23.

West, Philip. "Confronting the West: China as David and Goliath in the Korean War." *The Journal of American-East Asian Relations* 1 (Spring 1993): 5–28.

Westad, Odd Arne, ed. *Brothers in Arms: The Rise and Fall of the Sino-Soviet Alliance, 1945–1963*. Stanford, Calif.: Stanford University Press, 1998.

——. *The Global Cold War*. New York: Cambridge University Press, 2007.

——. "The Sino-Soviet Alliance and the United States." In *Brothers in Arms*, ed. Odd Arne Westad, 165–188. Stanford, Calif: Stanford University Press, 1998.

Whiting, Allen S. *China Crosses Yalu: The Decision to Enter the Korean War*. New York: Macmillan, 1960.

Wilcox, Emily. "Performing Bandung: China's Dance Diplomacy with India, Indonesia, and Burma, 1953–1962." *Inter-Asia Cultural Studies* 18, no. 4 (2017): 518–39.

Wilhelm, Alfred D., Jr. *The Chinese at the Negotiating Table: Style and Characteristics.* Washington, D.C.: National Defense University Press, 1994.

Williams, Lea E. "Sino-Indonesia Diplomacy: A Study of Revolutionary International Politics." *The China Quarterly* 11 (September 1962): 184–99.

Wilson, David A. "China, Thailand and the Spirit of Bandung (Part I)." *The China Quarterly* 30 (June 1967): 149–69.

——. "China, Thailand and the Spirit of Bandung (Part II)." *The China Quarterly* 31 (September 1967): 96–127.

Windrow, Martin. *The Last Valley: Dien Bien Phu and the French Defeat in Vietnam.* London: Weidenfeld and Nicolson, 2003.

Wingrove, Paul. "Mao's Conversation with the Soviet Ambassador, 1953–1955." Cold War International History Project, working paper #36, 2002.

Wint, Guy. "China and Asia." *The China Quarterly* 1 (March 1960): 61–71.

Wolff, David. " 'One Finger's Worth of Historical Events': New Russian and Chinese Evidence on the Sino-Soviet Alliance and Split, 1948–1959." Cold War International History Project, working paper #30, August 2000.

Wright, Richard. *The Color Curtain: A Report on the Bandung Conference.* New York: World Publishing Company, 1956.

Wu, Lengxi. *Yi Mao Zhuxi: Wo Qinzi Jingli de Ruogan Zhongda Lishi Shijian Pianduan* (Remembering Chairman Mao: My Personal Experience of Several Important Historical Events). Beijing, China: Xinhua Chubanshe, 1995.

Wu, Xiuquan. *Zai Waijiaobu Banian de Jingli, 1950 Nian 1 Yue–1958 Nian 10 Yue* (My Eight-year Experience in the Foreign Ministry: January 1950–October 1958). Beijing, China: Shijie Zhishi Chubanshe, 1983.

Xia, Liping. "Wanlong Huiyi Qianhou Zhongguo Zhengfu Dakai yu Yafei Guojia Guanxi de Nuli" (Chinese government's efforts to open relations with Asian and African states before the Bandung Conference). *Waijiao Xueyuan Xuebao* (Journal of China Foreign Affairs University) 81 (April 2005): 74–80.

Xia, Yafeng. *Negotiating with the Enemy: U.S.-China Talks During the Cold War, 1949–1972.* Bloomington: Indiana University Press, 2006.

Xia, Yafeng and Zhihua Shen. "Leadership Transfer in Asian Revolution: Mao and the Asian Cominform." *Cold War History* 14, no. 2 (2014): 195–213.

——. *Mao and the Sino-Soviet Partnership, 1945–1959*. New York: Lexington, 2015.

Xiong, Huayuan. *Zhou Enlai Chudeng Shijie Wutai* (Zhou Enlai's First Appearance on the World Stage). Shenyang, China: Liaoning Renmin Chubanshe, 1999.

——. *Zhou Enlai Wanlong zhi Xing* (Zhou Enlai's Trip to Bandung). Beijing, China: Zhongyang Wenxian Chubanshe, 2002.

Xiong, Huayuan, and Liao Xinwen, *Zhou Enlai Zongli Shengya* (Zhou Enlai's Career as Premier). Beijing, China: Renmin Chubanshe, 1997.

Xu, Yan. *Jinmen zhi Zhan* (The War for Jinmen). Beijing, China: Zhongguo Guangbo Chubanshe, 1992.

Xue, Mouhong, et al. *Dangdai Zhongguo Waijiao* (Contemporary Chinese Diplomacy). Beijing, China: Zhongguo Shehui Kexue Chubanshe, 1990.

Yang, Kuisong. "Changes in Mao Zedong's Attitude Toward the Indochina War, 1949–1973." Cold War International History Project, working paper #34, 2002.

——. "Liushi Nianqian de 'Zhongguo Daolu' " ('The Chinese Road' of Sixty Years Ago). *Tongzhou Gongjin* 1 (2010): 30–33.

——. *Mao Zedong yu Mosike de Enen Yuanyuan* (Hate and Love between Mao Zedong and Moscow). Nanchang, China: Jiangxi Renmin Chubanshe, 2005.

——. "Xinzhongguo Cong Yuanyue Kangfa dao Zhengqu Yinduzhina Heping de Zhengce Yanbian" (Shift of the New China's Policy from 'Assist Vietnam, Resist France' to Striving for Peace in Indochina). Zhongguo Shehui Kexue (Social Sciences in China) 1 (2001): 193–203.

Yao, Chunling. "Meiguo yu Dongnanya Tiaoyue Zuzhi de Jianli" (The U.S. and the Establishment of SEATO). *Meiguo Yanjiu* (American Studies Quarterly) 3 (1995): 110–26.

Yao, Yu, and Guo Youxin. "1953–1956 Nian Meiguo de Xiangjiao Zhengce and Guonei Zhengzhi" (U.S. Policy toward Rubber and Its Domestic Politics, 1953–1956). *Shijie Lishi* (Journal of World History Studies) 6 (2007): 60–68.

Ye, Fei. *Ye Fei Huiyilu* (Ye Fei's Memoir). Beijing, China: Jiefangjun Chubanshe, 1988.

Young, John W. "Churchill, the Russians and the Western Alliance: The Three-Power Conference at Bermuda, December 1953." *The English Historical Review* 101, no. 401 (October 1986): 889–912.

——. "German Rearmament and the European Defense Community." In *The Foreign Policy of Churchill's Peacetime Administration, 1951–1955*, ed. John W. Young, 83–95. Leicester, UK: Leicester University Press, 1988.

——. *The Foreign Policy of Churchill's Peacetime Administration, 1951–1955*. Leicester, UK: Leicester University Press, 1988.

Young, Kenneth. *Negotiating with the Chinese Communist: The United States Experience, 1953–1967*. New York: McGraw-Hill, 1968.

Yuan, Ming, and Harry Harding, eds. *Zhongmei Guanxi Shishang de Chengzhong Yiye* [A Bleak Period in Sino-American Relations]. Beijing, China: Peking University Press, 1989.

Zhai, Qiang. "Britain, the United States, and the Jinmen-Mazu Crises, 1954–1955 and 1958." *Chinese Historians* 5, no. 2 (Fall 1992): 25–48.

——. "China and the Geneva Conference of 1954." *The China Quarterly* 129 (March 1992): 103–22.

——. *China and the Vietnam wars, 1950–1975*. Chapel Hill: University of North Carolina Press, 2000.

————. "Crisis and Confrontation: Chinese-American Relations During the Eisenhower Administration." *The Journal of American-East Asian Relations* 9, no. 3/4 (Fall/Winter 2000): 221–49.

————. *The Dragon, the Lion & the Eagle: Chinese-British-American Relations, 1949–1958.* Kent, Ohio: Kent State University Press, 1994.

————. "The Making of Chinese Communist Foreign Relations, 1935–1949: A New Study from China." *The Journal of American-East Asian Relations* 1, no. 4 (Winter 1992): 471–77.

————. "Transplanting the Chinese Model: Chinese Military Advisers and the First Vietnam War, 1950–1954." *The Journal of Military History* 57 (October 1993): 689–715.

Zhang, Baijia. "The Changing International Scene and Chinese Policy Toward the United States." *Re-examining the Cold War: U.S.-China Diplomacy, 1954–73*, ed. Robert S. Ross and Jiang Changbin, 46–76. Cambridge, Mass.: Harvard University Asia Center, 2001.

Zhang, Baijia, and Jia Qingguo. "Duikang zhong de Fangxiangpan, Huanchongqi he Tanceyi: Zhongmei Dashiji Huitan." In *Cong Duishi Zouxiang Huanhe*, ed. Jiang Changbin and Robert Ross, 169–94. Beijing, China: Shijie Zhishi Chubanshe, 2000.

Zhang, Baijia, and Niu Jun, eds. *Lengzhan yu Zhongguo* [Cold War and China]. Beijing, China: Shijie Zhishi Chubanshe, 2002.

Zhang, Shu Guang. *Beijing's Economic Statecraft During the Cold War, 1949–1991.* Washington, D.C.: Woodrow Wilson Center; Baltimore, MD: Johns Hopkins University Press, 2014.

————. "Constructing 'Peaceful Coexistence': China's Diplomacy Toward the Geneva and Bandung Conferences, 1954–55." *Cold War History* 7, no. 4 (November 2007): 509–28.

————. *Deterrence and Strategic Culture: Chinese-American Confrontations, 1948–1958.* Ithaca, N.Y.: Cornell University Press, 1992.

————. *Economic Cold War: America's Embargo Against China and the Sino-Soviet Alliance, 1949–1963.* Washington, D.C.: Woodrow Wilson Center Press; Stanford, Calif.: Stanford University Press, 2001.

Zhao, Huijun. "Guonei dui 1954 Nian Rineiwa Huiyi Huifu Yinduzhina Heping de Yanjiu" (Review of the Research on the Geneva Conference of 1954 Restoring Peace in Indochina). *Dongnanya Zongheng* (Around Southeast Asia) 8 (2003): 31–35.

Zhao, Xuegong. *Juda de Zhuanbian: Zhanhou Meiguo dui Dongya de Zhengce* (Great Shift: U.S. Policy toward East Asia after WWII). Tianjing, China: Tianjing Renmin Chubanshe, 2002.

Zubok, Vladslav M. *A Failed Empire: The Soviet Union in the Cold War from Stalin to Gorbachev.* Chapel Hill: University of North Carolina Press, 2007.

————. "Soviet Intelligence and the Cold War: The 'Small' Committee of Information, 1952–53." CWIHP working paper #4, 1992.

Zubok, Vladslav, and Constantine Pleshakov. *Inside the Kremlin's Cold War: From Stalin to Khrushchev.* Cambridge, Mass.: Harvard University Press, 1996.

INDEX

Page numbers in *italics* denote figures.